Julia A. Lamm
Schleiermacher's Plato

Julia A. Lamm

Schleiermacher's Plato

DE GRUYTER

ISBN 978-3-11-126244-4
e-ISBN (PDF) 978-3-11-069506-9
e-ISBN (EPUB) 978-3-11-069516-8

Library of Congress Control Number: 2021945472

Bibliographic Information published by the Deutsche Nationalbibliothek
The Deutsche Nationalbibliothek lists this publication in the Deutsche Nationalbibliografie; detailed bibliographic data are available on the Internet at http://dnb.dnb.de.

© 2023 Walter de Gruyter GmbH, Berlin/Boston
This volume is text- and page-identical with the hardback published in 2021.
Cover image, collage: "Herm of Plato from the Academy," Altes Museum Berlin, photo by Zdenek Kratochvil (commons.wikimedia.com, CC-BY-SA 3.0). "Schleiermacher," bust by Christian Daniel Rauch, 1829, image from AKG-images (AKG106372), used with permission.
Printing and binding: CPI books GmbH, Leck

www.degruyter.com

For my husband, Alan

Preface

> *May everything beautiful that my grateful heart wishes for you only grow during this year.*
> —Schleiermacher to Eleanore Grunow, 1802

The project of *Schleiermacher's Plato* began a quarter century ago, when an outside reader for my book *The Living God: Schleiermacher's Theological Appropriation of Spinoza* (1996) raised the simple but daunting question: What about Plato? After initial inquiry into the topic, I added a brief section entitled "A Platonized Spinozism." Although those initial reflections have stood up to time, they were cursory at best and merely opened the gate to a vast estate ready to be explored. At the time, I rightly assumed that this would be a long-term project but imagined that to be ten years, not twenty-five.

My greatest professional debt in relation to *Schleiermacher's Plato* is to the *Alexander von Humboldt Stiftung*, which awarded me a grant to begin my research in Berlin in 1996–1997 and which later followed through with three subsequent shorter research grants. The Humboldt Foundation prides itself in supporting scholars not projects, in establishing a lifetime relationship with Humboldtians, and in fostering a worldwide network of scholars. The value of such support, especially for scholars in the Humanities, is incalculable. I am deeply grateful to the foundation, its staff, and the various academic hosts and institutions with which the foundation works. Kurt-Victor Selge, who was then director of the *Schleiermacherforschungsstelle* (Schleiermacher Research Center) at the *Berlin-Brandenburgische Akademie der Wissenschaften* (BBAW, Berlin-Brandenburg Academy of Sciences), was a most gracious academic host during that initial research year. He arranged a space for me at the Academy and an office for me in the Theology Faculty of Humboldt University (then located in the Waisenstrasse), but even more importantly he did me the honor of reading *The Living God* and respected me as a scholar, despite my halting German. He knew what it was to work in a foreign land and to think in a different language, and for that I shall always be thankful. I am also grateful to the special assistance given by Wolfgang Virmond during that year. He taught me how to navigate the BBAW and the *Staatsbibliothek zu Berlin* (State Library, Berlin), both of which were undergoing major transitions in those years following reunification. At that time in the *Staatsbibliothek*, it took enormous perseverance to track down the needed eighteenth- and nineteenth-century texts: one card in a drawer would refer to another card-catalogue, and that to yet another, and so on back into history; then it would take days for the staff to locate the relevant volume or to discover that it had been "lost in the war." Wolfgang Virmond initiated me into that system with patience and good cheer. I was so happy to be reunited with him again at the *Schleiermacher-Kongress* in Münster in 2015. Sadly, he died this past year. We all stand indebted to him for the advancements he made in Schleiermacher scholarship. In subsequent years, Andreas Arndt (2010) and Wilhelm Gräb (2015, 2019) have generously hosted me at the Academy and the University, respectively. I thank them both. I have especially enjoyed the theological conversations with Wilhelm Gräb.

My greatest personal debt is to my husband, Alan C. Mitchell, to whom this book is dedicated. We had our courtship in Berlin during that Humboldt year, when he too was enjoying a sabbatical year. The city itself was undergoing transformation as Germany was in the process of moving its capital from Bonn to Berlin. The skyline was filled with cranes, and Potsdamer Platz, a recent no-man's-land, was one big construction site. We would meet for the tradition of cake and coffee in the afternoons and spend weekend days exploring Berlin's many neighborhoods. In the quarter century since then, we have built a beautiful life together. Our son, Aidan, turns twenty next month and is studying neurobiology. Like his father, he is smart, witty, and loving. I thank them both for their love and support. Every day I give thanks that I get to spend my life with them. Alan, especially, has been supportive of this project on Schleiermacher and Plato. I could not have done it without him. No doubt, they will both be happy now that it is done. I have also benefitted from Alan's professional connections. A New Testament scholar, he was a guest researcher at the *Institut für Christentum und Antike* (Institute for Christianity and Antiquity) in the Theology Faculty of Humboldt University, then under the direction of Cilliers Breytenbach, whose warm welcome and collegiality have continued over these many years. We are both grateful, too, for the long friendship and professional relationship with Jens Schröter, now professor of New Testament and co-director of the Institute for Christianity and Antiquity, and with Christine Schröter.

Closer to home, I stand deeply indebted to colleagues here at Georgetown University who have supported me in this project over these many years. Faculty in the German Department have kindly indulged me as I pester them with questions about special terms or phrases: Friederike Eigler, Astrid Weigert, Mary Helen Dupree, and Peter Pfeiffer. In my home department of Theology, I have relied on the insights and encouragement for this project offered by Leo Lefebure, Daniel Madigan SJ, John O'Malley SJ, Peter Phan, Stephen Fields SJ, Ariel Glucklich, Lauve Steenhuisen, and Paul Heck. Our dear and brilliant colleague Gerard Mannion was especially enthusiastic in his support of my work on Schleiermacher and Plato. He died suddenly and far too young in September 2019, and we feel his loss terribly. I shall miss having that shot of whiskey with him—as he always so enjoyed celebrating with his friends. A great benefit about working at a university is, of course, that there are conversations to be had with colleagues from many different disciplines. I thank the following friends and colleagues for their expert feedback and ongoing support: Sarah McNamer, John Glavin (English); Alisa Carse, Bill Blattner, Alfonso Gomez-Lobo (†2011), Wayne Davis (Philosophy); and Kathy Olesko (History). I thank Georgetown University itself for summer research grants along the way. I had the good fortune of having a superb research assistant, Kirsty Jones, during the year in which I completed the book. She was helpful beyond measure, and I appreciate her hard work and responsiveness. My colleagues at Lauinger Library and Woodstock Theological Library at Georgetown did heroic work in getting needed material to me during lockdown due to the pandemic; I am especially grateful to Leon Hooper SJ and Jeffrey Popovich.

Beyond Healey Gates and D.C., I enjoy the good fortune of belonging to larger circles of Schleiermacher scholars who are amazingly generous, gifted, and fun. I have relied on their expertise and honest criticisms over the years. Many of us go back to the *Arbeitskreis* formed under B. A. Gerrish at The Divinity School of The University of Chicago: Dawn DeVries, Brent Sockness, Ted Vial, Walt Wyman, and Paul Capetz. We have grown in friendship as we have continued our debates about Schleiermacher and theology over the course of three decades. We all owe deep professional and personal debts to Brian Gerrish for the model of scholarship and teaching that he provided us—as well as for his wisdom, wit, and kindness. Beyond the Chicago circle, I am grateful for the scholarship of, and friendship with, four other extraordinary Schleiermacher scholars: Albert Blackwell, Richard Crouter, Francis Fiorenza, and Christine Helmer.

It is never easy to burden colleagues with the request to read a book manuscript, yet of course such review and critique is an essential aspect of scholarship. Walt Wyman, who has the eyes of a hawk, generously read the entire book manuscript. Richard Crouter, who knows Schleiermacher's *Speeches* probably better than anyone else, read the lengthy two chapters on Plato in the *Speeches*; it was he who had been that outside reader all those years ago, so this in a sense closed the circle. Lutz Käppel, a philologist and the editor of the critical edition of *Platons Werke*, served as a reader for De Gruyter. Peter Albert, an expert editor, has looked at it with an eye on stylistic matters. All offered suggestions that have made this a better book than it would have been. I am honored by their willingness to take the time and energy for such a task, and I thank them all profusely. All mistakes or infelicities are my own.

I acknowledge and thank the following journals and presses for permission to use essays and articles previously published. *The Journal of Religion* (University of Chicago Press), for "Schleiermacher as Plato Scholar," *JR* 80/2 (April 2000): 206–39, and "Schleiermacher's *Christmas Dialogue* as Platonic Dialogue," *JR* 92/3 (July 2012): 392–420, which form the bases of chapter 2 and 5, respectively. *Zeitschrift für Neuere Theologiegeschichte / Journal for the History of Modern Theology* (Walter de Gruyter), "Reading Plato's Dialectics: Schleiermacher's Insistence on Dialectics as Dialogical," *ZNThG/JHMTh* 10/1 (April, 2003): 1–25, which forms the basis for chapter 4. Cambridge University Press, for "The Art of Interpreting Plato," in *The Cambridge Companion to Schleiermacher*, edited by Jacqueline Mariña (2005): 91–108, parts of which form the basis of chapter 3. Academia Verlag, for "Plato's Dialogues as a Single Work of Art: Friedrich Schleiermacher's *Platons Werke*," in *Lire les Dialogues, mais lesquels et dans quel ordre? Définitions du corpus et interprétations de Platon*, edited by Anne Balansard and Isabelle Koch (2013): 173–188, parts of which have been distributed throughout chapters 2 and 3. Walter de Gruyter Press, for "Schleiermacher's Re-Writing as Spiritual Exercise, 1799–1806," in *Der Mensch und seine Seele. Bildung—Frömmigkeit—Ästhetik*, edited by Arnulf von Scheliha and Jörg Dierken (2017): 293–302, and "Schleiermacher's Modern Platonism," in *Reformation und Moderne. Pluralität—Subjektivität—Kritik*, edited by Jörg Dierken, Arnulf von Scheliha, and Sarah Schmidt (2018): 675–697, parts of which have been distributed throughout chapters 6 and 7.

Finally, I thank De Gruyter Press, and especially Albrecht Doehnert in Berlin and Aaron Sanborn-Overby in Boston. Their professionalism, expertise, support, and kindness have helped to make the publication process a smooth and enjoyable one. Finally, I feel honored to have the opportunity of my book appearing in this fine publishing house, the heir of Schleiermacher's own publisher, Reimer.

This book was finished during the year of COVID-19, a time of grievous loss, anxiety, and social upheaval. As I write this, the death count due to COVID in the United States stands at 592,413. It simply did not have to be that bad, and that is part of our shared grief and frustration. Alan and I have lost several friends and acquaintances in the past year, among them: Trish Walsh, Herb Bloom, Dora Richardson, Jim Carse, Jim Gustafson, and Günter Meckenstock. Although to my knowledge only one of them died of coronavirus disease, it is hard not to view their deaths in light the so-called "excess deaths" associated with COVID-19. Part of our sadness is that we could not mourn them properly, since funerals were not allowed for safety reasons. In addition to the tragedy of the pandemic, the whole country, and indeed much of the world, was rocked by what happened in Minneapolis, Minnesota on 25 May 2020 and in Washington, D.C. on 1 June 2020 and on 6 January 2021. Those events were acutely personal to me, since those are the two cities that I call "home." George Floyd died under the knee of a merciless man one mile from where I grew up; Lafayette Square, where peaceful protestors were attacked with military force, and the U. S. Capitol Building, which was breached and desecrated by insurrectionists who supported a lie, are close by. Two beautiful cities, scarred and shaken. I mention this not to elicit sympathy (my family and I have been fortunate in health and job security during this time) but instead to anchor completion of this book in a particular historic moment. Most scholarly books, especially historical books such as this, become stripped of their own context even as they try to contextualize the works of earlier scholars. This book has wound up being my instance of what has been called "therapies of granularity"—those focused tasks that have helped get us through each day during a shut-down. This historic year has demanded a tenuous balancing act of embracing the concrete simple things of everyday life while bearing witness to the horrors of a pandemic. Now, in the spring of 2021, about fifteen months after it all began, there are signs of hope due to vaccinations. We are hopeful but wary. May those who have died rest in peace, may their loved ones know consolation, and may peace and justice roll down.

Julia A. Lamm
Washington, D.C.
May 8, 2021

Contents

List of Tables —— XVII

Abbreviations —— XIX

1 Introduction: Schleiermacher's Plato —— 1
  1.1 Schleiermacher's Achievement —— 1
  1.2 The Question: Schleiermacher and Plato —— 3
  1.3 Thesis and Approach of *Schleiermacher's Plato* —— 8
  1.4 The Decade of Plato in Schleiermacher's Life —— 11
    1.4.1 Exile in Stolp, Pomerania (1802–1804) —— 13
    1.4.2 Academic Life in Halle (1804–1807) —— 17
  1.5 On Texts, Translations, and Editions —— 19

2 Schleiermacher's *Platons Werke* and Its Legacy —— 21
  2.1 Introduction —— 21
  2.2 Conception of the Plato Project —— 23
  2.3 Central Themes in Schleiermacher's "General Introduction" —— 32
    2.3.1 Internal Method —— 32
    2.3.2 Plato as Artist —— 37
    2.3.3 The Dialogue Form —— 41
    2.3.4 The Authenticity and Order of the Dialogues —— 44
  2.4 Controversial Issues in the *Introductions* —— 48
    2.4.1 Placement of the *Phaedrus* —— 48
    2.4.2 The Ordering and Chronology of the Dialogues —— 51
    2.4.3 The Validity of the Esoteric Tradition —— 53
  2.5 Concluding Remarks —— 56

3 Practicing on Plato: Interpretation, Socratic Clues, and the Emergence of Schleiermacher's Hermeneutics —— 58
  3.1 Introduction —— 58
  3.2 The New Criticism and the Plato Renaissance —— 59
  3.3 The *Phaedrus:* Socratic Clues and Hermeneutical Principles —— 64
  3.4 Principles for Determining Authenticity of Plato's Dialogues —— 71
  3.5 Principles for Ordering Plato's Dialogues —— 75
    3.5.1 Provisional Whole: A Trilogy of Trilogies —— 75

　　　　3.5.2　The Pedagogical Progression of Ideas —— 78
　　　　3.5.3　The Two Series: Ethics and Physics —— 82
　　3.6 Concluding Remarks: The Interpreter as Artist —— 84

4　Reading Plato's Dialectics: Schleiermacher's Insistence on Dialectics as Dialogical —— 86
　　4.1 Introduction —— 86
　　4.2 Basic Interpretive Principles in the "General Introduction" —— 89
　　4.3 The First Trilogy and the Method of Philosophy —— 91
　　4.4 The Trilogy at the Center and the Object of Philosophy —— 97
　　4.5 An Inconclusive Concluding Trilogy —— 102
　　4.6 Concluding Remarks: From Reading Plato's Dialectics to Lecturing on *Dialectics* —— 105

5　Schleiermacher's *Christmas Dialogue* as Platonic Dialogue —— 107
　　5.1 Introduction —— 107
　　5.2 The *Phaedrus* and the Opening Scene of the *Christmas Dialogue* —— 115
　　　　5.2.1　Gifts —— 116
　　　　5.2.2　Conversation —— 117
　　　　5.2.3　The 'Seeds' —— 118
　　　　5.2.4　Impulse and Method —— 122
　　5.3 The *Symposium* and the Women's Stories —— 128
　　　　5.3.1　Ernestine's Story —— 130
　　　　5.3.2　Agnes's Story —— 132
　　　　5.3.3　Karoline's Story —— 134
　　5.4 The *Republic* and the Men's Speeches —— 136
　　5.5 Josef's Unsaying —— 139
　　5.6 Concluding Remarks —— 141

6　The Presence of Plato in the *Speeches* (1806), Part 1: Revising, Reconceiving, and Recasting —— 143
　　6.1 Introduction —— 143
　　6.2 Re-Writing as Spiritual Exercise: Holding together Theory and *Praxis* in the *Speeches* —— 148
　　　　6.2.1　The Two Impulses (*Triebe*) —— 149
　　　　6.2.2　Rhetorical Shifts —— 153
　　　　6.2.3　Intuition as the 'Hinge' of the Argument —— 154

6.3 Revised Block N° 1: A New Three of Thinking, Doing, and Feeling —— 155
    6.3.1   A More Complex Typology —— 156
    6.3.2   Acting: Life and Art —— 158
    6.3.3   Thinking About Nature—and About Human Nature —— 160
6.4 Revised Block N° 2: "Contemplation is Essential to Religion" —— 163
    6.4.1   Appearances, Education, and the Higher Nature of Knowing —— 164
    6.4.2   The Science of Being, the Infinite, and Contemplation —— 169
    6.4.3   Plato's Middle Dialogues on the Infinite and the Finite —— 174
    6.4.4   Plato's Middle Dialogues on Contemplation —— 178
    6.4.5   Return to the Science of Being in Revised Block N° 2 —— 183
    6.4.6   The Science of Acting and Piety —— 184

7 The Presence of Plato in the *Speeches* (1806), Part 2: Being, Non-Being, and Intuition —— 187
  7.1 Introduction —— 187
  7.2 Revised Block N° 3: "… go and learn it from your Socrates" —— 189
    7.2.1   Socratic Ignorance, Being and Non-Being —— 190
    7.2.2   *Platons Werke*: The *Sophist* on Being and Non-Being —— 194
    7.2.3   The Second Speech and the *Sophist*: The Two Series, Physics and Ethics —— 199
    7.2.4   Intuition and the Unity of Theory and *Praxis*, Reason and Nature —— 201
  7.3 Revised Block N° 4: "the original relation of feeling and intuition" —— 206
    7.3.1   The Replaced 1799 Version: Intuition as the "Hinge" of the Second Speech —— 207
    7.3.2   Contemplation and the Innermost Sanctuary of Life, *Redux* —— 210
    7.3.3   The "Original Relation of Feeling and Intuition" —— 212
    7.3.4   Intuition in *Platons Werke* and the Second Speech —— 217
    7.3.5   The Three Series and Their Association —— 220
    7.3.6   Religion and Contemplation —— 222
  7.4 Concluding Remarks on the *Speeches* (1806) and the *Introductions* —— 226

8 Conclusion: Schleiermacher's Plato —— 227

Bibliography —— 233
  1   Primary Sources —— 233
      German Editions of Schleiermacher's Texts Cited —— 233
      English Translations of Schleiermacher's Texts Cited —— 234
      English Translations of Plato's Dialogues —— 235
  2   Secondary Sources —— 235

Index —— 248

List of Tables

Table 1: Chronology of Schleiermacher's Decade of Plato —— 14–15
Table 2: Schleiermacher's Ordering of the Platonic Dialogues —— 45–46
Table 3: A Trilogy of Trilogies: The 'Stock' of First-Ranked Dialogues —— 78
Table 4: Parallel Structures of *Platons Werke* and *Christmas Dialogue* —— 112
Table 5: The First Trilogy and the 'Seeds' of the *Christmas Dialogue* —— 116
Table 6: The Second Trilogy and the Women's Stories —— 128
Table 7: The Third Trilogy and the Men's Speeches —— 136
Table 8: Revised Blocks in the Second Speech, 2nd Edition (1806) —— 146
Table 9: Reciprocal Relations of Opposites in the *Speeches:Thinking* (*Denken*) and *Acting* (*Handeln*) —— 200

Abbreviations

I Volumes from the Critical Edition of Schleiermacher's Works (*KGA*)

Friedrich D. E. Schleiermacher Kritische Gesamtausgabe, ed. Hans-Joachim Birkner, Hermann Fischer, Günter Meckenstock, et al., 58 vols. (67 vols. projected) (Berlin, NY, Boston: De Gruyter, 1980–).

KGA 1/2   (Part) I, (vol.) 2: *Schriften aus der Berliner Zeit 1796–1799*, ed. Günter Meckenstock (Berlin and New York: Walter de Gruyter, 1984).

KGA 1/3   (Part) I, (vol.) 3: *Schriften aus der Berliner Zeit 1800–1802*, ed. Günter Meckenstock (Berlin and New York: Walter de Gruyter, 1988).

KGA 1/4   (Part) I, (vol.) 4: *Schriften aus der Stolper Zeit (1802–1804)*, ed. Eilert Herms, Günter Meckenstock, and Michael Pietsch (Berlin and New York: Walter de Gruyter, 2002).

KGA 1/5   (Part) I, (vol.) 5: *Schriften aus der Hallenser Zeit 1804–1807*, ed. Hermann Patsch (Berlin and Boston: De Gruyter, 2011).

KGA 1/6   (Part) I, (vol.) 6: *Universitätsschriften. Herakleitos. Kurze Darstellung des theologischen Studiums*, ed. Dirk Schmid (Berlin and New York: Walter de Gruyter, 1998).

KGA 1/11 (Part) I, (vol.) 11: *Akademievorträge*, ed. Martin Rößler (Berlin and New York: De Gruyter, 2002).

KGA 1/12 (Part) I, (vol.) 12: *Über die Religion (2.–)4. Auflage. Monologen (2.–)4. Auflage*, ed. Günter Meckenstock (Berlin and Boston: Walter de Gruyter, 1995).

KGA 1/13,1+2 (Part) I, (vol.) 13 (in 2 books): *Der Christliche Glaube nach den Grundsätzen der evangelischen Kirche im Zusammenhange dargestellt (1830–31)*, ed. Rolf Schäfer (Berlin and Boston: De Gruyter, 2003).

KGA 2/4   (Part) II, (vol.) 4: *Vorlesungen zur Hermeneutik und Kritik*, ed. Wolfgang Virmond, with Hermann Patsch (Berlin and Boston: De Gruyter, 2013).

KGA 2/10,1+2 (Part) II, (vol.) 10 (in 2 books): *Vorlesungen über die Dialektik*, ed. Andreas Arndt (Berlin and New York: De Gruyter, 2002).

KGA 4/3   (Part) IV, (vol.) 3: *Platons Werke I,1: Einleitung · Phaidros · Lysis · Protagoras · Laches (Berlin 1804. 1817)*, ed. Lutz Käppel und Johanna Loehr (Berlin and Boston: Walter de Gruyter, 2016).

KGA 4/5   (Part) IV, (vol.) 5: *Platons Werke II,1: Gorgias · Theaitetos · Menon · Euthydemos (Berlin 1805. 1818)*, ed. Lutz Käppel und Johanna Loehr (Berlin and Boston: De Gruyter, 2020).

KGA 5/1–12 (Part) V, (vols.) 1–12: *Briefwechsel*, ed. Andreas Arndt, Wolfgang Virmond, Simon Gerber, and Sarah Schmidt (Berlin and New York: De Gruyter, 1985–2020).

II Cited Works

Br.	Schleiermacher, *Briefwechsel*, in *KGA* 5/1–12.
CD	Schleiermacher, *Christmas Dialogue* (1806), in *Schleiermacher: Christmas Dialogue, The Second Speech, and Other Selections*, trans. Julia A. Lamm, Classics of Western Spirituality (Mahwah, NJ: Paulist Press, 2014), 101–151.
Dc	Schleiermacher, *Dialectic, or the Art of Doing Philosophy, A Study Edition of the 1811 Notes*, trans. Terrence N. Tice (Atlanta: Scholars Press, 1996).
Dk	Schleiermacher, *Vorlesungen über die Dialektik*, in *KGA* 2/10,1+2.
DWB	*Deutsches Wörterbuch von Jacob und Wilhelm Grimm*, 16 vols. (Leipzig 1854–1961; Quellenverzeichnis Leipzig 1971). Digitale Publikationsumgebung / Wörterbuchnetz.de, Trier Center for Digital Humanities, Universität Trier. http://www.woerterbuchnetz.de
EÜP	Schleiermacher, *Die Einleitungen zur Übersetzung des Platon (1804–1828)*, in *Friedrich Daniel Ernst Schleiermacher: Über die Philosophie Platons*, ed. Peter M. Steiner, 21–387 (Hamburg: Felix Meiner, 1996).
HC	Schleiermacher, *Hermeneutics and Criticism and Other Writings*, ed. Karl Ameriks and Desmond M. Clarke, trans. Andrew Bowie (Cambridge: Cambridge University Press, 1998).
HK	Schleiermacher, *Hermeneutik und Kritik*, ed. Manfred Frank (Frankfurt am Main: Suhrkamp, 1977).
IDP	Schleiermacher, *Introductions to the Dialogues of Plato*, trans. William Dobson (Cambridge and London, 1836; reprint, New York: Arno Press, 1973).
OR¹	Schleiermacher, *On Religion: Speeches to its Cultured Despisers* (1st ed., 1799), trans. Richard Crouter (Cambridge: Cambridge University Press, 1988).
OR²	Schleiermacher, "The Second Speech" (2nd ed., 1806), in *Schleiermacher: Christmas Dialogue, The Second Speech, and Other Selections*, trans. Julia A. Lamm, Classics of Western Spirituality (Mahwah, NJ: Paulist Press, 2014), 152–223.
OR³	Schleiermacher, *On Religion: Speeches to its Cultured Despisers* (3rd ed., 1821), trans. John Oman (New York: Harper & Row, 1958; reprint, 1986).
PDL	*Perseus Digital Library*, edited by Gregory R. Crane. Tufts University. http://www.perseus.tufts.edu.
PW	*Platons Werke von F. Schleiermacher*, 6 vols. (Berlin: Reimer, 1804–1828; 2nd ed. of vols. 1–5, 1817–1826).
PW 1/1	Schleiermacher, *Platons Werke*, (Part) I, (vol.) 1 (1804), in *KGA* 4/3.
PW 2/1	Schleiermacher, *Platons Werke*, (Part) II, (vol.) 1 (1805), in *KGA* 4/5.
PW (Eigler)	*Platon. Werke in acht Bänden, Griechisch und Deutsch*, 8 vols., trans. Friedrich Schleiermacher, ed. Gunther Eigler (Darmstadt: Wissenschaftliche Buchgesellschaft, 1970; 2nd ed., 1990).
R	Schleiermacher, *Über die Religion. Reden an die Gebildeten unter ihren Verächtern 1799/1806/1821*, ed. Niklaus Peter, Frank Bestebreurtje, and Anna Büsching (Zürich: Theologischer Verlag, 2012). When used without superscript specifying edition, it means that the particular edition is immaterial, that a passage remains stable throughout all editions, or that passages from both editions can be found on same page.

R^1	Schleiermacher, *Über die Religion* (1st ed., 1799), Peter edition: *Über die Religion. Reden an die Gebildeten unter ihren Verächtern 1799/1806/1821*, ed. Niklaus Peter, Frank Bestebreurtje, and Anna Büsching (Zürich: Theologischer Verlag, 2012).
R^2	Schleiermacher, *Über die Religion* (2nd ed., 1806), Peter edition: *Über die Religion. Reden an die Gebildeten unter ihren Verächtern 1799/1806/1821*, ed. Niklaus Peter, Frank Bestebreurtje, and Anna Büsching (Zürich: Theologischer Verlag, 2012).
WG	Schleiermacher, *Die Weihnachtsfeier: Ein Gespräch* (1st ed., 1806), in *KGA* 1/5:43–98.

1 Introduction: Schleiermacher's Plato

> There is no author who has so affected me and so initiated me into the sanctum, not only of philosophy but also of humanity generally, as has this divine man.[1]

1.1 Schleiermacher's Achievement

Friedrich Schleiermacher (1768–1834) wrote these words as he commenced his deep scholarly engagement with Plato, which resulted in his six-volume masterpiece *Platons Werke* (*Plato's Works*).[2] His decades-long intensive work of translating and interpreting Plato would not stifle this early enthusiasm. Praise became virtual identification: "Plato is indisputably the author whom I know best and with whom I have almost coalesced."[3] The depth of the imprint on the subjective side, which such personal attestations capture, mirrored the breadth of influence on the objective side. Since the publication of the first volume of *Platons Werke* in 1804 until now, more than two centuries later, scholars have competed to find the best metaphor to convey what Schleiermacher accomplished. Already in 1816, Immanuel Bekker dedicated his critical edition of Plato's dialogues to Schleiermacher as the "restorer of Plato" (*Friderico Schleiermachero Platonis Restitutori*).[4] Heinrich von Stein (1833–1896) claimed that Schleiermacher's introductions to Plato's dialogues signaled a "geological fault" or "tectonic shifting" (*Verwerfung*) in the philological world.[5] As recently as 2019, in *Brill's Companion to German Platonism*, Schleiermacher's *Platons Werke* is described as "an extra-

---

[1] Friedrich D. E. Schleiermacher to Carl Gustav von Brinckmann, 9 June 1800 (#883, lines 103–108), in *Schleiermacher Kritische Gesamtausgabe* (hereafter cited in text as "*KGA*"), Pt. 5: *Briefwechsel*, 12 vols., ed. Andreas Arndt, Wolfgang Virmond, Simon Gerber, and Sarah Schmidt (Berlin and New York: De Gruyter, 1985–2020), 4:82 (hereafter cited in text as "*Br.*").
[2] *Platons Werke von F. Schleiermacher* (hereafter cited in text as "*PW*"), 6 vols. (Berlin: Reimer, 1804–1828; 2nd ed. of vols. 1–5, 1817–1826). The *KGA* is currently producing a new, critical edition of *PW*, edited by Lutz Käppel und Johanna Loehr. To date, two volumes have appeared: *Platons Werke I,1: Einleitung · Phaidros · Lysis · Protagoras · Laches* (Berlin 1804. 1817), in *KGA* 4/3 (Berlin and Boston: De Gruyter, 2016); and *Platons Werke II,1: Gorgias · Theaitetos · Menon · Euthydemos* (Berlin 1805. 1818), in *KGA* 4/5 (Berlin and Boston: De Gruyter, 2020); hereafter cited in text as "*PW* 1/1" and "*PW* 2/1," respectively.
[3] Schleiermacher to Eleanore Grunow, 3 Sept. 1803 (#1327, lines 40–42), *Br.* 6:113.
[4] Immanuel Bekker, ed., *Platonis Dialogi graece et latine*, 3 vols. (Berlin: Reimer, 1816–18), n.p.
[5] Heinrich von Stein, *Sieben Bücher zur Geschichte des Platonismus: Untersuchungen über das System des Plato und sein Verhältniss zur späteren Theologie und Philosophie*, 3 vols. (Göttingen, 1862, 1865, 1875; reprint, Frankfurt am Main, 1965), 3:409.

ordinary turning point in Plato studies"[6] and as "the most far-reaching revolution in Plato-interpretation since Marsilio Ficino's translation and commentary in the fifteenth century."[7] That Schleiermacher changed the course of Plato studies is beyond doubt. Simply put, he changed how we understand Plato.

Unlike other philologists at the time, Schleiermacher set out to translate not just a dialogue or two but the entire Platonic *corpus* instead.[8] His German translation of Plato's dialogues dominated for over two centuries and even now continues to be influential as the "classic" one.[9] More than that, however, he was determined to apply the newly emerging historical-critical method to Plato, which entailed identifying the authentic works of Plato and ordering those chronologically. That raised fundamental questions for a new, modern era: Who was

---

[6] Vittorio Hösle, "The Tübingen School," in *Brill's Companion to German Platonism*, ed. Alan Kim (Leiden: Brill, 2019), 332.

[7] Thomas A. Szlezák, "Friedrich Schleiermacher's Theory of the Platonic Dialogue and Its Legacy," in Kim, *Brill's Companion to German Platonism*, 163.

[8] He would not live to complete *PW*. He published the sixth volume, which includes the *Republic*, in 1828, but never translated the *Timaeus, Critias, Laws*, or the *Letters*.

[9] Adam Schnitzer, "A History in Translation: Schleiermacher, Plato, and the University of Berlin," *The Germanic Review* 75, no. 1 (2000): 53. For more on Schleiermacher's translation, see also Hermann Gauss, *Philosophischer Handkommentar zu den Dialogen Platos*, 6 vols. (Bern: Herbert Lang, 1952–61), 1:20–21; Jörg Jantzen, "Schleiermachers Platon-Übersetzung und seine Anmerkungen dazu," in *Über die Philosophie Platons*, ed. Steiner, xlv-lviii (see below, n. 10); and Theo Hermans, "Schleiermacher and Plato, Hermeneutics and Translation," in *Friedrich Schleiermacher and the Question of Translation*, ed. Larisa Cercel and Adriana Serban (Berlin and Boston: De Gruyter, 2015), 77–106. Schleiermacher was famous, too, for his *theory* of translation, which like his hermeneutics emerged out of his study of Plato. See Piotr de Bończa Bukowski, "Zur Übersetzungstheorie bei Friedrich Daniel Ernst Schleiermacher und Friedrich Schlegel in der Zeit ihrer Zusammenarbeit," in *Wissenschaft, Kirche, Staat und Politik: Schleiermacher im Preußischen Reformprozess*, ed. Andreas Arndt, Simon Gerber, and Sarah Schmidt (Berlin: Walter de Gruyter, 2019), 119–144. Ulrich von Wilamowitz-Moellendorff's minority position that Schleiermacher's translation is "unbearable" stems in part from his conviction that Plato is "untranslatable" and must be read in the Greek (*Platon: Sein Leben und seine Werke* [Berlin, Frankfurt am Main: Weidmannsche, 1948], xii).

As recently as 1990, an edition of the complete works of Plato in Greek and German used Schleiermacher's translation, although without his introductions and not in the order he had assigned: *Platon. Werke in acht Bänden, Griechisch und Deutsch*, 8 vols., trans. Friedrich Schleiermacher, ed. Gunther Eigler (Darmstadt: Wissenschaftliche Buchgesellschaft, 1970; 2nd ed., 1990); hereafter cited in text as "*PW* (Eigler)." Schleiermacher's translation has influenced even English translators. Allan Bloom, in the introduction to his own translation of the *Republic*, wrote, "Schleiermacher's old German version was the most useful translation I found. Although his text was inferior to ours, he seems to have had the best grasp of the character and meaning of the dialogues" (quoted and cited by Albert L. Blackwell, *Schleiermacher's Early Philosophy of Life: Determinism, Freedom and Phantasy* [Greenville: Scholars Press, 1982], 132–33).

Plato, and what is Platonic philosophy, once the accretions of centuries of Platonisms are scraped away? As important as Schleiermacher's translation, therefore, was his interpretation of Plato developed in the accompanying introductions to the dialogues.[10] In his famous "General Introduction" (*Einleitung*), he
set forth his basic interpretive and methodological principles, which he then continued to apply in his introductions to the individual dialogues, as he painted a
new portrait of Plato. As Stein put it, Schleiermacher "created a Platonic question."[11] And yet, in Schleiermacher studies, surprisingly little is known about
how Schleiermacher understood Plato or how that may have influenced his
own thinking.

1.2 The Question: Schleiermacher and Plato

The question of Schleiermacher and Plato may be approached from two different
perspectives: from *Plato studies*, which seeks primarily to understand Plato better by asking how Schleiermacher might aid in that endeavor; or from *Schleiermacher studies*, which seeks primarily to understand Schleiermacher (or his era)
better by asking how his Plato-interpretation might grant keener insight. The latter approach cannot be done without the former. Therefore, in chapter two, I examine what was new about Schleiermacher's portrait of Plato and how his *Platons Werke* influenced philology, classics, and philosophy over the course of two
centuries. Schleiermacher continues to be influential in Plato studies even now,
although much of that discussion is relegated to notes and shorter forays. A notable exception is the attention given to Schleiermacher in recent decades by the

---

10 Schleiermacher's introductions to Plato's dialogues came to be separated from his translations of those dialogues, although they are being reunited in the *KGA*. As early as two years
after Schleiermacher's death, the introductions were gathered together and translated into English: Schleiermacher, *Introductions to the Dialogues of Plato*, trans. William Dobson (Cambridge
& London, 1836; reprint, New York: Arno Press, 1973); hereafter cited in text as "*IDP*." In 1996,
Felix Meiner Press made the introductions available as a single work: *Die Einleitungen zur Übersetzung des Platon (1804–1828)*, in Friedrich Daniel Ernst Schleiermacher, *Über die Philosophie
Platons*, ed. Peter M. Steiner (Hamburg: Felix Meiner, 1996), 21–387; hereafter cited in text as
"*EÜP*." See below, 1.5 for more on these texts and editions. From this point forward, I refer to
his introductions to the dialogues as a single work, as his *Introductions*.
11 Stein, *Geschichte des Platonismus*, 3:375. According to Holger Thesleff, "Outside the German
sphere of influence there was no 'Platonic Question.' Plato and Platonism were as a rule interpreted along inherited lines, and little question was paid to questions of dating or authenticity"
(*Studies in Platonic Chronology*, Commentationes Humanarum Litterarum 70 [Helsinki: Societas
Scientiarum Fennica, 1982], 2).

so-called Tübingen School (*Tübinger Platonschule*), which is fiercely critical of Schleiermacher's rejection of the unwritten Platonic doctrines.[12] Although scholars associated with the Tübingen School represent a minority view, they tend to be vocal and prolific; somewhat ironically, precisely in their opposition to Schleiermacher, they have resurrected him as a Plato scholar. The publication of the new Schleiermacher critical edition of *Platons Werke* will most certainly stimulate renewed interest.[13] In short, as a scholar of Plato, Schleiermacher still cannot be ignored.

The perspective taken in the present volume is that of Schleiermacher studies. Let us take a moment to orient ourselves in that field's literature so as to assess the need for a full-length study of Schleiermacher and Plato. In general, German scholarship on Schleiermacher has demonstrated much greater awareness of the significance of Plato for him than has the secondary literature in English (or other languages), in no small part because of Germans' greater access to the primary texts but also because Schleiermacher's translation of Plato was *the* authoritative one in German. When Germans read Plato, they also held Schleiermacher in their hands. German-speaking students and scholars have thus enjoyed a more immediate acquaintance with Schleiermacher in relation to Plato than have we Anglophone students and scholars, who have had to arrive at that connection as a piece of information. Nonetheless, the work on Schleiermacher and Plato has remained surprisingly sparse given how significant and compelling the question is.

Wilhelm Dilthey (1833–1911), in his monumental biographical study of Schleiermacher's thought, gave considerable weight to the importance of Plato.[14] He argued that Plato, along with Spinoza and Shaftesbury, was a determining philosophical force in Schleiermacher's thought. Also in the late nineteenth century, there was a published dissertation comparing Schleiermacher and Plato on virtue, but that relied mainly on Schleiermacher's later essay on ethics, not on *Platons Werke*.[15] A general lack of full-scale studies of the topic continued throughout most of the twentieth century. That is not to say, however,

---

[12] See Hösle, "The Tübingen School."
[13] See above, n.2.
[14] See Wilhelm Dilthey, *Leben Schleiermachers* (Berlin: Reimer, 1870), 3rd ed., edited by Martin Redeker (Berlin: Walter de Gruyter, 1970; reprint, 2019), 1/2:37–75; also, *Leben Schleiermachers*, vol. 2: *Schleiermachers System als Philosophie und Theologie*, ed. Martin Redeker (Berlin: De Gruyter, 1966; reprint, De Gruyter, 2011), sub-vol. 3: 680–83.
[15] See Paul Kroker, *Die Tugendlehre Schleiermachers, mit spezieller Berücksichtigung der Tugendlehre Platos* (Erlangen: Junge & Sohn, 1889).

1.2 The Question: Schleiermacher and Plato — 5

that there were not insightful contributions to the conversation.[16] A significant shift occurred around the turn of this century due in part, no doubt, to the publication of the Meiner edition of Schleiermacher's lectures on Socrates and Plato and, importantly, his *Die Einleitungen zur Übersetzung des Platon*, which were collected for the first time in German in one place.[17] Scholarly attention to Schleiermacher and Plato has increased dramatically in the first two decades of the twenty-first century.[18] Jan Rohls has investigated in some depth the influence of Schleiermacher's *Introductions* (in particular, his "Introduction to the *So-*

---

16 See (in chronological order), Rudolf Odebrecht, "Der Geist der Sokratik im Werke Schleiermachers," in *Geistige Gestalten und Probleme: Eduard Spranger zum 60. Geburtstag*, ed. Hans Wenke (Leipzig: Quelle & Meyer, 1942), 103–118; Martin Redeker, *Schleiermacher: Life and Thought*, trans. John Wallhausser (Philadelphia: Fortress Press, 1973), 181–85; Werner Schultz, "Das griechische Ethos in Schleiermachers Reden und Monologen," *Neue Zeitschrift für systematische Theologie und Religionsphilosophie* 10 (1968): 261–88; Norbert Vorsmann, *Die Bedeutung des Platonismus für den Aufbau der Erziehungstheorie bei Schleiermacher und Herbart* (Düsseldorf: A. Henn, 1968); Hans-Georg Gadamer, "Schleiermacher Platonicien," *Archives de Philosophe* 32, no. 1 (1969): 28–39; Wolfgang Virmond, "Der fiktive Autor: Schleiermachers technische Interpretation der platonischen Dialoge (1804) als Vorstufe seiner Hallenser Hermeneutik (1805)," *Archivo di Filosofia* 52, nos. 1–3 (1984): 225–32; Franz Christ, "Schleiermacher zum Verhältnis von Mythos und Logos bei Platon," and Gunter Scholtz, "Schleiermacher und die Platonische Ideenlehre," in *Internationaler Schleiermacher-Kongress 1984*, ed. Hermann Fischer and Kurt-Victor Selge (Berlin: Walter de Gruyter, 1985), 837–48, 849–74, respectively; Hermann Patsch, "Poetische Nachbildungen in der Platon-Übersetzung," in *Alle Menschen sind Künstler: Friedrich Schleiermachers poetische Versuche* (Berlin: Walter de Gruyter, 1986), 68–76; and Eilert Herms, "Platonismus und Aristotelismus in Schleiermachers Ethik," in *Schleiermacher's Philosophy and the Philosophical Tradition*, ed. Sergio Sorrentino (Lewiston: Edwin Mellen Press, 1992), 3–26, and *Menschsein im Werden: Studien zu Schleiermacher* (Tübingen: Mohr Siebeck, 2003), 167–71.
17 See Steiner, *Über die Philosophie Platons* (see above, n.10). The three introductory essays in the Meiner edition also mark important contributions: Andreas Arndt, "Schleiermacher und Platon," vii–xxii ; Steiner, "Zur Kontroverse um Schleiermachers Platon," xxiii–xliv; and Jörg Jantzen, "Schleiermachers Platon-Übersetzung und seine Anmerkungen dazu," xlv–lviii.
18 See, e.g., Andrea Follak, *Der 'Aufblick zur Idee': Eine vergleichende Studie zur Platonischen Pädgogik bei Friedrich Schleiermacher, Paul Natorp und Werner Jaeger* (Göttingen: Vandenhoeck & Ruprecht, 2005); Christoph Asmuth, *Interpretation–Transformation: Das Platonbild bei Fichte, Schelling, Hegel, Schleiermacher und Schopenhauer und das Legitimationsproblem der Philosophiegeschichte* (Göttingen: Vandenhoeck & Ruprecht, 2006); Andreas Arndt, "'Das Unsterbliche mit dem Sterblichen verbinden': Friedrich Schleiermacher und Platons 'Symposion'," and "Ueber den Werth des Sokrates als Philosophen: Schleiermacher und Sokrates," in *Friedrich Schleiermacher als Philosoph* (Berlin: De Gruyter, 2013), 275–84 and 285–96, respectively; and Virmond, "*interpretari necesse est*: Über die Wurzeln von Schleiermachers *Hermeneutik und Kritik*," in *Friedrich Schleiermacher in Halle (1804–1807)*, ed. Andreas Arndt (Berlin: Walter de Gruyter, 2013), 67–76.

phist") and his lectures on the history of philosophy (1807–1823) on the development of his own *Dialectics*.[19] More and more, Schleiermacher scholars mention his work on Plato and underscore the importance of that, even though that may not be the main topic of their work.[20] For the most part, those German scholars who have explored the influence of Plato on Schleiermacher have focused on his philosophy, in particular his *Dialectics* and *Hermeneutics*. Lutz Käppel, a classicist and editor of *Platons Werke* for the *KGA*, has been doing probing work on Schleiermacher as a philologist.[21]

In the Anglophone world, the story is similar, albeit thinner. There was a mid-twentieth-century dissertation that explored "Platonic Dialectics and Schleiermacher's Thought" in depth, but it was never published and thus did not have the influence it could or should have had.[22] In the third quarter of the twentieth century, as interest in Schleiermacher was growing in North America, three influential monographs did point to the significance of Plato for him

---

19 Jan Rohls, "'Der Winckelmann der griechischen Philosophie': Schleiermachers Platonismus im Kontext," in *200 Jahre "Reden über die Religion": Akten des 1. Internationalen Kongresses der Schleiermacher-Gesellschaft Halle 14.–17. März 1999*, ed. Ulrich Barth and Claus-Dieter Osthövener (Berlin: Walter de Gruyter, 2000), 467–496; "Wahrheit, Dialog und Sprache in Schleiermachers *Dialektik*," in *Schleiermachers Dialektik: Die Liebe zum Wissen in Philosophie und Theologie*, ed. Christine Helmer, Christiane Kranich, and Birgit Rehme-Iffert (Tübingen: Mohr Siebeck, 2003), 181–206; and "Schleiermachers Platon," in *Schleiermacher und Kierkegaard*, ed. Niels Jørgen Cappelørn, Richard E. Crouter, Theodor Jørgensen and Claus-Dieter Osthövener (Berlin, Boston: De Gruyter, 2006), 709–731.
20 A good example of this is Sarah Schmidt's study of Schleiermacher's philosophy of reciprocity, *Die Konstruktion des Endlichen: Schleiermachers Philosophie der Wechselwirkung* (Berlin and New York: Walter de Gruyter, 2012), 6, 9, 19, 38, 44, 53, 106, 108, 111–12, 115, 217–19, 248, 262, 290.
21 See Lutz Käppel, "Schleiermachers Hermeneutik zwischen zeitgenössischer Philologie und 'Phaidros'-Lektüre," in *Schleiermacher-Tag 2005. Eine Vortragsreihe*, ed. Günter Meckenstock (Göttingen: Vandenhoeck & Ruprecht, 2006), 65–74; "Die frühe Rezeption der Platon-Übersetzung Friedrich Schleiermachers am Beispiel der Arbeiten Friedrich Asts," in *Geist und Buchstabe: Interpretations- und Transformationsprozesse innerhalb des Christentums. Festschrift für Günter Meckenstock zum 65. Geburtstag*, ed. Michael Pietsch und Dirk Schmid (Berlin and Boston: De Gruyter, 2013), 45–62; and "(Re-)Konstruktion von Antike als (Neu-)Konstruktion von Moderne. Schleiermachers Auseinandersetzung mit Platon und Heraklit," in *Reformation und Moderne. Pluralität—Subjektivität—Kritik*, ed. Jörg Dierken, Arnulf von Scheliha, and Sarah Schmidt (Berlin and Boston: Walter de Gruyter, 2018), 699–717.
22 Gustav-Adolf Krapf, "Platonic Dialectics and Schleiermacher's Thought: An Essay Towards the Reinterpretation of Schleiermacher," Ph.D. diss., Yale University, 1953. In his abstract, Krapf stressed the simple but overlooked fact that "Schleiermacher can be interpreted more adequately if he is read in the light of Plato" (n.p.).

but did not dwell on the matter,[23] and the Anglophone world remained in a relative state of ignorance concerning one of Schleiermacher's greatest achievements. That situation began to change in the 1980s with Albert Blackwell's penetrating study of the early Schleiermacher, all the more impressive since it preceded the *KGA*, and therefore he had to work with manuscripts and Schleiermacher's miniscule handwriting. Blackwell devoted a chapter to "Schleiermacher's Debt to Spinoza and Plato," where he rehearsed the translation project and drew a preliminary (yet insightful) sketch of how Schleiermacher was influenced by Plato.[24] I have tried to make my own contribution with several essays, some of which have been revised and incorporated here in *Schleiermacher's Plato*.[25] It has become much more commonplace than it had been for scholars to note the Plato connection and even to expand on it somewhat.[26] To this day, however, there is still no full-length study of Schleiermacher's Plato, and most certainly not when it comes to his theology. The topic indeed appears a rich one to pursue.

---

23 As we shall see in chap. 5, Richard R. Niebuhr demonstrated keen awareness of the importance of Plato: "the long labor with Plato more than any other experience tempered and sharpened the systematic bent of his mind" (31–32) and asked the question of the Platonic nature of Schleiermacher's *Christmas Dialogue* (*Schleiermacher on Christ and Religion: A New Introduction* [New York: Charles Scribner's Sons, 1964; reprint, Eugene: Wipf & Stock, 2009]). Richard B. Brandt mentioned Plato frequently but in only passing, with no real examination of actual texts (*The Philosophy of Schleiermacher: The Development of His Theory of Scientific and Religious Knowledge* [New York: Greenwood, 1968]). Robert R. Williams reminded us that Schleiermacher had been the translator of Plato (14) and compared features of Schleiermacher's theology with the *Parmenides* (60–64), but he did not examine what Schleiermacher actually wrote about that dialogue; his primary concern was to compare Schleiermacher and Cusanus, whom he took to represent a type of Platonism (*Schleiermacher the Theologian: The Construction of the Doctrine of God* [Philadelphia: Fortress, 1978]).
24 Blackwell, *Early Philosophy of Life*, 123–36.
25 See Julia A. Lamm, "Schleiermacher as Plato Scholar," *Journal of Religion* 80, no. 2 (April 2000): 206–39; "Reading Plato's Dialectics: Schleiermacher's Insistence on Dialectics as Dialogical," *Zeitschrift für Neuere Theologiegeschichte/Journal for the History of Modern Theology* 10, no. 1 (April 2003): 1–25; "The Art of Interpreting Plato," in *Cambridge Companion to Schleiermacher*, ed. Jacqueline Mariña (Cambridge: Cambridge University Press, 2005), 91–108; "Plato's Dialogues as a Single Work of Art: Friedrich Schleiermacher's *Platons Werke*," in *Lire les Dialogues, mais lesquels et dans quel ordre? Définitions du corpus et interprétations de Platon*, ed. Anne Balansard and Isabelle Koch (Sankt Augustin: Academia Verlag, 2013), 173–88; and "Schleiermacher's Modern Platonism," in Dierken, Scheliha, and Schmidt, *Reformation und Moderne*, 675–697.
26 See, e.g., Ruth Jackson Ravenscroft, "A Platonic Scheme?" in *The Veiled God: Friedrich Schleiermacher's Theology of Finitude* (Leiden: Brill, 2019), 179–83.

1.3 Thesis and Approach of *Schleiermacher's Plato*

Schleiermacher's Plato seeks to fill this lacuna in Schleiermacher studies. For the first half of the book (chapters 2–4), my guiding question is, *How did Schleiermacher understand Plato?* There I focus almost exclusively on Schleiermacher's *Introductions* to Plato's dialogues, treating them as a single work. In the second half of the book (chapters 5–7), my guiding question is, *In what ways might Schleiermacher's religious thought have been influenced by Plato?* There I shift attention to two of Schleiermacher's signature works on religion, both of which he published in 1806 while still so diligently translating and interpreting Plato: *The Christmas Celebration: A Dialogue* (*Die Weihnachtsfeier: Ein Gespräch*), and the second edition of his famous *On Religion: Speeches to Its Cultured Despisers* (*Über die Religion. Reden an die Gebildeten unter ihren Verächtern*). I examine both texts in light of his interpretation of Plato and alongside of his *Introductions*. Once again, answers to this latter question inescapably presupposes answers to the prior question.

My thesis is a necessarily complex one, given the enormity of the topic. Schleiermacher's thought, including his thinking about religion and Christian faith during the first decade of the nineteenth century, was profoundly influenced by Plato—by, that is, his rather distinctive understanding of Plato, which is not necessarily immediately recognizable as Platonic and is therefore better termed "Schleiermacher's Plato." That influence, moreover, was not unidirectional insofar as Schleiermacher's interpretation was shaped not only by views cultivated earlier during his Romantic period in Berlin (1796–1802), but also (and especially) by philosophical commitments he assiduously developed while in Stolp (1802–1804) and Halle (1804–1807). In other words, Schleiermacher's Plato is much more definite than the more generalized affinity he and other Romantics had felt with Plato—when, for instance, he wrote the first edition of his *Speeches* in 1799. The first decade of the nineteenth century was a critical time for Schleiermacher's development as a scholar. In those years he was simultaneously engaged in several intellectual pursuits on many fronts: intensively interpreting and translating Plato, which resulted in the publication of five volumes of *Platons Werke* in six years (1804–1809); systematically working out the basic principles of his ethics and epistemology in his *Grundlinien* (1803);[27] lecturing on ethics, hermeneutics, New Testament exegesis, fundamental theology, theological encyclopedia and methodology, and dogmatics; and preaching in his capacity as university chaplain. It was a period of astonish-

---

[27] See n. 30 below.

ing creativity and systematization amidst multi-disciplinary engagement. Plato inspired him, and his portrait of Plato was in turn shaped by this unique confluence of scholarly activities. Once we see that, we will recognize Schleiermacher's Plato not in his philosophical works alone but in his religious writings as well. This more formal thesis is given specificity in each of the following chapters.

In chapter two, "Schleiermacher's *Platons Werke* and Its Legacy," I consider Schleiermacher as a Plato scholar, laying out the principles of interpretation which he enunciated in his "General Introduction." I explain his early collaboration with Friedrich Schlegel (1772–1829), how he viewed himself in relation to previous Plato interpreters, and how later interpreters responded to him. There we encounter Schleiermacher's Plato as the "perfect artist" whose art form is the dialogue and whose doctrines cannot be known apart from the written text; more to the point, Plato as philosopher can be found *only* in the text as written, and never by circumventing its dialogic form.

In chapter three, "Practicing on Plato: Interpretation, Socratic Clues, and the Emergence of Schleiermacher's Hermeneutics," I delve deeper in his interpretation of Plato—more particularly, into *how* he interpreted Plato. Schleiermacher's ground-breaking lectures on *Hermeneutics and Criticism* arose out of his struggle to translate Plato. I argue that it was more than the act of translating; it was, rather, that he found actual clues for interpreting Plato in the dialogues themselves, and he then took up those Socratic clues into his more general theory of interpretation. I detail how Schleiermacher ordered the dialogues and determined their authenticity, and why that was key to his understanding of Plato. There we encounter Schleiermacher's Plato as that of the *Phaedrus* and as the consummate pedagogue.

In chapter four, "Reading Plato's Dialectics: Schleiermacher's Insistence on Dialectics as Dialogical," I tease out certain sustained reflexes which Schleiermacher exercised in interpreting the content of Plato's philosophy and which distinguish his Plato from more commonly recognizable forms of Platonism. The investigation there shifts somewhat from how Schleiermacher interpreted Plato to how he began to shape a new form of Platonism. I suggest how Schleiermacher's Plato is distinctly modern in the sense that, at the very least, it is not tied to a hierarchically arranged, dualistic metaphysics divorced from historical forces. There we encounter Schleiermacher's Plato as colored by the middle dialogues (the *Sophist*, *Symposium*, and *Phaedo*): the contemplative philosopher and, simultaneously, the gregarious world-loving Socrates.

In chapter five, "Schleiermacher's *Christmas Dialogue* as Platonic Dialogue," I begin considering whether his work on Plato influenced his thinking about religion, theology, or Christian faith. I move beyond the *Introductions* and into his *The Christmas Celebration: A Dialogue*, which he wrote under inspiration in December 1805 and published the following month. I address the long-standing question of whether his *Christmas Dialogue* can properly be seen as a Platonic dialogue, arguing that it is indeed Platonic, as Schleiermacher understood that. I make the case that, contrary to the usual ways of answering that question, the Platonic character can neither be reduced to one dialogue (e.g., the *Symposium*) nor restricted to one small part of his *Christmas Dialogue* (e.g., the men's speeches toward to the end); rather, the structure of his entire *Dialogue* reflects how Schleiermacher understood the structure of the entire Platonic *corpus*. There we have the first inklings of how his work on Plato affected his religious thought, as we can also observe another way in which Schleiermacher's Plato was distinctly modern: democratic and inclusive, insofar as women and children are included in the dialogue. Still, the influence of Plato is more formal than substantive: in the dialogue form, obviously, but also in the structure of the whole; the content, however, has to do with the incarnation and a particularly Christian form of joy. In the *Christmas Dialogue*, we encounter Schleiermacher's Plato as an undercurrent in conversation, aesthetics, celebration, ritual, and life-affirming apophasis.

In chapters six and seven, "The Presence of Plato in the *Speeches* (1806)," parts 1 and 2, I turn to Schleiermacher's *On Religion: Speeches to Its Cultured Despisers*, which he revised and published as a second edition in 1806, while continuing to work on *Platons Werke*. The issue of Schleiermacher's revisions to the second Speech, on "The Essence of Religion," has been another matter of pointed debate in the history of Schleiermacher studies. In these chapters, I read blocks of revised and added passages in the second edition of the *Speeches* alongside passages from his *Introductions*. I argue that Schleiermacher's Plato-interpretation directly and substantively influenced those revisions—indeed, that it even informed significant changes to his argument about religion. Plato is present in the *Speeches*, but it is very much Schleiermacher's Plato, which is perhaps why that presence has not been detected in this way before. The Schleiermacher's Plato we encounter there is the philosopher who holds together theory and practice, who systematically interweaves ethics and physics, and who presupposes the unity of being and knowing.

Schleiermacher's Plato does not exhaust the topic of Schleiermacher's Plato —nor could it, given how vast the issue is, how voluminous the material, and how polymath the man. There is much work yet to be done. My hope is that this book will establish a baseline and spark further conversation, questions, and ideas. I do not assess Schleiermacher's interpretation of Plato but seek instead to examine how he understood Plato and what he did with that Plato. The argument I present here remains focused on a particular period in Schleiermacher's life, what I call his decade of Plato.

1.4 The Decade of Plato in Schleiermacher's Life

Any comprehensive study of the influence of Plato on Schleiermacher would have to distinguish among and treat at least five periods in his life. In each period, he encountered Plato in various and distinct ways:
1. *His school-boy days at Niesky* (1783–1785), when he first learned Latin and Greek and read ancient literature.
2. *His university days at Halle* (1787–1789), a university known at the time for its unique confluence of Pietistic and Enlightenment sensibilities, where he studied philosophy, including new critical philosophy of Immanuel Kant (1724–1804), but where he also took a keen interest in Aristotle's *Nicomachean Ethics*.
3. *His Romantic period, the first period in Berlin* (1796–1802), when he served as the Reformed chaplain at the famed Charité hospital, was drawn into the social world of the Berlin salons, and emerged as a key figure in the early German Romantic circle.
4. *His time in Stolp and Halle, the inter-Berlin period* (1802–1807), when he established himself as a scholar, including as a Plato scholar, and held his first university appointment.
5. *His second Berlin period* (1808–1834), when he was a founding faculty member of the University of Berlin and reached maturity as a renowned theologian, church leader, member of the Royal Prussian Academy of Sciences, and political activist.[28]

The temptation is to dive into the third period, since Plato was indeed so important to the Romantics and their embrace of him represented a new, modern form of Platonism. Frederick Beiser names this a "hyperrational" Platonic mystical tradition, which competed with a Protestant (and Kantian) "suprarationalism."[29]

---

28 During this extended period, Schleiermacher also worked on the pre-Socratics (especially Heraclitus) and lectured on the history of philosophy. See, e.g., Käppel, "(Re-)Konstruktion von Antike."
29 Frederick C. Beiser, *The Romantic Imperative: The Concept of Early German Romanticism* (Cambridge, MA and London: Harvard University Press, 2003), 64. Beiser explains, "The object of their intellectual intuition is indeed the archetypes, the forms, or ideas underlying all phenomena. While the romantics are indeed skeptical of the powers of the intellect to know these forms, they still believe that they exist, and that we can have some intuition of them, however vague and fleeting" (64). Beiser intends this as an important corrective to the influential position of Manfred Frank, who failed to recognize the Platonic dimension of the early Romantics. The result, Beiser argues, has been the injection of "an unnecessary element of obscurantism into *Frühromantik*, which makes it vulnerable to all the old charges of antirationalism"

When it comes to the influence of Plato on Schleiermacher in particular, Beiser makes the following case:

> Various aspects of Schleiermacher's philosophy have much of their origins in his study of Plato: his conception of dialectic, his organic view of nature, his skepticism about foundationalism, and his theory of religious experience. It is this final aspect of Plato's influence that is especially relevant here. If we carefully read Schleiermacher's analysis of religious experience in the second speech of the *Reden*, its Platonic roots soon reveal themselves.[30]

The evidence he offers is from the first edition of the *Speeches* (1799), written before *Platons Werke* was conceived. Yet, while this may be the Romantics' Plato, which is of course hugely important for understanding Schleiermacher and Plato, it is not yet Schleiermacher's Plato.

In the present book, I focus almost exclusively on the fourth period, when Schleiermacher was working most intensively on *Platons Werke*—and when, therefore, Schleiermacher's Plato came to be. Understanding this decade of Schleiermacher's intellectual development is critical for understanding why the influence of Plato on Schleiermacher's thinking cannot be construed as unidirectional, or even bidirectional, inasmuch as Schleiermacher was involved in a myriad of other scholarly pursuits which were themselves ground-breaking, both personally for him and also for modern philosophy and theology. This same decade marked an intellectual transition for Schleiermacher from Romanticism to a more academic, systematic style. As John Wallhausser puts it, "The Halle years consolidated his thinking,"[31] except that, I would add, such consolidation began earlier, in Stolp. The significance of this decade for Schleiermacher's thought is receiving fuller treatment, and deservedly so.[32]

(65–66). Elsewhere Beiser adds, "The romantic doctrine of the primacy of aesthetic experience over the forms of discursive thinking was not meant as a rejection or limitation of reason in general but was intended to elevate intuitive forms of reason over discursive ones. It was never intended as a rejection of rationality as such" ("Romanticism and Idealism," in *The Relevance of Romanticism: Essays on German Romantic Philosophy*, ed. Dalia Nassar [New York 2014], 37).
30 Beiser, *Romantic Imperative*, 70.
31 Wallhausser, "General Introduction" to Schleiermacher, *Brouillon zur Ethik/Notes on Ethics (1805/1806)*, trans. John Wallhausser (Lewiston, Queenston, Lampeter: The Edwin Mellen Press, 2003), 4.
32 See Arndt, *Schleiermacher in Halle*. Two volumes of the *KGA* have helped spur interest in this period of his life: *KGA* 1/4: *Schriften aus der Stolper Zeit (1802–1804)*, ed. Eilert Herms, Günter Meckenstock, and Michael Pietsch (Berlin and New York: Walter de Gruyter, 2002); and *KGA* 1/5: *Schriften aus der Hallenser Zeit (1804–1807)*, ed. Hermann Patsch (Berlin and Boston: De Gruyter, 2011).

Here I perform two preliminary tasks in order to lay some groundwork for my argument. First, I provide a visual overview of his many overlapping activities and accomplishments during this period of his life (see table 1). Second, I sketch some biographical contours of Schleiermacher's life in Stolp and Halle, along with some pertinent passages from two other works written during that time, both of which have direct relevance for understanding Schleiermacher's Plato. This should serve to underscore how Schleiermacher was not influenced by some abstract, ahistorical form of Platonism; rather, he himself shaped an understanding of Plato that in turn profoundly shaped his emerging thought.

1.4.1 Exile in Stolp, Pomerania (1802–1804)

Schleiermacher left Berlin in 1802 to take a position as head pastor for the Reformed congregation in (and smaller congregations around) Stolp, in Eastern Pomerania, for a kind of self-imposed exile. The work was hard and the existence lonely, but it afforded him the opportunity to devote himself to his scholarship in an unprecedented way. During his sojourn there, he worked intensively on two major works simultaneously: the lengthy, somewhat tortuous study of ethical theories, *Grundlinien einer Kritik der bisherigen Sittenlehre* (*Baselines of a Critique of Previous Ethics*),[33] and the first two volumes of *Platons Werke*. The *Grundlinien* had been conceived back when he was rooming with Schlegel in Berlin, but it took a different shape in Stolp as Schleiermacher worked on it between June 1802 and August 1803; it was published in October 1803.[34] At the same time, he was collaborating on the Plato project until Schlegel withdrew in May 1803 and the project became Schleiermacher's alone.[35] After completing the *Grundlinien* that summer, Schleiermacher immediately turned his full attention to *Platons Werke*, submitting the final manuscript for the first volume in April 1804. Hence, within a span of seven months (between October 1803 and May 1804), he published his first two scholarly works: the *Grundlinien* and *Platons Werke I,1*. Although representing different genres, the two works were intricately connected.

The *Grundlinien*, while certainly not one of his successful or better-known works, was nevertheless crucial for Schleiermacher in thinking through some

---

[33] Schleiermacher, *Grundlinien einer Kritik der bisherigen Sittenlehre* (1803), in *KGA* 1/4: 27–350.
[34] He finished Bk 1 in Feb. 1803; Bk 2 in Apr. 1803; and the final part, Bk 3, in Aug. 1803.
[35] See below, 2.2.

Table 1: Chronology of Schleiermacher's Decade of Plato

Date/Place	Life Events	Publications	University Lectures
1799–1802/ Berlin		*Speeches on Religion* (1799)	
		Soliloquies (1800)	
1802–1804/ Stolp	June 1802: S. begins new position in Stolp as head pastor	("Notes on Plato")	
1802		"Review of Ast's *Phaedrus*"	
1803		*Grundlinien* (Oct.)	
1804	Aug. 31, 1804: S. departs Stolp	*PW I,1* (May)	
1804–1807/ Halle	Oct. 12: S. begins new position at University of Halle		
1804			Winter 1804/05: 1) systematic theology; 2) encyclopedia & methodology; 3) ethics (*Brouillon*).
1805	Mar.: S. preaches for first time in Halle	*PW I,2* (early 1805)	
			Summer 1805: 1) hermeneutics; 2) encyclopedia; 3) fundamental theology
		PW II,1 (Nov.)	Winter 1805/06: 1) ethics (*Brouillon*); 2) dogmatics; 3) exegesis (*Gal.*)
1806		*Christmas Dialogue* (Jan.)	
		Speeches, 2nd ed. (Sept.)	Summer 1806: 1) exegesis (*Thess., Cor., Rom.*) 2) Christian ethics 3) method: church history
	Oct. 17: Halle falls to Napoleon		Halle University is closed

1.4 The Decade of Plato in Schleiermacher's Life — 15

Table 1: Chronology of Schleiermacher's Decade of Plato *(continued)*

Date/Place	Life Events	Publications	University Lectures
1807		"Review of Fichte" (Jan.) *PW II,2* (April) *I Timothy* (May)	Private lectures in Berlin on history of ancient philosophy
	Dec.: S. makes final departure from Halle for Berlin		
1808–1810/ Berlin			
1808		*Occasional Thoughts on Universities in the German Sense* *Heraclitus*	
1809		*PW II,3*	
1810	University of Berlin opens		

key philosophical issues.[36] As Beiser puts it, "the *Grundlinien* was only a critical preparation for his system."[37] As such, it provides an instructive entry point into Schleiermacher's Plato. André Laks demonstrates that, whereas in his *Grundlinien* Schleiermacher dealt with the content of Plato's philosophy, in *Platons Werke* he focused more on form.[38] In the *Grundlinien*, Plato and Benedict (Baruch) Spinoza (1632–1677) win the highest praise, but Plato the highest still.[39] Comparing the two, Schleiermacher wrote:

---

36 See John Wallhausser, "Schleiermacher's Critique of Ethical Reason: Toward a Systematic Ethics," *The Journal of Religious Ethics* 17, no. 2 (fall 1989): 25–39.
37 Frederick C. Beiser, "Schleiermacher's Ethics," in Mariña, *Cambridge Companion to Schleiermacher*, 53.
38 See André Laks, "Schleiermacher on Plato: From Form (*Introduction to Plato's Works*) to Content (*Outlines of a Critique of Previous Ethical Theory*)," in Kim, *Brill's Companion to German Platonism*, 146–64; and "Platonicien malgré lui? Le statut de l'éthique platonicienne dans les Grundlinien," *Archives De Philosophie* 77, no. 2 (April–June 2014): 259–79.
39 For more on Spinoza's infuence on the early Schleiermacher, see Julia A. Lamm, *The Living God: Schleiermacher's Theological Appropriation of Spinoza* (University Park: Pennsylvania State University Press, 1996).

Of the latter, everyone somewhat acquainted with [Plato] must know how from the beginning on he proceeded from the presentiment [*Ahndung*] to pursue a common ground for the science of the true and of the good, for physics and ethics; and how he constantly sought [that ground], drawing ever nearer to its origin over time. Yes, it can be said that, in all his significant expositions, this striving is the place out from which light disseminates itself throughout the whole. For [Plato], the infinite being [*Wesen*] appears not only as existing [*seiend*] and generating [*hervorbringed*] but also as poeticizing [*dichtend*], and the world [appears] as a becoming, from works of art into the infinite, [into a] composed work of art of the godhead. For that reason, too, everything individual and real is only becoming [*werdende*], while the infinite, forming [*bildende*] [being] alone [can be said to be] *existing* [*seiend*]. [These] are also for him the universal ideas [*Begriffe*]—not, as for [Spinoza], mere appearance and illusion [on the part] of humans; rather, by the opposite method, they become for [Plato] the living thoughts of the godhead, which are to be presented in things, the eternal ideals [*Ideale*], in which and for which everything *is*. Since he now posits for all finite things a beginning of its becoming, and a progression of the same in time, thus emerges also necessarily in all who are given a relationship with the highest being [*Wesen*] the demand to draw near to the ideal of the same. No fuller expression for this demand can be given than this: to become like God [*Theaetetus* 176b]. It is clear, therefore, that here [with Plato] a yet firmer connection of ethics to the supreme science occurs [than with Spinoza]. This is not the place to evaluate, however, whether the highest science itself has a firm basis that is logical, as Spinoza constructs it, or is in accordance with a poetic presupposition of the highest being, as Plato portrays it. The end of the investigation is just this: that, among all those who have grasped the idea to establish ethics out of a higher science, the only ones to perhaps be successful until now are those who have philosophized objectively—that is to say, who have taken as their starting point the infinite as the sole necessary object.[40]

---

40 Schleiermacher, *Grundlinien*, in *KGA* 1/4: 65.8–66.13 (*Von diesem muß Jeder, der ihn einigermaßen kennt, es wissen, wie er von Anfang an von der Ahndung ausgegangen ist für die Wissenschaft des Wahren und des Guten, für die Physik und Ethik einen gemeinschaftlichen Grund zu suchen, und wie er diesen, ihrem Ursprünge sich je länger je mehr annähernd, beständig aufgesucht hat. Ja man kann sagen, daß es keine bedeutende giebt unter seinen Darstellungen, worin nicht dieses Bestreben die Stelle wäre, von welcher aus sich Licht über das Ganze verbreitete. Ihm nun erscheint das unendliche Wesen nicht nur als seiend und hervorbringend, sondern auch als dichtend, und die Welt als ein werdendes, aus Kunstwerken ins Unendliche zusammengesezteS Kunstwerk der Gottheit. Daher auch weil Alles Einzelne und wirkliche nur werdend ist, das unendliche bildende aber allein seiend, sind auch ihm die allgemeinen Begriffe, nicht etwa nur wie jenem, Schein und Wahn der Menschen, sondern bei dem entgegengesezten Verfahren werden sie ihm die lebendigen Gedanken der Gottheit, welche in den Dingen sollen dargestellt werden, die ewigen Ideale, in welchen und zu welchen Alles ist. Da er nun allen endlichen Dingen einen Anfang sezt ihres Werdens, und ein Fortschreiten desselben in der Zeit, so entsteht auch nothwendig in allen, denen eine Verwandschaft mit dem höchsten Wesen gegeben ist, die Forderung dem Ideale desselben anzunähern, für welche es keinen andern erschöpfenden Ausdruck geben kann, als den der Gottheit ähnlich zu werden. Daß also hier eine noch festere Anknüpfung der Ethik an die oberste Wissenschaft statt finde, als dort, ist offenbar. Ob aber die höchste Wissenschaft selbst so logisch, als Spinoza sie aufbaut, oder so wie Platon sie nur nach einer poetischen Voraussezung des höchsten*

We will find Schleiermacher returning to some of these same insights, although using slightly different terminology, in *Platons Werke*.

In early 1804, Schleiermacher, miserable and lonely, received and hesitantly accepted an academic position at the newly reconstituted University of Würzburg, in Bavaria.[41] The Prussian king, Friedrich Wilhelm III, interrupted that plan by offering him instead a position at the University of Halle, which Schleiermacher had attended as a student. It was his first academic appointment. He had yet to publish anything in the field of theology.

1.4.2 Academic Life in Halle (1804–1807)

On 12 October 1804, five months after the first volume of *Platons Werke* had appeared and just as he was completing the second volume, Schleiermacher arrived in Halle for his new position as professor of theology and philosophy and as university preacher. That first semester he lectured on fundamental doctrines of the theological system; on theological encyclopedia and methodology; and on ethics (it was billed as a course on Christian ethics but wound up being more general and philosophical, what he called the *Brouillon*, meaning a sketch or rough draft). I quote here three passages from the *Brouillon* on the relationship between ethics and physics:

> Ethics is thus one entire side of philosophy. Everything in it appears as a producing, just as in natural science everything appears as a product. Each of these two must accept something else from the other as positive, for even knowing and acting are natural faculties and must be authenticated as such. Accordingly, all real knowing divides into these two sides.[42]

Wesen hinzeichnet, einen festen Stand habe, dieses zu beurtheilen, ist nicht des gegenwärtigen Orts. Nur dies ist das Ende der Untersuchung, daß unter Allen, welche den Gedanken gefaßt haben, die Ethik aus einer höheren Wissenschaft her zu begründen, es nur denen bis izt vielleicht gelungen ist, welche objectiv philosophirt haben, das heißt von dem Unendlichen als dem einzigen nothwendigen Gegenstande ausgegangen sind).

41 See Albert L. Blackwell, "Three New Schleiermacher Letters Relating to His Würzburg Appointment of 1804," *Harvard Theological Review* 68, nos. 3–4 (1975): 333–56.

42 Schleiermacher, *Notes on Ethics*, 33–34; see *Brouillon zur Ethik (1805/06)*, ed. Hans-Joachim Birkner (Hamburg: Meiner, 1981), 3–4 (*Die Ethik ist also die ganze eine Seite der Philosophie. Alles erscheint in ihr als Produciren, wie in der Naturwissenschaft als Product. Jede muß etwas anders aus der andern als positiv aufnehmen. Denn auch Wissen und Handeln sind als Vermögen Natur und müssen als solche nachgewiesen werden. Sonach theilt sich alles reale Wissen in diese beiden Seiten).*

> We have found ethics to be the polar contrast to physics.[43]
>
> The two sides stand in a relation of reciprocal dependence, mediated by the mutual necessity of the moral disposition and the scientific attitude; thus, the two also approximate completeness only together and by parallel development.[44]

As we will see, this understanding of the polar yet reciprocal relationship between ethics and physics played an important function in his Plato-interpretation. Indeed, it is a defining feature of Schleiermacher's Plato.

It was in Halle that Schleiermacher first lectured on hermeneutics (summer 1805), and it was in Halle that Schleiermacher became a theologian. He lectured on a wide range of theological topics (in the sub-fields of dogmatics, church history, Christian ethics, and exegesis), and he published arguably his first theological works: his *Christmas Dialogue*, and a historical-critical study of *I Timothy*.[45] In addition to his formal lectures and publications, he thought deeply about the natural sciences in extended dialogue with his friend and colleague, the Danish scientist and theologian Henrik Steffens (1773–1845), professor of natural philosophy, physiology, and minerology.[46] Physics, in other words, was not just an abstraction for Schleiermacher.

Halle fell to Napoleon on 17 October 1806, almost exactly two years after Schleiermacher had arrived in the city. His apartment just off the main marketplace (Große Märkerstraße 21/22) was ransacked and occupied, the university was closed, and Schleiermacher became unemployed.[47] Even so, he continued his scholarship. In short, during the three short years he spent in Halle, before returning to Berlin and eventually becoming a founding faculty member of the

---

[43] Schleiermacher, *Notes on Ethics*, 39; *Brouillon*, 10 (*Wir haben die Ethik gefunden als den ganzen Gegensaz zur Physik*).
[44] Schleiermacher, *Notes on Ethics*, 40; *Brouillon*, 10–11 (*Beide Seiten stehen in einem Verhältniß gegenseitiger Abhängigkeit vermittelst der gleichen Nothwendigkeit der Gesinnung und der Wissenschaftlichkeit; können sich also auch nur gemeinschaftlich und parallel der Vollkommenheit nähern*).
[45] On Schleiermacher's theological writings from the Halle period, see Hermann Patsch, " '… mit Interesse die eigentliche Theologie wieder hervorsuchen': Schleiermachers theologische Schriften der Hallenser Zeit," in Arndt, *Schleiermacher in Halle*, 31–54; and "Vom Pseudo-Paulus über den Sammler Lukas zum johanneischen Erlöser," in Dierken, Scheliha, and Schmidt, *Reformation und Moderne*, 749–57.
[46] See Sarah Schmidt, ed., *System und Subversion: Friedrich Schleiermacher und Henrik Steffens* (Berlin, Boston: De Gruyter, 2018); and Schmidt, "Analogie versus Wechselwirkung—Zur 'Symphilosophie' zwischen Schleiermacher und Steffens," in Arndt, *Schleiermacher in Halle*, 91–114.
[47] Steffens and his wife took Schleiermacher and his sister into their home.

newly established University of Berlin,⁴⁸ Schleiermacher was actively developing his own ideas in several fields and sub-fields at once. Plato was an integral part of that formative decade of Schleiermacher's intellectual life. Yet, as much as he absorbed Plato, he also poured much back into his reading of Plato. The influences were reciprocal, multidirectional, and pluriform.

1.5 On Texts, Translations, and Editions

This book is written for both English- and German-speaking audiences. Most of Schleiermacher's primary texts quoted here (except for his correspondence) are given first in translation and then in German. So that pages do not become too cluttered, I have adopted the following practice. Individual terms and short phrases are given in both English and German in the main text; extended passages are given in indented block quotations, first in English, followed by the German in italics; other, mid-sized quotations are given in English in the main text, with the German provided in the footnote in italics. The purpose of the italics is to make it easier for the eye to move across the page without too much delay or distraction. As much as possible, I use the *KGA* for the German texts and, when I do, provide the line numbers along with page numbers. For example, "23.5 – 9" indicates page 23, lines five through nine.

For Schleiermacher's works that have been translated, I use the English version of the title after the first use (hence, *Speeches* rather than *Reden*); for those that have not yet been translated, I stay with the German title (hence, *Platons Werke* or *Grundlinien*); one exception is his *Brouillon*, since I find the translation *Notes on Ethics* to be lacking.

I refer to Schleiermacher's introductions to Plato's dialogues simply as *Introductions*, because part of my approach is to treat them as a single work.

For *Platons Werke*, I use the *KGA* whenever possible, but to date only two volumes have been published in the new critical edition (*KGA*): *PW* 1/1 and *PW* 2/1.⁴⁹

---

48 Friedrich Wilhelm University was established in 1809 and opened in 1810 (it is now Humboldt University, named after the brothers Alexander and Wilhelm von Humboldt, two contemporaries of Schleiermacher). Schleiermacher himself was instrumental in conceiving the modern university. In 1808 he published *Gelegentliche Gedanken über Universitäten in deutschem Sinn. Nebst einem Anhang über eine neu zu errichtende* (in *KGA* 1/6:19 – 100); trans. Terrence Tice and Edwina Lawler, *Occasional Thoughts on Universities in the German Sense: With an Appendix Regarding a University Soon to Be Established (1808)* (Edwin Mellen Press, 1991).
49 See n. 2 above.

Otherwise, I use "*EÜP*"[50] when quoting from the *Introductions*, and *PW* (Eigler)[51] when citing Schleiermacher's German translation from the Greek.

The only English translation of Schleiermacher's *Introductions* is Dobson's from 1836: *Introductions to the Dialogues of Plato* (*IDP*).[52] Dobson's translation is relatively accessible through reprints and electronic copies available online. While Dobson's translation is serviceable, it also proves problematic when it comes to certain technical terms and sometimes when it comes to style. As much as possible, however, I want to encourage Anglophone readers to read along and familiarize themselves with the text. Towards that end, when I use Dobson's translation, my citation will first be to *IDP* and then to the corresponding German text; slight modifications of his translation will be signaled by a substitute word in brackets. Where I find his translation too problematic for whatever reason, I provide my own translation, in which case my citation will first be to the German text and then to the corresponding page number in *IDP*, preceded by "cf.," so that readers may cross-check the textual evidence and follow the argument.

For English translations of Plato's dialogues, I use those provided in the *Perseus Digital Library*[53] so that Anglophone readers will have ready and common access and so that Germanophone readers, too, might make their own comparisons.

---

50 See n. 10 above.
51 See n. 9 above.
52 See n. 10 above.
53 *Perseus Digital Library*, ed. Gregory R. Crane. Tufts University. http://www.perseus.tufts.edu (accessed July 17, 2020).

2 Schleiermacher's *Platons Werke* and Its Legacy

In fifty years, someone else will probably do it better.[1]

2.1 Introduction

Schleiermacher's prediction regarding *Platons Werke*, if sincere, could not have been more wrong. Not only would his translation of Plato's dialogues prove authoritative for over two centuries,[2] but the portrait of Plato he painted would continue to shape the field in profound ways even as particular points were challenged. "Through it," Dilthey declared, "the knowledge of Greek philosophy first became possible."[3] Somewhat more poetically, Ulrich von Wilamowitz-Moellendorff (1848–1931) made a similar point: among the many great philologists of his day, Schleiermacher was the most "far-sighted," since "his German Plato chased away the mystique and mist which, really since Plato's death, enshrouded the authentic image."[4] Simply put, Schleiermacher "revolutionized" how people viewed Plato and his philosophy.[5]

The very idea of undertaking so massive a project as a new translation of the entire *corpus* of Plato emerged in the context of a philological renaissance in late eighteenth-century Germany. Like the humanism of the fifteenth and sixteenth centuries, this new humanism occupied itself with translating classic texts. Unlike the earlier Renaissance, however, the new renaissance was not international in character but was specifically German. Homer, Plato, Shakespeare, and ancient Sanskrit texts were translated into a self-conscious and romantic style of German. Such philological activity was permeated by the sense that only a German, and only the German language, could uncover the soul of the classics. This new, German renaissance, moreover, was fuelled by the emergence of the new historical consciousness. Since the revolutionary work on the nature of language

---

[1] Schleiermacher to G. A. Reimer, June 1803 (#1502, lines 23–24), *Br.* 6:392.
[2] See above, chap. 1, 2.
[3] Dilthey, *Leben Schleiermachers*, 1/2:37.
[4] Ulrich von Wilamowitz-Moellendorff, *Geschichte der Philologie* (Leipzig: Teubner, 1921), 51.
[5] Rohls, "Schleiermachers Platon," 731. Schleiermacher's influence extended beyond Germany. See, e.g., Tomasz Mróz, "The Reception of Schleiermacher's View on Plato in 19th Century Poland," in John F. Finamore and John Phillips, eds., *Literary, Philosophical, and Religious Studies in the Platonic Tradition: Papers from the 7th Annual Conference of the International Society for Neoplatonic Studies*, Academia Philosophical Studies 45 (Baden-Baden: Academia, 2013), 179–89.

by J. G. Hamann (1730–1788) and J. G. Herder (1744–1803) in the 1770s, not just texts but language itself came to be viewed as fundamentally historical in nature. Schleiermacher and the other Romantics were heirs to this literary movement of the *Sturm und Drang* (*Storm and Stress*) era. They brought a bold willingness to challenge older classifications. In the Romantic canon, Plato, an ancient philosopher who had attacked the poets, was a Romantic poet and artist; Shakespeare, a modern poet, was a Romantic philosopher; and Spinoza, a modern rationalistic philosopher, was a Romantic poet and mystic. The motivation behind such reclassifications was, in part, iconoclastic: to challenge deep prejudices and tenaciously held assumptions.[6]

Inspired by the new movement and destined to bring it further, Friedrich Schlegel deemed the time ripe in terms of the development of the German language for a new, artistic translation of Plato. To help him in this project he solicited the aid of none other than his close friend and flatmate at the time, the young preacher at Charité Hospital in Berlin, Friedrich Schleiermacher. In the end, the Plato-project would outlive the friendship and would become Schleiermacher's enterprise alone. It would also significantly alter the course of Plato research.

In this first chapter, I focus on Schleiermacher as a scholar of Plato. That Schleiermacher changed the course of Plato scholarship is incontrovertible and hardly makes for a new thesis—except it is a neglected and forgotten one, especially by those of us who are not classicists. My aim, therefore, is to argue the thesis anew by means of an analysis of Schleiermacher's "General Introduction" to *Platons Werke* and a review of modern scholarship on Plato. Toward that end, I offer here a description of the translation project itself—its conception, tumultuous progress, and published product (section 2.2); an exposition of four central themes in Schleiermacher's "General Introduction" which were fairly novel to Plato studies at the time and which had a profound impact on subsequent Plato-interpretation (section 2.3); and a discussion of three points of controversy in Schleiermacher's Plato-interpretation, one of which remains contro-

---

[6] As A. Leslie Willson puts it, the aim of Romantic criticism was not just "to overthrow and demolish the *ancien régime* of classicist theory. But we should keep in mind that the real target of the romantic assault was not classicism, but the aesthetic system of neoclassicism and the classicist tradition of the *ars poetica*. The origins of Romanticism in Germany reveal a strong affinity to Greek and Roman antiquity. At best one can speak of a shift of emphasis in the relationship to classicism, which can be described as a departure from the dominant Roman and Aristotelian influence upon European criticism in exchange for a closer bond with the Greeks and especially the Platonic tradition" ("Introduction" to *German Romantic Criticism* [New York: Continuum, 1982], viii).

versial (section 2.4). To understand how Schleiermacher understood Plato is to begin to understand Schleiermacher's Plato.

2.2 Conception of the Plato Project

In 1799, just as he "penned the last stroke"[7] to his *On Religion: Speeches to Its Cultured Despisers*, Schleiermacher wrote to his friend Henriette Herz that he was taking on an even more formidable project in collaboration with their mutual friend:

> Schlegel wrote to me ... about a great *coup* which he wishes to propose with me, and that is nothing less than to translate Plato. Oh! It is a divine idea, and I fully believe that few are as well suited to the task. However, I dare not undertake it until some years hence, and then it must be undertaken free from every external dependency ... and how many years it takes ought to be given no notice. Indeed, that is a mystery and still lies far away.[8]

Their original plan for the Plato project was fourfold: Schlegel and Schleiermacher would each select the dialogues that suited him best, translate those, and send the translation complete with annotation to the other, who would offer a critical commentary; Schlegel would write an introduction, a "Study of Plato" (*Studium des Plato*) using the newest scientific method; Schleiermacher would write a concluding piece, a "Characterization of Plato" (*Charakteristik des Plato*); and, finally, they would organize the dialogues for the first time according to a historical ordering, which, Schlegel was convinced, was only waiting to be discovered.[9] Each of these points would become a matter of contention between the two collaborator-friends.

Schlegel had clearly been the leader of the project.[10] His name gave weight to the project. It was he who invited Schleiermacher to help in the project, he who evidently dictated the original plan, and he who undertook negotiations

---

7 Schleiermacher to Herz, 15 Apr. 1799 (#629, lines 18–19), *Br.* 3:90.
8 Schleiermacher to Herz, 29 Apr. 1799 (#640, lines 9–11), *Br.* 3:101.
9 See F. Schlegel to Schleiermacher, 10 and 28 Mar. 1800 (#808, lines 25–42; #824, lines 32–35), *Br.* 3:412, 443, respectively; and the announcement of the Plato-translation in *Intelligenzblatt der Allgemeinen Literatur-Zeitung*, 29 Mar. 1800 (in *KGA* 4/3:xvii, n.8) and in *Poetisches Journal* 1/2 (1800): 493–94.
10 There is some evidence to suggest that the two conceived the project together during the first year of rooming together, but Ernst Behler, original editor of *Kritische Friedrich-Schlegel-Ausgabe* (München, Paderborn, Wien: Schöningh, 1958–), argues that Schlegel had been occupied with a translation of Plato as early as 1796, before he met Schleiermacher (*KFSA* 19:536).

with the publisher Karl Frommann. According to the agreement reached by Schlegel and Frommann in late winter 1800, the Plato translation was to be a two-volume work, with the first volume appearing around Easter 1801. Schlegel communicated the details of the agreement in a letter to Schleiermacher and inquired whether he, too, would like to be named both in the announcement and on the title page.[11] That Schlegel even had to ask such a question is curious; that, rather than waiting for a reply, he unilaterally decided that only his name would appear in the announcement is startling. His explanation after the fact was that "in the current announcement I prefer to be named alone; two names—that is too motley for people and unnerves them."[12] Schlegel's reaction to Schleiermacher's protest, which arrived too late to effect any change, was one of "astonishment." He saw no need to apologize and remained convinced that he had done nothing wrong, although he did express regret that the beginning of the project had been tainted by Schleiermacher's displeasure and offered reassurance that his friend would be named on the title page and in a special foreword. He tried to justify his decision with a rhetorical question which anticipated the eventual fate of the project: "How can two translate Plato together?"[13]

In a letter to another friend, Carl Gustav von Brinckmann, Schleiermacher mentioned the episode over the announcement without any apparent bitterness.[14] Nevertheless, the episode remained a sensitive issue between Schlegel and Schleiermacher, and in retrospect it proved to be a telling sign of tensions that had already crept into the friendship during the summer of 1799, as well as an omen of profound disagreements that would define their collaboration on the Plato project. Schlegel's constant need for money led to his taking on more projects than he could complete, which often resulted in Schleiermacher's having to pick up the slack. Furthermore, Schlegel's personal life and erratic work habits, coupled with the physical distance between them, made it virtually impossible for them to meet any of their deadlines.[15] Most profound of all, how-

---

[11] See Schlegel to Schleiermacher, 10 Mar. 1800 (#808, lines 15–24), *Br.* 3:412.
[12] Schlegel to Schleiermacher, 21 Mar. 1800 (#816, lines 17–19), *Br.* 3:431–32.
[13] Schlegel to Schleiermacher, ca. 4 Apr. 1800 (#830, lines 46–47), *Br.* 3:455.
[14] He went on to say that the work on Plato "thrills me, for I am deeply, inexpressibly imbued with veneration of Plato ever since I have known him—but at the same time I stand in holy awe before him, and I fear having gone beyond the limits of my powers. May heaven help us" (Schleiermacher to Brinckmann, 22 Apr. 1800 [#847, lines 107–11], *Br.* 3:486).
[15] Dilthey was harsh in his assessment, attributing the difference between them to the "opposition between the immature, divinatory thought of Schlegel and the solid, foundational work on Plato by Schleiermacher" (*Leben Schleiermachers*, 1/2:48). Hans Stock tried to defend Schlegel by pleading that the falling-out between the two friends needs be interpreted in a broader context than is usually the case and that the tensions between them cannot be attributed solely to Schle-

ever, were their diverging interpretations of Plato and ideas of what their study of Plato should look like. During the course of the next year—between the appearance of the public announcement in March 1800 and the scheduled publication date of Easter 1801—these differences would become more pronounced, and an unacknowledged reversal of roles occurred. Whereas Schlegel had begun the project as the acknowledged expert and Schleiermacher as the awestruck novice,[16] the latter's enthusiasm and diligence produced a new expertise that would surpass that of the former. In the end, Schlegel would himself admit that "the translation is perhaps really not my strength."[17]

Already by the summer of 1800, Schleiermacher became aware that their friend Friedrich "seems not to think very seriously about"[18] the Plato translation, and he found a more congenial partner in Ludwig Friedrich Heindorf (1774–1816), who was working on a critical edition of the *Phaedrus*.[19] Schlegel, for his part, reported that he was still reading in order to decide which texts he wanted to choose for himself but insisted that he nonetheless had the "chief ideas."[20] He had, however, begun to cut corners, for he suggested that his introduction could wait until the end. Schleiermacher's long letter of response marked the first major turning point in their collaborative effort. "I just do not see it," he reproved Schlegel, adding, "I hope, since you are reading diligently and already have the chief ideas and the form in your head, ... you can write it down."[21] Clearly, Schleiermacher had begun to challenge Schlegel's leadership: Did Schlegel really intend to remain silent about other scholarship on Plato? If Schlegel could not produce the introduction, should Schleiermacher un-

---

gel's personal faults; he argued, instead, that the drift was a result of the different ways in which each internalized the Romantic notion of individuality; surprisingly, he did not treat the Plato project in his biographical approach ("Friedrich Schlegel und Schleiermacher," Ph.D. diss., Philipps-Universität zu Marburg, 1930 [Marburg: Joh. Hamel, 1930]). In his more recent biography, Nowak does not dwell on the point, simply asserting that the motivation was but personal: "love and worship" (*Schleiermacher*, 137; see also 133).

16 Schleiermacher confessed to Brinckmann, "What studies I will have to do in order to be Schlegel's worthy companion in the translation of Plato! ... So inspired I am by the whole venture, so much holy reverence have I also, and never would I forgive myself, were I to produce something mediocre" (9 June 1800 [#883, lines 98–103], *Br.* 4:82).
17 Schlegel to Schleiermacher, 5 May 1803 (#1490, line 47), *Br.* 6:363. For further discussion of this letter, see Bukowski, "Zur Übersetzungstheorie," 137–38.
18 Schleiermacher to Herz, 5 July 1800 (#901, line 44), *Br.* 4:119.
19 See L. Heindorf, *Platonis Dialogi Quattuor. Lysis, Charmides, Hippias Maior, Phaedrus* (Berlin, 1802). For more on their collaboration, see Virmond, "*interpretari necesse est*"; and Käppel, "Schleiermachers Hermeneutik."
20 Schlegel to Schleiermacher, early July 1800 (#903, line 71), *Br.* 4:122.
21 Schleiermacher to Schlegel, 10–11 July 1800 (#910, lines 99–101), *Br.* 4:149.

dertake it instead? Schlegel accepted the challenge, explaining that he was "Platonizing" very intensely, reading the dialogues again and again in order to discover authenticity and order; he also reasserted his leadership, incredulous that Schleiermacher would claim to have more expertise in the *Phaedrus* and stubborn in his belief regarding the authenticity of certain dialogues, despite arguments to the contrary.[22] Schleiermacher, however, remained unconvinced. He criticized Schlegel for offering fragments rather than arguments and pressed for a more systematic approach to the dialogues. He had clearly grown impatient over Schlegel's "known passivity."[23] Schlegel, in turn, became suspicious that Schleiermacher just wanted to confiscate the most important material for himself.

A second turning point occurred in December 1800, when Schlegel finally came through with his "Complexus of Hypotheses," in which he offered a brief chronology of Plato's dialogues (divided according to three periods of Plato's career) and an even briefer explanation of his fundamental principles. Taking the concept of irony as his guiding principle, he arrived at the unusual conclusion that the *Theages* is authentic and the *Apology* inauthentic. "Never before," he proclaimed, "was I more pleased with myself."[24] Schleiermacher, neither pleased nor impressed, warned that using irony as one's basic principle will only lead to "incoherencies."[25] Indifference can be harder to bear than harsh criticism. Although at first seemingly unfazed by Schleiermacher's reception of his "Hypotheses," Schlegel later recalled the incident with some resentment, declaring that "the coldness with which you received my theory of ordering ... excuses anything on my part."[26] Schleiermacher simply thought that Schlegel occupied himself too much with the more theoretical question of how the dialogues should be ordered, while he himself was certain that the philological task was the fundamental one. The precise and painstaking work of translation, which like Schlegel he understood to be an art, would yield the rest: "Philosophy and the higher grammar should therein revise each other."[27]

---

[22] See Schlegel to Schleiermacher, early Aug. 1800 (#922, lines 36–48), *Br.* 4:181.

[23] Schleiermacher to Schlegel, 13 Sept. 1800 (#949, lines 39–40), *Br.* 4:258; see another letter dated 20 October 1800 (#968), *Br.* 4:299–300.

[24] Schlegel to Schleiermacher, 8 Dec. 1800 (#993, lines 55–56), *Br.* 4:352. For Schlegel's ordering, see *Br.* 4:353–59.

[25] Schleiermacher to Schlegel, 10 Jan. 1801 (#1008, line 16), *Br.* 5:8.

[26] Schlegel to Schleiermacher, 26 Oct. 1801 (#1115, lines 52–57), *Br.* 5:232.

[27] Schleiermacher to Schlegel, 7 Feb. 1801 (#1019, lines 88–89), *Br.* 5:47. Years later Schleiermacher gave a fuller explanation of his own method for determining authenticity and order in the dialogues (see letter to Schlegel, 10 Oct. 1804 [#1829], *Br.* 7:467–69).

The final turn in the partnership came in April 1801, when Schleiermacher, distressed that the publication date had come and gone, finally called Schlegel to task: "I must frankly confess to you, that, given the way in which you treat the Plato project and my part therein, you do everything possible to spoil any desire for the whole thing.... You show no consideration for my activity: no replies to my criticisms of you, no shadow of a judgment about anything from me, ... so that I do not even know whether you have read it or not. This lies beyond all excuse."[28] In short, Schleiermacher arrived at the conclusion that Schlegel had not only lost control of the material but had lost credibility as the chief contributor as well.

The rest of 1801 brought further disagreements but also some concessions and new promises. The two were reunited in Berlin for a few weeks over the new year and were able to reaffirm their friendship. According to Schleiermacher, however, no progress was made on the Plato project during that visit. In 1802, more deadlines were missed, Schlegel moved to Paris with Dorothea Mendelssohn Veit (1764–1839), Schleiermacher took a pastoral position far away in Stolp, and Frommann gave more than one ultimatum. In March 1803, Schleiermacher broached the subject of the inevitable and gently urged Schlegel to hand the project over, which Schlegel finally did in a letter dated May 5, 1803: "Friend, I lay [the Plato project] in your hand.... I now entrust to you the decision of the whole affair, according to the specifications which here follow."[29] In what followed, Schlegel assumed responsibility for the money owed to Frommann, retained his right to write the introduction should Schleiermacher choose to adopt his ordering, and tried to persuade Schleiermacher to resist the temptation to find "completeness" (*Vollständigkeit*) in the dialogues.[30] That summer, Frommann, too, pulled out of the project. Schleiermacher was therefore free to arrange a new contract with his friend and publisher, Georg Andreas Reimer. "At least," Schleiermacher wrote to Reimer, "there will be more unity in the whole because Friedrich has pulled out."[31] The new deadline was set for Easter 1804, three years after the original target date.

In his November 1803 "Advertisement Regarding the Translation of Plato" for the forthcoming translation of Plato, Schleiermacher emphasized the continuity of his translation with the project announced three-and-a-half years earlier, in large part because he had to gain the respect of the literary and philological world that had eagerly been anticipating Schlegel's translation and study of

---

28 Schleiermacher to Schlegel, 27 Apr. 1801 (#1051, lines 4–7,16–21), *Br.* 5:108.
29 Schlegel to Schleiermacher, 5 May 1803 (#1490, lines 24–28), *Br.* 6:362–63.
30 Schlegel to Schleiermacher, 5 May 1803 (#1490, line 89), *Br.* 6:364.
31 Schleiermacher to Reimer, 11 Nov. 1803 (#1590, lines 23–24), *Br.* 7:93.

Plato.³² Schleiermacher explained that, although Schlegel had failed to mention it, he was involved in the project since its inception and has gained the respect of two established philologists, Heindorf and G. L. Spalding (1762–1811). Whereas Schlegel had felt it necessary to end the contract, Schleiermacher found himself "incapable of leaving the work; to the contrary, I find myself compelled in every way to venture it alone."³³ He was confident that this "feeling of necessity" (*das Gefühl der Nothwendigkeit*) would carry him through whatever difficulties, including his own limitations, he may encounter.³⁴ Such modest disclaimers, however, belied the fact that Schleiermacher had in the previous three years gained tremendous confidence as a translator and interpreter of Plato. He concluded his advertisement saying that if, as hoped, Schlegel would soon complete his own critique of Plato, the friends of philosophy would be able to see for themselves where Schlegel and Schleiermacher were agreed and where they deviated from one another.³⁵

How precisely did they deviate? As Schleiermacher understood it, it had less to do with their different opinions regarding the ordering and authenticity of the dialogues than with different views of the method and task of philology itself. Schleiermacher reproached Schlegel and Schlegel's student, Friedrich Ast (1778–1841), for neglecting the painstaking, detailed historical-critical work of philology.³⁶ In 1802, Schleiermacher published his first piece on Plato: a sharply

---

32 Schleiermacher, "Anzeige die Übersetzung des Platon betreffend," in *Intelligenzblatt der Allgemeinen Literatur-Zeitung* no. 212, 12 Nov. 1803 (and elsewhere); in KGA 4/3:xxviii–xxx.
33 Schleiermacher, "Anzeige," xxix.
34 Schleiermacher, "Anzeige," xxix.
35 For more on the collaboration between Schleiermacher and Schlegel and on their respective interpretations of Plato, see Käppel and Loehr, "Historische Einführung," KGA 4/3:xv–xxvii; Dilthey, *Leben Schleiermachers*, 1/2:42–49, 52–55; Hermann Patsch, "Friedrich Schlegels 'Philosophie der Philologie' und Schleiermachers frühe Entwürfe zur Hermeneutik," *Zeitschrift für Theologie und Kirche* 63 (1966): 434–472; Laks, "Schleiermacher on Plato," 149; Bukowski, "Zur Übersetzungstheorie," 133–43. See also Marie-Dominique Richard, ed., *Friedrich Daniel Ernst Schleiermacher. Introductions aux dialogues de Platon (1804–1828). Leçons d'histoire de la philosophie (1819–1823). Suivies des textes de Friedrich Schlegel, relatifs à Platon* (Paris: Éditions du Cerf, 2004); "La Critique d'A. Boeckh de l'Introduction Générale de F. Schleiermacher aux Dialogues de Platon," *Les Études Philosophiques* 1 (January–March 1998): 11–30; and "Plato and the German Romantic Thinkers: Friedrich Schlegel and Friedrich Daniel Ernst Schleiermacher," *Faculty Philosophy Journal* 36, no. 1 (2015): 91–124.
36 Friedrich Ast was a student of F. Schlegel and F. W. J. Schelling. According to Dilthey, it was only through his personal influence on Ast that Schlegel left his mark on Plato scholarship (see *Leben Schleiermachers*, 1/2:44–45). Ast went on to make a name for himself as a Plato researcher, but Schleiermacher remained as critical of his later work as of his early work. In the second edition of his *Platons Werke* (1817), Schleiermacher added numerous criticisms of Ast. In two

critical, anonymously-written review of Ast's book on the *Phaedrus*.[37] There he articulated the task, method, and identity of the philologist, contrasting it with that of the idealist philosopher. There are, of course, the predictable criticisms that are grist for the mill in most book reviews: Ast claims for himself a discovery made by someone else, he does not always substantiate his claims, he is immodest and immature, etc. In Schleiermacher's harsher criticisms of Ast, however, we find careful formulations of various complaints voiced in his correspondence with Schlegel. Echoing his earlier admonition to Schlegel that "philosophy and the higher grammar should therein revise each other," Schleiermacher in his review of Ast drew a fundamental distinction between *philosophy*, which assigns its own meaning, and *philology*, which tries to recover original meaning. Schleiermacher charged that "the chief striving of [Ast] is to comment on the thought of Plato from the idealistic philosophy," which only leads him "to misunderstand and completely misinterpret Plato."[38]

If the task of the philologist is to understand and interpret (in this case) Plato, then the method employed by the philologist must be critical and historical. This means, first, the philologist can bring no content, no prior doctrinal commitments, to the text. Ast's goal, however, was to find "his own ideas in Plato,"[39] and he took "as his starting point the principles of idealist philosophy and gladly ascribes this to Plato."[40] Second, the philological method for Schleiermacher involves close grammatical and comparative work within the text. Each part must be isolated and worked through with "exactitude and completeness" because "the field of philology is so infinite, and its entire thriving rests on each part,"[41] so much so that if the careful work of attending to the details is

---

Academy Addresses from 1829, "On the Concept of Hermeneutics, with Reference to F. A. Wolf's Instructions and Ast's Textbook," Schleiermacher was still contending with Ast's views ("Über den Begriff der Hermeneutik, mit Bezug auf F. A. Wolfs Andeutungen und Asts Lehrbuch," in *KGA* 1/11:599–641; also in *Schleiermacher: Hermeneutik und Kritik*, ed. Manfred Frank [Frankfurt am Main: Suhrkamp, 1977], 309–46, trans. by James Duke and Jack Forstman in *Hermeneutics: The Handwritten Manuscripts*, ed. Heinz Kimmerle, [Missoula, Montana: Scholars Press, 1977], 175–214). For more on Schleiermacher and Ast, see Käppel, "Die frühe Rezeption der Platon-Übersetzung," and "Schleiermachers Hermeneutik"; and Gunter Scholtz, "Ast and Schleiermacher: Hermeneutics and Critical Philosophy," in *The Routledge Companion to Hermeneutics*, ed. Jeff Malpas and Hans-Helmuth Gander (Oxfordshire, England: Routledge, 2016), 62–73.
37 Schleiermacher, "Rezension von Friedrich Ast: *De Platonis Phädro* (Jena, 1801)," *Erlanger Litteratur-Zeitung* 7, no. 30 (1802): 233–40; in *KGA* 1/3:469–81.
38 Schleiermacher, "Rezension von Ast," 474.5–7,18–19. On this point, see Richard, "Plato and the German Romantic Thinkers," 98.
39 Schleiermacher, "Rezension von Ast," 477.5–6.
40 Schleiermacher, "Rezension von Ast," 471.25–26.
41 Schleiermacher, "Rezension von Ast," 470.25–28.

not done, the whole cannot be understood. Ast, however, "quietly lays aside the difficulties of interpretation and the historical tasks that intrude."[42] Third, as this last criticism suggests, the philological method is inescapably historical in that it requires a deep and thorough investigation of the linguistic, literary, and conceptual background of the texts in question, as well as an acquaintance "with everything that has already been said about the topic."[43] Yet in Ast's work there is "a complete lack of historical investigations."[44] In sum, Ast's *De Platonis Phädro* was an interesting expression of the newest philosophy but had little to do with "what Plato says."[45] Ast practiced *conjectural criticism (Conjecturalkritik)*,[46] whereas the true philologist is one who engages in historical and textual criticism. That task Schleiermacher took upon himself in his *Platons Werke*.

The first volume of *Platons Werke* appeared in May 1804 and included the *Phaedrus*, *Lysis*, *Protagoras*, and *Laches*, along with Schleiermacher's *Einleitung* ("General Introduction") and his introductions to those four individual dialogues. The second volume appeared the next winter (1805), and included the *Charmides*, *Euthyphro*, *Parmenides*, as well as an Appendix with dialogues which he took to be secondary to the core canon or inauthentic.[47] It was hailed as a major achievement. In his review of the first two volumes, the respected philologist August Boeckh (1785–1867), declaring that it had been "left to our time" to present Plato as philosophical artist, identified Schleiermacher as that one "rare talent" who could accomplish what was demanded:

> No philologist by profession, he does not yet have the knowledge of archeology going into the most specialized knowledge. How could so broadly [educated] a person have developed this particular virtuosity so impressively? Yet antiquity itself he does indeed know; we see here exceptional insight into Hellenic language and custom and completely new results of the most astute philological critique.... No one has so fully understood Plato or has taught others to understand Plato as this man.[48]

---

42 Schleiermacher, "Rezension von Ast," 469.19–20.
43 Schleiermacher, "Rezension von Ast," 470.32–33.
44 Schleiermacher, "Rezension von Ast," 473.12.
45 Schleiermacher, "Rezension von Ast," 478.6.
46 Schleiermacher, "Rezension von Ast," 469.10
47 See table 2.
48 August Boeckh, "Rezension," in *Heidelbergische Jahrbücher der Literatur für Philologie, Historie, Literatur und Kunst* 1, no. 1 (1808): 83; see https://digi.ub.uni-heidelberg.de/diglit/hdjb1808_5/0089. R. Steven Turner contends that it was through Boeckh that Schleiermacher's hermeneutical principles were "communicated" to, and thereby made "common currency of German philologists" ("Historicism, *Kritik*, and the Prussian Professoriate, 1790–1840," in *Philologie und Hermeneutik im 19. Jahrhundert II*, ed. Mayotte Bollack and Heinz Wismann [Göttingen: Vandenhoeck & Ruprecht, 1983], 471). See also Richard, "La Critique d'A. Boeckh."

Boeckh's review was not without points of criticism, but he praised the genius behind the work as a historic accomplishment—not just of a single person, but of a nation. "Let us be proud of ourselves," he enjoined, "even though foreigners should pay no attention: for which nation is as able as we are to understand the Hellenic ways? Certainly not the neighbors."[49] Schleiermacher's *Platons Werke*, in many ways the culminating mark of the German philological renaissance, quickly became the standard by which all other studies of Plato were to be judged.[50]

Even though it would be only a matter of a few years before Schleiermacher's ordering of the dialogues would be rejected, such acclaim as Boeckh's for the philological achievement of *Platons Werke* resounded well into the twentieth century. Dilthey rated it "among the great forces which the modern scientific consciousness has precipitated,"[51] and Stein praised Schleiermacher for having created "a Platonic question" and for his "conscientious diligence, philological genius, and the maturity of his philosophical education."[52] More recently, although some scholars dismiss Schleiermacher's *Introductions* as little more than an item of historical curiosity, others are revisiting Schleiermacher's Plato and critics are still forced to engage with it.[53] In what ways, therefore, did Schleiermacher's *Introductions* mark something so fundamentally new and important?

---

[49] Boeckh, "Rezension," 120.
[50] See, e.g., Boeckh's review of P. G. van Heusde, *Specimen criticum in Platonem* (Leiden, 1803) in *Jenaische Allgemeine Literatur-Zeitung* 6, no. 1 (Jan.–Mar., 1809): 161–68.
[51] Dilthey, *Leben Schleiermachers*, 1/2:37.
[52] Stein, *Geschichte des Platonismus*, 3:395, 341.
[53] Four relatively recent examples: in her hefty monograph, Catherine Zuckert mentions Schleiermacher once in her main text but discusses him in several notes (*Plato's Philosophers: The Coherence of the Dialogues* [Chicago: University of Chicago Press, 2009], 2, 216n2, 386n190, 483n2); in Kim, *Brill's Companion to German Platonism*, three essays address Schleiermacher in substantive ways; in her study of modern German philology, Constanze Güthenke devotes an entire chapter to Schleiermacher ("'So That He Unknowingly and Delicately Mirrors Himself in Front of Us, As the Beautiful Often Do': Schleiermacher's Plato," chap. 3 in *Feeling and Classical Philology: Knowing Antiquity in German Scholarship, 1770–1920* [Cambridge: Cambridge University Press, 2020], 72–95); and William H. F. Altman engages so deeply with Schleiermacher that he entitles the introduction to his most recent book "Schleiermacher and Plato" (*Ascent to the Beautiful: Plato the Teacher and the Pre-Republic Dialogues from Protagoras to Symposium* [Lanham, Boulder, New York, and London: Lexington Books, 2020], 1–25).

2.3 Central Themes in Schleiermacher's "General Introduction"

According to Schleiermacher, the goal of his new exposition was not so much to offer an analysis of Plato's philosophy itself as it is "to make it possible for every [reader], by means of an immediate and more exact knowledge of [Plato's works], to come to their own view of Plato's mind [*Geist*] and teaching, whether that view be entirely new or just more complete."[54] This is possible only if the "natural sequence and a necessary relation [of] these dialogues to one another" is discovered.[55] Schleiermacher therefore took upon himself the task of restoring the original order and relation of the dialogues—a task which he considered to be his unique contribution to the field. As it turned out, it was his method, more than his ordering, that came to be recognized as his lasting contribution to Plato studies. That method was characterized by four interconnected themes: a development and special application of the *internal method*; an interpretation of Plato as *artist*; an insistence on the necessary relation between *form and content*; and, finally, a determination of *authenticity and order* in light of the first three themes. In developing each of these themes, Schleiermacher departed decisively from his predecessors—even, and perhaps most consciously, his immediate predecessor Wilhelm Gottlieb Tennemann (1761–1819), whose study of Plato nevertheless informed his own.[56]

2.3.1 Internal Method

The first methodological moment in Schleiermacher's "General Introduction" involves a philological task, which could no longer be understood as a strictly grammatical exercise insofar as it demanded historical tools of investigation. The modern philologist had to have so intimate a knowledge of the language

---

[54] *PW* 1/1:19.1–4 (... *durch die unmittelbare genauere Kenntniß derselben allein jedem eine eigne, sei es nun ganz neue oder wenigstens vollständigere, Ansicht von des Mannes Geist und Lehre möglich zu machen*); cf. *IDP* 3–4.
[55] *IDP* 19; *PW* 1/1:32.21–22 (*eine natürliche Folge und eine nothwendige Beziehung dieser Gespräche auf einander*).
[56] This assessment differs from that of Szlezák, who challenges the "masterpiece" status of Schleiermacher's "General Introduction" by listing twelve ways in which Schleiermacher's insights are dependent on Tennemann's (see Thomas A. Szlezák, "Schleiermachers 'Einleitung' zur Platon-Übersetzung von 1804: Ein Vergleich mit Tiedemann und Tennemann," *Antike und Abendland* 43, no. 1 [December 1997]: 46–62, esp. 51–53).

as to recognize the particular ways in which an author had used and modified it. This entailed a historical knowledge of the language and so of the culture that produced it. The goal, Schleiermacher explained, is "to adduce something about the scientific state of the Hellenes at the time when Plato began his career, about the progress of the language in relation to philosophical ideas, about texts of the same genre that were available at the time and the probable extent of their circulation."[57] What Schleiermacher called for was a rigorous application of the new criticism, not unlike that being done in biblical scholarship, to Plato studies.[58] He wanted to get behind the tradition in order to discover the authentic Plato. Such criticism in turn required an examination of the philosophical grounds of interpretation, something Plato scholars had not yet undertaken. In answer to his own call, Schleiermacher developed an internal approach to the Platonic texts.

Schleiermacher's development of an internal method is best understood against the backdrop of eighteenth-century Plato research and what E. N. Tigerstedt has termed "The New Situation" in Germany: "In the second half of the eighteenth century, the rejection of the Neoplatonic interpretation of Plato thus became more and more accepted by scholars and the general public.... It was now taken for granted that any interpretation of Plato had to be based above all upon his own works—exclusively even, some would have added. This implied a new situation."[59] According to Tigerstedt, that new situation reached back to Gottfried Wilhelm von Leibniz (1646–1716) but really began, at least on the popular level, with Jacob Brucker (1696–1770), whose program was carried out in a more philosophically responsible manner by Dietrich Tiedemann (1748–1803) and his successor at Marburg, Tennemann. It was Tennemann's major work, *System der platonischen Philosophie* (1792), that proved to be most influential on Schleiermacher's own approach to the dialogues.[60]

---

[57] PW 1/1:17.19–24 (... *einiges beizubringen über den wissenschaftlichen Zustand der Hellenen zu der Zeit, als Platon seine Laufbahn betrat, über die Fortschritte der Sprache in Absicht auf die Bezeichnung philosophischer Gedanken, über die damals vorhandenen Schriften dieser Art und den muthmaßlichen Grad ihrer Verbreitung*); cf. IDP 2.

[58] See, e.g., Harald Schnur, *Schleiermachers Hermeneutik und ihre Vorgeschichte im 18. Jahrhundert. Studien zur Bibelauslegung, zu Hamann, Herder und F. Schlegel* (Stuttgart and Weimar: J. B. Metzler, 1994); and William Baird, *History of New Testament Research*, vol. 1: *From Deism to Tübingen* (Minneapolis, Minn.: Fortress Press, 1992).

[59] E. N. Tigerstedt, *The Decline and Fall of the Neoplatonic Interpretation of Plato: An Outline and Some Observations*, Commentationes Humanarum Litterarum 52 (Helsinki-Helsingfors: Societas Scientiarum Fennica, 1974), 63.

[60] For Schleiermacher's debt to this longer history, see Leo Cantana, "Afterword: Schleiermacher and Modern Plato Scholarship," chap. 6 in *Late Ancient Platonism in Eighteenth-Century Ger-*

Tennemann acknowledged the important contributions of Brucker and Tiedemann, but he claimed that his own study of Plato was entirely new because he was the first who, eschewing all dogmatic interests and relying on Plato alone to be his guide, sought "the system and the history of the philosophy of Plato."[61] Tennemann was right in claiming something new for himself, but perhaps the significant difference between his work and that of his predecessors had less to do with setting aside neo-Platonism (since they had attempted that, too) than with his conviction that Kant's critical philosophy had inalterably changed our understanding of philosophy, hence of Plato. So convinced was he of the new philosophy that he stated in his foreword, "One can therefore accept that the more truth a system contains, the more it must approach the critical philosophy, and conversely, the more it approaches the critical philosophy, the truer it must be. And this relation is found in the Platonic philosophy."[62]

Schleiermacher expressed appreciation for the "modern criticism" (*spätere Kritik*)[63] of the preceding century insofar as it had removed the worst misunderstandings of Plato, made some progress toward a historical understanding of the dialogues, and removed the most obviously inauthentic dialogues from the list of Plato's works. Nevertheless, the new research had not gone far enough and thus lacked "perfect understanding."[64] The problem was that, in their reluctance to question the old canon and in their failure to give reasons for accepting some dialogues as authentic, modern critics remained uncritical. Only Tennemann's work stood apart because it broke with the conventional categories and sifted through the vast body of biographical material on Plato. This, coupled with the fact that his was at least "the first somewhat thorough attempt to discover the chronological sequence of the Platonic dialogues from various historical traces left in them,"[65] offered a real chance for finding a "natural sequence"[66] in the dialogues.

---

man *Thought*, Archives internationales d'histoire des idées/International Archives of the History of Ideas Archives 227 (Cham, Switzerland: Springer, 2019), 165–69; and Szlezák, "Schleiermachers 'Einleitung'."
61 Wilhelm Gottlieb Tennemann, *System der platonischen Philosophie*, 2 vols. (Leipzig, 1792), 1: x.
62 Tennemann, *System der platonischen Philosophie*, 1:v.
63 IDP 27; PW 1/1:41.2.
64 IDP 5; PW 1/1:19.27 (*vollständiges Verstehen*).
65 PW 1/1:38.8–11(… *wenigstens dort zuerst mit einiger Vollständigkeit angestellte Versuch, die chronologische Folge der platonischen Gespräche aus mancherlei ihnen eingedrükten historischen Spuren zu entdekken*); cf. IDP 24.
66 PW 1/1:32.21, 33.4, 40.12, 49.5.

Indeed, Schleiermacher so respected Tennemann's historical method that he opened his "General Introduction" by referring the reader to the first part of Tennemann's study: "*Leben des Plato*" ("Life of Plato").[67] Because he saw no way to improve on Tennemann's biography of Plato, Schleiermacher decided against undertaking his own and described his study as a "necessary counterpart" [*Gegenstük*][68] to Tennemann's. Such a description, however, is not unambiguous. His pair of direct references to Tennemann in the "General Introduction" certainly suggest that by "*Gegenstük*" he meant a "companion-piece" in the sense of a work that complements Tennemann's work.[69] This interpretation is supported by another, indirect reference, where Schleiermacher, in calling his investigation *ein nothwendiges Ergänzungsstük*, seemed to be describing his internal method as a "necessary supplement" to Tennemann's method.[70] The chief difference between them, as Schleiermacher saw it, was that Tennemann's intention was "directed less to discover, by the method he adopts, the real and essential relation of the works of Plato to one another, than to discover in general the dates of their composition, in order to avoid confounding early and imperfect attempts with an exposition of the Philosophy of the mature and perfect Plato."[71] In fact, the difference between them would prove to be more marked than this passage indicates—so marked that, much more than supplementing Tennemann's work, Schleiermacher's study superseded it.

Whereas Tennemann had relied on external evidence or historical traces, Schleiermacher planned to rely primarily on internal evidence, using external evidence as a "natural test" (*die natürliche Probe*).[72] Although necessary, external traces are not in themselves sufficient because they do not address the natural relations among dialogues, they are more subject to accidental conditions, and, strictly speaking, they may not "extend beyond the life of Socrates."[73] More to the point, Schleiermacher was skeptical about what we can learn from historical traces. So little is known of Plato's life "that little can be gained for the dating and ordering of his writings, and at the very most, we can conjec-

---

67 Tennemann, *System der platonischen Philosophie*, 1:1–80.
68 *IDP* 24; *PW* 1/1:38.19.
69 See *IDP* 1, 24; *PW* 1/1:16, 38.
70 *PW* 1/1:28.34; cf. *IDP* 14.
71 *IDP* 24; *PW* 1/1:38.13–18 (*Zwar ist seine Absicht dabei weniger darauf gerichtet gewesen, auf diesem Wege die wahre und wesentliche Beziehung der Werke des Platon zu entdecken, sondern nur im Allgemeinen die Zeiten zu unterscheiden, um nicht in eine Darstellung der Philosophie des reifen und vollendeten Platon auch frühere Unvollkommenheiten mit aufzunehmen*).
72 *IDP* 24; *PW* 1/1:38.23.
73 *IDP* 25; *PW* 1/1:39.10–11 (*... dürften sich die historischen Spuren nicht über das Leben des Sokrates hinaus erstrecken*).

ture where the former series interrupts the latter."[74] Not only is the internal method less subject to what is accidental or circumstantial, it also allows the entire *corpus* to be viewed together. Nevertheless, Schleiermacher was aware that the internal method by itself is also insufficient. He cited the example of James Geddes who, although he had come upon the promising idea "that certain dialogues of Plato reciprocally [illuminate] each other,"[75] made no attempt to offer a chronology, thereby rendering his conclusions useless. The internal investigation needs the counterweight of whatever external evidence there is.

Ideally, when viewed together and compared with precision, the external and the internal series should corroborate each other. Yet in reality, because there are so few external historical markers, the internal indicators (the authentic words and texts of Plato) become the primary source for understanding Plato. For Schleiermacher, the external and internal methods are held together in the philological task. Although clearly indebted to the new historical methods that had emerged in the wake of the Enlightenment, Schleiermacher was wary of undue confidence in our being able to know the past. He therefore developed a method which, while historical and critical, respected the scarcity of empirical evidence without falling into skepticism.[76] In applying his internal method, Schleiermacher promised to frame new questions, to suspect any assumptions, and to let the authentic Platonic texts be his guide. Indeed, he rejected many accepted schemas and authorities; and although he sometimes relied on Aristotle, he gave philosophical and historical reasons for doing so. Most importantly, he supplied the hermeneutical theory that previous attempts lacked. A key element to that theory, which would have a profound effect on subsequent scholarship, was the view of Plato as artist.

---

[74] PW 1/1:17.11–15: (... *daß nicht sonderlicher Gewinn daraus zu machen ist für die Zeitbestimmung und Anordnung seiner Schriften, und daß man höchstens hie und da den Ort wahrscheinlich machen kann, wo jene die Reihe von diesen unterbrechen*); cf. IDP 2.

[75] IDP 22; PW 1/1:36.13–14 (... *daß gewisse Dialogen des Platon sich wechselseitig erläutern*). See James Geddes, *An Essay on the Composition and Manner of Writing of the Antients, Particularly Plato* (Glasgow, 1748).

[76] For an example of where he followed the external method to the extent possible and then turned to the internal method, see "Introduction to the *Protagoras*," in IDP 85–86; PW 1/1:575–76.

2.3.2 Plato as Artist

Schleiermacher hoped that his new method would not only lead the lay reader into a more profound encounter with the dialogues but would also alter the experts' understanding, since it took as its fundamental orientation the view of Plato "as philosophical artist" (*als philosophischen Künstler*).[77] The reader's insights, he promised, even if not completely altered, would at least be "better interconnected and gain more range and unity."[78] This understanding of Plato as artist was the interpretive key that would unlock the mysteries of the dialogues because with it, and only with it, could Plato's work be viewed as a *whole*, and not just as any whole but as an *artistic whole*. In other words, there is an "essential unity" (*wesentliche Einheit*)[79] of all the dialogues to which previous interpreters had been blind because their approach to Plato's thought was either too fragmentary or overly systematized.

At one extreme, there were those who had presented the dialogues in a piecemeal fashion and who thus characterized Plato as a mere dialectician, "more eager to refute others than capable of, or inclined toward, producing a well-grounded edifice of his own."[80] Schleiermacher quickly dismissed such an approach because it betrayed "a disguised confession of total not-understanding of the Platonic works."[81] At the other extreme, there were those who appealed to some hidden, unwritten (esoteric) tradition of Plato in order to fill the gaps and inconsistencies left in the public, written (exoteric) tradition. Schleiermacher distinguished ancient varieties of esotericism, judging the "so-called neo-Platonists" (*die sogenannten Neu-Platoniker*)[82] to be the most praise-worthy, but he was more concerned with the modern version, the main proponent of which was none other than Tennemann.[83] Schleiermacher's suspicions of the esoteric tradition follow logically from his methodological commit-

---

[77] *PW* 1/1:19.15; cf. *IDP* 4.
[78] *PW* 1/1:19.13–14 (... *oder wenigstens sich besser verknüpfen und mehr Umfang und Einheit gewinnen*); cf. *IDP* 4.
[79] *IDP* 7; *PW* 1/1:21.28.
[80] *PW* 1/1:22.17–19 (... *mehr begierig Andre zu widerlegen als fähig oder gesonnen ein eignes wohlgegründetes Lehrgebäude aufzuführen*); cf. *IDP* 8.
[81] *PW* 1/1:22.22–23 (... *ein verkleidetes Geständniß des gänzlichen Nichtverstehens der platonischen Werke*); cf. *IDP* 8.
[82] *PW* 1/1:26.11; cf. *IDP* 11.
[83] Tennemann maintained that Plato "had a double philosophy, an external one and an internal or secret one" (*System der platonischen Philosophie*, 1:137); see below, 46n127. Tigerstedt also identifies Tennemann as the main subject of Schleiermacher's criticisms on this point (see *Decline and Fall*, 6).

ments. In a word, whether in its ancient or modern form, the appeal to an esoteric Platonic tradition was (in fact or in effect) pre-critical. Privileging the oral over the written tradition simply does not lend itself to textual- or historical-criticism.[84]

Modern interpreters of Plato faced a serious dilemma. In rejecting neo-Platonism, did they also have to relinquish the notion of there being a unity to Plato's thought? Most scholars at the time did not think so. Some tried to ground that unity in what Schleiermacher considered to be too subordinate a principle;[85] others, convinced that there was some unifying system but unable to find it, imposed their own. Schleiermacher deemed both such attempts as untenable as conceding that Plato's philosophy was fragmentary. The essential unity of Plato's thought was rather to be found not in a particular doctrine, but in Plato himself—in his artistic genius. Hence, his works are to be interpreted not so much as a *system*, but as an *artistic whole*. Whereas in a system the various parts are often randomly arranged,[86] in a work of art the parts are arranged according to "a natural sequence and a necessary relation" (*eine natürliche Folge und eine nothwendige Beziehung*).[87] What is more, an artistic whole, unlike a system, requires an aesthetic response on the part of the beholder in order to be understood. Readers, Schleiermacher warned, must investigate with their own inner activity, otherwise the dialogues will remain foreign objects, unrelated to each other and inconsequential to the reader.

To illustrate further what he meant by this, Schleiermacher employed one of his favorite metaphors, that of an organic body. When we view something as a living body, we realize that the passive knowledge produced by "dissection" or "dismemberment" (*Zerstükelung*)[88] is not adequate, and we are driven to discover the natural and essential relations and thus to acknowledge the vital role of seemingly insignificant parts.[89] When we apply this method to the Platonic dia-

---

[84] At the same time, it is probably also true that Schleiermacher's move in rejecting oral tradition was not due solely to historical-critical interests but was an authentically Protestant move: *sola Scriptura*. As Martin Luther had done, Schleiermacher insisted that what is necessary is already given in the written word, not some subsequent tradition. M.-D. Richard criticizes Schleiermacher for radicalizing the theory of *sola scriptura* ("La Critique d'A. Boeckh," 29).
[85] He cited the example of Johann August Eberhard (1739–1809), his former professor at the University of Halle, who had appealed to the didactic function of the dialogues—namely, the formation of youths into virtuous citizens (see *PW* 1/1:37; *IDP* 22).
[86] See *IDP* 5–6; *PW* 1/1:20–21.
[87] *IDP* 19; *PW* 1/1:32.21–22.
[88] *IDP* 14; *PW* 1/1:28.35.
[89] Schleiermacher takes his cue here from Socrates: "every discourse must be organized, like a living being, with a body of its own, as it were, so as not to be headless or footless, but to have a

logues, we can finally re-member or restore the "limbs" (*Glieder*)—the particular dialogues—to their "natural connection" (*in ihren natürlichen Zusammenhang*).[90] Then the dialogues will finally be seen as constituting "increasingly more complete presentations which gradually developed Plato's ideas, so that, with each dialogue being comprended not only as a whole in itself but also in its connection with the rest, Plato may at last be understood as a philosopher and artist."[91] The somatic metaphor also allowed Schleiermacher to account for occasional or accidental pieces, which do not necessarily express the free activity of the author, and to address other notorious difficulties in Plato-interpretation, such as the relation between the two parts of the *Phaedrus*. The "triumph of [Plato's] artistic understanding," Schleiermacher argued in his introduction to that dialogue, is that he "leaves nothing to chance or blind fate, but with him everything is proportioned to, and active in accordance with, the full range"[92] of his thought. Even in the most trivial of passages, Plato's art may be discerned.

This view of Plato as artist includes one further and quite important dimension that distinguished Schleiermacher's interpretation from both eighteenth- and nineteenth-century interpretations. When Schleiermacher argued that the dialogues are essentially connected, he meant that they lead naturally and necessarily from one to the other. There is in the dialogues, he insisted, a *pedagogical progression of ideas* proceeding "from the first excitement of the original and guiding ideas, up to an all but perfected presentation of particular sciences."[93] To view Plato as an artist is to view him as the consummate pedagogue who already had in mind the full body of material to be communicated to the student,

---

middle and members, composed in fitting relation to each other and to the whole" (*Phaedrus* 264c; trans. Howard N. Fowler, in *Perseus Digital Library*, ed. Gregory R. Crane [Tufts University]: http://www.perseus.tufts.edu; hereafter cited in text as "*PDL*").

90 *IDP* 14; *PW* 1/1:29.1–3.

91 *PW* 1/1:29.3–7 (... *wie sie als immer vollständigere Darstellungen seine Ideen nach und nach entwikelt haben, damit, indem jedes Gespräch nicht nur als ein Ganzes für sich, sondern auch in seinem Zusammenhange mit den übrigen begriffen wird, auch er selbst endlich als Philosoph und Künstler verstanden werde*); cf. *IDP* 14.

92 *PW* 1/1:70.21–26 (*Das ist aber eben die Weise des Platon und der Triumph seines künstlerischen Verstandes, daß in seinen großen und reichhaltigen Formen doch nichts leer ist, und daß er nichts dem Zufall oder einer blinden Willkühr zu bestimmen anheimstellt, sondern bei ihm alles nach Maaßgabe seines Umfanges auch zwekkmäßig und mitwirkend sein muß*); cf. *IDP* 56–57.

93 *PW* 1/1:32.18–21 (... *von der ersten Aufregung der ursprünglichen und leitenden Ideen bis zu einer wenn auch nicht vollendeten Darstellung der besonderen Wissenschaften*); cf. *IDP* 19.

as well as the course best suited to carry the student along, before he sat down to write the dialogues.[94]

This pedagogical theory of the sequence of the dialogues stands in contrast to a developmental interpretation, according to which Plato's doctrines are presumed to have changed and matured throughout the course of his life and writing.[95] Those who held such a developmental view, such as Tennemann and, later, Karl Friedrich Hermann (1804–1855),[96] sought the original order of the dialogues in part so they could isolate the mature works of the real Plato. This served to diminish the weight of the earlier dialogues. Schleiermacher allowed no such diminishment. For him, the first dialogue, the *Phaedrus*, contained the "seeds" (*Keime*)[97] from which all philosophical doctrines unfolded. If an idea is not fully formed in an early dialogue, that is because the student is not yet prepared to receive it, not because anything is lacking in Plato's philosophy. Schleiermacher's ordering is therefore reader-centered, even as it presumes the established genius of the author.[98]

From this follows yet another principle for discovering the original ordering of the dialogues—namely, the progressive relation between *myth* and *dialectics*. Inasmuch as myth stands in tension with history, it became a hermeneutical co-

---

[94] For further elaboration on Schleiermacher's notion of the pedagogical progression of ideas and how it informed his ordering of Plato's dialogues, see below, 3.5.2.

[95] Zuckert wrongly identifies Schleiermacher as the originator of the developmental theory (*Plato's Philosophers*, 2).

[96] In a lengthy discussion of the relation of his work to Schleiermacher's, Hermann explained that, whereas he was firmly convinced of Schleiermacher's "image of a living organic development" and of the need for a scientific approach beginning from this assumption, he (unlike Schleiermacher) took that to mean that the notion of development had to be applied to Plato himself. Plato, Hermann argued, could not have had the full scope of his philosophical doctrines in mind before he began writing. A "purely historical" (in contrast to Schleiermacher's "pseudo-historical") perspective forces us to admit that Plato must have come under the influences of his time, which is to say, his own understanding must have undergone development (see *Geschichte und System der Platonischen Philosophie* [Heidelberg, 1839], 351). Schleiermacher was not unambiguous on this point. He conceded that a historical-critical approach necessarily had to view its object as any other piece of literature, and he claimed to reject any position that "deprived [Plato] of a right enjoyed by every one else, that of correcting or changing his opinions even after he has publicly explained them" (*IDP* 34; *PW* 1/1:47.18–20 [... den Platon eines Rechtes berauben, dessen sich jeder andere erfreut, nemlich seine Gedanken zu berichtigen oder zu vertauschen, auch nachdem er sie schon öffentlich geäußert]). At the same time, his view of Plato as artist did not, in fact, allow for essential change.

[97] *PW* 1/1:80.4; cf. *IDP* 68.

[98] Laks identifies a "radical" difference between Schlegel and Schleiermacher on this point: Schlegel "read[s] Plato as a philosopher who, because he is a philosopher, i.e. is in search of wisdom, is not yet actually in possession of a system" ("Schleiermacher on Plato," 149).

nundrum for those engaged in historical-critical research. Schleiermacher's notion of the pedagogical progression of ideas helped him solve the problem of myth in Plato rather tidily. Plato, fully understanding the power of myth to excite ideas, would introduce a philosophical principle at first mythically and then, having aroused the student's imagination, would develop that myth into scientific, or dialectical, form. Hence, what "is anticipated mythically more often than not appears later in its scientific form."[99] Schleiermacher goes on to argue that individual myths are developed and formed out of a single, Platonic "fundamental myth" (*Einem Grundmythos*).[100] Interpreting Plato therefore requires close attention to form.

2.3.3 The Dialogue Form

Before Schleiermacher, the common assumption had been that the dialogical form proved a hindrance to understanding Plato's essential philosophical doctrines. Even Tennemann was not able to break from this older model of interpretation. His overriding interest was to discover the system in Plato's thought, and he considered the dialogical form to be the chief difficulty in achieving his goal.[101] To his credit, Tennemann acknowledged the advantages of the dialogical form: it allowed "for the presentation of truths, for the development of concepts and propositions, for the refutation of objections, and overall for the production of persuasion";[102] moreover, it allowed Plato to utter dangerous truths. Yet for Tennemann it remained the case that this form "becomes somewhat rambling and boring; ... Why did Plato choose precisely this form?"[103] The only answer he could come up with was simply that Plato "could not do everything" and therefore had left much of his task to Aristotle![104] Tennemann, having made a distinction between a philosophical and an aesthetic point of view, clearly opted for the former, using *content, language, sequence*, and *chief ideas*, rather than *form*, as his criteria for judging what belongs to the Platonic system. The

---

[99] *PW* 1/1:54.31–55.2 (... *indem nach dieser nicht selten mythisch anticipirt wird, was erst später in seiner wissenschaftlichen Gestalt erscheint*); cf. *IDP* 43.
[100] *IDP* 43; *PW* 1/1:55.11. See also his introductions to the *Phaedrus* (*IDP* 71; *PW* 1/1:83.7) and to the *Gorgias* (*IDP* 177; *PW* 2/1:16.9). For more on the movement from myth to dialectics, see below, chap. 3, 81–82.
[101] See Tennemann, *System der platonischen Philosophie*, 1:xv–xvi, xxiv.
[102] Tennemann, *System der platonischen Philosophie*, 1:126.
[103] Tennemann, *System der platonischen Philosophie*, 1:126.
[104] Tennemann, *System der platonischen Philosophie*, 1:147.

dialogical form, he said, is only the "dressing" or outer garment (*Einkleidung*)[105] for pure doctrine.

Although he did not mention Tennemann, Schleiermacher vehemently rejected such a "depreciating view" (*geringschäzige Ansicht*)[106] of the dialogue form as an utter failure to understand Plato's work. If, as modern research claimed, we must rely entirely on the authentic writings of Plato, it would not do to be so dismissive of them. Rather than presuming the dialogical form to be some easily discarded embellishment, Schleiermacher proposed that the meaning of the dialogues' content be sought precisely through an appreciation of their form. Such a bold approach was really a natural consequence of the view of Plato as artist: it simply made no sense to judge a work of art apart from its form. Here again the somatic metaphor comes into play. Just as the parts of a living body can be understood only in vital connection with one another, so Plato's philosophy "is inseparable in regard to its form and content, and each sentence is rightly understood only in its own place, and within the connections and restrictions, that Plato established for it."[107] Hence, in stark contrast to Tennemann, Schleiermacher insisted that *language* and *content* were not sufficient for judging authenticity or order. Another criterion, *form* ("the form and composition in the whole"[108]), was also required. Schleiermacher's ground-breaking recognition of the philosophical significance of Plato's literary brilliance proved to be one of his most enduring contributions to Plato studies, acknowledged even by his detractors.

Such an appreciation of form followed from the historical task, as Schleiermacher understood that. Again, the interpreter must have so comprehensive grasp of the language during a given era as to be able to recognize an author's innovative use of the language: "whoever does not possess a competent knowledge of the deficient state of the language for philosophical purposes, to feel where and how Plato is cramped by it, and where he himself laboriously extends its grasp, must necessarily misunderstand his author, and that, for the most part,

---

105 Tennemann, *System der platonischen Philosophie*, 1:86, 89, 117, 127.
106 *IDP* 8; *PW* 1/1:22.26–27.
107 *PW* 1/1:28.25–27 (... so ist in ihr Form und Inhalt unzertrennlich, und jeder Saz nur an seinem Orte und in den Verbindungen und Begränzungen, wie ihn Platon aufgestellt hat, recht zu verstehen); cf. *IDP* 14.
108 *PW* 1/1:48.25 (... *die Form und Composition im Ganzen*); cf. *IDP* 35. Hermann was convinced by Schleiermacher on this point, but he used form as a tool to strengthen his own position regarding the development of Plato's thought.

in the most remarkable passages."[109] The *feeling* to which Schleiermacher here refers should not be mistaken for something arbitrary or purely subjective. By it he meant "the philological feeling" (*das philologische Gefühl*),[110] which only the most expert and talented philologists enjoy.

Schleiermacher's novel appreciation of the dialogue form also functioned in his critique of the esoteric (unwritten) tradition. By *form* (*Form*) he meant the dialogue form, yes, but also the *written* form. His preference for written over oral communication, however, seemed to contradict the passage in the *Phaedrus* (274b–278e) where Socrates expresses preference for the oral. Aware of this discrepancy, Schleiermacher turned to the subtleties of Socrates's argument, finding therein support for his own claim regarding the necessity of the dialogical form. The purpose of the Socratic method of oral instruction, Schleiermacher explained, was pedagogical. In other words, it is not oral instruction *per se*, but oral instruction as an exercise of the dialogue form that defines the Socratic method. What is more, even though Plato's method was Socratic, Plato surpassed his teacher in "educational dialectics" (*in der bildenden Dialektik*).[111] Consequently, Plato successfully captured the essence of oral instruction in his written dialogues. Hence, Plato's written dialogue (since it, too, is an "emulation of that original and mutual communication"[112]) is as valid as his oral instruction. The aim of both is the same: Plato wanted to "bring the not-yet-knowing reader to knowledge [*Wissen*],"[113] or, failing that, to compel the reader to "the feeling of having found nothing and understood nothing."[114]

Schleiermacher did not explicitly say it, but the implication was that the written Platonic tradition is to be trusted because of the complete integrity (moral, artistic, intellectual) of its author. Throughout his *Introductions*, he granted Plato the benefit of the doubt whenever inconsistencies arose and refused to

---

109 *IDP* 3; *PW* 1/1:18.16–21 (... *wer nicht von dem dürftigen Zustande der Sprache in philosophischer Hinsicht soviel Kenntniß hat, daß er fühlt, wo und wie Platon durch sie beschränkt wird, und wo er sie selbst mühsam weiter bildet, der wird ihn, und zwar an den merkwürdigsten Orten am meisten, nothwendig mißverstehen*).
110 *PW* 1/1:44.5–6; cf. *IDP* 30 ("philological consciousness"). For further discussion of what Schleiermacher meant here by "philological feeling," see Güthenke, *Feeling and Classical Philology*, 79–80.
111 *PW* 1/1:30.16–17; cf. *IDP* 16.
112 *PW* 1/1:30.28–29 (... *zur Nachahmung jenes ursprünglichen gegenseitigen Mittheilens*); cf. *IDP* 17.
113 *PW* 1/1:31.6–7 (... *daß Platon doch auch den noch nicht wissenden Leser wollte zum Wissen bringen*); cf. *IDP* 17.
114 *PW* 1/1:31.13–14 (... *oder dazu gezwungen werde, daß er sich dem Gefühle, nichts gefunden und nichts verstanden zu haben*); cf. *IDP* 17.

attribute anything to him that was "not otherwise peculiar to him," as he put it in his "Introduction to the *Euthydemus*."[115] In his "Introduction to the *Parmenides*," Schleiermacher even went so far as to refer to Plato as a "forerunner of the sacred writers" (*Vorläufer der heiligen Schriftsteller*).[116] The same integrity applied to Plato's oral instruction, but such "immediate teaching" (*das unmittelbare Lehren*)[117]—the true meaning, according to Schleiermacher, of the esoteric tradition—belonged strictly to the past. Everything that is necessary to know about Plato's philosophy is contained in the written form. Herewith, in the words of Lloyd Gerson, "the modern separation of Plato from Platonism begins."[118]

2.3.4 The Authenticity and Order of the Dialogues

Schleiermacher's internal method, his view of Plato as artist, and his emphasis on the dialogical form—each and all of these principles together aided him in determining the authenticity and order of the dialogues. If Schleiermacher saw his chief contribution as reconstructing, as nearly as possible, the sequence of the Platonic dialogues, he understood his first task as being the determination of authenticity. Unless and until the "surest canon" (*den sichersten Kanon*)[119] is secured, it makes no sense to speak of ordering. In determining that canon, Schleiermacher made a distinction between on the one hand dialogues of the "first rank" (*erste Rangordnung*),[120] or those dialogues of indisputable origin and importance, and on the other hand those of second and third ranks. Once those of the first rank are identified, he claimed, they immediately fall naturally into groups of three. In his notebook, Schleiermacher sketched these three groups: "In the end, one can put everything in Plato into *three trilogies:* Phaedrus Protagoras Parmenides—Theaetetus Sophist Philosopher—Republic Timaeus Critias. The rest are outflows."[121] This basic structure of three trilogies, what I

---

115 PW 2/1:1052.16 – 17. (*Man ist wenigstens nicht genöthiget, hiebei stehen zu bleiben, und dem Platon bei diesem Gespräch ein Verfahren zuzuschreiben, das ihm sonst nicht eigen ist*); cf. IDP 226. See also "Introduction to the *Protagoras*," PW 1/1:574; IDP 84.
116 EÜP 132; cf. IDP 117.
117 PW 2/1:32.9; cf. IDP 18.
118 Lloyd P. Gerson, *From Plato to Platonism* (Ithaca: Cornell University Press, 2013), 34n1.
119 IDP 36; PW 1/1:49.12.
120 IDP 32; PW 1/1:45.18.
121 Schleiermacher, note #118, "Zum Platon," in KGA 1/3:373.9 – 11, emphasis added (*Man kann am Ende Alles im Plato auf drei Trilogien bringen[:] Phaedrus Protagoras Parmenides—Theaetet Sophist Philosoph—Respublica Timaeus Critias. Das Uebrige sind Ausflüsse*).

2.3 Central Themes in Schleiermacher's "General Introduction" — 45

call a "Trilogy of Trilogies," is that armature around which Schleiermacher's Plato was formed.[122] With this structure in place, Schleiermacher maintained, we have a secure basis for "deciding the [authenticity] of the rest, and investigating the place which belongs to each of them."[123] In the next chapter, I explain in detail the interpretive process Schleiermacher underwent in determining the authenticity and ordering of specific dialogues and how the principles he thereby developed contributed to his hermeneutics. Here in table 2, I simply lay out his ordering of the dialogues alongside the volumes of *Platons Werke* and his basic structure of the three trilogies.[124]

Table 2: Schleiermacher's Ordering of the Platonic Dialogues

Platons Werke (1st and 2nd eds.)	Order of Dialogues* (*PW* Table of Contents)	Three Trilogies (1st-ranked) (The main "trunk"/*Stamm*)
PW I,1 (1804; 1817)	*Phaedrus*	First Trilogy:
	Lysis	1. *Phaedrus*
	Protagoras	2. *Protagoras*
	Laches	3. *Parmenides*
PW I,2 (1805; 1818)	*Charmides*	
	Euthyphro	
	Parmenides	
	Appendix:	
	Authentic but occasional:	
	Apology	
	Crito	
	Dubious:	
	Ion	
	Inauthentic:	
	Hippias Minor	
	Hipparchus	
	Minos	
	Alcibiades II	
PW II,1 (1805; 1818)	*Gorgias*	Second Trilogy:
	Theaetetus	1. *Theaetetus*
	Meno	
	Euthydemus	

---

122 Even though he thereby departed from ancient orderings according to tetralogies or a series of trilogies, his notion of three trilogies nonetheless aided him in seeing a basic structure.
123 IDP 32; PW 1/1:45.23–24 (... *die Aechtheit der übrigen zu entscheiden, und die Stelle welche jedem gebührt auszumitteln*).
124 For comparison with recent orderings, see Altman, *Ascent*, xviii; and Zuckert, *Plato's Philosophers*, 8–9.

Table 2: Schleiermacher's Ordering of the Platonic Dialogues *(continued)*

Platons Werke (1st and 2nd eds.)	Order of Dialogues* (*PW* Table of Contents)	Three Trilogies (1st-ranked) (The main "trunk"/*Stamm*)
PW II, 2 (1807; 1824)	Cratylus Sophist Statesman Symposium	2. (sub-trilogy): (i) *Sophist* + (ii) *Statesman* + (iii) *Symposium*

PW II, 3 (1809; 1826)	Phaedo
	Philebus
	Appendix:
	  Inauthentic or dubious:
	    Theages
	    Erastae
	    Alcibiades I
	    Menexenus
	    Hippias Major
	    Clitophon
		3. *Phaedo* + *Philebus*

PW III,1 (1828) (left incomplete)	Republic (*Timaeus*) (*Critias*)	Third Trilogy: 1. *Republic* 2. *Timaeus* 3. *Critias*

Upon review of the central themes of the "General Introduction," it becomes apparent that Schleiermacher's study of Plato was much more than a "companion-piece" to Tennemann's. Although to some degree Schleiermacher's internal method can indeed be said to complement Tennemann's external method, Schleiermacher's other interpretive principles—his view of Plato as artist, his sole reliance on the written works, and his emphasis on the dialogical form—all stand in opposition to Tennemann's principles. Moreover, despite the fact that Tennemann's *System der platonischen Philosophie* has generally been recognized as "the first modern monograph on Plato,"[125] it never engaged in the same level of criticism that Schleiermacher's *Platons Werke* had for at least three reasons. First, although Tennemann promised to look to Plato's writings as the only legitimate source, he wound up claiming that "generally in [Plato's] writings we do not encounter his complete philosophy."[126] Incredulous at the very thought that Plato had no system, he concluded that Plato must have had a "double philosophy";[127] and, unable to reject the idea of an esoteric tradition but unwilling

---

[125] Tigerstedt, *Decline and Fall*, 65.
[126] Tennemann, *System der platonischen Philosophie*, 1:264.
[127] Tennemann, *System der platonischen Philosophie*, 1:137; see above, 37n83.

to assign to it a neo-Platonic content, he assigned to it instead a Kantian one. Second, although he promised to examine as never before the authenticity of the dialogues, he wound up accepting most of what the tradition had already accepted as genuinely Platonic. Third, although he set out to give a strictly historical ordering of the dialogues, his discussion of the chronology was brief and underwhelming.[128] In the end, Tennemann's chief contribution was his biography of Plato.

Schleiermacher, who had set out to accomplish many of the same goals listed by Tennemann, was more successful in achieving those goals. His "General Introduction" was nothing less than a revolution. Not only did he fulfil his promises to question the conventional assumptions and to raise entirely new questions, but out of this project he also developed an interpretive theory that would itself prove revolutionary.[129] Consequently, he proceeded without hesitation in rejecting the esoteric tradition, eliminating several dialogues from the *corpus*, and assigning others to secondary or even questionable status. Moreover, through the description of his methodology in the "General Introduction" and the detailed explanations in each introduction, he carefully made his argument for a new ordering of the dialogues, criticizing along the way Tennemann's reasons for a later dating of the *Phaedrus*.[130] Even though, as we shall soon see, Schleiermacher's ordering would be called into question by the next generation of Plato scholars, his thoughtful reflections on each dialogue and on their interrelations would remain relevant and illuminating to later generations. In the end, Tennemann stood in the background with the other eighteenth-century Plato scholars, while Schleiermacher set a new course in Plato research.

It is more difficult to determine the degree to which Schleiermacher had been influenced by, or had departed from, Schlegel in his interpretation of Plato. Schlegel clearly thought that Schleiermacher had stolen his chief ideas. Unfortunately, Schlegel left no finished or extensive study of Plato that would provide a means of comparison. More complicated yet is the fact that the question of Schlegel's and Schleiermacher's interpretations of the Platonic dialogues is intricately bound up with the development of their respective hermeneutical theories.[131] Nevertheless, there was one particular theme that had proved an on-

---

128 See Tennemann, *System der platonischen Philosophie*, 1:115–25.
129 See below, chap. 3.
130 See *PW* 1/1:78–79; *IDP* 66–67.
131 The literature on the relation between their respective hermeneutics is extensive. In addition to works cited in nn. 15 and 35 above, see H. Jackson Forstman, "The Understanding of Language by Friedrich Schlegel and Schleiermacher," *Soundings* 51 (1968): 146–65; Hendrik Birus, "Hermeneutische Wende? Anmerkungen zur Schleiermacher-Interpretation," *Euphorion* 74, no. 2

going issue of contention between them and that therefore might provide some measure by which we may judge the degree to which Schleiermacher's interpretation of Plato's dialogue was new—namely, the placement and significance of the *Phaedrus*. Their disagreements over the *Phaedrus* are all the more interesting since Schleiermacher's treatment of it would become one of the most controversial issues in the debates of the mid-nineteenth century.

2.4 Controversial Issues in the *Introductions*

2.4.1 Placement of the *Phaedrus*

Indignant that Schleiermacher had called his work on Plato into question, Schlegel retorted, "On the *Phaedrus* do you really wish [to claim] more expertise than I?"[132] Thereafter the *Phaedrus* was a focal point of their growing disagreements. In his hypotheses, Schlegel identified the *Phaedrus* as the earliest.[133] Schleiermacher, who at the time was more preoccupied with producing a careful translation of the *Phaedrus* than with fretting about its placement, cited two reasons for doubting its early dating: Plato would not have reproached Lysis for being youthful were he himself still young, and the discourse on writing could not be the work of a novice; nor was he convinced, however, by Tennemann's much later dating for it, the reasons for which he considered "dumb."[134] In the winter of 1801, therefore, Schleiermacher was open to the possibility that the *Phaedrus* was the first dialogue, but he also stressed that a later dating would not undermine his support of Schlegel's "system," since at that point he remained in basic agreement with Schlegel's principles.[135] A year later, reviewing Ast's *De Platonis Phädro*, Schleiermacher continued to resist the placement of the *Phaedrus* as the first dialogue, at least on the basis of its "dramatic form."[136] Nevertheless, within the next two years Schleiermacher, too, arrived at

---

(1980): 213–22; Reinhold Rieger, *Interpretation und Wissen: Zur philosophischen Begründung der Hermeneutik bei Friedrich Schleiermacher und ihrem geschichtlichen Hintergrund* (Berlin and New York: Walter de Gruyter, 1988); and Schnur, *Schleiermachers Hermeneutik und ihre Vorgeschichte*, 139–59.

132 Schlegel to Schleiermacher, early August 1800 (#922, lines 46–47); *Br.* 4:181.
133 See Schlegel to Schleiermacher, early Sept. 1800 (#942, lines 17–18) and 8 Dec. 1800 (#993, line 86); *Br.* 4:244, 353, respectively.
134 Schleiermacher to Schlegel, 10 Jan. 1801 (#1008, lines 44–53); *Br.* 5:10.
135 See Schleiermacher to Schlegel, 7 Feb. 1801 (#1019, lines 24–26); *Br.* 5:45.
136 See Schleiermacher, "Rezension von Ast," 472.18

2.4 Controversial Issues in the *Introductions* — 49

the conclusion that the *Phaedrus* must have been Plato's first dialogue, although he was careful to distinguish his reasons from those of "that ancient tradition" (*jene alte Ueberlieferung*)[137] of Diogenes and Olympiodorus. He made passing reference to Ast but made no mention of Schlegel.

Shortly after the publication of the first volume of Schleiermacher's *Platons Werke*, Schlegel wrote to Reimer, the publisher, complaining that Schleiermacher had stolen his ideas. Schleiermacher denied any such dependence. Responding directly to Schlegel, he countered that he could not have taken his ideas from Schlegel since he had "never heard from you any real reasons for the priority of the *Phaedrus*."[138] Schlegel's accusations did not go away, and Schleiermacher had to defend himself again four years later in a lengthy, detailed letter to Boeckh.[139] There he explained that Schlegel and he had agreed that the *Phaedrus* and *Protagoras* were both early dialogues, and he conceded that Schlegel had pronounced it first, since at the time he had himself been preoccupied with translating. Still, Schleiermacher contended, Schlegel had never given any reasons other than style and tradition for the *Phaedrus* being first. What is more, he himself never had any interest in taking up the "quite uncritical thoughts about the *Phaedrus*"[140] propounded by Schlegel. In short, although a quick glance at his ordering might lead one to believe it similar to Schlegel's, Schleiermacher insisted that, when examined in its particulars, it clearly owed no debt to Schlegel.

As it turned out, each was claiming credit for a theory that would soon be proven false. Already in 1820 with Joseph Socher's *Ueber Platons Schriften*[141] and more definitively in the 1830s with the works of Gottfried Stallbaum

---

137 *PW* 1/1:80.13; cf. *IDP* 68. In his "Introduction to the *Phaedrus*," Schleiermacher expanded on the reasons given in the General Introduction: "For it is of course undeniable that the seeds of his entire philosophy are all but in the *Phaedrus*, although just as clear is its undeveloped state, and the incompleteness particularly betrays itself in that indirect conduct of the dialogue" (*PW* 1/1:80.4–7 [*Denn die Keime seiner ganzen Philosophie fast sind im Phaidros freilich nicht zu läugnen, aber auch ihr unentwikkelter Zustand ist eben so deutlich, und zugleich verräth sich die Unvollkommenheit in jener indirecten Führung des Gespräches*]; cf. *IDP* 68). See also the "Introduction to the *Gorgias*," where, he said, that seed continues to grow (*PW* 2/1:17; *IDP* 178–79).
138 Schleiermacher to Schlegel, 10 Oct. 1804 (#1829, lines 16–17), *Br.* 7:467.
139 See Schleiermacher to Boeckh, 18 June 1808 (#2701), *Br.* 10:116–24.
140 Schleiermacher to Boeckh, 18 June 1808 (#2701, line 122), *Br.* 10:119
141 Joseph Socher, *Ueber Platons Schriften* (München: Ignas Joseph Lentner, 1820).

(1793–1861)¹⁴² and Hermann, the *Phaedrus* came to be seen as a later work.¹⁴³ Hermann, citing Stallbaum and Socher, agreed with Schleiermacher that the *Phaedrus* contained the seeds of the Platonic doctrines but averred that, rather than being the first of the entire series of the dialogues, it functioned as the beginning program for Plato's Academy and therefore could not be the first, or even among the earliest.¹⁴⁴ In Germany in the 1880s, Hermann's genetic methodology was itself superseded by stylometry (the statistical examination of words, grammar, and style), which nevertheless reached the same basic conclusion regarding the *Phaedrus*.¹⁴⁵ Today the consensus is that the *Phaedrus* is a middle or later dialogue.

The question remains whether Schleiermacher's incorrect identification of the *Phaedrus* as the first dialogue subverts the rest of his interpretation of Plato. Somewhat predictably, Schleiermacher scholars have argued that it does not. Gustav-Adolf Krapf and Karl Pohl have both made the case that in Schleiermacher's treatment of the *Phaedrus* we find not only a profound grasp of Plato's dialectics but also the key to understanding Schleiermacher's own theory of dialectics.¹⁴⁶ Given the fact that so often when Schleiermacher was mentioned in twentieth-century commentaries on Plato it was in passing reference to his outdated view of the *Phaedrus*, it would seem that Plato scholars generally assume his interpretation of Plato to be an antiquated one. Yet some have concurred in the judgment that Schleiermacher's Plato-interpretation does not "stand or

---

142 Gottfried Stallbaum, *Platonis Dialogos selectos recensuit et commentariis in usum scholarum instruxit Godofredus Stallbaum*, 10 vols. (Gotha and Erfurt: Hennings, 1827–); later entitled: *Platonis Opera omnia* (reprint: New York & London: Garland, 1980).
143 Werner Jaeger (1888–1961) attributes the discovery of the later placement of the *Phaedrus*, hence the first attack on Schleiermacher's ordering, to Hermann and his 1839 study, *Geschichte und System* (see Jaeger, "Der Wandel des Platobildes im 19. Jahrhundert," in *Humanistische Reden und Vorträge* [1936; 2nd ed., Berlin: Walter de Gruyter, 1960], 133). Virmond pushes the discovery back to Stallbaum in 1832 but argues that it was Hermann who, in his review of Stallbaum in 1833, recognized the significance of the new ordering, welcomed the end of Schleiermacher's tutelage, and developed this position more fully in 1839 (see Virmond, "Der fiktive Autor," 232). Thesleff locates the break with Schleiermacher earlier still, in Socher's 1820 study of Plato's works, and contends that it was Socher who first employed the new genetic method that would be developed by Hermann (see Thesleff, *Studies in Platonic Chronology*, 2, 8).
144 See Hermann, *Geschichte und System*, 513–14.
145 For more on the genetic approach, see E. N. Tigerstedt, *Interpreting Plato* (Uppsala: Almquist & Wiksell, 1977), 25–51. For more on the stylometric method, see Leonard Brandwood, *The Chronology of Plato's Dialogues* (Cambridge and N. Y.: Cambridge University Press, 1990).
146 See Krapf, "Platonic Dialectics," 56, 61–62; and Karl Pohl, "Die Bedeutung der Sprache für den Erkenntnisakt in der 'Dialektik' Friedrich Schleiermachers," *Kant-Studien* 46, no. 4 (1954–55): 308–15.

fall"¹⁴⁷ with his placement of the *Phaedrus*. For instance, two translators of the *Phaedrus* are persuaded by Schleiermacher's basic insight regarding the relatedness of the two parts of the dialogue;¹⁴⁸ similarly, Albin Lesky holds that, "for the task of determining the relative chronology of the Platonic writings, Schleiermacher's attempt is still of fundamental importance."¹⁴⁹ This leads to another, yet related, contentious issue in Schleiermacher's Plato—namely, whether it is possible to give specific dates for the dialogues.

2.4.2 The Ordering and Chronology of the Dialogues

Like the debates over the placement of the *Phaedrus*, the controversy over the ordering of the dialogues goes back to the very beginning of the Plato project. Schlegel had been chiefly interested in establishing an *"historical* ordering"¹⁵⁰ which, he was convinced, would correspond with a more artistic or literary ordering. In contrast, Schleiermacher apparently proposed what Schlegel termed "a construction of [Plato's] *Geist.*"¹⁵¹ Schleiermacher clearly seems to have been skeptical early on about the possibility of a strictly historical ordering and described his point of departure as "the viewpoint of non-ordering [*NichtOrdnung*]."¹⁵² As already noted, he thought that the task of translating necessarily preceded that of chronologizing, so much so that Schlegel criticized him for being so willing to drop the ordering just to meet a deadline.¹⁵³ Schleiermacher, far from ignoring the job of ordering, was the first to offer a chronological ordering of the dialogues, or at least a compelling one. *Sequential*, however, might be a more accurate term than *chronological*, in as much as the internal method alone yields "only a sequence and no point in time."¹⁵⁴ While the external method does yield certain definite chronological points of reference, those are limited. In other words, Schleiermacher's ordering (as suggested by his view of Plato as artist and of the dialogues as a living body) was primarily based on what he

---

147 Stein, *Geschichte des Platonismus*, 1:67.
148 See Alexander Nehamas and Paul Woodruff, trans., Plato, *Phaedrus* (Indianapolis: Hackett, 1995), "Introduction,"xxvii.
149 Albin Lesky, *A History of Greek Literature*, trans. James Willis & Cornelis de Heer (London: Methuen, 1966), 515.
150 Schlegel to Schleiermacher, 10 Mar. 1800 (#808, line 36); *Br.* 3:412, emphasis added.
151 Schlegel to Schleiermacher, 28 Mar. 1800 (#824, line 33); *Br.* 3:443.
152 Schleiermacher to Schlegel, 13 Sept. 1800 (#949, lines 13–14); *Br.* 4:257.
153 See Schlegel to Schleiermacher, (mid-) Nov. 1800 (#977, lines 2–5); *Br.* 4:317.
154 *PW* 1/1:40.7–8 (... *nur eine Folge und keinen Zeitpunkt*); cf. *IDP* 26.

called the *natural, internal* relations within the dialogues, and only secondarily did it enjoy a probability of correspondence with chronological sequences. Of course, logically speaking, his natural ordering implied a before-and-after relation ("… both must be one and the same"[155]), but Schleiermacher did not emphasize that, and he certainly made no pretense at being able to date certain dialogues. The evidence, he thought, was simply not always there.

It was inevitable that such boundaries set by Schleiermacher would be challenged, since, as Klaus Oehler explains, "The interest in the historical individuality of the person Plato was too powerful."[156] Thus Hermann, beginning with the basic assumption that development and change must be applied to Plato, set out to determine the "history of the development of [Plato's] life and thought" by unearthing the "most important moments of his life,"[157] beginning with the day of his birth. The stages of development of Plato's philosophy were to be traced to stages in his life that could be determined by certain major events (e. g., the death of his teacher, political events in Athens). Schleiermacher, too, had relied on whatever external, historical traces there were. Nevertheless, Hermann's (and his followers') overwhelming confidence in our ability to reconstruct history approached a psychologizing of Plato (which, incidentally, paralleled the psychologizing in various nineteenth-century attempts to discover the historical Jesus) that could not be supported by the historical evidence.

Eduard Zeller (1814–1908), much like Hermann, tried to assign fairly precise dates for the dialogues but also acknowledged the inherent difficulties in getting behind the anachronisms. He concluded, not unlike Schleiermacher, that in Plato we are dealing with an artist and therefore can never find certainty regarding our claims to history.[158] By and large, however, the trend throughout the latter part of the nineteenth century was increasingly positivistic. After 1867 and the emergence of the stylometric method, it seemed that the empirical evidence Schleiermacher thought lacking was finally available in statistical analysis. Plato scholars felt confident in their division of Plato's life and works into three periods, even though they continued to debate the dates of particular dialogues.

The reaction against positivism in Plato scholarship was first voiced by an American graduate student in Munich, Paul Shorey (1857–1934), who went on

---

155 Schleiermacher to Boeckh, 18 June 1808 (#2701, line 36), *Br.* 10:117.
156 Klaus Oehler, "Der entmythologisierte Platon: Zur Lage der Platonforschung," *Zeitschrift für philosophische Forschung* 19, no. 3 (1965): 395.
157 Hermann, *Geschichte und System*, 9–10; see also 384.
158 See Eduard Zeller, *Die Philosophie der Griechen in ihrer geschichtlichen Entwicklung*, 3 vols. (Tübingen, 1856, 1859), 98–99.

to become a founding faculty member of the University of Chicago. In an influential essay, *The Unity of Plato's Thought* (1903), Shorey criticized the stylometric approach because "the attempt to base such a chronology on the variations and developments of Plato's doctrine has led to an exaggeration of Plato's inconstancy that violates all sound principles of literary interpretation and is fatal to all genuine intelligence of his meaning."[159] Thus, ninety-nine years after the publication of Schleiermacher's "General Introduction," the essential unity of the written dialogues was reaffirmed. In concluding his essay, Shorey wrote, "My thesis is simply that Plato on the whole belongs rather to the type of thinkers whose philosophy is fixed in early maturity (Schopenhauer, Herbert Spencer), rather than to the class of those who receive a new revelation every decade (Schelling)."[160]

2.4.3 The Validity of the Esoteric Tradition

Schleiermacher's rejection of an esoteric tradition, unlike his placement of the *Phaedrus* and his ordering of the dialogues, did not become truly controversial until more than a century after his death. With a couple of exceptions, his insistence that scholars rely on the exoteric tradition alone became the dominant interpretation. Even Georg W. F. Hegel (1770–1831), who criticized Schleiermacher's work on Plato for being superfluous and hypercritical and who rejected the notion of Plato as an artist, nonetheless agreed with Schleiermacher that "Plato's philosophy was left to us in the writings which we have from him."[161] The momentum began to shift in the period between the world wars, when classicists began to address the problem of Plato's unwritten doctrines.[162] For the most part, this new scholarly attention to the Platonic *agrapha* did not challenge the authority of the dialogues, although it did lead some scholars to reconsider the validity of neo-Platonism as an authentic expression of Platonic doctrine.[163]

---

159 Paul Shorey, *The Unity of Plato's Thought*, vol. 6: The Decennial Publications of the University of Chicago (Chicago: University of Chicago, 1904), 5.
160 Shorey, *Unity of Plato's Thought*, 88.
161 G. W. F. Hegel, *Vorlesungen über die Geschichte der Philosophie*, in *Werke in zwanzig Bänden*, ed. Eva Moldenhauer and Karl Michel (Frankfurt: Suhrkamp Verlag, 1971), 19:19.
162 Most notably: Werner Jaeger, John Burnet, A. E. Taylor, and Cornelia J. de Vogel. De Vogel gives an historical overview of this renewed interest in the *agrapha* in "Plato: The Written and Unwritten Doctrines. Fifty Years of Plato Studies, 1930–1980," chap. 1 in *Rethinking Plato and Platonism* (Leiden: E.J. Brill, 1986), 3–56.
163 De Vogel refers obliquely to Schleiermacher and his legacy when she writes, "a more radical change in Platonic studies took place in the nineteenth century: only then was Plato sepa-

The real controversy over the *agrapha* erupted in 1959, when the publication of Hans Joachim Krämer's *Arete bei Platon und Aristoteles* inaugurated the new esotericism and along with it the Tübingen School.[164] Krämer placed Schleiermacher right at the center of the controversy: "It was the authority of Schleiermacher alone that brought this well-founded view [of an esoteric special teaching of Plato] almost completely to a standstill."[165] Tigerstedt has ridiculed such an attack on "the evil genius of Schleiermacher,"[166] but several scholars of note concurred with Krämer's assessment.[167] These proponents of esotericism, more than simply arguing for the validity of the esoteric tradition, insist on its supremacy. Although they cannot reject the written tradition, they nevertheless insist that the central tenets of Plato's philosophy are not to be found in it,[168] that it is "inferior to the oral process,"[169] and that it sometimes even serves to "mask"[170] the true teachings of Plato. Consequently, Plato's written doctrines can be understood only in light of the esoteric philosophical principles. Krämer

---

rated from Neoplatonic interpretation" (Cornelia J. de Vogel, "On the Neoplatonic Character of Platonism and the Platonic Character of Neoplatonism," *Mind* [1953], 44). She did not intend this as a compliment, her thesis being that "... *Platonism must be understood in a Neoplatonic sense, and that Neoplatonism should be regarded, in its essence, as a legitimate Platonism*" (54).

164 Hösle summarizes its position: "it accepts the Aristotelian and the other pupils' reports, while rejecting the dating of the unwritten doctrines to the last phase of Plato's life. In respect of the content, it in a way returns to the first paradigm, for it accepts a systematic doctrine of principles, although methodologically it accepts all the innovations that philology underwent in the nineteenth and twentieth centuries" ("Tübingen School," 336). He lists Krämer, Konrad Gaiser, and Thomas Szlezák as the leading figures, and he counts himself as belonging as well (341).

165 Hans Joachim Krämer, *Arete bei Platon und Aristoteles. Zum Wesen and zur Geschichte der platonischen Ontologie* (Heidelberg: Carl Winter Universitätsverlag, 1959), 18.

166 Tigerstedt, *Decline and Fall*, 5.

167 See J. N. Findlay, *Plato: The Written and Unwritten Doctrines* (London: Routledge & Kegan Paul, 1974), 406; Konrad Gaiser, *Platons ungeschriebene Lehre. Studien zur systematischen und geschichtlichen Begründung der Wissenschaften in der Platonischen Schule* (Stuttgart: Ernst Klett Verlag, 1963), 335; Oehler, "Der entmythologisierte Platon," 399; Thomas A. Szlezák, *Platon und die Schriftlichkeit* (Berlin: de Gruyter, 1985), 331–2n3, and *Aufsätze zur griechischen Literatur und Philosophie*, International Plato Studies 139 (Baden-Baden: Academia, 2019), 488–508, 689–91; and Jürgen Wippern, "Einleitung," in *Das Problem der ungeschriebenen Lehre Platons: Beiträge zum Verständnis der Platonischen Prinzipienphilosophie* (Darmstadt: Wissenschaftliche Buchgesellschaft, 1972), vii.

168 See, e.g., Gaiser, *Platons ungeschriebene Lehre*, 3.

169 Hans Joachim Krämer, *Plato and the Foundations of Metaphysics: A Work on the Theory of the Principles and Unwritten Doctrines of Plato with a Collection of the Fundamental Documents*, trans. John R. Catan (Albany: State University of New York Press, 1990), 70.

170 Findlay, *Written and Unwritten Doctrines*, 4.

and others associated with the Tübingen School have therefore assigned to themselves the task of reconstructing the esoteric tradition on the basis of the *Phaedrus*, the *Seventh Letter*, and the unwritten oral teachings handed down by Plato's inner circle of disciples. It is not surprising, therefore, that they would appreciate Tennemann's Plato more than Schleiermacher's.

Krämer does indeed offer some compelling criticisms of what he refers to as the Romantic paradigm and of Schleiermacher's Plato in particular.[171] Yet problematic is the fact that his reconstruction of the Platonic esoteric tradition turns out to be suspiciously Hegelian in nature.[172] It was precisely such an interpolation of content into Plato's philosophy that Schleiermacher tried to guard against by insisting on a new, critical examination of the authentic, written dialogues. Thomas Szlezák's subsequent criticisms of Schleiermacher focuses on the "Introduction to the *Phaedrus*" and his handling of Socrates' critique of writing.[173] Szlezák faults Schleiermacher for insinuating that "Plato in his maturity [i.e. in the *Letter*] no longer believes in the stern youthful verdict concerning the scant value of writing"; and he goes so far as to charge Schleiermacher's "utterly inadequate approach" as being "not merely *un-Platonic*—it is, in spirit, *anti-Platonic*."[174] Szlezák has a point, although he takes it too far.

Schleiermacher himself had an important point about the basic principle being the *dialogical form*, whether written or unwritten, although he did evade the jagged edge of the suspicion of writing voiced by Socrates. Nevertheless, Schleiermacher did not deny the validity of an esoteric tradition *in toto*; he suggested, rather, that the oral teachings to which Aristotle referred add nothing to what we can learn from the written dialogues, and it is therefore pointless "to lament over, or to dream of, other lost riches of Platonic wisdom."[175] According

---

[171] See, e.g., Hans Joachim Krämer, *Gesammelte Aufsätze zu Platon*, Beiträge zur Altertumskunde 321 (Boston and Berlin: De Gruyter, 2014), 402–404, 534.
[172] See Krämer, *Plato and the Foundations*, 157–67; also, Findlay, *Written and Unwritten Doctrines*, 399–401.
[173] See, e.g., Thomas A. Szlezák, *Reading Plato* (New York: Routledge, 1999; and Florence: Taylor & Francis Group, 1999), 31; "Schleiermacher's Theory," esp. 172–78, 187; and "Schleiermachers 'Einleitung'," 51–61.
[174] Szlezák, "Schleiermacher's Theory," 170, 179.
[175] *IDP* 13; *PW* 1/1:28.5–6 (... *es sei vergeblich, über einen andern verlorenen Schaz platonischer Weisheit zu klagen oder zu träumen*). While Leo Strauss (1899–1973) agreed with Schleiermacher's insistence on the written dialogues for understanding Plato's philosophy, he disagreed with him on the unity, and by extension the continuity, of Plato's thought. See Hannes Kerber, "Strauss and Schleiermacher on How to Read Plato: An Introduction to Exoteric Teaching'," in *Reorientation: Leo Strauss in the 1930s*, ed. by Martin D. Yaffe and Richard S. Ruderman (New York: Palgrave Macmillan, 2014), 203–214.

to Schleiermacher, when it comes to Plato's philosophy we have no choice but to stick with the written texts we have.[176] Gerson has termed this approach "Schleiermacherism."[177]

2.5 Concluding Remarks

In retrospect, Schleiermacher's Plato project occupied a unique decade in the history of German philology. In 1799, the field was open for so daring and monumental an enterprise as the one conceived by Schlegel and Schleiermacher; after 1809, the year in which Schleiermacher published the penultimate volume of *Platons Werke*, philology became increasingly professionalized as an independent discipline, and the older generation of translators—F. A. Wolf, A. W. Schlegel, and L. Tieck—came under attack by a new generation. The result, according to R. Steven Turner, was an "alienation of a professional and esoteric philology from broader channels of cultural humanism."[178]

How did Schleiermacher understand Plato? Thus far we have learned that Plato was for him the Plato of the (written) dialogues, the artist whose philosophy was a unified whole. Yet this framework, while necessary, remains rather formal, thus providing only a partial answer to the question at hand. It needs to be complemented by a discussion of Schleiermacher's substantive analysis of Plato's philosophy. The problem is that Schleiermacher apparently saw his role as a philologist as one which required him to avoid just such a task; his objective in writing the "General Introduction" was to give each reader new and immediate access to Plato's works.[179] Nevertheless, his introductions to individual dialogues can offer crucial insights into Schleiermacher's more substantive interpretation of Plato.

These insights can also function as a bridge to the other question, *In what ways was Schleiermacher influenced by Plato or Platonism?* Andreas Arndt is without doubt right in cautioning that Schleiermacher's intermittent proclama-

---

[176] Szlezák criticizes Schleiermacher's silence over the *Seventh Letter* in the "General Introduction" (see "Schleiermachers 'Einleitung'," 57). Because *Platons Werke* was left unfinished, we do not know how Schleiermacher would have treated the question of the authenticity of the *Letter*.
[177] Gerson, *From Plato to Platonism*, 40n12. For Schleiermacher, the issue was methodological. Yet the fact is that it carried implications for philosophical content as well, since the esoteric tradition was associated with more dualistic interpretations of Platonic philosophy. In contrast, the new esotericists are divided regarding monistic or dualistic interpretations.
[178] Turner, "Historicism, *Kritik*, and the Prussian Professoriate," 468.
[179] See *IDP* 3–4; *PW* 1/1:18.24–19.4.

tions of veneration for Plato do not in themselves substantiate the claim for Plato's philosophy having had a "decisive influence" on Schleiermacher's thought.[180] Yet Schleiermacher's *Introductions* just might substantiate what proclamations cannot. It makes a difference, in other words, that Schleiermacher recognized in the dialectics of the *Sophist* "the essence of all true Philosophy";[181] that he resisted a dualistic interpretation of Plato's teaching on the relation between body and soul; that he was critical of Plato in the *Republic*; and that he carefully distinguished various schools of Platonism, rather than simply dismissing neo-Platonism out of hand. The answer, therefore, lies somewhere between Arndt's insistence that what we find in Schleiermacher after 1803 is at most "vague Platonism"[182] and Shorey's accolade that "the only true Platonic tradition ... [is] liberal theology and natural theology. The true and typical Platonists in this domain are such men as Cicero, Plutarch, Schleiermacher, Matthew Arnold, and Martineau."[183] In the next two chapters, we move out of the "General Introduction" and into the *Introductions* as a whole.

---

180 Arndt, *Schleiermacher als Philosoph*, 263.
181 EÜP 250 (*das Wesen aller wahren Philosophie*); cf. IDP 253.
182 Arndt, *Schleiermacher als Philosoph*, 274.
183 Paul Shorey, *Platonism Ancient and Modern* (Berkeley: University of California Press, 1938), 44; see also 16. Szlezák blames Shorey for importing the "Schleiermacherian creed" into "the Anglo-Saxon interpretation of Plato" ("Schleiermacher's Theory," 186).

3 Practicing on Plato: Interpretation, Socratic Clues, and the Emergence of Schleiermacher's Hermeneutics

> *Thus, indeed, all principles of higher criticism, the entire art of understanding, must be worked into the analytical reconstruction.*[1]

3.1 Introduction

Schleiermacher wrote these words concerning the interplay of criticism and understanding in the winter of 1805, during his first semester as a professor at the University of Halle and while working on the third volume of *Platons Werke* (see table 1). The following semester, he would lecture on hermeneutics for the first time.[2] He is famous, of course, for the "turn" (*Wende*) his *Hermeneutics* inaugurated, which was as significant as the one he initiated in Plato studies.[3] The intersection of these two turns is beyond doubt: his theory of interpretation and criticism emerged (at least in part) out of his struggle to translate, interpret, and understand Plato. Dilthey established that fact a century-and-a-half ago;[4] it has since become commonplace to assert the connection, although less common for scholars to examine it. More recently, Wolfgang Virmond has enriched our understanding of the deeper background of Schleiermacher's hermeneutics by pointing to Schleiermacher's early studies of the classics during his student days at Halle and, crucially, to his close collaboration with Heindorf on translat-

---

1 Schleiermacher to J. C. Gaß, 3 Feb. 1805 (#1914, lines 33–35); *Br.* 8:125.
2 He went on to lecture on hermeneutics and criticism eight more times in Berlin, between 1809 and 1833. Most scholarly attention has been paid to the later lectures on hermeneutics, but there has been increased awareness of the significance of his earliest lectures. See KGA 2/4: *Vorlesungen zur Hermeneutik und Kritik*, ed. Wolfgang Virmond, with Hermann Patsch (Berlin and Boston: De Gruyter, 2013).
3 See, e.g., Manfred Frank, "Einleitung," *Hermeneutik und Kritik*, ed. Manfred Frank (Frankfurt am Main: Suhrkamp, 1977), 7–10 (hereafter cited in text as "*HK*"); and Hendrik Birus, "Hermeneutische Wende?" Regarding *Platons Werke* as a "turn," see Szlezák, "Schleiermacher's Theory," 165.
4 See Dilthey, *Leben Schleiermachers*, 1/2:38, and 2/3:680–83.

ing Plato,[5] and Lutz Käppel has led us yet further into Schleiermacher's painstaking work on ancient texts and its effects on his own thought.[6]

In this chapter, I argue that Schleiermacher practiced on Plato as he simultaneously drew insight from Plato. I focus not so much on Schleiermacher's *Hermeneutics* as on his *Introductions to the Dialogues of Plato*, treating those as a single work. In chapter two, we examined the formal principles of the Plato-interpretation which Schleiermacher enunciated in his "General Introduction": his view of Plato as artist; his development of an internal method; his emphasis on the exoteric tradition and elision of the esoteric tradition; and his insistence on the dialogue form as a signature of Plato's philosophy. Now we need to turn our attention to how those principles actually functioned when Schleiermacher made concrete decisions about authenticity and ordering, and when he tried to solve age-old conundrums in Plato-interpretation.

I proceed by discussing how Schleiermacher faced the challenge of famous difficulties of interpreting the *Phaedrus* by means of Socratic clues, which he applied as hermeneutical principles for understanding that dialogue (section 3.3); how he employed the new criticism in order to determine which dialogues are authentic (section 3.4); how he arrived at an ordering of the dialogues, and why he thought that ordering was so crucial for understanding Plato's philosophy (section 3.5). Readers familiar with his *Hermeneutics* will recognize incipient formulations of that theory in these interpretive decisions, but familiarity with his hermeneutics is not required to follow the argument. Nevertheless, to make that connection a little more explicit, I begin with a general orientation related to interpretation and criticism at the turn of the nineteenth century (section 3.2).

3.2 The New Criticism and the Plato Renaissance

We have already looked at the late-eighteenth century German renaissance and its implications for Plato studies. There was a growing consensus that the new historical-critical method had to be applied to Plato's works, which had been largely neglected in Germany, especially in comparison to England and France. Consequently, a fundamental shift in orientation regarding Plato's philosophy

---

[5] See Virmond, "Der fiktive Autor"; "*interpretari necesse est*"; and "Neue Textgrundlagen zu Schleiermachers früher Hermeneutik: Prolegomena zur kritischen Edition," in Fischer and Selge, *Schleiermacher-Kongreß 1984*, 575–90.
[6] See Käppel, "Schleiermachers Hermeneutik," and "Die frühe Rezeption der Platon-Übersetzung."

occurred, a shift that mirrored work starting to be done in the interpretation of the New Testament.[7] This meant, first, that claims about Plato's philosophy had to be grounded in the writings themselves—undefiled by dogmatic commitments, theological agendas, or other philosophical systems. Second, the writings had to be set in historical context. This required, third, that the chronological sequence and dates of the dialogues be discovered. This newly stated ideal had yet to be achieved by 1800, when Schleiermacher entered the scene of Plato studies.

Unquestionably indebted to this "new situation,"[8] Schleiermacher was the one who carried it forward by relentlessly pursuing its ideals and commitments. What was it that set his study of Plato apart from that of the other modern critics? On this point it may be instructive to return to Schleiermacher's acknowledgment of debt to, and pointed criticism of, two of the most important Plato interpreters of his day: the Kantian philosopher, W. G. Tennemann; and the Romantic critic, F. Schlegel. In the previous chapter, we considered Schleiermacher's relation to these men from a biographical vantage point; now let us do so from a comparative one. Both Tennemann and Schlegel were committed to approaching Plato *via* new methodologies. Yet each represented one side within the new situation: Tennemann the more historical (and philosophical); Schlegel the more literary (and philological). The limitations of each demonstrated to Schleiermacher the weakness of any one-sided approach.

The strength and weakness of Tennemann's *System der platonischen Philosophie* (1792) was his historical method, what Schleiermacher referred to as an "external" method—external, because it relied exclusively on historical evidence, or external markers. What defined Tennemann's scholarship as being truly modern was that he had sifted through all previous scholarship and had sorted out the historical from the conjectural. As a result, he was able to isolate certain dates and facts about Plato's life and works. As we have seen, Schleiermacher considered Tennemann's "*Leben des Plato*" ("Life of Plato") so authoritative that he saw no need to revisit it. Yet the great weakness of Tennemann's external method was that it could neither accomplish its own goals of dating and ordering the dialogues nor tell us much that is substantive about Plato or his philosophy. There were simply not enough external markers. This created a problem for Tennemann, who, unable or unwilling to relinquish the notion of a Platonic system, wound up betraying his own methodological commitments. He asserted

---

[7] Interestingly, Friedrich Schlegel did not think that the Bible could be criticized since it was not a "classic," a conviction that Patsch attributes to what he calls Schlegel's "catholicizing" ("Schlegels 'Philosophie der Philologie'," 449).

[8] Tigerstedt, *Decline and Fall*, 63.

that Plato must have had a "double philosophy"—an "external" one found in the extant writings and a "secret" one.⁹ Since Tennemann's presentation of Plato's so-called system was therefore not based exclusively on the close examination of texts, he strayed from the new criticism. He did not forsake dogmatic tendencies after all, despite his intentions: having found no system in the written dialogues, he wound up imposing his own philosophical (Kantian) system. Schleiermacher proposed that, given the paucity of historical evidence, the external method needed to be supplemented by an *internal* (by which he meant, in part, literary) method.

Schlegel, too, was convinced that an internal method was necessary. An artistic translation of Plato, he proclaimed, was waiting to be discovered. Schleiermacher agreed. Increasingly, however, the two friends and collaborators diverged on what this internal method involved. Schlegel focused more and more on irony as the *leitmotiv* that would help determine authenticity and order. Schleiermacher, in response, warned that such an approach would produce only fragments and inconsistencies, not argument. Although Schlegel began the Plato project committed to the very historicism he himself had advanced, Schleiermacher was concerned that Schlegel had come to occupy himself too much with the more theoretical questions. In contrast, Schleiermacher emphasized that the precise, painstaking work of the *higher grammar* was the more fundamental and necessary task. In his view, the new criticism involved close grammatical and comparative work within the text(s) whereby each part is worked through with precision and thoroughness. Such attention to the particulars would begin to yield the rest—the relation among the particulars, as well as the relation between particulars and the whole. They needed to have the translations before them, Schleiermacher urged, before they could begin to determine the order and connection of the dialogues: "Philosophy and the higher grammar should therein revise each other."¹⁰

Ironically, although Tennemann and Schlegel represented two different sides of the new modern approach to Plato, their respective forms of one-sidedness arrived at the same problematic result: the imposition of their own philosophies onto Plato. Both resulted, that is, in a form of idealism. Tennemann reached beyond the authentic texts to some hidden philosophy (which he had originally rejected) in order to find the Platonic *system*. Schlegel, although anti-system, also departed from (historical and textual) criticism in order to follow his literary theory, a theory which yielded false conclusions regarding the authenticity of

---
9 Tennemann, *System der platonischen Philosophie*, 1:137. See above, chap. 2, 37n83.
10 Schleiermacher to Schlegel, 7 Feb. 1801 (#1019, lines 88–89), *Br.* 5:47.

certain texts (e.g., that the *Apology* is inauthentic). To Tennemann, Schleiermacher responded that the historical must be balanced by the internal or literary; to Schlegel, he responded that the literary needed to be balanced by historical investigations and philological details. In other words, the science of the new criticism would restrain philosophical and idealistic urges.[11] For Schleiermacher it was the text, the written text, the authentic text.

Schleiermacher, like Tennemann and Schlegel, began the art of interpreting Plato committed to the new criticism; unlike them, however, he continued to adhere to the rules of criticism, as he himself forged those rules, using them as a touchstone. As the *sine qua non* of Schleiermacher's interpretation of Plato, criticism restrained different tendencies and temptations to stray from the texts and to import foreign meanings. Criticism, however, while an art, is not itself the art of interpreting. Later, in his lectures on hermeneutics, Schleiermacher explained the relation between criticism and interpretation:

> Hermeneutics and criticism, both philological disciplines, both theories belong together, because the practice of one presupposes the other. The former is generally the art of understanding particularly the written discourse of another person correctly, the latter the art of judging correctly and establishing the authenticity of texts and parts of texts from adequate evidence and data. Because criticism can only recognize the weight to be attached to evidence in its relationship to the piece of writing or the part of the text in question after an appropriate correct understanding of the latter, the practice of criticism presupposes hermeneutics. On the other hand, given that explication can only be sure of its establishing of meaning if the authenticity of the text or part of the text can be presupposed, then the practice of hermeneutics presupposes criticism.
>
> Hermeneutics is rightly put first because it is also necessary when criticism hardly takes place at all, essentially because criticism should come to an end, but hermeneutics should not.[12]
>
> *Hermeneutik und Kritik, beide philologische Disziplinen, beide Kunstlehren, gehören zusammen, weil die Ausübung einer jeden die andere voraussetzt. Jene ist im allgemeinen die Kunst, die Rede eines andern, vornehmlich die schriftliche, richtig zu verstehen, diese die Kunst, die Echtheit der Schriften und Schriftstellen richtig zu beurteilen und aus genügenden Zeugnissen und Datis zu konstatieren. Da die Kritik die Gewichtigkeit der Zeugnisse in ihrem Verhältnis zum bezweifelten Schriftwerke oder zur bezweifelten Schriftstelle nur erkennen kann nach gehörigem richtigen Verständnis der letzteren, so setzt ihre Ausübung die Hermeneutik voraus.*

---

11 On the significance of the notion of "science" at this time, see Kathryn M. Olesko, "Germany," in *The Cambridge History of Science*, vol. 8: *Modern Science in National, Transnational, and Global Context*, ed. H. R. Slotten, R. L. Numbers, and D. N. Livingstone (Cambridge: Cambridge Univ. Press, 2020), 233–277.

12 *Friedrich Schleiermacher: Hermeneutics and Criticism and Other Writings*, ed. and trans. Andrew Bowie, Cambridge Texts in the History of Philosophy, ed. Karl Ameriks and Desmond M. Clarke (Cambridge: Cambridge University Press, 1998), 3–4 (hereafter cited in text as "*HC*").

3.2 The New Criticism and the Plato Renaissance — 63

Wiederum, da die Auslegung in der Ermittlung des Sinnes nur sicher gehen kann, wenn die Echtheit der Schrift oder Schriftstelle vorausgesetzt werden kann, so setzt auch die Ausübung der Hermeneutik die Kritik voraus.

Die Hermeneutik wird billg vorangestellt, weil sie auch da nötig ist, wo die Kritik fast gar nicht stattfindet, überhaupt weil Kritik aufhören soll, ausgeübt zu werden, Hermeneutik aber nicht.[13]

How did the relation between these two philological disciplines take shape in *Platons Werke*?

In his "General Introduction," Schleiermacher explained that the translator-interpreter must have so thorough a knowledge of the history of Greek language and thought as to be able "to adduce something about the scientific state of the Hellenes at the time when Plato began his career, about the progress of the language in relation to philosophical ideas, about texts of the same genre that were available at the time and the probable extent of their circulation."[14] This expert knowledge of the whole—that is to say, of the language shared by the author and his original audience, and thus of the historical and intellectual context—is what in his *Hermeneutics* Schleiermacher would come to call the "grammatical" part of the explication, the first canon of which is: "*Everything in a given utterance which requires a more precise determination may only be determined from the language area which is common to the author and his original audience.*"[15] Only with such thorough knowledge and expertise can the interpreter then move to the part, to the uniqueness of an individual's expression of the language. Regarding the Platonic dialogues, this means that the interpreter must be able to "feel where and how Plato is restricted by [the state of the language], and where he himself laboriously expands it."[16] In his *Hermeneutics*, Schleiermacher would come to call this the "technical" or "psychological" part of the explication. He always insisted, from this early articulation of it in his "General Introduction" through to his later lectures on hermeneutics, that these two must co-exist and are interdependent, that each presupposes and requires the other.

This is why interpretation and explication are an art: "*The successful practice of the art depends on the talent for language and the talent for knowledge of individual people.*"[17] Much more than learning a foreign language, therefore, the interpreter must have a "living awareness of language, the sense of analogy

---

13 *HK* 71.
14 *PW* 1/1:17.19–24; cf. *IDP* 2. For German text, see above, chap. 2, 33n57.
15 *HC* 30; *HK* 101. See *KGA* 2/4:9.17–21.
16 *IDP* 3; *PW* 1/1:18.18–19. For German text, see above, chap. 2, 43n109.
17 *HC* 11; *HK* 81.

and difference."[18] Hence the art of understanding Plato begins in science (*Wissenschaft*)—in particular, in philology—but such a science always requires art. This view dovetails with Schleiermacher's twofold goal in *Platons Werke*. He wanted "to make it possible for every [reader], by means of an immediate and more exact knowledge of [*Plato's works*], to come to their own view of Plato's *Geist* and teaching, whether that view be entirely new or just more complete,"[19] as he also hoped that other experts would "experience an alteration"[20] in their set views on Plato. In all this, the key is to recognize Plato as "philosophical artist."[21]

3.3 The *Phaedrus:* Socratic Clues and Hermeneutical Principles

Schleiermacher clearly felt the weight of the long history of Plato-interpretation. He decided to begin his own interpretation with misunderstanding—that is to say, with the question of why Plato had previously been so misunderstood. Understanding, in other words, sometimes begins in misunderstanding. He identified two "incorrect judgments" (*unrichtigen Urtheile*)[22] about Plato and, with them in mind, developed his own method for surmounting them. First, there is the complete "not understanding" (*Nichtverstehen*) that stems from viewing Plato as a "dialectician" (*Dialektiker*) more intent upon tearing down arguments than on constructing his own.[23] Second, there are the "misunderstandings" (*Mißverständnisse*) that result from the appeal to some supposed esoteric Platonic tradition.[24] The former line of interpretation failed because of its arbitrary division of Plato's works, the latter because of its equally arbitrary uncritical appeal to some esoteric system. Schleiermacher avoided both mistakes by distinguishing between *system* and *unity*. Whether or not there is a Platonic system, there is clearly a unity in Plato's thought and works. Yet, on what basis could Schleiermacher affirm any unity? After all, at the beginning of his quest to understand Plato he had only, on the one side, the particulars and details established by the "higher grammar" and, on the other side, the woeful misunder-

---

18 *HC* 11; *HK* 81.
19 *PW* 1/1:19.1–4; cf. *IDP* 3–4. For German text, see above, chap. 2, 32n54.
20 *IDP* 4; *PW* 1/1:19.13 (... *seine Ansichten eine Abänderung erleiden*).
21 *PW* 1/1:19.15; cf. *IDP* 4. See above, chap. 2.3.2.
22 *PW* 1/1:22.10; cf. *IDP* 7.
23 *PW* 1/1:22.23,16; cf. *IDP* 8.
24 *PW* 1/1:24.19; cf. *IDP* 10.

3.3 The *Phaedrus*: Socratic Clues and Hermeneutical Principles — 65

standings of previous interpreters. The new criticism should eschew prior philosophical and dogmatic commitments. Schleiermacher's answer was to locate that unity not so much in Plato's philosophy as in his person, in his artistic genius.

Preliminarily, the view of Plato as artist accomplished two things. First, it conveyed an initial, albeit cursory, sense of some whole. He explained in his *Hermeneutics*, "*Even within a single text the particular can only be understood from out of the whole, and a cursory reading to get an overview of the whole must therefore precede the more precise explication.*"[25] Yet, because it is only cursory, it needs to be tested in relation to the texts. Second, the view of Plato as artist permitted Schleiermacher to turn to Plato himself for hints by seeking interpretive clues in the Platonic texts. Most especially, he turned to the *Phaedrus*, a notoriously difficult dialogue to interpret, and yet a dialogue the importance of which was beyond dispute.

As we have seen, Schleiermacher, in his ordering of the Platonic dialogues, erroneously identified the *Phaedrus* as the first dialogue. Among the reasons he offered for this placement was that it is logically prior, has a youthful character, and contains the "seeds of almost his entire philosophy."[26] Schleiermacher explained that his "Introduction to the *Phaedrus*," which immediately follows the "General Introduction" in the first volume of *Platons Werke*, is the longest of all the individual introductions because it is in the *Phaedrus* that Plato sets forth his basic method, a method that is inseparable from content.[27] It is hardly accidental that, partly through discovering and explicating Plato's philosophical method, Schleiermacher came to articulate and develop his own method of interpretation. It thus makes sense to begin with Schleiermacher's "Introduction to the *Phaedrus*." Although his "General Introduction" is nothing less than his methodological prolegomenon for the art of interpreting Plato, it was in struggling with the challenges of understanding the *Phaedrus* that Schleiermacher had arrived at many of those very principles and guidelines which he then developed in the "General Introduction."

Three of the most notorious problems of Plato-interpretation arise in the *Phaedrus*: What is the main topic of the *Phaedrus*? Relatedly, how are the two parts of the dialogue related? Finally, how seriously are we to take Socrates's stated preference for oral communication over writing? Schleiermacher an-

---

25 *HC* 27; *HK* 97.
26 *PW* 1/1:80.4 (for German text, see above, chap. 2, 49n137); cf. *IDP* 68.
27 See *IDP* 48–73; *PW* 1/1:63–85.

swered each of these questions in a novel way and, in the process, discovered three Socratic clues which he then applied to the entire Platonic canon.

Schleiermacher began his "Introduction to the *Phaedrus*" by addressing the felt need on the part of countless interpreters to assign various subtitles, and he warned that we must set aside all prejudice and look anew at the issue. In doing so, he found a Socratic clue. Paraphrasing Socrates in *Phaedrus* 264c,[28] he noted that a speech "must be fashioned like a living creature, having a body proportioned to the mind, with parts also in due proportion."[29] This principle of the organic body became for Schleiermacher a guiding principle of interpretation: a speech, a text, or a body of texts must be seen as an organic body with essential, natural connections and proportions. Nothing is accidental. That is "the manner of Plato and the triumph of his artistic understanding."[30] Where this principle does not apply, the speech (or text) is not worthy of our attention. Yet we know, as even his detractors admit, that Plato's dialogues are worthy of attention and that the *Phaedrus*, in particular, commands our attention. Therefore, we are compelled to look further, past the appearance of unrelated parts, for essential relations.

Schleiermacher decided that he should search for the real subject matter of the *Phaedrus* in the second part, rather than in the famous third speech of the first part. The second part, however, presents another obstacle to understanding. Socrates' criticism of rhetoric as a false art is not unexpected, but his redefinition of it in terms of dialectics is. In carefully considering what Plato means by making dialectics "the true foundation of rhetoric,"[31] Schleiermacher came across a second Socratic clue: dialectics is an art, a systematic art (see *Phaedrus* 276e, 265d). Dialectics is "true science" (*eine wahre Wissenschaft*) and "true art"

---

[28] Socrates: "But I do think you will agree to this, every discourse must be organized, like a living being, with a body of its own, as it were, so as not to be headless or footless, but to have a middle and members, composed in fitting relation to each other and to the whole" (*Phaedrus* 264c; trans. Fowler, in *PDL*). Schleiermacher's translation: *Aber dieses, glaube ich, wirst du doch auch behaupten, daß eine Rede wie ein lebendes Wesen müsse gebaut sein und ihren eigenthümlichen Körper habe, so daß sie weder ohne Kopf ist, noch ohne Fuß, sondern eine Mitte hat und Enden, die gegen einander und gegen das Ganze in einem schiklichen Verhältniß gearbeitet sind* (*PW* 1/1:317.23 – 28, 319.1 – 4).

[29] *IDP* 49; *PW* 1/1:64.22 – 24 (... *daß es wie ein lebendiges Wesen gebildet sein und einen dem Geiste angemessenen Körper mit verhältnißmäßigen Theilen haben müsse*). See above, chap. 2, 38, 42, 51.

[30] *PW* 1/1:70.21 – 22 (*Das ist aber eben die Weise des Platon und der Triumph seines künstlerischen Verstandes*); cf. *IDP* 56.

[31] *IDP* 52; *PW* 1/1:66.28 – 29 (*daß also die Dialektik das wahre Fundament der Rhetorik sei*). See Plato, *Phaedrus* 269b.

(*Wahre Kunst*)[32] because it proceeds by a twofold process of *combining* (*zusammenfassen*) what appears scattered and of *dissecting* (*zertheilen*) a body along its natural joints (265d-e).[33] Schleiermacher's translation of *technē* as *Kunst* communicates a double meaning of "art" as scientific method and aesthetic principle.[34] The dialectical method, he explained, is one that brings the many, the parts, together "in a systematic and completely exhaustive manner."[35] This also serves as an aesthetic principle in that the *body* is conceived as an artistic unity, which for the Romantics meant everything is internally, harmoniously, complexly, and beautifully related. This second, aesthetic clue is really an extension of the first, but whereas the somatic metaphor tells us how to view a speech or text, this principle of dialectics as art informs us how to proceed. The Socratic method is to begin with well-known particulars and, by connecting similar concepts, to arrive at higher, more unified concepts; then, by means of dialectical movements between the inner and the outer, to propel ourselves "to the innermost soul of the whole work."[36] When these two basic movements are joined, this *scientific method* belongs to *art*.

These first two interpretive principles did not allow Schleiermacher to rest in his interpretation of the *Phaedrus*. Otherwise, he would have had to conclude that part one (with its speeches as three examples of rhetoric) is merely the playground for part two (with its redefinition of rhetoric in terms of dialectics), but that would imply that the relationship between the two parts is neither essential nor internal. Schleiermacher thus knew that he had not yet arrived at the "correct view" and that he had to push further inward.[37] This drove him back to the first part, especially to Socrates's famous speech.[38] There Schleiermacher recognized *erōs* as the "impulse" (*Trieb*)—or, the originating inward force of the soul. Not accidentally, the innermost soul of the text concerns the innermost spirit of

---

32 *IDP* 53; *PW* 1/1:68.1–2.
33 See Schleiermacher's translation, *PW* 1/1:327.3,18, respectively.
34 Schleiermacher's translation of *Phaedrus* 26e: *Weit herrlicher aber denke ich ist noch der Ernst mit diesen Dingen, wenn Jemand nach den Vorschriften der dialektischen Kunst, eine gehörige Seele dazu wählend, mit Einsicht Reden säet und pflanzt, ...* (*PW* 1/1:397.20–25). Nehamas and Woodruff make a similar decision in English: "But it is much nobler to be serious about these matters, and use the art of dialectic. The dialectician chooses a proper soul and plants and sows within it discourse accompanied by knowledge ..." (82). Fowler chooses *method* rather than *art*: "... in my opinion, serious discourse about them is far nobler, when one employs the dialectic method and plants and sows in a fitting soul intelligent words ..." (*PDL*).
35 *PW* 1/1:68.8 (*auf eine systematische und vollständig erschöpfende Weise*); cf. *IDP* 53.
36 *PW* 1/1:71.18 (*immer weiter getrieben bis zur innersten Seele des ganzen Werke*); cf. *IDP* 58.
37 *IDP* 57; *PW* 1/1:70.29–30 (*die richtige* [*Ansicht*]).
38 For more on Schleiermacher's comparison of the three speeches, see below, 4.3.

the human person. "Thereby all problems are solved," Schleiermacher concluded, "and this commends itself as the true unity of the work—bringing out, vivifying, and connecting everything."[39]

The subject matter of the *Phaedrus* is therefore nothing less than philosophy itself. The *Phaedrus* is not about one philosophical theme or another, whether that be beauty, love, or rhetoric. Rather, in it (along with the *Protagoras* and *Parmenides*, the other two dialogues which together with the *Phaedrus* constitute the first trilogy) Plato develops "the first presentiments" (*die ersten Ahndungen*)[40] of his philosophy. The first part of the *Phaedrus* speaks to philosophy's impulse (*erōs*), while the second part introduces its method (dialectics). According to Schleiermacher, these two, impulse and method, are always present in Socrates's exchanges and permeated his entire thought. Their separate presentation in the *Phaedrus* is one of the reasons why Schleiermacher determined the dialogue to be the first: Plato first presents separately what are ultimately united so that the novice learner might recognize each for itself; throughout the remaining dialogues, Plato increasingly reincorporates and reunites what in reality is not separate.

Having found, he thought, the unity of the dialogue, Schleiermacher still faced the further obstacle of Socrates's suspicion of writing, introduced toward the end of the *Phaedrus*. The perceived danger is that writing will introduce forgetfulness and make knowledge external rather than internal (275c–276a). Socrates himself employs only the "word which is written with intelligence in the mind of the learner, which is able to defend itself and knows to whom it should speak, and before whom to be silent."[41] This was so problematic for Schleiermacher that he found the need to address it in both his "General Introduction" and the separate "Introduction to the *Phaedrus*."[42] In addition to appearing to undermine Plato's very act of writing the dialogues, it also stood at odds with Schleiermacher's own critical insistence that Plato is to be found in the extant documents alone. Those espousing the esoteric tradition appealed (and continue to appeal) to this passage as evidence that Plato's true philosophical teachings

---

39 *PW* 1/1:72.13–15 (*Hiedurch also lösen sich alle Aufgaben, und dieses bewährt sich als die wahre alles hervorbringende belebende und verknüpfende Einheit des Werkes*); cf. *IDP* 59.
40 *PW* 1/1:56.11; cf. *IDP* 45. Dobson has "first breathings." See *DWB*, s.v. AHNDUNG: "*f. praesagium, vorgefühl, heute ahnung*."
41 Plato, *Phaedrus* 276a, trans. Fowler, in *PDL*. Schleiermacher's translation: *Welche [Reden] mit Einsicht geschrieben wird in des Lernenden Seele, wohl im Stande sich selbst zu helfen, und wohl wissend zu reden und zu schweigen, gegen wen sie beides soll* (*PW* 1/1:391.15–20).
42 See *IDP* 15–17; *PW* 1/1:29–31.

were handed down orally (and secretly) to an intimate circle of disciples and that the written dialogues were merely a decoy for the masses.⁴³

Schleiermacher addressed the challenge by interpreting Socrates's preference for *oral* communication as supporting evidence for his own claim regarding the importance of the dialogue form in Plato's *written* texts. Importantly, this difficult passage from the *Phaedrus* provided him with yet another Socratic clue: it speaks to the purpose of philosophy, which is none other than communication. Even though ideally the communication of ideas is done through dialogue, Schleiermacher suggested that Socrates nonetheless concedes that the risk of writing should be taken since the real purpose of dialogue is pedagogical. Its importance rests in this:

> that the teacher—standing in the presence of, and in lively interaction with, the student—can know in each moment what the student grasps or does not grasp, and so can assist the activity of the understanding whenever it falters; this advantage, however, is really based on, as everyone realizes, the *form of the dialogue*, which a truly living instruction must necessarily have.
>
> *daß hier der Lehrende in einer gegenwärtigen und lebendigen Wechselwirkung mit dem Lernenden stehend, jeden Augenblick wissen könne, was dieser begriffen und was nicht, und so der Thätigkeit seines Verstandes nachhelfen, wo es fehlt; daß aber dieser Vortheil wirklich erreicht werde, beruht, wie Jeder einsieht, auf der Form des Gesprächs, welche der recht lebendige Unterricht sonach nothwendig haben muß.*⁴⁴

Plato's method was a Socratic method insofar as his written dialogue was nothing less than a "living composition" (*lebendige Composition*),⁴⁵ which perfectly imitated Socrates' own "oral, living instruction."⁴⁶ The imitation is necessary because the learner, who is now the reader, although no longer in the presence of the teacher, must nevertheless be brought through the same processes of understanding. If the method of philosophy is dialectics and its impulse *erōs*, then its purpose is the kind of communication that brings the student-reader to knowledge. What is important, in other words, is the *form of the dialogue*, whether it be spoken or written.

Together, these three Socratic clues—the somatic metaphor, dialectics as art, and the dialogue form—all point to Plato as artist. Whatever proclivities Schleier-

---

43 For the Tübingen School's criticism of Schleiermacher on this point, see Szlezák, "Schleiermacher's Theory," 172–78; *Reading Plato*, 31; "Schleiermachers 'Einleitung'," 51–61. See above, 2.4.3.
44 *PW* 1/1:29.26–32; cf. *IDP*, emphasis added.
45 *IDP* 53; *PW* 1/1:68.16.
46 *PW* 1/1:29.20 (... *den mündlichen lebendigen Unterricht*); cf. *IDP* 15.

macher-the-Romantic may have had to interpret a genius like Plato as an artist, he believed he found warrants for just such an interpretation in Plato's texts, foremost in the *Phaedrus*. Those clues became interpretive principles that he extended to the entire Platonic *corpus*, for the *Phaedrus* does not "stand isolated."[47]

Sticking closely to Socrates's elaboration of the process of collection and dissection (*Phaedrus* 265d-e), Schleiermacher argued that viewing Plato's works as a "living creature" or organic body means that no part is dispensable, that the various parts are organically (which is to say, essentially and vitally) connected, and that those connections can only be understood if "the whole nature of a body" is recognized.[48] Interpretation must therefore begin with an acquaintance with the whole—a body, a text or set of texts—and then must proceed to dismember or dissect [*zerstuckeln*] that body. Schleiermacher applied the first and second Socratic clues as he set about determining authenticity (which dialogues constitute the body?) and then restoring the original order of those (how do they fit together so as to form a living body?). The "vessels" and "bones" must be separated out and compared with each other.[49] The end, however, of this process of dismemberment, dissection, or de-composition is not to leave a corpse behind. There is another part of the process of understanding that completes the dissection—namely, a restoration of the original connections, a re-composition. It is this part of the interpretive process that distinguishes the artist from the mere analyst. Once each "limb" is understood (through the process of separation and dismemberment) as a whole in itself, its place in and contribution to the "body" can also be understood. Those "limbs" or parts must then be re-joined to the body, and only then can the body itself can be understood.[50] When applied to Plato's dialogues, this process of dis-membering and re-membering, de-composing and re-composing, allows us to restore the individual dialogues to the natural connection according to which "they, as continually more complete expositions, gradually developed Plato's ideas; the end being that, each dialogue is simultaneously seen as a whole in itself as well as in its connection with the rest, so Plato himself can finally be understood as philosopher and artist [*Philosoph und Künstler*]."[51]

---

47 *IDP* 57; *PW* 1/1:71.1–3 (*oder … der Phaidros stände dann so isolirt da*).
48 *IDP* 14; *PW* 1/1:28.16–17 (*die ganze Natur eines Körpers*).
49 *IDP* 14; *PW* 1/1:28.17 (*Gefäße oder Knochen*).
50 *IDP* 14; *PW* 1/1:29.1 (*Glieder*).
51 *PW* 1/1:29.3–7 (*wie sie als immer vollständigere Darstellungen seine Ideen nach und nach entwikelt haben, damit, indem jedes Gespräch nicht nur als ein Ganzes für sich, sondern auch in sei-*

We are now in a better position to judge what work Plato-as-artist actually did for Schleiermacher's interpretation of Plato. As we have seen, two convictions defined the new criticism and its application to Plato: Plato is to be found only in those texts determined to be authentic; and discovering the original (chronological) ordering of the texts is crucial for understanding Plato's philosophy. The view of Plato as artist guided Schleiermacher in his carrying out of these two important philological tasks. Let us now turn back to Schleiermacher's "General Introduction."

3.4 Principles for Determining Authenticity of Plato's Dialogues

Included in the view of Plato as artist is the view of Plato's writings as works of art—indeed, as *one* work of art. Schleiermacher stressed, "we have no other tangible proof of his greatness and pre-eminence except these writings."[52] One of the profound contradictions of the esoteric interpretation of Plato, as Schleiermacher saw it, was that, in either altogether denying the importance of the extant written dialogues or in assigning to them a secondary status, it undermined the very genius its adherents sought to extol and perpetuate. It is useless, Schleiermacher scolded, to "to lament over, or to dream of, other lost riches of Platonic wisdom"[53] or to search in desperation for some hidden truth. Plato's extant writings are all we have—and all we really need to have. Schleiermacher's argument regarding the exclusive authority of the authentic, written texts (hence his rejection of the esoteric tradition) was so persuasive that it became the dominant scholarly assumption in Plato studies for the next century and a half.[54] It seemed the logical conclusion drawn from the central tenets of the new criticism, the first task of which is the determination of authenticity.

According to Schleiermacher, the necessary task of determining which are the authentic dialogues is a philological, not a philosophical, task. It requires a close examination of *language* (*Sprache*), *content* (*Inhalt*), and *form* (*Gestalt/*

---

nem Zusammenhange mit den übrigen begriffen wird, auch er selbst endlich als Philosoph und Künstler verstanden werde); cf. *IDP* 14.
52 *IDP* 9; *PW* 1/1:23.16–17 (*Da wir nun von seiner Größe und Treflichkeit keinen andern zeiglichen Beweis haben, als diese Schriften...*).
53 *IDP* 13; *PW* 1/1:28.4–6 (*es sei vergeblich, über einen andern verlorenen Schaz platonischer Weisheit zu klagen oder zu träumen*).
54 Hösle notes some exceptions to that in the 1820s ("Tübingen School," 334).

Form).⁵⁵ It takes a certain artistic sense to be able to recognize the proportional relations among the three. Although no one criterion is in itself sufficient, *form* is especially important. "As the clarity of form diminishes," he noted, "so also does the conviction of authenticity in every regard."⁵⁶ His insistence that *form* be considered along with (and indeed that it is the unitive ground of) *language* and *content* is significant in that, as noted above, it marks yet another departure from his predecessors.

Language. For Schleiermacher, the philological task could no longer be understood as a strictly grammatical exercise insofar as it demanded new historical tools of investigation. As we have seen above, the modern philologist had to have so intimate a knowledge of the language as to recognize the distinctive ways in which an author had used and modified it.⁵⁷ This entailed a historical knowledge of the language and so of the culture that produced it.

Content. With this criterion, Schleiermacher meant simply the philosophical topics and questions which had preoccupied Plato and which he addressed in a certain characteristic manner; of course, these were fairly wide-ranging, and, in some cases, Plato wrote occasional pieces that did not reflect his own chief interests. Hence, content alone cannot determine authenticity. The key to Schleiermacher's theory of interpreting Plato lay in the interplay of the three criteria, and how skilled the interpreter is in balancing them: "… we can judge neither by the content alone nor by the language alone; rather, we must judge by a third and more certain criterion, in which those two also unite—namely, the form and composition altogether."⁵⁸ Here again, Schleiermacher returned to the basic principle of Plato-as-artist. And here, too, he underscored how the interpreter must be both scientist and artist, able to judge proportion, "the whole tone and peculiar hue" of a work.⁵⁹

Form and Composition. As we have seen, Schleiermacher's view of Plato as artist instructed him to pay attention to form. Along with his insistence that we adhere only to the extant written texts, Schleiermacher's attention to the dialogue form was perhaps his greatest contribution to Plato-interpretation. It was inconceivable to him that a work of art would be considered apart from its form.

---

55 *PW* 1/1:46.8–9; cf. *IDP* 32.
56 *PW* 1/1:51.19–21 (*So nimmt mit der Klarheit der Form auch von allen Seiten die Ueberzeugung von der Aechtheit ab*); cf. *IDP* 39.
57 See above, 2.3.1, 3.2.
58 *PW* 1/1:48.22–25 (… *daß wir weder vom Inhalt allein noch von der Sprache allein urtheilen dürfen, sondern auf ein drittes und sicherers sehen müssen, in welchem sich auch jene beide vereinigen, nemlich auf die Form und Composition im Ganzen*); cf. *IDP* 35.
59 *PW* 1/1:48.26–27 (*der ganze Ton und die eigenthümliche Farbe derselben*); cf. *IDP* 35.

3.4 Principles for Determining Authenticity of Plato's Dialogues — 73

The dialogue form is none other than Plato's "art form" (*Kunstform*).[60] Yet most interpreters had considered the dialogue form to be either a nuisance or, worse, a deliberately placed obstacle intended to veil the real meaning and content of Plato's philosophical doctrines. In Schleiermacher's judgment, those who disparaged the dialogue form as mere embellishment could claim no understanding of Plato whatsoever. Schleiermacher was only being consistent. His view of the unity of Plato's dialogues held as much for the indissolubility of form and content as for the continuity of its parts. More even than tolerating or appreciating the dialogue form, we are to relish it. Schleiermacher praised the "mimetic and dramatic property" of the dialogue form, "by virtue of which persons and circumstances are individualized, and which, by general confession, radiates so much beauty and charm throughout the dialogues of Plato."[61] Although this form is sometimes (but not always) less copious when Plato ventures "into the darkest seriousness of speculation,"[62] it is never totally absent. The dialogue form, beautifully and exquisitely executed, was Plato's signature. So committed was Schleiermacher to this principle that he held that the absence or diminishment of this signature form correlates to inauthentic and ambiguous status. He concluded "that this distinct form can never be wholly lacking, and that Plato, even in the most insignificant pieces (what he wrote as a study or on someone's order) will have turned something of this art."[63] Attention to the form of the dialogues thus "yields the surest canon for judging their [authenticity]."[64]

According to Schleiermacher, where these three characteristics—language, content, and form—are clearly present and intricately inform one another, without any doubt, you have authentically Platonic dialogues of what he called the *first rank* (*die erste Rangordnung platonischer Werke*).[65] In contrast, dialogues of the *second rank* are those in which such clarity and co-inherence begin to fade. The second stage of the ranking process presents the most difficulties, since the characteristic marks of Plato are by definition not as clearly present

---

60 *PW* 1/1:21.19; cf. *IDP* 7.
61 *PW* 1/1:49.20 – 23 (*nemlich jene mimische und dramatische Beschaffenheit, vermöge deren Personen und Umstände individualisirt werden, und welche nach dem allgemeinen Geständniß so viel Schönheit und Anmuth über die Dialogen des Platon verbreitet*); cf. *IDP* 36.
62 *PW* 1/1:49.27–28 (*in den dunkelsten Ernst der Speculation*); cf. *IDP* 37.
63 *PW* 1/1:49.29 – 50.3 (*... daß diese eigenthümliche Form nirgends ganz fehlen darf, und daß Platon auch an das unbedeutendste, was er als Studium oder auf Veranlassung abfaßte, etwas von dieser Kunst wird gewendet haben*); cf. *IDP* 37.
64 *IDP* 36; *PW* 1/1:49.12–13 (*was den sichersten Kanon zur Beurtheilung ihrer Aechtheit abgiebt*).
65 *IDP* 32; *PW* 1/1:45.18 – 19.

as they are in dialogues of the first rank. At this stage of interpretation, the criterion of form becomes the chief one because it is always present. These authentic dialogues of the first and second rank are

> that critical ground upon which every further investigation must build, and in fact no better is required. For the Dialogues thus authenticated form a stock [Stamm] from which all the rest seem to be but offshoots, so that [kinship] with them affords the best test whereby to judge of their origin.... when we have that stock we are at once in possession of all the essential grounds of general connection.[66]

> *Denn die so beurkundeten Gespräche bilden einen Stamm, von welchem alle übrige nur Schößlinge zu sein scheinen, so daß die Verwandtschaft mit jenen das beste Merkmal abgiebt, um über ihren Ursprung zu entscheiden.... in jenem Stamme schon alle wesentlichen Momente des allgemeinen Zusammenhanges gegeben sein.*[67]

Schleiermacher reserved his arguments regarding other dialogues (whether inauthentic or ambiguous) for his separate introductions to those dialogues, which he placed in two appendices;[68] there he also included authentic dialogues that he categorized as occasional (such as the *Apology* and *Crito*), hence as not containing Plato's actual philosophy. He determined the following to be inauthentic: *Hipparchus, Minos, Theages, Alcibiades I* (despite how well liked) and *II, Erastae, Clitophon*, and (probably) *Hippias Major*. He identified the following dialogues to be ambiguous in origin, by which he meant they could have been written by a student or were unfinished by Plato's hand: *Hippias Minor, Ion, Menexenus*. In the second edition of *Platons Werke I,1* (1817), Schleiermacher updated his appendices with supplementary adjustments as he took into consideration views of classicists published in the interim, which demonstrates his continued engagement with scholarship in the field.

This determination of the critical ground of the authentic dialogues, although necessary, is not yet sufficient for understanding Plato's philosophy. The question of their ordering, of how they are related to one another, immediately arises. The task of arranging the dialogues was of such fundamental importance to Schleiermacher that he did not think the task of determining authenticity could be done apart from it. The two tasks, he maintained, "mutually support and verify each other."[69]

---

66 *IDP* 31.
67 *PW* 1/1:45.7–13.
68 See *IDP* 134–68, 321–49; *EÜP*, 147–176, 313–336. See table 2.
69 *IDP* 38; *PW* 1/1:50.26–27 (*einander gegenseitig unterstüzen und bewähren*).

3.5 Principles for Ordering Plato's Dialogues

As he took on the task of determining the order of Plato's dialogues, Schleiermacher kept in mind Socrates's dictum that a speech be seen as an organic body, only now he applied the somatic metaphor not just to a single dialogue but to all the authentic dialogues. The Platonic dialogues form a written *corpus*, in the strong sense of that term. For him, restoring the original order of the dialogues was one and the same thing with explicating the essential, necessary, and natural relations among them. Meaning and content are revealed through the discovery of interconnections. Indeed, that was why Schlegel and Schleiermacher had set out to translate *all* of Plato's works rather than just a few. The organic metaphor broadly speaking, of course, functioned as an aesthetic principle for the Romantics. We see that reflected clearly in Schleiermacher's ordering, with his emphasis on harmonization, unity, and continuity.

3.5.1 Provisional Whole: A Trilogy of Trilogies

According to Schleiermacher, the identification of the authentic dialogues, especially those of the first rank, together with established external markers, almost immediately allow that "the first main features of their connection and the arrangement resting thereon be submitted in the manner of a *provisional overview of the whole in general*."[70] Here, precisely in his notion of beginning with a provisional whole and discerning therein clusters of smaller wholes, we can appreciate how the various methodological moments functioned together for him. Schleiermacher explained that we have a body of material before us (dialogues determined to be authentic and of the first rank) and that these constitute what he called that certain "*stock*." Here emerges his Trilogy of Trilogies.[71]

Almost immediately, we recognize three among them (the *Republic*, *Timaeus*, and *Critias*) that distinguish themselves by their "objective, scientific presentation" (*eine objective wissenschaftliche Darstellung*).[72] Although tradition had long held these three to be later dialogues, Schleiermacher offered new reasons for considering them so: their internal similarities suggest that they belong together; the fact that they presume investigations already made in other dialogues

---

[70] *PW* 1/1:52.26–29, emphasis added (... *so auch nun die ersten Grundzüge ihres Zusammenhanges und der darauf beruhenden Anordnung zu vorläufiger Uebersicht des Ganzen im Allgemeinen vorgelegt werden*); cf. *IDP* 40.
[71] See above, chap. 2, 44–46, and below, table 3.
[72] *PW* 1/1:53.1; cf. *IDP* 41.

indicates that they are not among the earliest; and their scientific-constructive form confirms that they are among the latest of the dialogues. He then sought to order this particular whole and concluded that the *Republic* must have been the first because it contains within it, and gives structure to, all the dialogues not belonging to this cluster of three; at the same time, it contains elements that are developed further in the *Critias* and *Timaeus*.[73] If we were to force the *Republic* into another place, he claimed, our cultivated sense of the matter (*Empfindungen*)[74] would resist such an inversion. It can have only one place in the artistic whole.

According to Schleiermacher, once we have discerned and outlined the three constructive dialogues, our gaze passes back naturally to the whole body of first-ranked dialogues, and we then immediately recognize by means of contrast another grouping of three (the *Phaedrus*, *Protagoras*, and *Parmenides*). The contrast between these and other dialogues is marked by their *character* (they have a "quite distinctive character of youthfulness"[75]), their *circumstance* (the constructive dialogues both presuppose and mention them), and their *inner content* ("in them the first breaths of the basis of everything that follows are emitted"[76]). All of this leads ineluctably to the conclusion that this group, or *whole*, of three (along with some dialogues of the second rank) form "the first, and, as it were, elementary part of the Platonic works."[77] In order to determine their

---

[73] In both his "General Introduction" and the separate "Introduction to the *Republic*," written over twenty years later, Schleiermacher referred to the *Republic* as the keystone of all that had gone before, but he emphasized that it was not Plato's crowning achievement. He concluded his "Introduction to the *Republic*": "It can hardly be doubted that when Plato wrote these books [of the *Republic*], he had already resolved to attach the *Timaeus* and the *Critias* to them"; *EÜP* 387 (*Nur daran ist kaum zu zweifeln, daß als Platon unsere Bücher schrieb, er auch schon beschlossen hatte den 'Timaios' und 'Kritias' daran zu knüpfen*); cf. *IDP* 415. Since he never got around to writing introductions to those final two dialogues, the *Letters*, or the *Laws*, this sentence wound up being the final one of his *Introductions*.

[74] *IDP* 43; *PW* 1/1:54.22. I use "sense of the matter" here to distinguish *Empfindung* from two other, more technical terms in Schleiermacher—*feeling* (*Gefühl*) and *perception* (*Wahrnehmung*)—in order to avoid conflation. Although "feeling" might well be used here, the meaning should not be confused with *Gefühl*, a term Schleiermacher used in a more technical way and with which he is associated. What he means here is that, if we tried to force something, we would "sense" just how forced it is.

[75] *PW* 1/1:55.26–27 (... *durch einen ganz eigenthümlichen Charakter der Jugendlichkeit*); cf. *IDP* 44.

[76] *PW* 1/1:56.9–12 (*Das wichtigste ist aber auch bei ihnen ihr innerer Gehalt, denn in ihnen entwikeln sich die ersten Ahndungen von dem, was allem folgenden zum Grunde liegt*); cf. *IDP* 44–45.

[77] *IDP* 45; *PW* 1/1:56.15–16 (... *den ersten gleichsam elementarischen Theil der platonischen Werke*).

inner ordering, Schleiermacher considered how each developed the dialectical method, the main preoccupation of the early dialogues. These early dialogues, and the *Phaedrus* especially, contain the seeds of all of Plato's philosophy—seeds that will take root, grow, and bear fruit in later dialogues.

With these two smaller wholes set in place, Schleiermacher was convinced that a more defined picture of the larger whole has emerged. They serve as bookends, so to speak. Because the outer-support systems that give meaning and coherence to all the rest has been established, the order of the dialogues falling between them could be discerned through their "progressive connection" (*in ihrem fortschreitenden Zusammenhang*),[78] by which he meant "the natural progression of the development of ideas" (*die natürliche Fortschreitung der Ideenentwiklung*).[79] The middle dialogues presented Schleiermacher with a problem insofar as—unlike the early (or "elementary"[80]) and the later (or "constructive"[81]) dialogues, which form the first and third trilogies, respectively—these do not form a clear trilogy, nor is the order among them easily discernible. Most problematic is the fact that there are five, not three, dialogues of the first rank. Yet there are other problems as well. Two guiding principles aided him in sorting through these difficulties. First, he attended to "a variety of particular allusions and references";[82] this task of intricately tracing the connections among the different dialogues in fact characterizes all his introductions. Second, he was convinced that, whereas the earlier dialogues are concerned with the *method* of philosophy (that is, with the "development of the dialectical method"[83]), the middle dialogues are concerned with the *object* of philosophy.[84]

On this basis, Schleiermacher carved out a rough trilogy: the *Theaetetus*, the *Sophist* (to which he annexed the *Statesman*, so that together they constitute "One Dialogue" (*Ein Gespräch*),[85] and the *Phaedo* (which, along with the *Philebus*, marks the transition to the final trilogy). He explained,

> In the second part, the explanation of knowledge [*Wissen*] and of the process of knowing in operation is the predominant subject, and at the head of that part stands the Theaetetus, beyond the possibility of a mistake, taking up as it does this question by its first root, the

---

78 *IDP* 45; *PW* 1/1:57.3.
79 *IDP* 46; *PW* 1/1:57.12–13.
80 *IDP* 45; *PW* 1/1:56.16 (*elementarischen*).
81 *IDP* 44; *PW* 1/1:55.14,21 (*darstellenden*).
82 *IDP* 46; *PW* 1/1:57.13–14 (*auf mancherlei einzele Andeutungen und Beziehungen*).
83 *PW* 1/1:57.16–58.1 (*die Entwicklung der dialektischen Methode*); cf. *IDP* 46.
84 See "Introduction to the *Gorgias*," *PW* 2/1:10.24–26; *IDP* 170.
85 *PW* 1/1:54.2; cf. *IDP* 42. Dobson's translation does not capture Schleiermacher's capitalization of the article for emphasis.

Sophistes with the annexed Politicus in the middle, while the Phaedo and Philebus close it as transitions to the third part; the first, from the anticipatory sketch of Natural Philosophy, the second, because in its discussion of the idea of the Good, it begins to approximate to a totally constructive exposition, and passes into the direct method.[86]

Im zweiten Theil ist die Erklärung des Wissens und des wissenden Handelns das herrschende, und ganz unfehlbar steht Theaetetos an der Spize, der diese Frage bei ihrer ersten Wurzel auffaßt, der Sophistes mit dem ihm zugehörigen Politikos in der Mitte, Phaidon aber und Philebos beschließen ihn als Uebergänge zum dritten Theil: der erste schon wegen der vorgebildeten Anlage der Physik, der andere weil er sich in Behandlung der Idee des Guten schon ganz einer constructiven Darstellung nähert, und in das directe übergeht.[87]

Schleiermacher lent further definition to this trilogy by identifying a sub-trilogy within it: the *Sophist*, *Symposium*, and *Statesman*. Consequently, this sub-trilogy constitutes not just the center of this middle trilogy but also the very center and heart of the Platonic *corpus*.[88] In the three chapters to follow, we shall revisit this ordering and its ramifications for Schleiermacher's Plato—that is to say, for Schleiermacher's interpretation of Plato's philosophy and for how he took that up into his own thought.

Table 3: A Trilogy of Trilogies: The "Stock" (*Stamm*) of First-Ranked Dialogues

First Trilogy (*PW* I)	Second Trilogy (*PW* II)	Third Trilogy (*PW* III)*
1. *Phaedrus*	1. *Theaetetus*	1. *The Republic*
2. *Protagoras*	2. Sub-trilogy: *Sophist, Statesman, Symposium*	2. (*Timaeus*)
3. *Parmenides*	3. *Phaedo + Philebus*	3. (*Critias*)
	*Incomplete: *PW* ended with the *Republic*.	

3.5.2 The Pedagogical Progression of Ideas

If the view of Plato as artist serves as a general hermeneutical principle in Schleiermacher's interpretation of the dialogues, the pedagogical progression of ideas is the hermeneutical thread, so to speak, that ties the dialogues together. For Schleiermacher, Plato-as-artist went hand in hand with Plato-as-master-

---

86 *IDP* 46.
87 *PW* 1/1:58.4–12.
88 As Schleiermacher put it in his "Introduction to the *Sophist*," the dialogue is "in the middle point of the second part of the Platonic works" (*IDP* 248; *EÜP* 247 [*in dem Mittelpunkt des zweiten Teils der Platonischen Werke*]).

3.5 Principles for Ordering Plato's Dialogues — 79

teacher. Plato's aim in the dialogues was "to bring the not-yet-knowing reader to knowledge."[89] The knowledge imparted, as well as the capacity of the student to acquire it internally and originally, comes about gradually.[90] What might be only implicit in one dialogue, because the student is not yet ready to grasp it, is later presented more explicitly. Schleiermacher explained,

> For [Plato] cannot advance further in another dialogue unless he supposes the effect proposed in an earlier one to have been produced, so that the same subject which is completed in the termination of the one, must be supposed as the beginning and foundation of another....[91]
>
> *Denn weiter fortschreiten kann er doch nicht in einem andern Gespräch, wenn er nicht die in einem früheren beabsichtigte Wirkung als erreicht voraussezt, so daß dasselbe, was als Ende des einen ergänzt wird, auch muß als Anfang und Grund eines andern vorausgesezt warden....*[92]

This pedagogical progression of ideas determined the natural order of the dialogues.

In Schleiermacher's interpretation of Plato, this principle of the pedagogical progression of ideas not only shaped the general contours of the Platonic *corpus* (from the *Phaedrus*, through the *Sophist* and *Statesman*, to the scientific presentations in the *Republic* and *Timaeus*), but it also informed smaller decisions and countless moves. For instance, Schleiermacher judged the *Protagoras* to be early (the middle of the first trilogy) due to the contrast Protagoras provided with Plato's pedagogical-artistic approach. Socrates, in exposing his interlocutor's contradiction, exposes how Protagoras "has not reflected even in the slightest degree upon the conditions necessary for the [education] of others, or upon the notion of virtue in which he would instruct them"; as a result, we gain insight as to "how far removed he must continue from that method, [which but aims at] bringing the nursling of philosophy to self-consciousness, and compelling

---

89 *PW* 1/1:31.6–7 (... *daß Platon doch auch den noch nicht wissenden Leser wollte zum Wissen bringen*); cf. *IDP* 17.
90 Güthenke captures Schleiermacher's idea well: "In Schleiermacher's reading, the strategy of the Platonic works is to encourage the reader to continue, mirroring the characters in the text, and in the act to confront the same reader with an equally continuing lack of knowledge. These are therefore texts, as we would say, which deliberately refuse closure, an assumption generally in line with Schleiermacher's understanding of interpretation as an ongoing and approximative undertaking, conscious of the radical distance between self and other" (*Feeling and Classical Philology*, 83).
91 *IDP* 19. I pick up the passage again in the following sub-section.
92 *PW* 1/1:32.23–27. I pick up the passage again in the following sub-section.

[them] to [thinking for themselves]."[93] The "dialogical" (*dialogische*)[94] pedagogy of Plato, Schleiermacher held, is just such a method, as becomes clear from early on in the sequence.

This is another reason why Plato never left the dialogical form behind. Its two-fold function is pedagogical in nature: to communicate content, and to stimulate the activity of thinking. Schleiermacher frequently employed phrases such as "spontaneous activity" (*Selbstthätigkeit*), an "original mode of acquisition" (*ursprüngliche Art des Erwerbes*),[95] and "one's own inner production of intended thought."[96] Plato's purpose was "not only to explain his own mind [*Sinn*] to others in a lively way, but precisely thereby to excite and uplift theirs in a lively way."[97] The content, once again, is given in and through the form. In the previous chapter, I discussed Schleiermacher's rejection of the esoteric Platonic tradition and his strict espousal of the exoteric tradition.[98] Here, it needs to be added that not all esotericists reject the dialogue form for obscuring a deeper truth. Some have viewed it as a pedagogical tool to stimulate thought. These softer adherents to the esoteric tradition in Platonism maintain that the dialogical form is introductory only, that it can be shed once the student has advanced, and thus that it is not tied to the content itself. Although in his criticism of the esoteric tradition Schleiermacher had in mind the stronger view, he would have rejected even this softer version of esoteric theory. Not only can a "progressive connec-

---

93 IDP 94; PW 1/1:583.15–22 (*Und wenn wir am Ende, wo Sokrates ihm seinen großen Widerspruch aufdekt, erfahren, daß er über die ersten Bedingungen der Bildung Anderer und über den Begriff der Tugend, die er ihnen anbilden will, auch nicht im mindesten nachgedacht hat: so sind wir unterdeß auch inne geworden, wie weit er entfernt bleiben mußte von derjenigen Methode, die es nur darauf anlegt den Zögling der Philosophie zum Selbstbewußtsein zu bringen und zum Selbstdenken zu nöthigen*).
94 PW 1/1:583.23; cf. IDP 94.
95 IDP 16, 17; PW 1/1:30.25,27.
96 PW 1/1:31.11–12 (*zur eignen inneren Erzeugung des beabsichtigten Gedankens*); cf. IDP 17.
97 PW 1/1:28.30–31 (*nicht nur seinen eignen Sinn Andern lebendig darzulegen, sondern eben dadurch auch den ihrigen lebendig aufzuregen und zu erheben*); cf. IDP 14. So taken was Schleiermacher with this pedagogical ideal that he appropriated it for himself. In his *Occasional Thoughts on Universities*, written while he was still working on PW, Schleiermacher proposed that the life of the university is to be found in lectures, the sole purpose of which is vital communication. The problem, of course, is that the style of the university lecture is not that of dialogue but rather of systematic, scientific presentation. Nevertheless, Schleiermacher adhered to what was for him the Platonic principle that, "because its first aim is to bring ideas to consciousness, university lecturing must in any case adhere in this respect to the nature of ancient dialogue, if not to its external form" (29); KGA 1/6:48.24–27. Even the most scientific of presentations is rooted in the dialogue and is essentially communicative.
98 See above, 2.4.3.

tion" (*fortschreitenden Zusammenhang*)[99] be clearly traced but the pedagogical function also always remains.

Schleiermacher's principle of the pedagogical progression of ideas is likewise related to his principle of the relation between myth and dialectics in Plato.[100] According to Schleiermacher, it is myth, not the dialogical form, that has a propaedeutic function. Myth is followed but not superseded by scientific formulation. Both mythical representations and scientific exposition remain essentially dialogical: both forms of presentation remain communicative, both evoke a desire for knowledge, and both seek to connect ideas. For Schleiermacher's Plato, the movement from myth to science is a fairly smooth and continuous one. If there is a shift in style between the early and the later dialogues, it is not due to a growing rift between dialogue (as propaedeutics) and dialectics (as pure thought); rather, it is due to a "transition of much that is mythical into the scientific."[101] Where myth conveys "simple principles" (in pregnant form), science offers a "composite presentation."[102] Therefore, consistent with a progressive dialectics, the dialogues that contain the most mythic elements are the earlier ones, while the more constructive, expository dialogues are the later ones. Myth, however, is never entirely abandoned. In fact, Schleiermacher argued, Plato returned to myth in Book I of the *Republic* as an act of remembrance before setting forth his scientific treatment of ethics. Myth contains and anticipates what will later be presented in scientific form. Schleiermacher described this relation as a "gradual development and cultivation of the Platonic myths out of One Fundamental Myth [*aus Einem Grundmythos*]."[103] Myth, in other words, is not speculative or merely fantastical in nature but is pre-scientific: its role is to excite the mind and to act as impetus and lure, mostly for the novice but

---

99 *IDP* 46; *PW* 1/1:50.3.
100 See above, chap. 2, 40–41.
101 *PW* 1/1:55.11–12 (*jenes Uebergehen manches Mythischen in Wissenschaftliches*); cf. *IDP* 43.
102 *PW* 1/1:55.7–8 (*... daß man bei dem eigentlichen Philosophiren nicht von einer zusammengesezten Darstellung, sondern von den einfachen Principien ausgehn müsse*); cf. *IDP* 43.
103 *PW* 1/1:55.9–11 (*die allmähliche Entwikklung und Ausbildung der platonischen Mythen aus Einem Grundmythos*); cf. *IDP* 43. This understanding of myth reflects his Romantic background and the early Romantics' appreciation of myth. For instance, Schlegel wrote in his *Dialogue on Poetry* (1799–1800), "Mythology has one great advantage. What usually escapes our consciousness can here be perceived and held fast through the senses and spirit like the soul in the body surrounding it, through which it shines into our eye and speaks to our ear" (trans. Ernst Behler, *Dialogue on Poetry and Literary Aphorisms* [University Park and London, Pennsylvania State University Press, 1968], 85). See Bruce Lincoln, *Theorizing Myth. Narrative, Ideology, and Scholarship* (Chicago and London: University of Chicago Press, 1999), for a salient discussion of myth in Plato (37–42) and in the *Sturm und Drang* and early Romantic movements in Germany (51–56).

even occasionally for the expert. Yet, at the same time, one cannot remain in myth. The goal is real knowledge.

3.5.3 The Two Series: Ethics and Physics

On its own, the principle of the pedagogical progression of ideas would remain merely formal. The question would inevitably arise: progression toward what? The matter of how something is taught depends, of course, on what is being taught.[104] The proper object of Plato's philosophy, Schleiermacher said, are the ideas (*Ideen*) and thus, intermediately, the "possibility and conditions of knowledge [*Wissen*]."[105] The two "real sciences" (*reale Wissenschaften*)[106] that bring us to true knowledge are *ethics* and *physics*. The "essence of knowledge" (*das Wesen der Erkenntnis*) falls under these two sciences: *ethics* studies the "human itself" (*den Menschen selbst*), while *physics* studies (non-human) "nature" (*die Natur*).[107] In Schleiermacher's Plato, each of these sciences forms a "series" (*Reihe*), and together they proceed by means of a "progressive connection" (*fortschreitenden Zusammenhang*).[108] This progressive connection of ethics and physics serves as the material principle, so to speak, for Schleiermacher's ordering of Plato's dialogues. He used it to trace the progress of each science toward knowledge and, as importantly, toward each other throughout the *corpus*.

Schleiermacher insisted that for Plato the two series, ethics and physics, were united because of the ultimate identity of being (*Sein*) and knowing (*Erkennen*) or consciousness (*Bewußtsein*). The passage on the pedagogical progression of ideas, which I began to quote in the indented block quotation in the previous sub-section (3.5.2), continues thusly:

> ... Now if Plato ended with separate expositions of the several philosophical sciences, it might then be supposed that he had also advanced each for itself in gradual progression, and we should be compelled to look for two [different series] of dialogues, an ethical and a physical series. But as he represents them as a connected whole, ... so also are the preparations for them united in like manner, and made by considering their common principles

---

104 See his "Introduction to the *Gorgias*," which he saw as the gateway into the middle dialogues (the second trilogy) and thus as the transition from the *method* to the *object* of Plato's philosophy.
105 *IDP* 45; *PW* 1/1:56.12–14 (... *von der Möglichkeit und den Bedingungen des Wissens*).
106 *IDP* 45; *PW* 1/1:56.20.
107 *PW* 1/1:53.10–13; cf. *IDP* 41.
108 *IDP* 45; *PW* 1/1:57.3.

and laws, and there are therefore not several unconnected and collaterally progressing series of Platonic Dialogues, but only one single [series], comprehending everything in it.[109]

> ... Endete nun Platon in abgesonderte Darstellungen der einzelnen philosophischen Wissenschaften, so wäre vorauszusezen, daß er auch jede für sich nach und nach weiter gebracht habe, und man müßte zwei verschiedene Reihen von Gesprächen aufsuchen, eine ethische und eine physische. Da er sie aber als ein verbundenes Ganzes darstellt, und es eben sein Eigenthümliches ist, sie überall als wesentlich verbunden und unzertrennlich zu denken, so sind auch die Zurüstungen zu ihnen eben so vereint und durch Betrachtung ihrer gemeinschaftlichen Gründe und Geseze gemacht, und es giebt daher nicht mehrere unabhängig neben einander fortlaufende Reihen platonischer Gespräche, sondern nur eine einzige alles in sich befassende.[110]

According to Schleiermacher, Plato developed these two basic series separately in the first trilogy but brought them together in the center of the second trilogy,[111] specifically in the *Sophist* and the *Statesman*, where it becomes clear "that all virtue was knowledge, and all vice ignorance."[112] Plato continued to develop the two series in close relation to each other, until each culminates in full scientific expression in the third and final trilogy: physics as knowledge of *being* (*Sein*) in the *Timaeus*, and ethics as knowledge of the *good* in the *Republic*. Schleiermacher traced these developments out in intricate ways, such that his ordering of the dialogues cannot be fully understood apart from this principle. For instance, he traced certain moral themes from the *Lysis*, *Protagoras*, *Laches*, *Charmides* to the *Gorgias* and *Meno*, where they begin to connect more explicitly to epistemological issues in the *Theaetetus*; and he traced epistemological themes from the *Parmenides* to the *Theaetetus*, and into the *Sophist*, but then also into the *Statesman* where they assume practical application. There and only there, in the center of the central trilogy, do the theoretical and the practical series come together and set the stage for the final trilogy; the *Sophist* and the *Statesman* thus together serve as the firmament for the *Timaeus* and the *Republic*.

Schleiermacher's notion of the two series, their progressive connection, and their final unity permeates almost every aspect of his interpretation of Plato.[113] It was the material principle that determined his ordering of the Platonic dialogues as, true to form, it structured his very understanding of Plato. In fact, it defines

---

109 *IDP* 19.
110 *PW* 1/1:32.27–33.3.
111 See Schleiermacher, "Introduction to the *Gorgias*," especially *IDP* 170–172; *PW* 2/1:10–12.
112 *IDP* 274; *EÜP* 269 (... daß alle Tugend Erkenntnis und alle Untugend Unkenntnis sei).
113 See Rohls, "Schleiermachers Platonismus," 485–91. For Schleiermacher's treatment of physics and ethics in his lectures on the history of philosophy (*Vorlesungen zur Geschichte der Philosophie*), delivered between 1807 and 1823, see Rohls, "Schleiermachers Platon," 727–28.

Schleiermacher's Plato. Depending on a particular dialogue and its subject matter, it may take a slightly different form, but always it is a rendition of the same theme. Ethics is a practical science whose object is the *good*; its basic human activity is doing or acting, which ideally realizes itself as virtue. Physics is a theoretical science whose object is *being* or the *true*; its basic human activity is thinking, which ideally realizes itself as knowledge (*Erkenntniß*, Schleiermacher's translation of *epistēmē*). This basic typology was of such importance to Schleiermacher that he would take it up and develop it in his own constructive work, especially in his revisions of the *Speeches*, as we shall explore in chapters six and seven (see table 9).

3.6 Concluding Remarks: The Interpreter as Artist

It takes an artist to interpret an artist. The scholarship required for translating, interpreting, and explicating Plato's dialogues necessarily includes art—a keen sense of analogy and proportion, of the whole, of what is fitting; an ability to engage in an almost infinite process of connecting and relating, of applying rules, of testing and challenging, of creating and even destroying, of communicating and mediating. Schleiermacher saw his role as one of painting a new image of Plato so that others might gain new access to Platonic philosophy. In other words, it is fair to say, Schleiermacher understood his own role in part as that of author and mediator. Dilthey, indeed, praised him for mirroring Plato's philosophical artistry in his presentation of Plato:

> If one seeks, however, to penetrate the hermeneutical standpoint of this work, to the extent it has been completed, through studying the *Introductions*, then it seems to the seeker also therein akin to his subject matter as through a mimetic reproduction. Indeed, the presentation itself moves forth uninterrupted in a clear and artful course, the fundamental intuition of the whole features yet with an always new charming economy only in fewer significant moves, so that one does not tire comparing these moves, in order thereby to divine at least the splendid entirety of the intuition, as it must have been in Schleiermacher's soul. And in this occupation, one would like to see oneself led to a perpetual *combination of the character of Platonic philosophizing with the artistic form of the work*.[114]

Schleiermacher endeavored not necessarily to provide a final, definitive account of Plato's philosophy so much as to recover the living and vital connections of the dialogues and to recapture thereby their spirit, all with the aim of awakening something in the (early nineteenth-century German) reader. He anticipated that

---

114 Dilthey, *Leben Schleiermachers*, 2/3:681.

future generations of Plato scholars would come to different findings, as indeed they have done.

Christopher Rowe is undoubtedly right when he states that there is no basis in Plato's writings for Schleiermacher's positing that the dialogues constitute a single work of art, yet he nonetheless sees something of value in the basic point:

> it is true *both* that the corpus is, by and large, an organic unity, *and* that we need to read it in a certain order—not just because some parts of it openly, or more or less openly, point backwards or forwards to other parts, but because of a particular feature that I claim to be characteristic of Platonic writing. His writing is, I propose, inherently *cumulative* in form.[115]

Another contemporary Plato scholar, Catherine Zuckert, likewise underscores the "coherence of the dialogues," locating it in what she calls the principle of "dramatic chronology."[116] Schleiermacher's view of Plato as artist and of the dialogues as a single work of art helped him overcome several stumbling blocks in interpreting Plato's dialogues: it pressed him to seek the relations among the dialogues, paying attention to all the dialogues and every detail therein; it inspired him to invite the reader to enter into a reading of the dialogues such that he or she would *enjoy* them; and it compelled him to remind student and scholar alike of the importance of the dialogue form in gaining knowledge and in becoming virtuous.

Schleiermacher's lectures on hermeneutics and criticism bear the imprint of his intensive scholarly activity translating and interpreting Plato's dialogues in *Platons Werke*. Just as true, and closely related, is the fact that his basic philosophy (his epistemology and ontology), as presented in his lectures on dialectics, also bear the imprint of his deep engagement with Plato, although in this case that imprint has to do with the actual content of Plato's own philosophical method.[117] Schleiermacher's take on Platonic dialectics is the topic of the next chapter.

---

115 Christopher Rowe, "One Dialogue or Two? Reading Plato's *Republic*," in Balansard and Koch, *Lire les Dialogues*, 248; see also 245.
116 Zuckert, *Plato's Philosophers*, 19.
117 On the relationship between Schleiermacher's dialectics and hermeneutics, see Arndt, "Dialektik und Hermeneutik: Zur kritischen Vermittlung der Disziplinen bei Schleiermacher," pt. 4 chap. 1 in *Schleiermacher als Philosoph*, 299–325.

4 Reading Plato's Dialectics: Schleiermacher's Insistence on Dialectics as Dialogical

Plato's method was a Socratic one.[1]

4.1 Introduction

Echoing Schleiermacher's words, taken here from the "General Introduction" to *Platons Werke*, it would not be unfair to say that his own method was a Platonic one. The connection between Schleiermacher's dialectics and Platonic dialectics is direct and without question, and it begins with his very choice of the title: *Dialectics*. Manfred Frank captures the point succinctly: "Instead of 'metaphysics,' Schleiermacher called his first philosophy, in the Platonic tradition, 'Dialectic'."[2] Almost a century ago, Krapf made the case that

> except for Plato, all names are either mentioned [in the *Dialectics*] casually or for the illustration of some point. Spinoza, Kant and Hegel are criticized with the purpose of drawing the limits between their philosophies and Schleiermacher's own thought. Plato, however, is always mentioned as being at the basis of what he himself develops. Plato is invoked as a witness for the genuineness of the dialectics which Schleiermacher unfolds.[3]

More recently, Rohls has published several essays closely examining the intricate connections between Schleiermacher's *Introductions*, his lectures on the history of philosophy, and his *Dialectics*.[4]

Commonly, when scholars speak of the Platonic character of Schleiermacher's *Dialectics*, they mean its essentially Socratic, dialogical nature, since the word derives from the Greek word *dialektikē*, meaning discourse or conversation.[5] There are, of course, good reasons for making that connection, not the least of which is the shift Schleiermacher made, beginning in the 1822 lectures,

---

[1] *PW* 1/1:30.13; cf. *IDP* 16. See below, n. 10.
[2] Manfred Frank, "Metaphysical Foundations: A Look at Schleiermacher's *Dialectic*," in Mariña, *Cambridge Companion to Schleiermacher*, 15.
[3] Krapf, "Platonic Dialectics," 153–54.
[4] See above, chap. 1, 6n19.
[5] See, e.g., Gerhard Spiegler, *Eternal Covenant: Schleiermacher's Experiment in Cultural Theology* (New York: Harper and Row, 1967), 35, 79.

from defining dialectics as the "art of philosophizing" (*Kunst zu philosophiren*)⁶ to defining it as "the art of conducting dialogue."⁷ The assumption, however, seems to be that there is only one kind of Platonic dialectics, when a case can fairly be made that there are competing forms of dialectics at work in Plato's dialogues.

Sometimes, as Julia Annas explains, Plato's dialectic is "something articulate" and thus "looks like a development of the Socratic conversations."⁸ At other times, she notes, Plato's "constant use of the imagery of vision and grasping" suggests that the activity of dialectics is "something non-verbal and non-articulate that each person has to do for himself or herself."⁹ Annas maintains that, even though "at first glance [these two ways of viewing dialectic] do not go very happily together,"¹⁰ there is no real tension between them. My intention here is not to take issue with so eminent a Plato scholar as Annas but to ask, rather, how another eminent Plato scholar, Schleiermacher, handled this issue. The brief answer is that, beyond admitting of no *real* tension in Plato, Schleiermacher denied even the *appearance* of tension. Whereas Annas says both forms of dialectic are needed, Schleiermacher's insistence on the vital necessity of one resulted in an elision of the other. The difference is not insignificant, as a longer answer to the question should demonstrate.

Throughout his *Introductions*, Schleiermacher held tenaciously to the controlling idea that "necessarily and by its very nature Plato's method was a Socratic one."¹¹ In this chapter, I argue that this controlling idea made it necessary for Schleiermacher to develop certain interpretive strategies that allowed him, consistently if not always consciously, to qualify and elide those dialogues and passages in Plato where a nonverbal, or what I shall term a speculative, view of dialectics is clearly present.

Since *speculative dialectics* is not Schleiermacher's term, some explanation of its meaning and justification of its use is called for. In its broadest sense, the term functions negatively to mean any non-dialogical form of dialectics. In

---

6 Schleiermacher, *Dialektik* (1811), in *KGA* 2/10,1–2: *Vorlesungen über die Dialektik*, ed. Andreas Arndt (Berlin & New York: Walter de Gruyter, 2002), 2:5.30–31(hereafter cited in text as "*Dk*"). English translation: *Dialectic, or the Art of Doing Philosophy, A Study Edition of the 1811 Notes*, trans. Terrence N. Tice (Atlanta: Scholars Press, 1996), 3 (hereafter cited in text as "*Dc*").
7 Dk (1822) 2:402.11–12 (... *in der Dialektik als der Kunst, das Gespräch zu führen*).
8 Julia Annas, *An Introduction to Plato's Republic* (Oxford: Oxford University Press, 1981), 282.
9 Annas, *Plato's Republic*, 283.
10 Annas, *Plato's Republic*, 282.
11 PW 1/1:30.12–13 (*nothwendig und seiner Natur nach ist seine Methode eine sokratische gewesen*); cf. *IDP* 16.

order to gain more specificity than this, *speculative dialectics* needs to be divided into two main categories, Platonic and non-Platonic. According to the logic of Schleiermacher's reading of Plato, non-Platonic forms of speculative dialectics would be what in his lectures on *Dialectics* he called "mere empty speculation" (*nur leere Speculation*),[12] by which he meant processes divorced from the empirical, from love for the real, from the process and rules of knowing, and from philosophical communication. How Schleiermacher understood a genuinely Platonic form of speculative dialectics is much more elusive—especially since, if I am correct that Schleiermacher elided precisely this kind of dialectics in Plato, it is hardly surprising that he would not offer a clear definition of it. Nevertheless, his *Introductions* provides us with a few hints. For instance, in his "Introduction to the *Parmenides*" he referred to that kind of philosophical "investigation, done on one's own, which precedes and is conducive to communication,"[13] wherein one gazes purely at the truth. Echoing the *Phaedo* 79c–d,[14] this would seem to fit neatly with at least two other references Schleiermacher made in his *Introductions* to a Platonic "glance" into that "higher sphere of speculation,"[15] where the higher spheres are those defined more by the identity of thought and being than by the oppositions of the empirical world. Plato, he insisted, connected "the higher speculation with the dialectical procedure."[16] Taken alone, these few excerpts might suggest that Schleiermacher's reading of Plato's dialectics is compatible with Annas's, insofar as both identify an independent and taciturn form of dialectics. Read in context, however, these passages provide interesting examples of how Schleiermacher, in his reading of Plato's dialectics, actually suppressed the more speculative strains in the dialogues and how, when he did allow them to emerge, they did so only briefly and, what is more, only from the shadows of dialogical dialectics.[17]

---

12 *Dk* (1811) 2:63.6; cf. *Dc* 62.
13 *EÜP* 129 (... *in Beziehung auf das der Mitteilung billig vorangehende eigene Forschen*); cf. *IDP* 114.
14 Socrates: "But when the soul inquires alone by itself, it departs into the realm of the pure, the everlasting, the immortal and the changeless ..." (*Phaedo*, 79c–d, trans. Fowler, in *PDL*).
15 Schleiermacher, "Introduction to the *Sophist*," *IDP* 253; *EÜP* 250 (*der Blick in jenes höhere Gebiet der Spekulation*); and "Introduction to the *Parmenides*," *EÜP* 139 (... *aus dem höheren Gebiete der Spekulation*); cf. *IDP* 125.
16 Schleiermacher, "Introduction to the *Parmenides*," *EÜP* 137 (*die höhere Spekulation mit dem dialektischen Verfahren verbindet*); cf. *IDP* 123.
17 Other scholars have also noted the non-speculative bent either in Schleiermacher's portrait of Plato or in his own *Dialectics*. Douglas Hedley, for instance, is critical of the non-speculative turn that Schleiermacher took in Plato scholarship: "Schleiermacher replaced the 'Attic Moses' with the much less speculative and more, as it were, Romantic Plato, one who believed that dia-

In this chapter, I investigate this tendency more fully by examining how, in his *Introductions*, Schleiermacher negotiated with the texts he was translating and interpreting, coaxing any other view of dialectics to fit comfortably under the rubric of dialogue without admitting any problem or tension. I proceed, first, by reviewing five basic interpretive principles, set forth in his "General Introduction," which pertain to the essentially dialogical character of Platonic dialectics (section 4.2). I then turn to the heart of my argument where, focusing on his introductions to individual Platonic dialogues, particularly those dialogues which he judged to be of the first rank and which seem to present a speculative dialectics: in the first trilogy, the *Phaedrus* and *Parmenides* (section 4.3); in the middle trilogy, the *Sophist*, *Symposium*, and *Phaedo* (section 4.4); and in the unfinished final trilogy, the *Republic* (section 4.5).

4.2 Basic Interpretive Principles in the "General Introduction"

Schleiermacher's "General Introduction" to the Platonic dialogues is more than just introductory; it is prolegomena. In it, Schleiermacher established and delineated the principles and methodology he would follow in translating and interpreting Plato. Having discussed his chief interpretative principles at some length in the two preceding chapters, I simply list them here so as to provide a helpful summary for quick reference points:

---

logue was the only proper way of communicating philosophical truth"; and "Schleiermacher sees Plato's dialogues as the expression of a certain metaphysical agnosticism" (*Coleridge, Philosophy and Religion: "Aids to Reflection" and the Mirror of the Spirit* [Cambridge: Cambridge University Press, 2000], 44, 45, respectively). Krapf decides, in his exposition of Platonic dialectics in Schleiermacher's *Dialectics*, to refer to Plato only "insofar as it is essential to point out how Schleiermacher's dialectics retains the character of the dialogue"; he adds, Schleiermacher's "insistence that dialectics itself must remain within the realm of the dialogue differentiates this dialectics from that of Hegel" ("Platonic Dialectics," 153, 163, respectively). My approach to Schleiermacher's dialectics comes closest to Krapf's in that, like him, I begin with an examination of Schleiermacher's *Introductions*. Our respective analyses, however, differ on at least three points: (1) like Schleiermacher, he defines Platonic dialectics simply in terms of its dialogical character, whereas I, following Annas, acknowledge at least one other strain of Platonic dialectics; (2) consequently, Krapf does not recognize where Schleiermacher made interpretive decisions that mitigate or suppress other possible (and more probable) interpretations, whereas I focus precisely on such decisions; and (3) he sees "... the height of Schleiermacher's art of interpretation" (92) in the "Introduction to the *Sophist*," whereas I hold that, in his translation and interpretation of this dialogue, there is clear evidence that Schleiermacher imposed some of his own commitments onto Plato's text.

1. *The necessary first step to understanding Plato is the discovery and restoration of the original, "natural," and "necessary" ordering of the dialogues.* This principle is primary in the sense that the others all serve it. Schleiermacher's insistence that each dialogue can be understood only in relation to other dialogues and only in relation to the place it occupies in the entire corpus operates in such a way as to mitigate and qualify instances of a more speculative type of dialectics. Whenever a speculative form of dialectics presents itself in the text, he inevitably argued that—if properly understood in terms of form, content, composition, and structure—it is essentially a communicative form of dialectics.
2. *There is a necessary relation between (dialogical) form and (philosophical) content.* The main point of this principle as it relates to the discussion at hand is that, according to Schleiermacher, the content of Plato's dialogues, his philosophy, cannot be understood apart from the art of Plato's dialogical form. It follows that Plato's philosophy is essentially dialogical, which is to say, social and communicative—as opposed to solitary and taciturn.
3. *Platonic dialectics, whether written or oral, and as opposed to sophistical dialectics, is necessarily rooted in dialogue.* This underscores the point that, for Schleiermacher, Platonic dialectics is inherently communicative, interactive, and social—not a purely speculative or isolated exercise.
4. *The original order of the Platonic dialogues can be determined by tracing the pedagogical progression of ideas.* If the view of Plato as artist serves as a general hermeneutical principle in Schleiermacher's interpretation of the dialogues, the pedagogical progression of ideas is the hermeneutical thread that ties the dialogues together. This notion further strengthens Schleiermacher's reading of Plato's dialectics as dialogical and communicative, since the purpose of even the most scientific of presentations is nevertheless educational.
5. *It is myth, not the dialogical form, that has a propaedeutic function; myth is followed, but not superseded, by scientific formulation.* The main point for our present purposes is that both mythical representations and scientific exposition remain essentially dialogical and dialectical, or better, dialogical-dialectical. Both forms of presentation, the mythical and the scientific, remain communicative, both evoke and respond to a desire for knowledge, and both seek to connect ideas. The movement from myth to science is a continuous and smooth one. If there is a shift in style between the early and the later dialogues, it is not, in Schleiermacher's reading, due to a growing rift between dialogue (as propaedeutics) and dialectics (as pure

thought); it is rather due to "that crossing over of many a mythical into something scientific."[18]
6. *The pedagogical progression of ideas is structured according to two series, ethics and physics.* These two series begin separately in the early dialogues, are brought together in the middle dialogues, and are brought ever closer in relation to each other until both are scientifically presented in the final trilogy, in the *Republic* and *Timaeus*.

These, then, are some of the principles that undergird, guide, and restrain Schleiermacher's reading of Plato's dialectics; they are the presuppositions that shape Schleiermacher's determination to read Plato's dialectics as essentially and unambiguously dialogical. More interesting, however, is how Schleiermacher applied these principles to concrete situations when, as he worked through each particular dialogue, he was faced with interpretive decisions about Plato's philosophy.

4.3 The First Trilogy and the Method of Philosophy

Part I of *Platons Werke* comprises the trilogy of the *Phaedrus*, *Protagoras*, and *Parmenides*. (The dialogues of the second rank included along with them are the *Lysis, Laches, Charmides, Euthyphro*). As Schleiermacher saw it, the chief purpose of these early dialogues is "the development of the dialectical method."[19] Keep in mind that, according to Schleiermacher's Plato and the principle of the pedagogical progression of ideas, the first trilogy seeks to train the reader-student in the early stages of the dialectical method. In his introductions to these early dialogues, Schleiermacher set the groundwork for his understanding of Platonic dialectics as dialogical.

His "Introduction to the *Phaedrus*" is disproportionately long because in it he lays out as clearly as possible the "Platonic composition."[20] In the previous chapter, we saw how Schleiermacher addressed the major interpretive problems for which the *Phaedrus* is notorious and how he did so by applying three Socratic clues: the somatic metaphor, the notion of dialectics as art, and the sovereignty of the dialogue form. Applying these clues to the *Phaedrus* itself, he concluded

---
[18] PW 1/1:55.11–12 (... *jenes Uebergehen manches Mythischen in Wissenschaftliches*); cf. IDP 43.
[19] PW 1/1:57.16–58.1 (*die Entwicklung der dialektischen Methode*); cf. IDP 46.
[20] PW 1/1:63.19 (*die platonische Bildungsweise*); cf. IDP 48. Whereas in chap. 3 I examined the "Introduction to the *Phaedrus*" in terms of Schleiermacher's hermeneutical principles, here I focus more closely on his understanding of Plato's dialectics.

that the topic of the dialogue is nothing less than philosophy itself: the first part is about the required driving impulse (*Trieb*)—*erōs*; the second part is about the proper method—*dialectics*. In the *Phaedrus*, Plato presents as separate (impulse and method) what in fact is united so that the novice learner might have somewhere to begin. Let us now examine more closely how exactly Schleiermacher understood Platonic dialectics.

In the second part of the *Phaedrus*, Schleiermacher claimed, Plato identifies dialectics "the true foundation of rhetoric" (*das wahre Fundament der Rhetorik*),[21] because the ideas are "the original object of dialectics."[22] That is why dialectics is both "a true science" (*eine wahre Wissenschaft*) and "true art" (*Wahre Kunst*).[23] It proceeds by means of a process of collection and division. In 265d-e, Socrates speaks of a method or "art" (*technē*)[24] involving a twofold activity: the first is "that of perceiving and bringing together in one idea the scattered particulars, that one may make clear by definition the particular thing which he wishes to explain"; the second is "that of dividing things again by classes, where the natural joints are, and not trying to break any part, after the manner of a bad carver."[25] In elaborating on this Socratic-Platonic notion of "dialectical art" (276e),[26] Schleiermacher concentrated on the first kind of activity described by Socrates. Rhetoric, he wrote, is "art in a higher sense" and "true art"[27] only when it is grounded in dialectics and thus only insofar as, by means of dialectics, the manifold "is connected in a systematic and perfectly exhaustive manner."[28] By connecting similar concepts we may arrive at "higher" (*höhere*) concepts, and when those in turn are connected with one another, this dialectical method belongs to science as it comes to know "the true and right" (*das Wahre und Richtige*).[29] That is the difference between rhetoric as art (hence, truly *Redekunst*) and "artless dispatch" (*kunstloses Verfertigen*).[30]

We have seen how Schleiermacher, having thus determined that the subject matter of the second part of the *Phaedrus* to be philosophical method (dialectics), turned his attention back to the first part of the dialogue and found in Soc-

---

21 *IDP* 52; *PW* 1/1:66.29. See *Phaedrus* 269b.
22 *PW* 1/1:71.31–32 (*Der ursprüngliche Gegenstand der Dialektik aber sind die Ideen*); cf. *IDP* 58.
23 *IDP* 53; *PW* 1/1:68.1–2.
24 Schleiermacher translates *technē* as *Kunst* (*PW* 1/1:324.21).
25 Plato, *Phaedrus* 265d–e; trans. Fowler, in *PDL*.
26 *dialektikē technē*, trans. Schleiermacher as "… *der dialektischen Kunst*" (*PW* 1/1:397.23).
27 *IDP* 53; *PW* 1/1:67.28 (*Kunst in einem höheren Sinne*), 68.1 (*Wahre Kunst*).
28 *IDP* 53; *PW* 1/1:68.8–9 (*auf eine systematische und vollständig erschöpfende Weise verbunden wird*).
29 *IDP* 52; *PW* 1/1:68.27,18, respectively.
30 *IDP* 53; *PW* 1/1:68.9,4, respectively. See *Phaedrus* 270a.

rates's second speech the necessary philosophical impulse (*erōs*).³¹ Now let us train our attention more intently on his comparison of the three speeches in light of what he had come to understand about the Platonic dialectical method in the second part. According to Schleiermacher, Plato, the young author of the *Phaedrus*, is the "budding artist" (*der angehende Künstler*)³² whose method it is to leave nothing to chance but instead to place everything in elegant proportion. For that reason, the first two speeches ought not be neglected simply because we happen to prefer the third. Schleiermacher noted that the three speeches present an example of the manifold: three apparently unrelated objects, or at best related through opposition. Only through the "most exact comparison"³³ can the speeches, and their relations one to another, be understood. So, for example, Lysias's speech (230e–234c), as "an example of the common undialectical method,"³⁴ serves as a counter example to the Socratic method. Yet there is a notable difference even between Socrates's speeches: the first, which mimics the common tendency of the day, is less polished and more worldly than the second, which is "inspired" (*Begeisterte*)³⁵ and more properly belongs to Socrates. In Socrates's second speech we find "the exaltation of beauty to an equal rank with the highest moral ideas, and its close connection with the Eternal and Infinite."³⁶ In other words, in the three speeches we find a progression, from the crass, to the more rhythmic albeit still "transparent and cold,"³⁷ and then on to the elegant mythic account of yearning, eternity, and the infinite.

This is not to say, however, that the first part is just a playground for practicing dialectics. On the contrary, it brings its own content: *erōs*. All three speeches are about love. *Erōs* provides the movement, the impulse, toward philosophical communication. *Erōs*, in other words, ensures that philosophy is not done in isolation but is essentially communicative:

> And precisely because philosophy here appears entirely not just as an inward state, but, according to its nature, as expressing and communicating itself, so also must the impulse [*Trieb*] be presented and brought to consciousness—the impulse which pushes it [philosophy] outward from within and which is nothing other than that authentic and divine love that elevates itself above every other …

---

31 See above, 3.3.
32 *PW* 1/1:67.16; cf. *IDP* 52.
33 *PW* 1/1:68.29 (*die genaueste Vergleichung*); cf. *IDP* 54.
34 *PW* 1/1:68.21–22 (*ein Beispiel von der gemeinen undialektischen Methode*); cf. *IDP* 54.
35 *PW* 1/1:69.1; *IDP* 54.
36 *IDP* 54; *PW* 1/1:69.1–3 (… *die Erhebung der Schönheit zu gleichem Range mit den höchsten sittlichen Ideen und ihre genaue Verbindung mit dem Ewigen und Unendlichen*).
37 *IDP* 54; *PW* 1/1:68.33–34 (*dennoch durchsichtig und kalt*).

> Und eben weil die Philosophie hier ganz erscheint, nicht nur als innerer Zustand, sondern als ihrer Natur nach sich äußernd und mittheilend, so mußte auch der Trieb zum Bewußtsein gebracht und dargestellt werden, welcher sie von innen herausdrängt, und welcher eben nichts anders ist, als jene ächte und göttliche Liebe, die sich über jede andere auf irgend einen Nuzen ausgehende eben so weit erhebt, ...[38]

Schleiermacher concluded that Plato's dialectics is really a combination of *impulse* and *method*. The impulse is something "original and ever-active in the soul,"[39] which, at the same time that it needs to be brought to consciousness, is itself the force that pushes towards consciousness. Although in the *Phaedrus* impulse and method are presented separately, they are both integral to an organic or artistic whole, and just how intertwined and inseparable they are is made clearer and clearer through the pedagogical progression of ideas and the development of dialectics in the other dialogues. Their entwinement guarantees that Plato's method remains Socratic, that is to say, dialogical, communicative, loquacious: "For these two, impulse and method, were in all [Socrates's] conversations the constant and ever unchanging element."[40]

Schleiermacher (erroneously) identified the *Phaedrus* as the first dialogue because it anticipates all that is to come.[41] In it are the "seeds [*Keime*] of [Plato's] entire philosophy," albeit in "undeveloped state."[42] These seeds, which will eventually grow into the "priceless fruit"[43] of the *Sophist*, are further developed in the middle dialogue of the first trilogy, the *Protagoras*. In his "Introduction to the *Protagoras*," Schleiermacher argued that the chief purpose of the dialogue is "to praise and extol the Socratic dialogue form as the proper form of all genuinely philosophical communication."[44] The *Protagoras* continues what was begun in the *Phaedrus*, insofar as, in it, Plato more tightly interweaves method with the communicative impulse as the lack thereof in Protagoras's approach is exposed.[45]

---

38 *PW* 1/1:71.36 – 72.6; cf. *IDP* 58.
39 *PW* 1/1:72.11 (*ein ursprüngliches, immer reges in der Seele*); cf. *IDP* 59.
40 *IDP* 59; *PW* 1/1:72.27 – 28 (*Denn dieses beides, Trieb und Methode, war in allen seinen Unterhaltungen das bleibende, sich immer selbst gleiche*).
41 See above, 2.4.1 and 3.5.
42 *PW* 1/1:80.4 – 6 (*Denn die Keime seiner ganzen Philosophie fast sind im Phaidros freilich nicht zu läugnen, aber auch ihr unentwikkelter Zustand ist eben so deutlich*); cf. *IDP* 68. See *Phaedrus* 277a.
43 *EÜP* 247 (*... einer köstlichen Frucht*); cf. *IDP* 249.
44 *PW* 1/1:581.20 – 22 (*... die sokratische Gesprächsform als die eigenthümliche Form jeder ächt philosophischen Mittheilung lobpreisend und verherrlichend zu verkündigen*); cf. *IDP* 91.
45 See *IDP* 93 – 95; *PW* 1/1:582–84.

4.3 The First Trilogy and the Method of Philosophy — 95

It is the last dialogue of this first trilogy, the *Parmenides*, that provides an interesting test case for seeing how Schleiermacher dealt with a form of dialectics that is not dialogical—a test case, that is, to see whether or not he even acknowledged a tension in Plato. For, besides the fact that the young Socrates's views are routinely undermined by Parmenides, the dialogical form itself is made merely perfunctory, so much so that it is all but eliminated in the deductions at the end. Still, Schleiermacher held to his line of interpretation as he rejected the conventional view that the *Parmenides* is a later dialogue:

> As the 'Phaedrus' had only in a general way inspired and admiringly praised the philosophical impulse and its organ, dialectics, and as the 'Protagoras', in artfully connecting the external and the internal, had presented by means of examples this philosophical impulse [*Trieb*] and the sophistical itch, as well as the methods produced by each of them, so the 'Parmenides' shows itself to be a similar outflow from the 'Phaedrus', inasmuch as it completes from another side, as a supplement and counterpart, what the 'Protagoras' had begun. In [the 'Protagoras'] the philosophical impulse is considered as communicating, while here it is presented in relation to the investigation, done on one's own, which precedes and is conducive to communication—namely, how [the impulse], in its purity, looks only at truth.
>
> *So wie nämlich der 'Phaidros' nur im Allgemeinen den philosophischen Trieb und sein Organ die Dialektik begeistert und bewundernd gepriesen hatte; der 'Protagoras' aber künstlich Äußeres und Inneres verknüpfend den philosophischen Trieb und den sophistischen Kitzel, und so auch die aus jedem von beiden hervorgehende Methode in Beispielen dargestellt hatte: so zeigt sich der 'Parmenides' als sein gleichmäßiger Ausfluß aus dem 'Phaidros', indem er, was der 'Protagoras' begonnen hatte, als dessen Ergänzung und Gegenstück auf einer andern Seite vollendet. In jenem zwar wird der philosophische Trieb betrachtet als mitteilend, hier aber dargestellt in Beziehung auf das der Mitteilung billig vorangehende eigene Forschen; wie er nämlich in seiner Reinheit nur auf die Wahrheit sieht.*[46]

In the *Parmenides*, then, Schleiermacher encountered a "side" of dialectics that is not communicative or dialogical but is instead speculative, isolated, pure. He claimed it flows from the *Phaedrus* and the *Protagoras*, although that connection is not exactly clear. Could it be that, even against his own impulses, Schleiermacher's interpretation of Plato here reflects tensions in Plato's thought itself? The answer would have to be "not really." As follows from his view of Plato as perfect artist, Schleiermacher would admit no such tensions. Unable to ignore the presence of another kind of dialectics, he made it fit through three moves.

Schleiermacher's first move was to present Plato as the perfect gentleman, so to speak. Plato is only giving credit where credit is due by acknowledging Soc-

---

[46] *EÜP* 129. cf. *IDP* 114.

rates's (hence his own) indebtedness to Zeno[47] and Parmenides[48] and by allowing the latter to "speak quite in his own spirit."[49] In other words, Plato wants "to bring Parmenides historically into connection with Socrates, and to derive the dialectics which he praised in [Socrates] from that of the first and universal father of this art."[50] Schleiermacher thus departed from interpreters who had read the proofs in the *Parmenides* either as mere "sophisms" (*Trugschlüssen*) or as an example of "false dialectics" (*ein Beispiel falscher Dialektik*).[51]

In a second move, Schleiermacher again departed from conventional wisdom by interpreting the *Parmenides* as an early dialogue.[52] That is not to say the work is immature or carries less weight, as those who espouse a developmental view might say of an early dialogue; yet it does serve to remind us that the significance of the work lies in its pedagogical function. For Schleiermacher, the *Parmenides* presented the dialectical method in its early phase, when Socrates was still young and his own dialectics not yet fully formed. Schleiermacher thereby draws a contrast between, on the one side, the dialectics of Socrates and Plato and, on the other side, a more speculative dialectics with which Plato is often confused.

In a third and related move, Schleiermacher argued that Plato also uses the *Parmenides* not so much to refute any particular view as to draw attention to the "highest philosophical task" (*die höchste philosophische Aufgabe*).[53] The problem itself, that of "finding an original identity of thinking and being,"[54] will not be solved until the *Sophist*. In his "Introduction to the *Sophist*," Schleiermacher compared the two dialogues: "one will indisputably recognize in the *Sophist* a surer hand and a grander method," and will at the same time "find the key to

---

47 "That Plato respected Zeno very highly as a dialectician, and has here adopted his method, he himself says clearly enough; just as certain, however, it also seems that he sets no great value on his philosophical genius [*Geist*]"/*Daß Platon den Zenon als Dialektiker sehr hoch geachtet, und seine Methode hier angenommen, sagt er selbst deutlich genug: eben so gewiß aber scheint auch, daß er auf seinen philosophischen Geist ... eben keinen großen Wert legt* (EÜP 139); cf. IDP 125.
48 Parmenides was "the first who made the attempt to break out from dialectics into the sphere of the higher philosophy"/... *daß er der erste gewesen der den Versuch gemacht von der Dialektik aus in das Gebiet der höheren Philosophie einzubrechen* (EÜP 140); cf. IDP 126.
49 IDP 126; EÜP 140 (... *daß Platon den Parmenides ganz in seinem Geiste reden läßt*).
50 EÜP 140 (... *das Bestreben des Platon, auch historisch den Parmenides in Verbindung mit dem Sokrates zu bringen, und die Dialektik welche er an diesem lobt von der des ersteren als des allgemeinen Vaters dieser Kunst abzuleiten*); cf. IDP 127.
51 IDP 120; EÜP 134, 135.
52 The *Parmenides* is now generally considered to be a middle dialogue, although Zuckert, employing her "dramatic dating," identifies it as early (*Plato's Philosophers*, 8).
53 EÜP 133; cf. IDP 188.
54 EÜP 133 (... *eine ursprüngliche Einerleiheit des Denkens und Seins zu finden*); cf. IDP 118.

everything in the *Parmenides* that appears as equivocation."⁵⁵ Nevertheless, before a problem can be solved, it has to be formulated as a problem, and it is in the *Parmenides* that "the question of the knowability of things"⁵⁶ is posed.

Schleiermacher did not explore at length the many intricacies and difficulties of the *Parmenides*, and he saved the full force of his criticism of Parmenides's dialectical method for the "Introduction to the *Sophist*." Giving an account of Plato's philosophy, however, was not the task of his *Introductions*; his task, rather, was to show the natural and necessary relations among the dialogues. As is true of every other dialogue, the full meaning of the *Parmenides* is intelligible only when it is viewed in relation to the whole. When we look at the whole, especially at the relation between the *Parmenides* and the *Sophist*, the implication is clearly that Parmenides could not answer his own question due to the inadequacy of his dialectical method, which remained purely speculative.

4.4 The Trilogy at the Center and the Object of Philosophy

Whereas the earlier dialogues are concerned with the *method* of philosophy (that is, with the "development of the dialectical method"⁵⁷), the middle dialogues are occupied with the *object* of philosophy. (See tables 2 and 3.) Because the *Sophist* and the *Phaedo* present particularly strong indications of speculative dialectics, I focus on Schleiermacher's interpretations of them, as I also follow him in taking a quick dive into the *Symposium*.

In the *Sophist*, Schleiermacher exclaimed, "for practically the first time in Plato's writings, the innermost sanctuary of philosophy discloses itself purely philosophically."⁵⁸ This sanctuary is perfectly, because centrally, located: it is at the very "core of the whole" (*Kern des Ganzen*);⁵⁹ at the very center, that is, of the *Sophist*, which is itself at the center of the middle trilogy, hence at the center of the entire Platonic *corpus*. Alluding to the somatic metaphor that he adopted from Socrates, Schleiermacher maintained that in the *Sophist* we arrive at the heart, structurally and substantively, of Plato's philosophy. Here, finally, in the

---

55 *EÜP* 256 (*so wird man ja unstreitig im 'Sophisten' eine sicherere Hand und eine größere Methode finden, ... findet man den Schlüssel zu allem, was im 'Parmenides' als Amphilogie erscheint*); cf. *IDP* 260.
56 *EÜP* 131 (*die Frage von der Erkennbarkeit der Dinge*); cf. *IDP* 116.
57 *PW* 1/1:57.16–58.1 (*die Entwicklung der dialektischen Methode*); cf. *IDP* 46.
58 *EÜP* 248 (*... sich hier fast zuerst in den Schriften des Platon das innerste Heiligtum der Philosophie rein philosophisch aufschließt*); cf. *IDP* 251.
59 *EÜP* 248, 249; cf. *IDP* 251, 252.

discussion of the association of ideas and the possibility of non-being and of error, we arrive at the realization that being is better and nobler than non-being, at "the intuition of the life of what-*is* [*Seienden*] and of the necessary being-one and being-in-another of being [*Sein*] and knowing [*Erkennen*]."[60] We see how being shows itself in the realm of oppositions and through the many forms of non-being, which need to be understood as difference. Reality has opened itself up to view, and the rigid confines of the *Parmenides* are thus dissolved. Dialectics, understood as dialogical and communicative, is shown to have ontological grounding: it reflects "the true life of what-*is* [*Seienden*], in which all opposites interpenetrate."[61]

The breakthrough comes by means "of the purest dialectics" (*der reinsten Dialektik*).[62] That is to say, the pedagogical aids of the earlier dialogues—the use of myth and drama to excite, the use of irony to frustrate—are laid aside. The question for us has to be, in what does this *purest dialectics* consist? Is it a higher stage of the dialectical method to which the dialogical form of dialectics is but a preparatory stage? After all, Schleiermacher on the same page referred to a "glance into that higher sphere of speculation."[63] Once again, Schleiermacher negotiated his way out of a potential conflict without acknowledging a tension. How he did this is clear if we attend carefully to how he traced the "necessary" and "natural" relations of the various parts of various wholes: the whole that is the dialogue, the whole that is the second trilogy, and the whole that is a single work of art.

Schleiermacher noted that the true connoisseur knows that the core or internal part of the "priceless fruit"[64] that is the *Sophist* cannot be tasted without the peel, without that external part of the dialogue, where the Stranger engages in the method of division and subdivision. Such a method, Schleiermacher pointed out, is ridiculed by Plato and is exposed as a false and impotent form of dialectics. Despite its many attempts, it fails to arrive at the very essence of the matter. The problem with this kind of dialectics is that it is cut off "from true knowing and being" (*von dem wahren Erkennen und Sein*).[65] The innermost sanctuary was reached not by the method of subdivision but by the true dialectics of the *The-*

---

60 ... *die Anschauung von dem Leben des Seienden und von dem notwendigen Eins- und Ineinandersein des Seins und des Erkennens* (*EÜP* 249); cf. *IDP* 251.
61 *EÜP* 249 (... *das wahre Leben des Seienden, in welchem sich alle Gegensätze durchdringen*); cf. *IDP* 252.
62 *IDP* 253; *EÜP* 250.
63 *IDP* 253; *EÜP* 250 (... *der Blick in jenes höhere Gebiet der Spekulation*).
64 See above, n. 43.
65 *EÜP* 246; cf. *IDP* 249.

4.4 The Trilogy at the Center and the Object of Philosophy — 99

aetetus and its distinction between "correct representation" (*richtigen Vorstellung*) and "immediate knowledge" (*unmittelbaren Erkenntnis*).[66] The *Sophist* is manifestly the "apex of all that is anti-sophistic in Platonic dialogues."[67]

It might be tempting to linger in the "Introduction to the *Sophist*" because in it Schleiermacher is so effusive and because it does remind us of aspects of his lectures on dialectics.[68] We need, however, to remember that, according to Schleiermacher's understanding of Plato, this revelation of the "innermost sanctuary" of philosophy is not itself the end of philosophy; it is really the necessary presupposition for the presentation of the two sciences presented in the third trilogy: ethics (in the *Republic*) and physics (in the *Timaeus*). We need, furthermore, to keep in mind that Schleiermacher viewed the *Sophist* as the first dialogue of a smaller trilogy within the middle of the second trilogy. Not only did Schleiermacher view the *Sophist* and the *Statesman* as "One Dialogue" (*Ein Gespräch*),[69] but he also saw them as the first two moments of a part of a subtrilogy that resolves in the *Symposium*.

Not until the *Symposium* does Plato present us with "an image of the philosopher depicted in the person of *Socrates*."[70] If at the center of the *Sophist* there is that moment of doubt (for us, if not for Schleiermacher) as to whether the Platonic dialectics is essentially dialogical, the issue is made perfectly clear now. Socrates is the true philosopher because of both his "tireless enthusiasm for contemplation" *and* the "joyous communication" of what he has contemplated.[71] Neither the idea of knowledge found in the *Sophist* nor the idea of wisdom found in the *Statesman* is sufficient. What we learn in the *Symposium* is that one object of Socrates's inquiry is

> not some idea of knowledge and wisdom, but is rather the philosopher, a man like any other who, although godlike in comparison with the lowly life of most, nevertheless strolls as a human among humans; thus what should be presented is not the absolute being and nature of wisdom, but its life and its appearance in the mortal life of the visible person, in whom wisdom itself—for this is clearly Plato's main point in all his explanations of philosophy—has put on mortality…
>
> *nicht etwa die Idee der Erkenntnis und Weisheit, sondern der Philosoph, auch ein Mann wie jene, der, obschon Göttergleich im Vergleich mit dem niederen Leben der meisten Menschen*

---

[66] Schleiermacher, "Introduction to the *Theaetetus*," PW 2/1:442.6 – 7; cf. *IDP* 194.
[67] *EÜP* 257 (*der Gipfel alles antisophistischen in Platonischen Gesprächen*); cf. *IDP* 261.
[68] See below, 7.2.2, for a closer analysis of Schleiermacher's "Introduction to the *Sophist*."
[69] PW 1/1:54.2; cf. *IDP* 42.
[70] *EÜP* 274 (*ein Bild des Philosophen darstellt in der Person des Sokrates*); cf. *IDP* 278.
[71] *IDP* 278; *EÜP* 274 (… *uns den Sokrates darstellt in dem unermüdlichen Eifer der Betrachtung und in der freudigen Mitteilung*). For more on *contemplation*, see below, 6.4.2, 6.4.4, and 7.3.6.

> doch als ein Mensch unter Menschen wandelt; also nicht etwa das absolute Sein und Wesen der Weisheit sollte dargestellt werden, sondern ihr Leben und ihre Erscheinung in dem sterblichen Leben des erscheinenden Menschen, in welchem sie selbst, denn dies is offenbar die Hauptansicht des Platon in allen seinen Erklärungen über die Philosophie, das sterbliche angezogen hat ...[72]

Here, we encounter an incarnational view according to which the very nature of wisdom is communicative, which returns us to love, to *erōs*, as the essential philosophical impulse: "To call this endeavor love ... is not some poetic comparison."[73] Schleiermacher insisted that, for Plato, *erōs* and knowledge cannot be separated. Love drives us to the other.

Schleiermacher's determination to read Plato's dialectics in this way—in a way that reins in the more speculative tendencies in such a manner that they remain communicative and social—continued even in his "Introduction to the *Phaedo*," which perhaps more than any other dialogue would seem to champion a speculative dialectics. In the *Phaedo*, Schleiermacher himself acknowledged, Plato reviews his own "advances in speculation"[74] and dialectical method. The chief dialectic is that between knowledge and immortality, the relation between which had theretofore not been fully treated in the dialogues but is the kernel of the whole speech.[75] In the *Phaedo*, Plato writes of the soul being released from the body—and presumably from the social relations in which the body unavoidably participates. On precisely this point, Schleiermacher was quick to note, the difference between sophistical and Socratic-Platonic dialectics becomes most clear: both types of dialectics engage in separation and combination, but whereas the sophist's activity is confined to the sense-world, the Socratic philosopher strives "to acquire what-*is* [*das Seiende*], and to preserve it pure in knowledge."[76] In short, because it recounts Socrates's "desire to become pure spirit,"[77] the *Phaedo* would seem to draw us ineluctably into the realm of pure speculation.

Once again, Schleiermacher managed to resist the draw. He did so by employing three strategies, two of which are new and peculiar to his "Introduction to the *Phaedo*." First, as he had in previous introductions, Schleiermacher ap-

---

[72] *EÜP* 275–276; cf. *IDP* 279–80. In his "Introduction to the *Phaedo*," Schleiermacher spoke of the advantage of "a vivid presentation of the Socratic life" in the *Symposium* (*eine anschauliche Darstellung des sokratischen Lebens*); *EÜP* 293; cf. *IDP* 298. See below, 6.4.3 and passage 6J.
[73] *EÜP* 276 (*Dieses Bestreben nun Liebe zu nennen ... ist nicht etwa ein dichterischer Vergleich*); cf. *IDP* 280.
[74] *IDP* 298; *EÜP* 293 (*Fortschritten in der Spekulation*).
[75] See *IDP* 300–301; *EÜP* 295–96.
[76] *IDP* 292; *EÜP* 288 (... *strebt sich das Seiende zu erwerben und rein zu erhalten in Erkenntnis*).
[77] *IDP* 292; *EÜP* 288 (*das Verlangen reiner Geist zu werden*).

pealed to the basic hermeneutical principles set out in the "General Introduction," especially those regarding *form* and *structure*. Just when the "Platonic Socrates" (*der platonische Sokrates*)[78] seems to take flight into that eternal realm, the "mimetic" (*mimische*) character resumes in its "highest glory" (*höchsten Glorie*).[79] Thus, when the content turns more speculative, there is a resurgence of the mimetic form: gestures, self-expression, imitation, inter-personal communication. The content, it will be recalled, cannot be separated from the form. Similarly, Schleiermacher pointed to the structural role of the *Phaedo* for the entire *corpus*. Since the dialogue prepares the way for the scientific presentations of the third trilogy, it provides an important transition. As such, it is a summation of all previous dialogues and maintains its connections thereto. In other words, even though Schleiermacher seemed to grant that in the *Phaedo* there is a shift toward the more speculative, he nevertheless maintained that this more speculative strain of dialectics, by virtue of its form and structural role, remains grounded in and essentially related to the dialogical dialectics of the earlier dialogues.

Second, Schleiermacher made a new interpretive move by calling attention to Socrates's praxis. He pointed out that, for all his serenity in the face of death and his talk of escape from the body in order to attain pure knowledge,[80] Socrates nevertheless decides to linger with his friends, engaging in dialogue and social intercourse. The act of taking the goblet is itself social insofar as Socrates thereby participates in ritual. As Schleiermacher put it, "likewise he does not disrupt the accustomed social life but wants still, with the fatal goblet, to celebrate the sacred ceremonies of the festive meal."[81] Thus, according to this line of interpretation, the philosophical significance of Socrates's actions has to do with the dialectic (which, for Schleiermacher, meant the necessary relation) between the mortal and the immortal. If we pay attention to Socrates's actions, and if we read the *Symposium* and the *Phaedo* in relation to each other (as Schleiermacher insisted that we should), we see that love, which is described in the former as "the endeavour to join the immortal with the mortal," is not inconsistent

---

78 *IDP* 301; *EÜP* 296.
79 *EÜP* 292–93; cf. *IDP* 297. Dobson has "dramatic" for *mimische*, but elsewhere Schleiermacher distinguishes *mimisch* and *dramatisch* (see, e.g., *PW* 1/1:49.20). *Mimisch* is narrower in meaning, referring as it does to physical and especially facial gestures in a theatrical context.
80 See, e.g., Plato, *Phaedo* 66d–e: "the body is constantly breaking in upon our studies and disturbing us with noise and confusion, so that it prevents our beholding the truth, and in fact we perceive that, if we are ever to know anything absolutely, we must be free from the body and must behold the actual realities with the eye of the soul alone" (trans. Fowler, in *PDL*).
81 *EÜP* 290 (... *unterbricht er auch so nicht das gewohnte Zusammenleben, sondern will noch mit dem tödlichen Becher die heiligen Gebräuche des festlichen Mahles begehen*); cf. *IDP* 295.

with the striving toward "pure contemplation" in the immortal, which is celebrated in the latter.[82] "The two," Schleiermacher insisted, "are clearly bound necessarily with each other."[83]

Third, Schleiermacher acknowledged the metaphysical dimension reflected in Socrates's praxis. His determination to maintain the dialectical relation between mortality and immortality was continued in his interpretation of Plato's portrayal of the relation between body and soul. Although in the *Republic* the struggle takes place among the various parts of the soul, in the *Phaedo* the main struggle is between body and soul (see, e.g., 65e–66e; 79b–80e). Schleiermacher, however, strenuously resisted any dualistic theory regarding the relation between body and soul, insisting instead on a vital relation. He chastised any who would interpret Plato as maintaining that the soul is essentially separate from the body, from the world of becoming, or from mortality. In contrast to such conventional views, Schleiermacher emphasized the embodied soul—which is to say, a soul not known apart from its manifestation in and through the corporeal world. According to Schleiermacher's reading of Plato's dialectics, the more the process of dialectics progresses throughout the Platonic dialogues, the "higher" the concepts become, which for Schleiermacher meant the more inclusive the concepts are, the tighter the dialectical relations become, and the more difficult they are to separate.

4.5 An Inconclusive Concluding Trilogy

It remains to consider how Schleiermacher read the more speculative strain of dialectics in Plato's *Republic*. After all, it is in her own *Introduction to the Republic* that Annas makes the distinction between two types of dialectics in Plato—a distinction that has framed the central question of this chapter. In particular, Annas cites the analogies of the sun (507a–509c), the line (509d–511e), and the cave (514a–520a) as prime examples of what I have termed Plato's speculative dialectics. In some ways, Schleiermacher's treatment of these analogies appears to challenge the thesis of this chapter insofar as he appears perfectly comfortable acknowledging a speculative kind of dialectics in Plato. In the end, however, the thesis holds, despite some ambiguities—ambiguities which stem partly from the uncertain status of Schleiermacher's "Introduction to the Republic" and its relation to the other introductions.

---

82 *IDP* 294; *EÜP* 289 (... *das Unsterbliche mit dem Sterblichen zu verbinden ... reine Betrachtung*).
83 *EÜP* 289 (*Und beide sind offenbar notwendig mit einander verbunden*); cf. *IDP* 294.

Three things separate Schleiermacher's "Introduction to the *Republic*" from the other introductions. First, Schleiermacher never completed the third trilogy, of which he considered the *Republic* to be the first part—a fact which, according to his own interpretive principles, compromises our understanding of the text (see above, principle n° 1). This in itself, however, is not an insurmountable problem in that elsewhere in his *Introductions* Schleiermacher discussed how he understood the interrelations of the *Republic* and the *Timaeus*, especially. Second, two decades separate this introduction from the others. The penultimate volume of *Platons Werke* (II,3) was published in 1809, while the introduction to and translation of the *Republic* (*PW* III,1) did not appear until 1828. Third, and relatedly, the tone of the "Introduction to the *Republic*" is notably different from that of the other introductions. Whereas Schleiermacher's approach to the earlier dialogues had been more hermeneutical than dialectical, in that he was trying to interpret Plato and understand the organic relations of his texts, his approach to the *Republic* was at least as dialectical as it was hermeneutical, in that he was more overtly conversing with, arguing with, evaluating, and criticizing Plato's views.[84] Therefore, although the introductions in volumes I and II of *Platons Werke*, published in five volumes between 1804 and 1809, arguably form an organic whole (to borrow another one of Schleiermacher's hermeneutical principles), the "Introduction to the *Republic*" is neither an integral part of that whole nor completely separate from it.

The continuities are clear. Throughout much of the "Introduction to the *Republic*," Schleiermacher employed the same interpretive principles he had developed two decades earlier. Eschewing the convention of dismembering the dialogue into ten books yet acknowledging the shift in style after Book I, Schleiermacher argued that the *Republic* is "*one* undivided whole" (*Ein ungeteiltes Ganze*).[85] Whereas now scholars generally concur that the difference between Book I and the other books can be attributed to the former being an earlier work, Schleiermacher recognized great literary and philosophical purpose in it: "... this first book of our work in every way recalls to the reader's memory those earlier ethical writings, whether one looks at the method of the investigation or the course of the composition or the style and language."[86] In other words, the

---

[84] In the intervening two decades Schleiermacher had more fully developed his own theory of dialectics, hermeneutics, ethics, and politics; he had also, of course, published the first edition of his dogmatic theology, *Der Christliche Glaube*, in 1821/22.
[85] *EÜP* 338; cf. *IDP* 351.
[86] *EÜP* 340 (... *daß dieses erste Buch unseres Werkes auf jede Weise jene früheren ethischen Schriften dem Leser ins Gedächtnis zurückruft, man sehe nun auf die Methode der Untersuchung oder auf den Gang der Komposition oder auf den Stil und die Sprache*); cf. *IDP* 355.

dramatic quality of the dialogue in Book I reminds us that content is inseparable from form, dialogue inseparable from scientific presentation. Furthermore, as the first part of a trilogy, the *Republic* contains what has gone before as it provides a transition to and anticipates what is to come. It is, therefore, the "keystone of all earlier ethical preliminary studies,"[87] although not the culmination of Plato's philosophy. The *Republic*, the scientific presentation of *ethics*, stands in dialectical (necessary) relation with the *Timaeus*, the scientific presentation of *physics*.

Yet there are noteworthy discontinuities. At some points in the "Introduction to the *Republic*" Schleiermacher departed from the principles and tendencies established earlier in his *Introductions*. Not insignificantly, the greatest departure occurs in his interpretation of Books V–VII, where the analogies of the sun, line, and cave are found. As part of his criticism of the conventional division of the *Republic* into ten books, Schleiermacher argued that Books V–VII form one section (according to him, the fourth main division) which is really an interruption of the "original thread" (*der ursprüngliche Faden*)[88] of Plato's philosophical argument. He interpreted this section as having been thrown in, as something intrusive, forced, and foreign. This stands in sharp contrast to his earlier tendency to look for the organic and necessary relations of parts that, to most eyes, do not seem to fit. (Recall his insistence on the close relation between the two parts of the *Phaedrus* and between the inner and outer parts of the *Sophist*.)

In thus departing from what had been for him a basic hermeneutical principle (namely, that a work, especially a work by a perfect artist such as Plato, be viewed as a living creature), Schleiermacher actually introduced a new strategy for eliding the speculative strain of dialectics in Plato. For, at the same time he conceded that Books V–VII have "significant scope" (... *bedeutenden Umfanges*),[89] he suppressed the authoritative status of that very content by classifying the entire section as an intrusion, thereby marginalizing it. This move freed him to discuss the analogies of the sun, line, and cave at length and with some ease because he could do so in a mostly descriptive manner. He further suppressed elements of a speculative dialectics by subsuming discussion of the analogies of the sun, line and cave under a larger discussion of Plato's pedagogical theory, thereby maintaining the connection between the speculative and the dialogical. Schleiermacher's Plato remained the Socratic Plato.

---

[87] *EÜP* 383 (... *der Schlußstein aller früheren ethischen Vorarbeiten*); cf. *IDP* 409.
[88] *IDP* 376; *EÜP* 357.
[89] *EÜP* 357; cf. *IDP* 376.

4.6 Concluding Remarks: From Reading Plato's Dialectics to Lecturing on *Dialectics*

In summary, Schleiermacher sometimes seemed simply to ignore the more speculative strains of Plato's dialectics—as, for instance, in his reading of the *Phaedrus*, where he interpreted the mythic elements not as speculation but as providing the impulse (*erōs*) necessary for initiating and sustaining the dialogical-dialectical process. At other times, when he could not altogether ignore the speculative strains of dialectics in Plato, Schleiermacher suppressed them by bringing them into *necessary* relation with the dialogical form of dialectics, thus granting them no independent status—as, for instance, in his readings of the *Sophist* and the *Phaedo*. Finally, when he had to admit of a certain independent status of Platonic speculative dialectics, he managed to marginalize those passages, thereby stripping them of a significant degree of authority—as, for instance, in his reading of Books V–VII of the *Republic*. To pursue the question of *why* Schleiermacher so resisted the speculative dialectics in Plato would be another study altogether. Part of the answer would seem to lie in the construction of his own dialectics, where the ideal, acting as both presupposition and boundary, does not occupy a separate sphere of existence.

In the strategic decisions Schleiermacher made in reading Plato's dialectics (1804–1809, 1828) we can detect the basic commitments he would later develop in his lectures on *Dialectics* (1811, 1814/15, 1818/19, 1822, 1828, 1831). "To do philosophy concerning these first principles without regard for what is real," Schleiermacher said in his very first lecture (April 22, 1811), "seems to be something unsatisfactory and for science dangerous, especially if that practice quite likely has as a result some sort of opposition between speculation and real knowing."[90] He went on to cite Socratic dialogue as a necessary guard against a form of speculation that is divorced from the empirical and from real knowing.[91] What he meant by this is clearer if we attend to Schleiermacher's reading of Plato's dialectics than if we only consider the occasional references to Socrates and Plato scattered throughout his *Dialectics*. Only in understanding Schleier-

---

90 Dc 2; Dk (1811) 2:5.8–11 (*Ueber diese ersten Principien ohne Rücksicht auf das Reale zu philosophiren, scheint etwas Unerfreuliches und für die Wissenschaft Gefährliches, besonders wenn es wohl gar eine Art von Gegensatz zwischen der Speculation und dem realen Wissen zur Folge hat*).
91 "In the Socratic school dialogue took the place of the arbitrary diatribes of the sophists" (*Dc* 6); Dk (1811) 2:7.16–18 (*In der sokratischen Schule trat der Dialog an die Stelle der willkührlichen Diatriben der Sophisten*).

macher's understanding of Plato, in other words, can we understand just how and to what extent Schleiermacher's dialectics is Platonic.

A question remains. Did Schleiermacher arrive at his understanding of the art of doing philosophy while reading Plato's dialectics, or was it already in place before 1804 and, if so, did it determine his reading of Plato? Schleiermacher's conviction of the need to curb purely speculative impulses characterized his philosophical essays of a decade earlier,[92] and his fascination with dialogue and its philosophical import deepened in conjunction with his experiences as a member of the Romantic circle in Berlin.[93] Thus, it seems that certain basic philosophical commitments had already been in place before Schleiermacher began the Plato project and had predisposed him to read Plato's dialectics in a certain way. Yet it is also true that Schleiermacher was studying and translating Plato during those first years of the new century when his philosophical commitments were taking shape in his *Grundlinien* (1803) and in his lectures on ethics and hermeneutics at the University of Halle (1804–1806). In short, the relational model of a direct, causal line of influence would be inadequate. A better model would be a dialogical-dialectical one: Schleiermacher's understanding of dialectics, or the art of doing philosophy, was profoundly influenced by his reading of Plato, just as his reading of Plato's dialectics was profoundly influenced by his suspicion of speculation and idealization of dialogue. In the next chapter, we can glimpse a degree of the influence of Schleiermacher's particular reading of Platonic dialogical dialectics in his own attempt to write a dialogue.

---

[92] On his early student essays (1788–94), see Lamm, *Living God*, 13–56; and "The Early Philosophical Roots of Schleiermacher's Notion of Gefühl, 1788–1794," *Harvard Theological Review* 87/1 (1994), 67–105. In his first edition of his *Speeches* (1799), Schleiermacher wrote, "And how will the triumph of speculation, the completed and rounded idealism, fare if religion does not counterbalance it and allow it to glimpse a higher realism ...?" (OR^1 103; R^1 49 [*KGA* 1:2:213.20–23]. See below, chap. 6, 143n2 for full bibliographical information).

[93] See Andreas Arndt, "Geselligkeit und Gesellschaft. Die Geburt der Dialektik aus dem Geist der Konversation in Schleiermachers *Versuch einer Theorie des geselligen Betragens*," in *Salons der Romantik: Beiträge eines Wiepersdorfer Kolloquiums zu Theorie und Geschichte des Salons*, ed. Hartwig Schultz (Berlin and New York: Walter de Gruyter 1997), 45–62.

5 Schleiermacher's *Christmas Dialogue* as Platonic Dialogue

> *I cannot grant any Platonic spirit to the first speech, since by its very nature it is really frivolous; yet perhaps Platonic form, which is just as good in the third speech, perhaps.*[1]

5.1 Introduction

Schleiermacher was here referring in a letter to a dialogue he had just published in the winter of 1806: *The Christmas Celebration: A Dialogue* (*Die Weihnachtsfeier: Ein Gespräch*).[2] Whereas the three previous chapters focused almost exclusively on his *Introductions to the Dialogues of Plato* and considered how his hermeneutics (chapter three) and dialectics (chapter four) emerged out of his Plato-interpretation, this chapter and the next two shift attention to two published works from 1806, written while he was still deeply immersed in Plato scholarship. With that shift comes another: from the philosophical to the religio-theological. Here in chapter five, I address the question of how Schleiermacher's Plato influenced his *Christmas Dialogue*; in chapters six and seven, I examine how Schleiermacher's Plato informed his revisions in the second edition of his *Speeches on Religion*.

Schleiermacher wrote his *Christmas Dialogue* in only three weeks and under considerable inspiration. Schleiermacher had been in despair during the autumn of 1805. His beloved, Eleanore Grunow, had broken off their relationship, deciding instead to remain in her loveless marriage.[3] Schleiermacher felt hopeless, suffering under what he described as a "grievous feeling" (*das schmerzliche Gefühl*).[4] In early December, he cancelled his lecture on ethics so that he

---

[1] Schleiermacher to Henriette Herz, 17 Feb. 1806 (#2145, lines 13–15), *Br.* 8:468–70.
[2] Schleiermacher, *Die Weihnachtsfeier: Ein Gespräch* (1806), in *KGA* 1/5: 43–98 (hereafter cited in text as "*WG*"). English translation: *The Christmas Celebration: A Dialogue*, in *Schleiermacher: Christmas Dialogue, The Second Speech, and Other Selections*, trans. Julia A. Lamm, Classics of Western Spirituality (New York: Paulist Press, 2014), 101–151 (hereafter cited in text as "*CD*" for *Christmas Dialogue*).
[3] See Schleiermacher to Heinrich Willich, 18 Oct. 1805 (#2046, lines 70–78), *Br.* 8:335–36. For more on the immediate circumstances of his penning the *Christmas Dialogue*, see Lamm, "Schleiermacher's Spirituality: An Introduction," in *Schleiermacher*, 26–30.
[4] Schleiermacher to the von Willichs, 26 Nov. 1805 (#2081, lines 4–5), *Br.* 8:375.

could attend a concert by the virtuoso Friedrich Dülon (1768–1826), a blind flutist. So transformed was Schleiermacher by the experience that, upon leaving the concert, the idea of writing something on the joy of Christmas came to him suddenly. He submitted the manuscript on Christmas Eve morning, and the little book was published in January 1806. He would himself acknowledge that its literary achievement was limited, due in part to having been so hastily written. Nevertheless, it has proven to be his most-printed work.

In two hundred years of interpretation of Schleiermacher's *Christmas Dialogue* an enduring puzzle and point of contention has been about its form, including whether it is (or was intended to be) a *Platonic* dialogue.[5] Most interpreters acknowledge a general influence of Plato—a rather obvious point, since Schleiermacher, when he penned the *Christmas Dialogue* that winter in Halle, was still working assiduously on *Platons Werke*.[6] Nevertheless, proving that his *Christmas Dialogue* is indeed Platonic has been a much more elusive task. Several interpreters have noted parallels in form (and to some extent content) between Plato's *Symposium* and Schleiermacher's *Christmas Dialogue*, and some have attempted comparison with the *Phaedo* or *Phaedrus*. Until fairly recently, most have assumed that only the men's speeches, towards the end of the *Christmas Dialogue*, can be understood as in any way genuinely Platonic. Schleiermacher's own words, given in the epigraph above, would seem to support that. In short, the reigning assumption has been that, on account of the opening narrative and the three Christmas stories told by women, the *Christmas Dialogue*, in its entirety, cannot be a Platonic dialogue, since it does not have a single form but is instead a mixed form of dialogue and novella.[7]

---

[5] This line of inquiry began with the first reviews of the *Weihnachtsfeier*. See Hermann Patsch, "Historische Einführung," *KGA* 1/5: xlviii–l, lv–lxiv. Ruth Drucilla Richardson offers the most comprehensive review of the history of interpretation of the *Weihnachtsfeier*, with special focus on the question of form, in "Friedrich Schleiermacher's *Weihnachtsfeier* as 'Universal Poetry': The Impact of Friedrich Schlegel on the Intellectual Development of the Young Schleiermacher" (PhD Dissertation, Drew University, 1985).

[6] *PW II,1* had appeared in November 1805 and he was already hard at work on *PW II,2* (1807), which included the *Cratylus*, *Sophist*, *Statesman*, and *Symposium*; meanwhile, he was also working on the *Theaetetus* and on fragments of Heraclitus. See Käppel and Loehr, "Historische Einführung," *KGA* 4/5:xxix–xxx.

[7] David Friedrich Strauss: "eine dialogisch-novellenartige Form," and "Novelle … nach Art des Platonischen Symposion" (*Charakteristiken und Kritiken. Eine Sammlung zerstreuter Aufsätze aus den Gebieten der Theologie, Anthropologie und Aesthetik* [Leipzig: Wigan, 1839], 5 and 39, respectively). Dilthey: "So wandelt sich das historische Drama des platonischen Dialogs hier zur Novelle" (*Leben Schleiermachers*, 1/2:152; see also 158). Kurt Nowak: "Die Gesprächsnovelle" (*Schleiermacher*, 164). See also Martin Rade, "Einleitung," in *Schleiermacher: Monologen, Die Weihnachtsfeier* (1954), xii. Patsch and Matthias Morgenroth have recently concurred in identify-

One problem with this way of reading of the *Christmas Dialogue* is that, in refusing to recognize the literary integrity of the piece, it ignores sixty percent of the text. Another problem is that it reflects deeply rooted philosophical prejudices (a Platonic dialogue involves only men) and cultural prejudices (women, children, and the home are philosophically insignificant).[8] Typical is the view of David Schenkel, a nineteenth-century interpreter who, after noting that Schleiermacher "concedes a very considerable voice" to the women, abruptly concluded nevertheless that the women "say barely anything meaningful."[9] Even those with enough awareness to give a nod to the importance of the opening scene have shown their hand by the interpretive weight given to the men's speeches.[10]

A fundamental shift in interpretation began about a half-century ago, first with the publication in 1964 of Richard R. Niebuhr's *Schleiermacher on Christ and Religion*,[11] a study that inaugurated a new appreciation of Schleiermacher in the Anglophone world, and then with Terrence Tice's translation of the *Christmas Dialogue* published three years later.[12] Niebuhr gave considerable attention to the earlier parts of the *Christmas Dialogue*, arguing for their significance:

---

ing the mixed nature of the form, although neither uses that as an excuse to neglect the earlier parts. Morgenroth explains, "Eine 'Dialognovelle' aus drei Teilen entsteht" (*Weihnachts-Christentum. Moderner Religiosität auf der Spur* [Gütersloh: Chr. Kaiser/Gütersloher Verlag, 2002], 93). See Patsch, "Einführung," *KGA* 1/5:xlviii–xlix.

8 In his 2001 biography of Schleiermacher, Nowak reiterates two hundred years of interpretation when he insists that only in the men's speeches does the *Weihnachtsfeier* gain "the character of a symposium in the manner of Plato," though it is "broken by the feminine listeners, who join in the discourse after each speech" (*Schleiermacher*, 169). Nowak further undermines the authority of the women by claiming that the three women who tell the stories are all young in years, still "young girls" [*junge Mädchen*] (168), even though their ages are never given, and even though Ernestine and Agnes are clearly portrayed as mature women with authority.

9 David Schenkel, *Friedrich Schleiermacher. Ein Lebens- und Charakterbild. Zur Erinnerung an den 21. November 1768* (Elberfeld, 1868), 272.

10 Karl Barth, for instance, claimed, "all this part of the book is not mere preparation or preface, but presents in its way ... the answer itself" ("Schleiermacher's 'Celebration of Christmas'," in *Theology and Church: Shorter Writings 1920–1928*, trans. Louise Pettibone Smith [New York and Evanston: Harper & Row, 1962], 142). Nevertheless, he devoted only three pages to the women's stories, while having given nine to the men's speeches.

11 See above, chap. 1, 6–7n23.

12 Schleiermacher, *Christmas Eve: Dialogue on the Incarnation*, trans. Terrence N. Tice (Richmond: John Knox Press, 1967). In an article published that same year, Tice recognized the problem of distorted readings due to "tendency to concentrate attention on the final section, where the men make speeches on the meaning of Christmas" ("Schleiermacher's Interpretation of Christmas: 'Christmas Eve,' 'The Christian Faith,' and the Christmas Sermons,'" *Journal of Religion* 47, no. 2 [April 1967]: 101). In his introduction to *Christmas Eve,* Tice tried to shift that attention to the earlier parts of the dialogue, but in expanding his argument he turned his attention

[T]he Christmas dialogue commences with real humanity as it is actually determined by relatively natural forces, such as sex and personal temperament, and by more ethical or historical factors, specifically education, relationship to Christianity, marriage and politics. Unless there is a preliminary discussion to this end, it will be impossible to evaluate the heightened sense of life, the transformation of pain though joy, the spirit of serenity and resignation that make up the mood and much of the efficacy of Christmas. Furthermore, the failure to develop such information would mean, in its turn, that the image of the author of this new life must remain little more than an empty symbol whose real historical, ethical significance can be neither affirmed nor denied.[13]

Niebuhr devoted several pages to the opening narrative and the conversation, albeit a little less to the women's stories.[14] His interpretation of these earlier parts of the *Christmas Dialogue* remains insightful in part because he took the time to consider what Schleiermacher himself understood by a Platonic dialogue, and central to that was the dialogue form.[15]

Another important shift in interpretation came in the 1980s, when feminist theory began to draw more attention to the voices of the women and the portrayal of gender in the *Christmas Dialogue*. In her 1985 dissertation, Ruth Richardson offered a detailed summary of the history of interpretation of the piece in which she exposed deep biases in favor of the men's speeches. She concluded that the *Christmas Dialogue* was not intended as a Platonic dialogue but rather as a "different type of literary form"—namely, "universal poetry"[16] as conceived by Schleiermacher's old friend and former collaborator, F. Schlegel. In another study, Richardson further established the importance of the women's stories by demonstrating a direct correlation between them and the men's speeches. "Each is limited in itself," she argued; "each can only be properly explained

---

instead to the real, historical women in Schleiermacher's life who may have inspired the various characters (see 102–106).

13 Niebuhr, *Schleiermacher on Christ and Religion*, 48–49.

14 Niebuhr concluded, "None of the earlier questions is answered in these narratives. Instead, the recollections [of the women] serve to crystallize these questions and motifs in such a way that it is clear no further progress can be made through simple observations. It is now time to apply analysis, therefore, specifically to the connection between these various experiences … and the unvarying background against which all have occurred, namely, the figure of Christ" (*Schleiermacher on Christ and Religion*, 59–60). In short, according to Niebuhr, the answers are still given in the men's speeches.

15 Three principles, Niebuhr argued, "merit particular attention": (1) "the dialogue form is a reflection of Plato's own idea of the nature of philosophical communication"; (2) "the dialogue is not a collection of discrete views; it is a living whole"; and (3) "the unfinished appearance of the dialogues is … an essential feature of the form itself" (*Schleiermacher on Christ and Religion*, 29–30).

16 Richardson, "Friedrich Schleiermacher's *Weihnachtsfeier*," 537, 539, respectively.

through the other."¹⁷ More recently, Elisabeth Hartlieb has developed this line of argument further.¹⁸ In making her case for the importance of the female characters and of the three stories told by women in the *Christmas Dialogue*, Hartlieb focuses on gender differences, arguing that Schleiermacher developed therein "a model of egalitarian complementarity of the sexes."¹⁹ Not all scholars using tools of feminist critique, of course, have been interested in retrieving or defending Schleiermacher's views of women or gender in the *Christmas Dialogue*. Marilyn Chapin Massey, for instance, criticized the ideal of femininity developed there was an attempt to domesticate and restrict women.²⁰

The reason why most attempts to address the question of whether Schleiermacher's *Christmas Dialogue* is a Platonic dialogue have in the end been so unfruitful is that they start with certain assumptions about what a Platonic dialogue is—assumptions that were neither shared nor informed by Schleiermacher himself.²¹ My contribution to this debate will be to take Schleiermacher's own

---

17 Ruth Drucilla Richardson, *The Role of Women in the Life and Thought of the Early Schleiermacher (1768–1806): An Historical Overview*, Schleiermacher Studies-and-Translations 7 (Lewiston: Edwin Mellen Press, 1991), 154. She expanded upon the point: "The three stories of the women that are embedded in the finite order would not be complete without a spiritual explanation. They need to be lifted out of the merely finite into the realm of the infinite. The three theological/philosophical discourses of the men need to be seen in relation to the three stories of the women, because without them they are only abstract flights into the world of the infinite, without any concrete, finite point of reference. The stories of the women give them their grounding in the finite order of the real world. The philosophy/*Anschauung* of the men serves to '*ausbilden*' the stories of the women. The phantasy/*Gefühl* of the women serve to '*befestigen*' the philosophy/*Anschauung* of the men" (154). See 154–164 for her full account of this.
18 See Elisabeth Hartlieb, *Geschlechterdifferenz im Denken Friederich Schleiermachers* (Berlin and New York: Walter de Gruyter, 2006), 41–47.
19 Hartlieb, *Geschlechterdifferenz*, 33; see also 37, 42, 45, and 53.
20 Marilyn Chapin Massey, *Feminine Soul: The Fate of an Ideal* (Boston: Beacon, 1985). In particular, she argued that, in Schleiermacher's treatment of the girl Sofie, we find evidence for his suppression of the goddess Sophia (pp. 136–146). See Dawn DeVries's response in "Schleiermacher's *Christmas Eve Dialogue*: Bourgeois Ideology or Feminist Theology?" *Journal of Religion* 69, no. 2 (1989): 169–183. For more on feminist interpretations of Schleiermacher, see Julie Ellison, *Delicate Subjects: Romanticism, Gender, and the Ethics of Understanding* (Ithaca: Cornell University Press, 1990), 17–102; Patricia Guenter Gleason, *On Schleiermacher and Gender Politics* (Harrisburg, Penn.: Trinity Press International, 1997); Iain G. Nicol, ed., *Schleiermacher and Feminism: Sources, Evaluations, and Responses* (Lewiston/Queenston/Lampeter: Edwin Mellen, 1992); and Thandeka, "Schleiermacher, Feminism, and Liberation," in Mariña, *Cambridge Companion to Schleiermacher*, 287–306.
21 The two exceptions here are Niebuhr and Richardson, both of whom were well acquainted with Schleiermacher's interpretation of Plato when they wrote their studies. The principles I shall be applying are even more specific and detailed than those mentioned by either of them.

very specific principles of interpreting Plato, as he laid those out in his groundbreaking *Introductions*, and apply those principles to his *Christmas Dialogue*. My main thesis in this chapter is that his *Christmas Dialogue* is Platonic in a uniquely Schleiermacherian sense: its strongest parallels are not with any one of Plato's dialogues but rather with the entire *corpus* of Platonic dialogues, as Schleiermacher understood that. In particular, if we take Schleiermacher's interpretation of the Platonic *corpus* as a trilogy of trilogies and superimpose that onto the *Christmas Dialogue*, then something startling happens. The order and (what Schleiermacher called) the "necessary" and "natural" relations of each part of the dialogue suddenly begin to emerge, and how his interpretative principles might be applied to his own dialogue becomes much clearer (see table 4).

Table 4: Parallel Structures of *Platons Werke* and *Christmas Dialogue*

Platons Werke		Christmas Dialogue
1st Trilogy	*Phaedrus* *Protagoras* *Parmenides*	The Opening scene (gifts & conversation): 1. Gifts: gift exchange, Sofie's diorama of Christian story and 'history' 2. The Conversation
2nd Trilogy (sub-trilogy)	*Theaetetus* *Sophist + Statesman +* *Symposium* *Phaedo + Philebus*	3. The Women's stories of Christmases past: Ernestine Agnes Karoline
3rd Trilogy	*Republic* *Timaeus* *Critias*	4. The Men's speeches on faith, Gospels, history: Leonhardt Ernst Eduard 5. The Unsaying of Josef

One immediate effect of this new template for reading the *Christmas Dialogue* is the shift of attention it demands from the end (the men's speeches) to the beginning and middle sections. I maintain that, when we apply Schleiermacher's own interpretative principles for understanding the Platonic *corpus*, we can find new evidence for just how essential the opening scene and the women's stories are for the whole. Hence, my primary thesis leads to a secondary thesis: More than playing a prefatory, supporting or even complementary role, the opening scene provides the *impulse* (joy) and *method* (dialogue) for the whole, and it is the women's stories, not the men's speeches, that are the proper analogue for the *Symposium*. Indeed, to extract the men's speeches from the rest of the *Christmas Dialogue* is to strip them of their deeper meaning and rich irony.

This approach thus lends new support to claims, most often by feminist interpreters, that neither the opening scene nor the women's stories can be incidental to Schleiermacher's *Christmas Dialogue*. At the same time, I want to take the point further: their significance is not based *only* on some complementarity and correlation with the men's speeches; rather, they do real philosophical work, according to Schleiermacher's understanding of Plato's dialectics. To argue this convincingly, I need first to review briefly some of Schleiermacher's more basic interpretive principles (as he worked those out through the arduous task of translating and ordering Plato's dialogues) as well as the structure of the *Christmas Dialogue*.

As we have seen, Schleiermacher's most basic principle in interpreting Plato was his understanding of Plato "as philosophical artist" (*als philosophischen Künstler*).[22] This carried several meanings at once for him. According to Schleiermacher, there is a unity to Plato's thought, and that unity is to be found in Plato's person, in his genius, rather than in a supposed philosophical system. It follows from this that the content of Plato's thought cannot be understood apart from its form, which means that the dialogue form cannot be dismissed as mere accoutrement; it is, in fact, crucial to understanding Plato.[23] Furthermore, Plato's works must thus be viewed as one single work of art, as an "essential unity" (*wesentliche Einheit*),[24] rather than as dissected pieces lying next to each other. This aesthetic principle was coupled with an organic model of what it is to be a living whole, with "natural" and "necessary" relations.[25] In seeking the ordering of Plato's works, Schleiermacher concluded that the authentic dialogues form one whole with three main parts, each of which is to be understood as an artistic whole in itself and each comprised of three chief dialogues—hence, a trilogy of trilogies. These principles lead to only one conclusion when it comes the matter of the Platonic character of the *Christmas Dialogue:* it must be considered as a whole, and its natural and necessary relations must be traced.[26]

---

22 *PW* 1/1:19.15; cf. *IDP* 4.
23 As we saw above in chap. 2, Plato's philosophy, Schleiermacher wrote, "is inseparable in regard to its form and content, and each sentence is rightly understood only in its own place, and within the connections and restrictions, that Plato established for it"/... *so ist in ihr Form und Inhalt unzertrennlich, und jeder Saz nur an seinem Orte und in den Verbindungen und Begränzungen, wie ihn Platon aufgestellt hat, recht zu verstehen* (*PW* 1/1:28.25–28; cf. *IDP* 14). Interpreters of Schleiermacher's *Christmas Dialogue* have made the opposite mistake of interpreters of Plato's dialogue: whereas the latter stressed content over form (dialogue), the former have stressed form (a narrow understanding of Platonic dialogue) over content.
24 *IDP* 7; *PW* 1/1:21.28
25 *IDP* 19; *PW* 1/1:32.21,23.
26 Ravenscroft supports this view with a different line of argument (see *Veiled God*, 179–83).

Conventionally, Schleiermacher's *Christmas Dialogue* has been divided into three parts: the opening narrative scene, the women's stories, and the men's speeches.[27] More often than not, this threefold division both derives from and supports the reigning assumption that the men's speeches are the most important part of the text. Such a division, without qualification, is problematic in that it ignores Schleiermacher's own principles of aesthetic proportion; it artificially "dissects" what is supposed to be a living whole and neglects the natural connections;[28] and consequently, it precipitately reduces more than half of the entire work to prefatory filler.

Hartlieb challenges that conventional division and, paying close attention to literary transitions within the text itself, argues instead for a five-fold division:

> ... the whole very clearly breaks down into a narrative, dialogical part and a discursive, monological part. In my view, under closer observation five sections can be distinguished of the different elements of genre ... Thereby the text more powerfully comes into view as a totality, and the first half is not pressed into the role of being a narrative launch pad for the philosophical-theological arguments of the second half. The dialogue of the circle of friends, like the stories of women, obtain a stronger weight ...[29]

With Hartlieb, I maintain that the *Christmas Dialogue* is better understood when broken down into five parts, to which I assign these titles: (1) 'Gifts,' (2) 'Conversation,' (3) 'Stories' (by the women), (4) 'Speeches' (by the men), and (5) 'The Unsaying of Josef' (see table 4). In addition to the reasons offered by Hartlieb, there are two further advantages for adopting this division, at least as an initial stage of (re)interpretation. First and most simply, this division challenges the *status quo*, calls forth a critical openness, and invites the reader into neglected parts of the text. Second, it reminds us that the prophetic and mystical unsaying of Josef at the end, even though his scene takes up but one page of the entire *Christmas Dialogue*, really is, paradoxically, the last word, and in Socratic fashion this last part forces us to question what we think we have grasped.

That being said, the interpretation of the *Christmas Dialogue* I offer here does not stand or fall with either a quint- or tri-partite division; actually, it employs both. It uses the former to open up the text and to stand as a corrective to interpretations that overemphasize the importance of the men's speeches; and, having made that move, it applies the latter division, albeit in a novel way. The tri-

---

[27] For example, Dilthey, Krapf, Barth, and Richardson all break it down into three parts; more recently, Morgenroth has also assumed this tripartite division.
[28] See *IDP* 13–14; *PW* 1/1:27–28.
[29] Hartlieb, *Geschlechterdifferenz*, 29. For the details of her breakdown of the five parts, see 29–30.

partite division I propose is informed by Schleiermacher's own trilogical division of Plato's dialogues. Thus, for example, this approach entails a close examination of 'Gifts' and 'Conversation' as distinct parts of the whole. At the same time, there is a reason why these two early parts have routinely been read together, in that they do form a single dramatic scene. Hence, I also refer to the 'Opening Scene,' which comprises the first two parts: 'Gifts' and 'Conversation.' Schleiermacher's interpretation of the *Phaedrus*, I maintain, will provide clues for understanding both the distinction and continuity between parts one and two.

The 'Opening Scene' plays the role for the *Christmas Dialogue* that the first trilogy, and most especially the *Phaedrus*, plays for the entire Platonic corpus, according to Schleiermacher's interpretation: it contains the 'seeds,' the impulse, and the method of the whole (section 5.2). The women's stories play the role that the second trilogy, most especially the *Symposium*, plays for Plato's *corpus:* they present the main 'object' of the whole in a concrete and vivid manner (section 5.3). The men's speeches play a similar role that the third trilogy, and especially the *Republic*, does: they offer a 'scientific' presentation of what has been developed thus far (section 5.4). Finally, the appearance of Josef at the very end undercuts the men's speeches as well as the motive behind them and returns the *Christmas Dialogue* back to the 'Opening Scene' albeit in a transformed manner, since so much has transpired; Josef is the embodiment of an apophasis that is not ascetic in nature but is instead immersive in the redemptive joys of multigenerational community, simple beauty, and religious chorus (section 5.5).

5.2 The *Phaedrus* and the Opening Scene of the *Christmas Dialogue*

Table 5: The First Trilogy of PW and the 'Seeds' of CD

Platons Werke	Role in Platonic *corpus*	Christmas Dialogue	Role in *Dialogue*
First trilogy: focus on *Phaedrus* (the first dialogue), the 'seeds' of Plato's philosophy, and dialectics as method	Part I of *Phaedrus*: 'impulse" (*erōs*) Part II of *Phaedrus*: 'method' (dialogical *dialectics*)	Opening scene: Part 1: gift exchange, music, diorama Part 2: Conversation	Impulse (joy) Method (loving communication)

5.2.1 Gifts

The opening scene begins with the description of a gathering of an intimate circle of friends on Christmas Eve in a home beautifully decked out for the holidays.[30] The hostess, Ernestine (married, and the mother of at least one child, Sofie),[31] has artfully arranged the gifts so as to heighten the sense of beauty, delight, and surprise associated with Christmas. The exchange of presents occurs complete with mirth, joviality, and gratitude—as well as with the kind of joking that takes place only among people well acquainted with each other. The deep-rooted affection each has for the others is communicated through the thoughtfulness of each present and the care that went into making or purchasing them. The daughter of the household, Sofie (a precocious child probably between six and ten years old) is given a book of Christmas music rather than instructions for needlework, which thrills her, as she declares, "O great Music! Christmas for a lifetime! Sing, children, the most wondrous things."[32] Sofie's gift to their guests is an elaborate diorama she has constructed in her room. Originally, the playset of miniatures was meant to display the first Christmas, but she has tucked the crèche in amidst a cacophony of other representations of events and figures from the history of Christianity.

When the party returns to the parlor, they re-examine their gifts and Karoline (a presumably young and unmarried woman) sits down to play the clavier; she, Eduard (the host, married to Ernestine), and Friederike (engaged to be married to Ernst) begin to sing for the others. There is a clear break at this point in the text, with a moment of silent communing:

> Soon they had everyone listening devoutly, and when they had finished, it happened, as it always does, that religious music effects first a silent satisfaction and withdrawal of the heart. There were a few silent moments in which everyone knew that each and every heart was lovingly directed toward all the rest, and toward something higher still.[33]
>
> *Bald hatten sie alle zu andächtigen Zuhörern, und als sie geendet hatten, geschah es, wie immer, daß religiöse Musik zuerst eine stille Befriedigung und Zurükgezogenheit des Gemüthes*

---

30 *CD* 101–108; *WG*, 43–50. For the purpose of approximating percentage of the entire text: 'Gifts' occupies fifteen percent of the entire text.
31 Since marital status is so important for Schleiermacher's theory of gender as presented in the *Christmas Dialogue*, and since most interpreters have focused more on the women's marital status than on the men's, I shall include a parenthetical note as to the marital status of each adult character introduced.
32 *CD* 104–105; *WG* 46.31–33 (... *o große Musik! Weihnachten für ein ganzes Leben! ihr sollt singen, Kinder, die herrlichsten Sachen*).
33 *CD* 107–108.

bewirkt. Es gab einige stumme Augenblikke, in denen aber Jeder wußte, daß eines Jeden Gemüth liebend auf die Uebrigen und auf etwas noch Höheres gerichtet war.[34]

5.2.2 Conversation

At this point, an extended conversation begins—a dialogue within the *Dialogue*. This 'Conversation' constitutes about thirty-six percent of the entire *Christmas Dialogue*,[35] which makes it significantly longer than either the 'Stories' or the 'Speeches.' It is therefore difficult to understand why, until fairly recently, it had been so neglected.[36] The conversation begins with an exchange over how to distinguish feelings of love and joy that can be exuberant yet ultimately transient in nature from feelings of love and joy that are enduring in depth and tenderness. This leads to consideration of Sofie's innocent, exuberant display of religiosity and concern on the part of Leonhardt (an attorney, presumably unmarried, who plays the role of skeptic and who delivers the first speech) that her religiosity either results from or will result in some sort of fanaticism. The conversation then turns to the nature of proper religious piety and its development, to whether piety develops differently in men and in women, and to a comparison of Catholic and Pietist forms of devotion. Here, interestingly, while many of the gender stereotypes of the day are reinforced, they are simultaneously subverted through the action of conversing—through verbal challenges, gestures, sarcasm, and humor.

Further insight into the importance of the 'Opening Scene' for the *Christmas Dialogue* and the specific role it plays for the whole can be gained when we read it in light of Schleiermacher's interpretation of the *Phaedrus* as the first dialogue in the Platonic *corpus* (see tables 4 & 5).

---

34 *WG* 50.4–9.
35 *CD* 108–126; *WG* 50–72.
36 Such neglect was likely related to the fact that all the adults, women and men, are active participants, and at one point even little Sofie is brought into the conversation. Consequently, because women and a (female) child are involved, it was not judged to be a proper Platonic dialogue. I shall return to this point later.

5.2.3 The 'Seeds'

> For there is certainly no denying that the seeds of [Plato's] entire philosophy are found in the Phaedrus, although their undeveloped state is also as clear ...
> —"Introduction to the *Phaedrus*"[37]

> Hence the Phaedrus establishes in the most general way the striving after the good as the ground, and the secure attainment of the good as the work of love.
> —"Introduction to the *Symposium*"[38]

Key to Schleiermacher's ordering of Plato's works, and indeed key to his understanding of Plato's philosophy overall, was his conviction that the *Phaedrus* was the first dialogue.[39] His reasoning was not just that it was first chronologically, but also that it was the first conceptually and pedagogically. The *Phaedrus* was first because it contains the "seeds" (*Keime*) of practically the entirety of Plato's thought and because it presents both the impulse and the method for doing philosophy. This notion of "seeds" was a peculiarly Romantic notion that connected the notion of an artistic whole with the biological understanding of a seed containing the entire mature organism within it, in incipient but potent form. It was critical to Schleiermacher's understanding of Plato as philosophical artist. This principle of interpretation is also suggestive regarding the significance of the opening scene of the *Christmas Dialogue*, for more than simply describing the setting in which three of the men will eventually give speeches on the meaning of Christmas, Schleiermacher here actually planted the seeds for the entire rest of the *Christmas Dialogue*. In 'Gifts' and 'Conversation' Schleiermacher introduced countless themes and sub-texts that he would take up again repeatedly, intricately interweaving them throughout the rest of the *Christmas Dialogue*, so much so that the men's 'Speeches' are not properly understood apart from these early seeds.

This attention to the particulars, to seeds, is true at the simplest level, at the level of things described in the opening scene: lighting, presents, pieces of art, "feminine" crafts, etc. It is also true in terms of actions and performances: the interplay of the characters, the playing of music, the joking and laughing, the exchange of gifts, Sofie's innocence and precociousness, gestures of joy and love, and most especially dialogue itself. It is, finally, true in terms of explicit conver-

---

[37] PW 1/1:80.4–6 (*Denn die Keime seiner ganzen Philosophie fast sind im Phaidros freilich nicht zu läugnen, aber auch ihr unentwikkelter Zustand ist eben so deutlich*); cf. IDP 68.
[38] EÜP 282 (*So stellt Phaidros am allgemeinsten das Streben nach dem Guten als den Grund und das sichrere Erreichen desselben als das Werk der Liebe auf*); cf. IDP 68.
[39] See above, 2.4.1, 3.3.

sational topics that are introduced here in the 'Opening Scene' and then revisited in the 'Stories' and again in the 'Speeches.' To trace them all out in their intricacy would be an entire essay in itself but allow me to offer three examples in order to illustrate the point.

First, the narrator's claim, in part one of *Christmas Dialogue*, that "Christmas is quite properly a children's holiday, and she [Sofie] lived in it in such a totally exceptional way"[40] is picked up several times in the 'Conversation';[41] it is echoed through the actions of children portrayed in all three of the women's 'Stories'; it is repeated with no little irony in Leonhardt's speech[42] and in Ernst's counter-speech;[43] finally, it is at the heart of Josef's 'Unsaying' in the conclusion:

> The speechless subject demands or generates in me a speechless joy, and in my joy I can only smile and cheer like a child. This day, all people are children to me, and for that very reason they are dear. For once, the serious wrinkles are smoothed out; for once, age and worries are not written on the forehead; for once, the eyes sparkle and live, and it is the presentiment of a beautiful and graceful existence [*Dasein*] in them. I myself have also become a child again to my good fortune. As a child stifles childish grief, holds back sighs, and draws in the tears when a childish joy is given, so on this day, the long, deep, undying grief of my life is soothed for me as never before. I feel myself at home and as if newly born in the better world, in which grief and lament have no sense and no space.[44]

> *Der sprachlose Gegenstand verlangt oder erzeugt auch mir eine sprachlose Freude, die meinige kann wie ein Kind nur lächeln und jauchzen. Alle Menschen sind mir heute Kinder, und sind mir eben darum so lieb. Die ernsthaften Falten sind einmal ausgeglättet, die Zahlen und die Sorgen stehen ihnen einmal nicht an der Stirn geschrieben, das Auge glänzt und lebt einmal, und es ist eine Ahndung eines schönen und anmuthigen Daseins in ihnen. Auch ich selbst bin ganz ein Kind geworden zu meinen Glükk. Wie ein Kind den kindischen Schmerz erstikt, und die Seufzer*

---

40 CD 105; WG 47.16–17 (*Wie nun Weihnachten recht eigentlich das Kinderfest ist, und sie ganz besonders darin lebt*).
41 For instance, Eduard later comments, "And that is why, dear Ernestine, we were so captivated by your arrangement this evening, because you expressed so well our sense of Christmas—the being rejuvenated, the return to the feeling of childhood, the serene joy in the new world—which we owe to the child being celebrated today" (CD 117)/*Und um deswillen, liebe Ernestine, waren wir so ergözt von deiner Anordnung diesen Abend, weil du unsern Weihnachtssinn so recht ausgedrükkt; das Verjüngtsein, das Zurükgehn in das Gefühl der Kindheit, die heitre Freude an der neuen Welt, die wir dem gefeierten Kinde verdanken* (WG 62.20–24).
42 Leonhardt declares, "To me, at any rate, the smallest thing is significant. For just as a child is the main subject of Christmas, so too here children are primarily the ones who lift and carry on the festival—and, in turn, through the fesitval, lift and carry Christianity itself" (CD 141)/*Mir wenigstens ist auch das Kleinste davon bedeutungsvoll. Denn wie ein Kind der Hauptgegenstand desselben ist, so sind es auch hier die Kinder vornemlich, welche das Fest, und durch das Fest wiederum das Christenthum selbst heben und tragen* (WG 88.10–13).
43 See CD 143; WG 90.
44 CD 150.

> zurükdrängt und die Thränen einsaugt, wenn ihm eine kindische Freude gemacht wird: so ist mir heute der lange tiefe unvergängliche Schmerz besänftiget, wie noch nie. Ich fühle mich einheimisch und wie neugeboren in der besseren Welt, in der Schmerz und Klage keinen Sinn hat und keinen Raum.[45]

Likewise, Sofie's announcement that "Christ is true guarantor that life and delight will never more perish in the world"[46] resurfaces in Agnes's story,[47] in Eduard's Johannine Christology in the third speech,[48] and finally is confirmed again in Josef's words.[49]

Second, the theme of the connection between art and religion, so central to the entire *Christmas Dialogue*, is introduced in myriad ways in the 'Opening Scene.' It is an explicit topic of discussion in 'Gifts,' but it is also a palpable part of the setting itself. It is Sofie who first introduces the image of the mother and divine child in her diorama; shortly thereafter she likens her own mother to Mary.[50] The iconic image is revisited in the 'Conversation' and then forms the center of each woman's story. In each instance, not just the idea of motherhood but also a very definite portrait of Madonna and child (and twice of the *Pietà*) is drawn.[51] For Schleiermacher, of course, the analogy between piety and music

---

45 WG 97.23 – 98.1.
46 CD 107; WG 49.13 – 14 (*Christ der rechte Bürge ist, daß Leben und Lust nie mehr untergehen werden in der Welt*).
47 Agnes's story is about a family deciding to baptize their infant (her nephew) at home in the midst of their Christmas Eve celebration. Her brother, a minister, went on about "how the very fact that a Christian child is received in love and joy, and always remains embraced in them, provides the guarantee that the Spirit of God will dwell in him, how the celebration of the birth of the new world must be a day of love and joy, and how the two united together are specially ordained to initiate a child of love into the higher birth of divine life" (CD 132); WG 77.29 – 78.1 (*wie eben dieß, daß ein christliches Kind von Liebe und Freude empfangen werde und immer umgeben bleibe, die Bürgschaft leiste, daß der Geist Gottes in ihm wohnen werde; wie das Geburtsfest der neuen Welt ein Tag der Liebe und Freude sein müsse, und wie beides vereinigt recht dazu auserlesen sei, ein Kind der Liebe auch zur höheren Geburt des göttlichen Lebens einzuweihen*).
48 See CD 146 – 147; WG 94 – 95.
49 For a detailed account of how Sofie's prophecy connects what DeVries considers the three sections of the *Christmas Dialogue*, see DeVries, "Schleiermacher's *Christmas Eve Dialogue*," 175 – 79.
50 See CD 107; WG, 49.18 – 19.
51 This is most evident in Ernestine's story (see 5.3.1). It is not out of the question that it was very convenient for interpreters to ignore what Hartlieb calls a "protestant Mariology" (*Geschlechterdifferenz*, 41, 52), in so far as most interpreters were male Protestant theologians interested primarily in Christological questions and involved, at least to some degree, in Catholic-Protestant polemics in the nineteenth and early- or mid-twentieth centuries.

5.2 The *Phaedrus* and the Opening Scene of the *Christmas Dialogue* — 121

was especially important, as is apparent in the *Christmas Dialogue*.[52] In the 'Opening Scene' it is presented in terms of objects (a clavier and book of music) and performance (singing and instrumentals), as well as in terms of an articulated theory of piety. Eduard declares,

> This closer affinity [between music and religion] ... probably lies in this: only in the immediate relation to the highest, to religion, and only in a definite form of the same, does music, without becoming tied to an individual fact, have enough of the given to be intelligible. Christianity is a single theme presented in infinite variations, which, however, are also united by an inner law, and which fall under definite, universal types.[53]
>
> *Diese nähere Verwandtschaft ... liegt wol mit darin, daß nur in der unmittelbaren Beziehung auf das Höchste, auf die Religion, und eine bestimmte Gestalt derselben, die Musik ohne an ein einzelnes Factum geknüpft zu werden, doch Gegebenes genug hat, um verständlich zu sein. Das Christenthum ist ein einziges Thema in unendlichen Variationen dargestellt, die aber auch ein inneres Gesez verbindet, und die unter bestimmte allgemeine Charaktere fallen.*[54]

Improvising on the clavier, Friederike accompanies all three of the women's stories. In the final scene, Josef scolds the men for having given speeches when they could have enjoyed listening to the women sing, and, in the very last sentence of the *Christmas Dialogue*, he bids the company, "Come then, and above all, if she is not already asleep, bring the child along, and let me see your splendors, and let us be merry and sing something pious and joyful."[55]

Third, the transcending of oppositions, which is introduced in the 'Opening Scene' in several ways, is developed throughout the *Christmas Dialogue:* it is set explicitly as an ideal in the 'Conversation,' is emphasized in Ernestine's and Karoline's stories, and is addressed in Ernst's and Eduard's speeches.[56] Indeed, in these two final speeches, redemption itself is described in terms of the lifting away, resolving, or transcending of the oppositions in life.[57] The theoretical culmination, however, is found not in the last speech but in the even higher inarticulate unity presented by Josef at the very end. Moreover, the concrete exam-

---

52 See Albert L. Blackwell, *The Sacred in Music* (Louisville, Ky: Westminster John Knox Press, 1999).
53 *CD* 118–119.
54 *WG* 64.12–18.
55 *CD* 151; *WG* 98.10–13 (*Kommt denn, und das Kind vor allen Dingen mit, wenn es noch nicht schläft, und laßt mich Eure Herrlichkeiten sehn, und laßt uns heiter sein und etwas Frommes und Fröhliches singen*).
56 As we shall see below in chap. 7 (esp. 7.2), the relating and transcending of opposites was a key element in his interpretation of the *Sophist* and, therefore, central to Schleiermacher's Plato.
57 As we shall see below in chaps. 6 and 7, this is closely related to Schleiermacher's interpretation of the association of kinds in the *Sophist*.

ples of how this is done and what it looks like are given in Ernestine's composure in 'Gifts' and in the women described in the 'Stories.' Without these powerful descriptions and concrete examples of what are (according to Schleiermacher) the highest form of Christian piety and the Christian experience of redemption, the men's speeches would remain too abstract and speculative to be as meaningful as they are when read in relation to the whole text.

Again, several other examples could be offered, but what these and other themes have in common is that they are introduced in the 'Opening Scene,' developed throughout the *Christmas Dialogue* (often by being brought into closer connection with other themes), concretely presented and articulated in the women's 'Stories,' brought to the level of theory (not always successfully) in the men's 'Speeches,' and then crystallized, so to speak, in the final page with 'Josef's Unsaying.'

5.2.4 Impulse and Method

> *And precisely because philosophy here appears entirely not just as an inward state, but, according to its nature, as expressing and communicating itself, so also the impulse, which presses it outward from within and which is nothing other than the authentic and divine love that raises itself about every other..., had to be presented and brought to consciousness.*
> —"Introduction to the *Phaedrus*"[58]

Although Schleiermacher would prove to be wrong about the *Phaedrus* being the first of Plato's dialogues, his solution to the perennial puzzle of how the two parts of the *Phaedrus* are related remains intriguing. As we have seen, he argued that in the first part, with the three speeches on *erōs*, Plato presents the *impulse* for doing philosophy—namely, *love*. This impulse, according to Schleiermacher's reading, is something "original and ever-active in the soul."[59] *Erōs* is that "authentic and divine love,"[60] and as impulse it inspires the movement of the soul toward the good and the eternal—and also, necessarily, toward philosophical communication and expression, thus ensuring that philosophy is not done in isolation.

---

[58] PW 1/1:71.36–72.3 (*Und eben weil die Philosophie hier ganz erscheint, nicht nur als innerer Zustand, sondern als ihrer Natur nach sich äußernd und mittheilend, so mußte auch der Trieb zum Bewußtsein gebracht und dargestellt werden*); cf. IDP 58.
[59] PW 1/1:72.10–11 (*... als ein ursprüngliches, immer reges in der Seele*); cf. IDP 59.
[60] PW 1/1:72.4–5 (*... als jene ächte und göttliche Liebe*); cf. IDP 58.

5.2 The *Phaedrus* and the Opening Scene of the *Christmas Dialogue*

In the second part of the *Phaedrus*, Plato presents the *method* for doing philosophy—dialectics, specifically *dialogical-dialectics*. For Schleiermacher's Plato, dialectics is the art of collecting particulars into a larger, living whole—and of collecting limited and conflicting ideas into higher, more unified concepts; furthermore, dialectics is almost always dialogical, thus inherently social. According to Schleiermacher's interpretative principle of the pedagogical progression of ideas, Plato first presents these two most fundamental aspects of philosophy—impulse and method—separately and then, in subsequent dialogues, he gradually integrates them. In short, in the *Phaedrus*, which so many interpreters have taken to be a bifurcated work, Schleiermacher actually found a principle of unity—a way to account for both the distinction of the parts and their unity.

If we keep in mind the importance the *Phaedrus* had for him as well as the specifics of how he interpreted it, then we can gain deeper insight into the importance of the 'Opening Scene' of the *Christmas Dialogue*. Like the first part of the *Phaedrus*, the first part of Schleiermacher's *Dialogue* ('Gifts') provides the impulse of the entire piece (and of the Christmas celebration itself): joy. And, like the second part of the *Phaedrus*, the second part of his *Dialogue* ('Conversation') presents the method of the entire work (and of the Christian life as exemplified in the celebration of Christmas): conversation as loving communication.

Interpreters of the *Christmas Dialogue* have characteristically tried to identify its main theme, usually including joy in their accounts.[61] I suggest that the main theme is given in the title itself—the celebration of Christmas. The *Christmas Dialogue* addresses why (out of what motivation, toward what ends), how, where, by whom and with whom Christmas is celebrated. In 1805, such an approach was novel from both a dogmatic and a literary point of view.[62] Joy is without doubt central to Schleiermacher's presentation, yet I suggest it would be better understood as the impulse within the celebration rather than as just another theme, however central. My cue here is taken from Schleiermacher's interpreta-

---

[61] Tice argued that the main theme is "the love and joy that may be known in the Christian life" ("Schleiermacher's Interpretation of Christmas," 102). For Niebuhr it was "the new life released in the nativity of Christ and the inward appropriation of the same as joy and peace through the feast of Christmas" (*Schleiermacher on Christ and Religion*, 43). Dilthey identified it as beauty and love (see *Leben Schleiermachers*, 1/2:153).
[62] Morgenroth argues that Schleiermacher's *Christmas Dialogue* heralded a modern shift in Protestant thought and practice—a shift from a focus on Christ's death on the cross to a more incarnational and joyful form of piety, one that reflected the emergence of a bourgeois culture and with it the privatization of the celebration of Christmas in Germany (see *Weihnachts-Christentum*, 16, 21, 27, 35–36, 99–101, 106).

tion of the *Phaedrus*, which sees *erōs* as the impulse behind all philosophizing. According to Schleiermacher, the joy evoked and renewed in the celebration of Christmas is the Christian's joy of the experience of having been redeemed; joy is the impulse behind the giving of gifts, as it is the intended effect of such gifts; joy is the impulse that brings to consciousness the meaning of Christmas and that reunites the Christian with the gift that is Christ; joy is the impulse toward conversation, genuine communication, hence community.

As is true of *erōs* in the three speeches that constitute the first part of the *Phaedrus*, so joy is described in several ways in 'Gifts.' By testing and comparing different kinds of joy, that ebullient joy of Christmas may be discovered, a joy that is no stranger to crushing grief. In 'Gifts' Schleiermacher depicts and seeks to arouse (the scene would have been readily recognizable to his intended audience) a sense of joy, but that joy is always also portrayed in terms of an impulse—an impulse that draws people closer, that evokes deeper appreciation and gratitude, that seeks expression, and that is brought to consciousness by means of dialogue. A few examples might be in order. The guests joke and tease as they wait to be let in the room where the gifts are laid out, and then again as they play a guessing game of who gave what to whom and why. This captures not only a light-hearted and playful kind of joy, but it also hints at the joy borne of the intimacy and trust of sharing a history together. Ernestine's gift to the others is to decorate the house and ingeniously arrange everyone's gifts precisely to arouse the joy of her family and friends.[63] There is clear joy over the thoughtfulness and uniqueness of each gift and "heartfelt joy in everything beautiful."[64] 'Gifts' concludes with the expression of the joy of being part of a loving community.

What is true of Schleiermacher's interpretation of *erōs* in the *Phaedrus* is therefore also true of his own depiction of joy in the *Christmas Dialogue*. In chapter three above, we saw how, in Schleiermacher's reading of Plato, *erōs* provides the movement, the impulse, toward philosophical communication and thus ensures that philosophy is not done in isolation but is essentially communicative. So, too, it can it be said of the *Christmas Dialogue* that *joy* provides the move-

---

[63] "So beautiful was the arrangement and so perfect an expression of her [Ernestine's] sense that feeling and eyes alike gravitated toward her, unconsciously and ineluctably. She stood there, half in the dark, intending, herself unnoticed, to take delight in the beloved figures and in their ebullient joy. Yet it was she in whom everyone first took delight" (*CD* 102); WG 44.25–29 (*So schön war die Anordnung und ein so vollkommner Ausdrukk ihres Sinnes, daß unbewußt und nothwendig Gefühl und Auge zu ihr hingezogen wurden. Halb im Dunkel stand sie da, und gedachte sich unbemerkt an den geliebten Gestalten und an der leichten Freude zu ergözen: aber sie war es, an der sich alles zuerst ergözte*).
[64] *CD* 105; WG 47.4 (*herzliche Freude an allem Schönen*).

5.2 The *Phaedrus* and the Opening Scene of the *Christmas Dialogue* — 125

ment, the impulse, toward religious, specifically Christian, communication and expression; *joy* ensures that Christian piety is not experienced in isolation but is essentially communicative and social. If joy is the impulse to the celebration of Christmas, conversation as reciprocal, loving communication is the vehicle, the method.

As is true with the speeches on *erōs* in the *Phaedrus*, so here the comparison of the many feelings and expressions of joy raises the question of authenticity. This, in turn, creates a transition to the 'Conversation,' to the need to sort it all out. The 'Conversation' is a dialogue within the *Christmas Dialogue*. It introduces the method of the celebration of Christmas. It is a sustained dialogue in the sense of a living, genuinely reciprocal conversation, and it picks up the scattered pieces of what had proceeded, putting them together and arriving at a higher understanding (and experience) of Christmas joy.

The 'Conversation' begins with a misguided presumption regarding joy. Ernst, overly exuberant, is pained by the fact that not all his friends can feel the elevated, lively joy that he and his fiancée, Friederike, feel in anticipation of their wedding day. Eduard protests such presumption, sarcastically chiding Ernst for his enthusiasm and pointing to an "authentic enthusiasm" (*jede ächte Begeisterung*),[65] by which he means the mature joy and intimate love that is always present and ever excitable in a long and loving marriage. Leonhardt, for his part, is concerned that Sofie's joy—as expressed through the cluttered diorama she has constructed—is a potentially fanatical distortion that springs from a conflation of the sacred story with mere fables. He asks whether it represents a state of intoxication or superstition like that which Catholics contract, in part because they so conflate art and religion. Karoline also distinguishes between particular joys and a deeper, universal joy:

> My feeling, at least, quite definitely distinguishes that higher, more universal joy from the most spirited participation in what is happening, or is about to happen, to you all, dear friends. If anything, I would say that the particular joy is heightened by means of the universal joy. If the beautiful and joyful stand out at a time when we are most deeply conscious of the greatest and most beautiful, then the latter communicates itself to the former, and, with respect to the great salvation of the world, all love and goodness receive a greater meaning. Yes, I still feel it vividly, just as I have once experienced it. That higher, more universal joy blossoms out in us unimpeded even next to the deepest sorrow, and it purges and soothes the sorrow without being destroyed by it—so original is this joy, and so immediately grounded in something imperishable.[66]

---

65 *CD* 109; *WG* 51.15.
66 *CD* 117–118.

> *Mein Gefühl wenigstens unterscheidet sehr bestimmt jene höhere allgemeinere Freude von der lebhaftesten Theilnahme an dem, was Euch Allen, ihr lieben Freunde, begegnet oder bevorsteht; und ich möchte eher sagen, diese wird durch jene erhöht. Wenn das Schöne und Erfreuliche zu einer Zeit vor uns steht, wo wir uns des Größten und Schönsten aufs innigste bewußt sind: so theilt sich dieses jenem mit, und in Beziehung auf das große Heil der Welt, bekommt alles Liebe und Gute eine größere Bedeutung. Ja ich fühle es noch lebhaft, wie ich es schon einmal erlebt habe, daß auch neben dem tiefsten Schmerz jene Freude ungehindert in uns aufblüht, und daß sie ihn reiniget und besänftiget, ohne von ihm gestört zu werden, so ursprünglich ist sie, und unmittelbar in einem Unvergänglichen gegründet.*[67]

Significantly, we find here in the voice of a woman a theory of Christian joy that arguably comes closest to Schleiermacher's own, which serves to highlight the mistake so many interpreters have made in seeking Schleiermacher's own view in one (or all) of the men's 'Speeches.'

In the *Christmas Dialogue*, the dialectical method remains essentially Socratic-Platonic, as Schleiermacher understood that, but the dialogue form has been expanded and modernized.[68] It is expanded in the sense that the reciprocal communication is no longer set as a form of instruction but as a conversation among equals (with the exception of Sofie) and in the sense that the circle of interlocutors now includes women and a child. Consequently, it is modernized in that women are full and equal participants in the conversation, which is characterized by the free revelation of ideas and emotions as well as the freedom to check another's ideas and emotions. What is striking here is the trust among friends (and lovers) and the respect for each person's inner freedom. The difference, for Schleiermacher, is that here, in the gathering of intimate friends on Christmas Eve, the dialogic method is anchored in a loving religious community.

This set of conditions, an even more idealized form of Platonic dialogue than that presented in his *Introductions*, seemed to grant Schleiermacher permission to introduce something that he had elided in *Platons Werke*. As we have seen in chapter four, although there are arguably two forms of dialectics (a speculative one done in isolation, and an inherently communicative one), Schleiermacher continually resisted and elided the former, emphasizing instead the latter, which he took to be the truly Socratic form: spoken, articulated dialogue. The bonds of trust, love, and intimacy that Schleiermacher depicted in the 'Opening Scene' of *Christmas Dialogue* allow for yet another form of expansion of the Pla-

---

67 WG 63.10–21.
68 In his introduction to the *Weihnachtsfeier*, Georg Wehrung used the term "der modernisierte Platonismus," but he was referring to Eduard's speech in particular and Eduard's insistence on a concrete form of the Redeemer ("Einführung," in *Die Weihnachtsfeier. Ein Gespräch* [Darmstadt: Wissenschaftliche Buchgemeinschaft, 1953], xv). I am using the term in another sense.

tonic dialogue. For, however crucial conversation is, it is not the full expression of Christmas joy, nor is it the sole mode of communicating Christmas joy. Schleiermacher only occasionally admitted something similar to this in Plato, for instance in the *Phaedo*, where he noted Socrates's affirmation of life simply by being present, by engaging in ritual in the presence of his friends.

In the *Christmas Dialogue*, however, such nonverbal forms of communication play an integral, not just a marginal, role. I have already given two instances of this: when the company silently beholds one other after singing, and when each beholds Ernestine and takes delight in her. Here, in the 'Conversation,' Eduard says,

> For each beautiful feeling comes forth perfectly only when we have found the sound for it. I do not mean the word but rather the sound in the strict sense, since the word can always only be a mediated expression, only a plastic element, if I may so put it. And religious feeling is most closely akin to music. People so often talk about how the corporate expression of this feeling could be again revived, but almost no one thinks about how easily the best outcome might occur if singing were reset in a more appropriate relationship to the word. What the word has made clear, the sound must make alive, capturing it as harmony and carrying it over immediately into the inner being.[69]

> *Denn jedes schöne Gefühl tritt nur dann recht vollständig hervor, wenn wir den Ton dafür gefunden haben; nicht das Wort, dies kann immer nur ein mittelbarer Ausdrukk sein, nur ein plastisches Element, wenn ich so sagen darf, sondern den Ton im eigentliehen Sinne. Und grade dem religiösen Gefühl ist die Musik am nächsten verwandt. Man redet so viel darüber hin und her, wie man dem gemein samen Ausdrukk desselben wieder aufhelfen könnte; aber fast Niemand denkt daran, daß leicht das Beste dadurch geschehen möchte, wenn man den Gesang wieder in ein richtigeres Verhältniß sezte gegen das Wort. Was das Wort klar gemacht hat, muß der Ton lebendig machen, unmittelbar in das ganze innere Wesen als Harmonie übertragen und festhalten.*[70]

Nonverbal forms of dialogue appear again later in the *Christmas Dialogue:* for instance, in the "half-unconscious dialogue of love and longing"[71] between the mother and child in the first story; in Friederike's claim that she is not good at storytelling and thus prefers to accompany the other women's stories with improvisation on the piano; and, fundamentally, in the very person of Sofie. Finally, nonverbal communication closes the entire dialogue, when the long-anticipated Josef shows up, chides the men for having tried to give scientifically articulated accounts of Christmas, and invites them into song. Yet the nonverbal

---

69 *CD* 118.
70 *WG* 63.30–64.6.
71 *CD* 128; *WG* 73.18 (... *in einem halb unbewußten Gespräch von Liebe und Sehnsucht*).

in the *Christmas Dialogue* remains dialogical: it is always communicative and interpersonal, never solitary or speculative.

5.3 The *Symposium* and the Women's Stories

Table 6: The Second Trilogy of *PW* and the Women's Stories in *CD*

Platons Werke	Role in Platonic *corpus*	Christmas Dialogue	Role in *Dialogue*
Second trilogy: focus on *Symposium*, the center of the center	The 'object' of philosophy: the ideas Vehicle: Love (*erōs*)	Part 3: Three stories by women	The object of Christmas: the Christ-child, new life Vehicle: Love (*Mutterlieb*)

One reigning assumption has been that, if Schleiermacher indeed modeled his *Christmas Dialogue* on a Platonic dialogue, the key to that would be found in the men's speeches, and the most likely archetype would be the *Symposium*, presumably because it includes speeches given by men at a celebratory feast. Schleiermacher's own interpretation of the *Symposium*, as developed in his "General Introduction" and his "Introduction to the *Symposium*," does not lend support to such assumptions. If we heed Schleiermacher's reading of Plato's *Symposium*, then it at once becomes evident that, with regard to the *Christmas Dialogue*, the proper analogue for the *Symposium* is neither the men's 'Speeches' at the end nor the *Dialogue* as a whole but is instead the section comprising the women's 'Stories.' This is true not only regarding structure and placement, but also regarding content, form, and function. The clues, again, are to be found in Schleiermacher's own interpretation of Plato.

Particularly revealing, for our present purposes, is how Schleiermacher viewed the *Symposium*'s place within the Platonic *corpus*. Schleiermacher located the *Symposium* within a sub-trilogy at the center of his middle trilogy—in other words, together with the *Sophist* and *Statesman*, it occupies the center of the center, the heart of the heart, of Plato's *corpus* (see table 3). Moreover, we know that, for Schleiermacher, place has everything to do with purpose and function. The *Symposium* completes the crucial sub-trilogy.

According to Schleiermacher, the main purpose of the middle trilogy in Plato's works is to present the *object* of philosophy—the ideas.[72] The climax of this philosophical presentation is found in the *Sophist*. The particular importance of

---

[72] See Schleiermacher, "Introduction to the *Gorgias*," *IDP* 170–71; *PW* 2/1:10–11.

the *Symposium* lies in how, after the more speculative flights of the *Sophist*, it humanizes Socrates once again by bringing the philosopher back to earth. Plato, Schleiermacher wrote, wanted to present "an image of the philosopher depicted in the person of *Socrates*."[73] So while the purpose of the middle trilogy in general is to present the object of philosophy, the purpose of the *Symposium* in particular is to present the philosopher who grasps the true and the good in a concrete, human way. Recall that, in Schleiermacher's words, the point is "not the absolute being and nature of wisdom, but its life and its appearance in the mortal life of the visible person, in whom wisdom itself … has put on mortality."[74] Schleiermacher proposed that Plato had wearied of the form used in the *Sophist* and *Statesman* and wanted to present Socrates in the "tireless enthusiasm for contemplation and in joyous communication."[75]

Later on in his "Introduction to the *Symposium*," reflecting on Diotima's speech, Schleiermacher concluded, it was clear that "in the entire proceeding is seen the uninterrupted progression, not only from the pleasure in the beauty of the body … up to the immediate pleasure in eternal beauty, … but also from the generation of natural life … up to the participation … in that immediate knowledge comprehending all other good in itself and alone making blessed."[76] Finally, Schleiermacher, in his "Introduction to the *Phaedo*," when summarizing the idea of *erōs* as portrayed in the *Symposium*, described it as the endeavour "to connect the immortal with the mortal."[77]

In his *Christmas Dialogue*, Schleiermacher pursued all of these same principles in the course of the women's 'Stories,' except this time as applied not to philosophy but to the Christmas celebration. First, with regard to placement in the overall structure of the work, the women's 'Stories' are at the center, at the heart, of the *Christmas Dialogue* (whether one employs the tripartite or quintpartite division). Second, the content of each story has to do with the main "object" of the Christmas feast—the Christ-child, the appearance of the Redeemer in the world,

---

[73] *EÜP* 274 (*ein Bild des Philosophen darstellt in der Person des Sokrates*); cf. *IDP* 278.
[74] *EÜP* 276; cf. *IDP* 279–80 (for German text see above, chap. 4, 99–100).
[75] *EÜP* 274; cf. *IDP* 278 (for German text see above, chap. 4, 99n71).
[76] *EÜP* 277–78 (*… in der ganzen Verhandlung die ununterbrochene Steigerung sowohl von dem Wohlgefallen an der Schönheit des Leibes durch das an jedem größeren Besonderen und Mannigfaltigen bis zu dem unmittelbaren an der ewigen Schönheit, welche sich, ohne daß das Besondere und Einzelne mehr gesehen werde, dem in dieser Ordnung geübten und geschärften Auge des Geistes darstellt, als auch von der Erzeugung des natürlichen Lebens durch die der richtigen Vorstellung und der bürgerlichen Tugend bis zu der über jede Meisterschaft im Einzelnen weit hinausgehenden Teilnahme an jener allein beseligenden und alles andere Gute unter sich begreifenden unmittelbaren Erkenntnis*); cf. *IDP* 281–82.
[77] *IDP* 294; *EÜP* 289 (*… das Unsterbliche mit dem Sterblichen zu verbinden*).

and the experience of new life. At the same time, third, the form of the stories, like that of the *Symposium* according to Schleiermacher's interpretation, is not dialectical in a sophistical sense (Leonhardt's approach), nor scientific, nor yet abstract. The women's stories are concrete, warm, familiar, and deeply human—incarnational in the sense in which he described Socrates in his "Introduction to the *Symposium*." Fourth, if one purpose of the 'Stories' is to present the incarnation in a vivid and accessible way so as to evoke an affective response, another purpose of all the stories taken together is to set forth a kind of progression and transformation: from pleasure in the physical beauty of mother and child to a participation in that "dialogue of love" (Ernestine's story); from a natural, human experience of love to a more eternal kind of love (Agnes's story); and from mortal suffering and loss into joy and new life (Karoline's story). Mother-love is the vehicle, so to speak, of such progression and transformation. And so, fifth and finally, the main topic of each story is love, in this case *Mutterlieb* rather than *erōs*, but like *erōs* it is a love that desires and transcends.

I shall touch briefly on each story, demonstrating, as space will allow, how each accomplishes the basic commitments of the *Symposium*, as Schleiermacher interpreted that dialogue. Particular focus will be on the joyful exchange of gifts, the holding together of oppositions, and Christian love as essentially mother-love.

5.3.1 Ernestine's Story

The first story is set against a background of tragedy, the crushing stress of tragedy on a family, and the experience of alienation from institutional religion.[78] Recalling an encounter in a church on a Christmas Eve when she was a child, Ernestine relates,

> There I spotted in an open choir stall, under a beautiful old monument, a woman with a small child in her lap. She appeared to pay little attention to the preacher, the songs, or anything around her, but rather to be deeply lost in her own thoughts, and her eyes were steadfastly directed to the child. I was drawn irresistibly to her, … The child, too, appeared to me uncommonly lovely. He moved in a lively way, but was quiet, and appeared to me to be grasped in a half-unconscious dialogue of love and longing with his mother. Now I had living figures of the beautiful pictures of Mary and the Christ-child.[79]

---

[78] *CD* 126–29; *WG* 72–74.
[79] *CD* 127–128.

> *Da erblikte ich in einem offnen Stuhl, unter einem schönen alten Monument, eine Frau mit einen kleinen Kinde auf ihrem Schooß. Sie schien des Predigers, des Gesanges und alles um sie her wenig zu achten, sondern nur in ihren eigenen Gedanken tief versenkt zu sein, und ihre Augen waren unverwandt auf das Kind gerichtet. Es zog mich unwiderstehlich zu ihr,... So schien mir auch das Kind ungemein lieblich, es regte sich lebendig aber still und schien mir in einem halb unbewußten Gespräch von Liebe und Sehnsucht mit der Mutter begriffen. Nun hatte ich lebendige Gestalten zu den schönen Bildern von Maria und dem Kinde.*[80]

Here beauty plays an important role, as it does in the *Symposium*. Before the girl is a beautiful, living image of the Madonna with babe in her lap. Ernestine reveals that the woman in the story would become her sister-in-law, hence the baby her nephew. At this point in the *Christmas Dialogue*, Friederike played a song about Mary set to verse by Novalis, and Sofie brings into the room two portraits of her Aunt Kornelia and cousin, one of which had been painted just before he was to "to fall as one of the last victims to the bloodthirsty time."[81] The narrator explains that this young man, the baby-boy Ernestine encountered in his mother's lap on that Christmas Eve, would die in battle and become "the son of sorrows" (*Schmerzenssohn*),[82] and so the scene also evokes the *Pietà*.

At the center of this story is a dialogue between strangers, a woman and a girl, who would later become friends as well as sisters-in-law. It takes place in a corner of the church that, because of the beauty of this mother and baby, stands in stark contrast to the rest of the scene. As Ernestine recounts it, elsewhere in the church there is no apparent joy, no genuine communication, no beautiful music—only a cacophony caused, on the outside, by rowdy boys with cheap Christmas toys, and on the inside, by the empty words of a preacher and a sorry lack of harmony on the part of the choir. (The grim, heavy grayness of institutional religion also stands in contrast to the illuminated home of the mature Ernestine and Eduard, which is described in such detail in 'Gifts.') Here, too, is Ernestine, the mother of Sofie, as a young girl—and apparently every bit as precocious as her own daughter would be, thereby underscoring that Ernestine was probably correct earlier in the evening when in the 'Conversation' she had insisted that Sofie's early piety was not a distortion, as Leonhardt feared. On the contrary, Sofie's intensity would inevitably grow into the serenity of Ernestine, whose own grace and wisdom was shaped by this woman she encountered on a Christmas Eve long before.

---

80 WG 72.35–73.5,16–20.
81 CD 129 (slightly altered); WG 74.28–29 (... *um als eins der lezten Opfer der blutdürstigsten Zeit zu fallen*). The threat of war and invasion is an undercurrent throughout the *Christmas Dialogue*. Napoleon's army would capture Halle in October 1806.
82 CD 129; WG 74.26.

In addition to this one quite articulate dialogue (between the woman and the girl), there are two nonverbal dialogues: a "half-unconscious dialogue of love and longing"[83] (between mother and baby), and another dialogue in the exchange of gifts (from the girl to the baby, and from the woman to the girl). As the mother says, "today everyone gives, and all for the sake of the child."[84]

In Ernestine's story, several oppositions are held together: *joy and grief*—the joy in and of the child, and the anticipated suffering because that child will die as a young man in war; *present and future*—the moment insofar as it was transformative for the young Ernestine, and the anticipated death of the son, as well as the future marriage of the girl and of the woman's younger brother, standing behind her undetected in the shadows. Mother-love is the ideal, but it is not restricted to the biological or to a particular gender. *Mutterlieb* extends to the stranger, to the friend, and to the spouse.

5.3.2 Agnes's Story

In the second story, Agnes (the mother of the two young boys at the party, who is pregnant but whose marital status is not given) recalls a Christmas Eve celebrated at her brother's house and the impromptu home baptism of her new-born nephew.[85] The focus is on Christmas joy, which is both expressed in and excited by the exchange of gifts. Again, we find Schleiermacher's emphasis on the holding together of oppositions, albeit on a much lighter note than in the previous story—jest and earnestness, the eternal and temporal, the present and the future, the individual and the community.

Agnes tells of an articulate dialogue that took place that Christmas—of a playful conversation among those there to celebrate the holiday, which led to a playful presentation of gifts to the baby. The playful, intimate form of joy she describes calls to mind the conviviality described in the 'Gifts.' Agnes also refers to an nonverbal form of communication in which the gathered company expresses its joy, gratitude, and hopes by means of religious ritual and communal gesture: "As we all laid hands on the child, according to the fine, old local custom, it was as if streams of heavenly love and delight converged on the head and heart of the child as a new focal point, and so would radiate again in all directions. It was certainly the *shared feeling* that they are there enkindling a

---

83 See above, n. 71.
84 *CD* 128; *WG* 73.27–28 (... heute giebt ja Jedermann, und alles um eines Kindes willen).
85 *CD* 129–33; *WG* 75–78.

new life."⁸⁶ She went on to reflect, "For *I do not have the words to describe* how deeply and inwardly I felt on that occasion that every serene joy is religion. Love, delight, and devotion are notes from one perfect harmony that can follow one another in any number of ways or can sound together."⁸⁷

Here religion, as expressed and performed in the warmth of a close circle of family and friends in a home, stands in contrast to the cold church presented in the first story. There is, therefore, a progression of sorts from exterior forms of worship to private, intimate, and interior forms.⁸⁸ And yet the institutional church is presented in a more positive light than in the previous story, since Agnes's brother is an ordained minister.

In Agnes's story, mother-love is presented in prophetic terms (not unlike the Lukan Mary). The mother is the prophet who sees the whole person in the child and the eternal in the present. Yet emphasis is also on communal love. Those present at the home baptism are all witnesses who thereby promise to be present as the child grows in Christian faith throughout his life. This familial love into which the child is born will lead to a "higher birth" (*zur höheren Geburt*)⁸⁹ and thus it remains a kind of maternal love.⁹⁰ In the final speech, Eduard will return to this theme of a higher birth.⁹¹

---

86 CD 132, emphasis added; WG 78.1–5 (*Als wir nun Alle dem Kinde die Hände auflegten, nach der dortigen guten alten Sitte, so war es als ob die Strahlen der himmlischen Liebe und Lust sich auf dem Haupt und Herzen des Kindes als einem neuen Brennpunkt vereinigten, und es war gewiß das gemeinschaftliche Gefühl, daß sie dort ein neues Leben entzünden*).
87 CD 132, emphasis added; WG 78.17–21 (*Denn ich weiß mit Worten nicht zu beschreiben, wie tief und innig ich damals fühlte, daß jede heitere Freude Religion ist, daß Liebe, Lust und Andacht Töne aus Einer vollkommnen Harmonie sind, die auf jede Weise einander folgen und zusammenschlagen können*).
88 See Nowak's brief discussion of the privatization of Christmas celebrations at that time and the new laws governing Christmas services in eighteenth-century German lands (*Schleiermacher*, 164–65).
89 CD 132; WG 77.34.
90 Schleiermacher had written in his *Speeches* (1799): "Religion was the maternal womb in whose holy darkness my young life was nourished and prepared for the world still closed to it" (OR¹ 84)/ *Religion war der mütterliche Leib in deßen heiligem Dunkel mein junges Leben genährt und auf die ihm noch verschloßene Welt vorbereitet wurde* (R¹ 17 [KGA 1/2:195.5–7]).
91 See CD 149; WG 96.29.

5.3.3 Karoline's Story

In the third story, told by Karoline, the theme of death and grief returns, although this time the death is imminent and the grief all too real.[92] She recounts a Christmas Eve spent at the home of a friend, Charlotte, known to and loved by many of those to whom she tells the story. As in the previous two stories, gift-giving plays an important role. Interestingly, Karoline describes a tradition of gift-giving as practiced in a particular locale, designed so as to heighten the sense of anticipation and joy. That year the exchange had to be suspended due to impending death of Charlotte's infant son, her "darling."

The Madonna image also returns in Charlotte's person. Leonhardt prods, is this not "an inverted Mary, who begins with the deepest sorrows of motherhood—with the *Stabat Mater*—and ends with joy in the divine child?"[93] Charlotte embraces within herself the essence of Christian piety, as Schleiermacher understood it: serenity, sensibility, steadiness, and a certain stoicism. Again, mother-love goes beyond the biological in that Charlotte, with calm resignation, hands over the desperately ill child to God. She is, in a sense, portrayed as a kind of Socrates. Indeed, the themes strongly call to mind Schleiermacher's interpretation of the *Phaedo*, in that we find here the joining of the mortal with the immortal, the giving of the mortal over to the eternal and immortal—except that in this case the child miraculously recovers, and so Charlotte and all those present find new life and joy. Karoline recounts Charlotte's words and actions:

> 'It touched me poignantly and sweetly to send an angel to heaven at the time when we celebrate the sending of the greatest one to earth. Now both come to me at the same time, given immediately by God. On the celebration of the new birth of the world, unto me is born to a new life the darling of my heart. Yes, he lives—there is no doubt about it,' [Charlotte] said, while she bent over him, hardly daring to touch him or to press his hand to her lips. 'Even so, he remains an angel,' she said after a while. 'He is purified through his pains. He is, as it were, drawn forth through death and sanctified to a higher life. He is to me a special gift of grace, a heavenly child, because I had already dedicated him to heaven.'[94]

> *Es rührte mich wehmüthig und versüßend, einen Engel zum Himmel zu senden, zu der Zeit, wo wir die Sendung des größten auf die Erde feiern. Nun kommen mir beide zugleich unmittelbar von Gott geschenkt. Am Feste der Wiedergeburt der Welt wird mir der Liebling meines Herzens zu einem neuen Leben geboren. Ja er lebt, es ist kein Zweifel daran, sagte sie, indem sie sich zu ihm überbog und doch kaum wagte ihn zu berühren, und seiner Hand ihre Lippe aufzudrücken.*

---

92 *CD* 133–36; *WG* 79–82.
93 *CD* 136; *WG* 82.5–7 (… *eine umgekehrte Maria, die mit dem tiefsten Mutterleiden, mit dem Stabatmater anfängt und mit der Freude an dem göttlichen Kinde endigt?*).
94 *CD* 135–36.

> *Er bleibe auch so ein Engel, sagte sie nach einer Weile, er ist geläutert durch die Schmerzen, er ist wie durch den Tod hindurchgedrungen und zu einem höheren Leben geheiligt. Er ist mir ein besonderes Gnadengeschenk, ein himmlisches Kind, weil ich ihn schon dem Himmel geweiht hatte.*[95]

The mother-love depicted in this last story could fairly be suspected as an attempt to restrict women by over-idealizing the feminine and motherhood. After all, Charlotte is lauded for attending to the needs of others and even to holiday festivities while she cared for a dying child, and then she relinquished the child with equilibrium. That notwithstanding, it should not go unnoted that Charlotte's paroxysm of grief, which is then quickly transformed into joy, mirrors Schleiermacher's own experience that served as a catalyst for penning the *Christmas Dialogue*. His intense, agonizing grief over the end of his relationship with Eleonore was suddenly broken when he attended that Dülon concert on a cold December night. For at least the second time in the *Christmas Dialogue*, we find Schleiermacher's own theory and sentiments expressed through a female character.[96]

In summary, the women's stories are narrated histories that present clear images, evoke specific emotional responses, set forth embodied ideals of Christian piety, raise serious questions, and prompt further conversation. Furthermore, each contains a dialogue concerning the meaning of Christmas and the significance of the Christ-child. In depicting the incarnation in warm, deeply human ways and in describing the transformative effects of these encounters with mother-love, the stories play an essential role in the *Christmas Dialogue*. Finally, the women—both the narrators and the women whose stories they narrate—play a similar role to that of Socrates in the *Symposium:* they themselves embody and present the ideal (in this case, "wisdom" as Christian piety) in their own characters, and they grasp in their understanding and in their very being the main "object" (in this case, the Christ-child and the gift of redemption).

---

95 WG 81.24–35.
96 Twenty-years later, in a sermon given at the graveside of his own beloved son, nine-year-old Nathanael, Schleiermacher would himself express and embody the very attitude he ascribed to Charlotte here in the *Christmas Dialogue*. See Albert L. Blackwell, "Schleiermacher's Sermon at Nathanael's Grave," *Journal of Religion* 57, no. 1 (1977): 64–75.

5.4 The *Republic* and the Men's Speeches

Table 7: The Third Trilogy and the Men's Speeches

Platons Werke	Role in Platonic *corpus*	Christmas Dialogue	Role in *Dialogue*
Third trilogy: focus on the *Republic*	Final scientific presentation of what had been presented in mythic form	Part 4: Three speeches by men on Christmas and the problem of history	'Scientific' (theological) presentation of basic themes in pts. 1–3

At last, we arrive at the later portion of the *Christmas Dialogue*, which has conventionally been so privileged by interpreters, most of whom have assumed that the Platonic dialogue form, if it is there at all, is to be found in the men's speeches at the end. The parallels to the *Symposium* seem clearly given in the fact that men at a celebratory feast give speeches on an assigned topic. Scholars have noted the passing allusions to the *Symposium* as further evidence of this parallel.[97] What is telling is that other allusions, which might support a more modernized and expanded understanding of the Platonic dialogue form, have gone apparently unnoticed. For instance, the fact that the women are not relegated to another room—indeed, that the women are drinking with the men, that they are to judge the speeches, that one of them sets the topic, and that they join in the conversation and offer critiques—all this stands in contrast to the *Symposium* (176e). Nevertheless, the argument that needs to be made here should be based not on passing allusions but instead on Schleiermacher's own principles for interpreting Plato.

Returning to the template suggested by Schleiermacher's ordering of Plato's dialogues (see tables 4 & 7), new insight into the men's 'Speeches' at the end of the *Christmas Dialogue* can be gained if we read them as performing a parallel role to that of the third trilogy—*The Republic*, *Timaeus*, and *Critias*. When undertaking a preliminary survey of all the authentic dialogues, Schleiermacher thought that these three alone stood out by their "objective scientific presenta-

---

[97] For instance, Leonhardt's wish to go first seems to allude to *Symposium* 177e: "[A]ccording to our custom, I, as the youngest, may not decline being the first to speak. And I prefer it that way, partly because the imperfect speech is most easily blown away by a better one, and partly because I will most surely experience the joy of anticipating the first thoughts of another" (*CD* 137); WG 83.23–27 (*nach unserer Gewohnheit werde ich, als der Jüngste, mich nicht weigern dürfen, auch der erste zu sein. Und ich bin es um so lieber, theils weil die unvollkommene Rede so am leichtesten von einer bessern verweht wird; theils weil ich so am sichersten die Freude genieße, einem Andern den ersten Gedanken vorwegzunehmen*).

tion" (*eine objective wissenschaftliche Darstellung*).⁹⁸ Hence, according to his interpretive principle of the pedagogical progression of ideas, they must certainly form the final trilogy.⁹⁹ According to Schleiermacher, Plato's aim was to bring the novice learner to knowledge, a process that begins by stimulating impulse and spontaneous activity (*Phaedrus*), progresses by transforming myth into progressive forms of dialectics until concepts become more clear and eventually more unified (the middle trilogy, including the *Symposium*), so that they become expressed and understood through scientific formulation (ethics and physics, as presented in the *Republic* and *Timaeus*, respectively). Anyone engaged in a serious study of Plato, he was convinced, will recognize "the gradual development and formation of the Platonic myths out of *one* fundamental myth [*aus Einem Grundmythos*], even as that transition of much that is mythic into the scientific."¹⁰⁰

This interpretive principle can be applied to the *Christmas Dialogue* and, in particular, to the relationship between the women's 'Stories' and the men's 'Speeches.' Sofie's diorama would thus play the role of myth, the women's stories the transformation of that myth as it matures through realization of the "object," and the men's speeches the final yet incomplete scientific formulation of the same. This interpretation, however, would seem once again to diminish the importance of the women's stories—unless we keep in mind Schleiermacher's understanding of the relation between myth and science. First and foremost, for him myth had a propaedeutic function in that it is followed, *but not superseded*, by scientific formulation.¹⁰¹ That is demonstrated not only in the ordering of the dialogues but also in the fact that Plato continued to employ myth in the *Re*-

---

98 *PW* 1/1:53.1; cf. *IDP* 41.
99 See above, 3.5.1, 3.5.2.
100 *PW* 1/1:55.9–12 (... *die allmähliche Entwikklung und Ausbildung der platonischen Mythen aus Einem Grundmythos, eben wie jenes Uebergehen manches Mythischen in Wissenschaftliches*); cf. *IDP* 43.
101 Schleiermacher would retain this basic idea and develop it into a theory of religious language. In his Introduction to *The Christian Faith* (1830–31), Schleiermacher distinguished the poetic, rhetorical, and descriptively didactic forms of expression. The last of these, he explains in §16.1, "remains distinct from the two others, and is made up of the two put together, as a derivative and secondary form" (*The Christian Faith*, trans. H. R. Mackintosh and J. S. Stewart [Edinburgh: Clark, 1928], 79)/... *darstellend belehrende von jenen beiden zurükbleibend und aus ihnen zusammengesezt als ein abgeleitetes und zweites* (*Der christliche Glaube nach den Grundsätzen der evangelischen Kirche in Zusammenhange dargestellt*, in *KGA* 1/13, ed. Rolf Schäfer [Berlin: Walter de Gruyter, 2003], 1:131.12–14). For a salient discussion of these forms of religious speech and their relationship, see Dawn DeVries, *Jesus Christ in the Preaching of Calvin and Schleiermacher* (Louisville, Kentucky: Westminster John Knox Press, 1996), 48–58.

public and in the *Timaeus*. Second, Schleiermacher, along with the other Romantics, held a positive attitude towards myth and did not reject it as either speculative or superstitious. Myth conveys simple principles in evocative and pregnant form, anticipating scientific formulation and exciting the mind as both lure and impetus. Third and finally, the women's stories are actual histories, not fables; they are not purely 'mythic' but are narratives that frame concepts clearly and concretely. They are therefore to be differentiated from the myths and fables referred to in the opening scene, not only because of their historical nature, but also because they are infused with reason, coherence, and clarity. In the women narrators and in the stories they tell, the two series of knowing and acting come together, as Schleiermacher argued they do in the middle dialogues. The two-fold meaning of the German word *Geschichte* (story and history) was itself a topic in the 'Conversation,' and how the new historical-critical method threatened the trustworthiness of the Christian narrative about the birth of Christ is the starting point for each of the men's speeches. Indeed, the underlying issue being addressed in the *Christmas Dialogue* is precisely the problem that modern historical consciousness posed to Christian faith.

In short, just as in his interpretation of Plato's dialogues Schleiermacher distinguished but never separated myth, knowing and acting, and theory—so, too, in his *Christmas Dialogue* he held together the content and principles of the stories and speeches, however different in form they may be. Nor is it the case, as Niebuhr argued, that the men's speeches provide answers to the questions raised by the women's stories. Nor yet is it, as Richardson maintained, that the stories are about the finite and the speeches about the infinite, since Agnes and Karoline discuss the infinite, and the men discuss the finite. The relationship is better understood, I suggest, as the relationship between the concrete (the 'Stories') and abstract (the 'Speeches').[102] None of this is to deny that the men's speeches were not intended to imitate Platonic speeches from the *Phraedrus* or *Symposium*, as Schleiermacher's comment in the epigraph above, where he distinguishes Platonic form and Platonic spirit, suggests. Yet there, notably, he undermines the status of Leonhardt's speech and, although Eduard's speech (the third) most closely mirrors his own interpretation of Plato and the coincidence of opposi-

---

[102] Throughout his career, Schleiermacher was consistent in his insistence that the concrete and the abstract be held together: it was there in his *Speeches on Religion*; in his lectures on dialectics, hermeneutics, and ethics; and in his theological *magnum opus*, *The Christian Faith*. Indeed, *The Christian Faith* is structured according to this relationship: the most concrete experience, he explained, is the Christian experience of having been redeemed by Christ, and the propositions describing that are found in part 2, which he insisted was the heart of his entire dogmatic system.

tions, he pulls it back from the speculative and purely theoretical. It is not the final word.

Space does not permit, nor does my double thesis require, an investigation of the three men's speeches. Nevertheless, a few hints may invite further discussion. The approach I propose here would entail at least three things: first, a close analysis of the connection of ideas presented in the three 'Speeches' with ideas already introduced and developed earlier in the *Christmas Dialogue*; second, a careful consideration of how Schleiermacher understood Plato's use of irony to frustrate the reader; and third, keen attention to the actual role of the women throughout this section of the *Dialogue*. And then, of course, with all this in view, further reflection is needed on the significance of Josef's 'Unsaying' for the men's 'Speeches.'

5.5 Josef's Unsaying

The brief conclusion of the *Christmas Dialogue* begins with the entrance of Josef and consists of an anti-speech he gives, ending with an invitation to song and celebration.[103] As noted above, one of the strengths of the quintpartite division is that demands proper attention be given to this final scene (part 5). Josef is first mentioned in the transition between 'Stories' and 'Speeches,' when Eduard, as the host, refused to let anyone of his party wander off with an interloping group of acquaintances that had briefly crashed their Christmas party: Josef was expected and had been promised he would find them all there.[104] Josef finally appears towards the end of the third (Eduard's) speech and, when asked to offer his own speech, declines. He chastises the men for having given speeches when they could have simply enjoyed the company of the women, and he singles out Leonhardt, the skeptic, as the 'bad principle' among them. "For me, all forms are too rigid," he declares, "and all speech too tedious and cold."[105]

Much of Josef's speech has already been quoted above, where I sketch out how the 'Seeds' of the opening scene are developed until the point when they reach full development and are crystallized in Josef's words and in his person (see 5.2.3). Josef's words are also significant for the complexity they introduce in interpreting the text and for how they reverberate back throughout the entire

---

103 See *CD* 150–51; *WG* 97–98.
104 See *CD* 136; *WG* 82. The rowdy party crashers are likely an allusion to *Symposium* 212c–d and 223b.
105 *CD* 150; *WG* 97.20–22 (*Alle Formen sind mir zu steif, und alles Reden zu langweilig und kalt*).

text, joining the end of the Christmas Eve celebration with its beginning. In chiding the men and exalting the women, Josef challenges the temptation to value the men's speeches more than the women's stories. It is the women who have grasped the meaning of Christmas, hence the essence of the Christmas celebration. While it would be far too simplistic to take this as the sole and final assessment of the men's speeches, it should not be simply ignored, and the degree to which it has been is telling.

Even more compelling is Josef's apophasis. He reminds his friends of the "speechless" nature of the subject matter (the incarnation), which, he admits, "demands or generates in me a speechless joy, and in my joy I can only smile and cheer like a child."[106] This is not necessarily to reject *any* attempt to articulate the meaning of the birth of Christ, or its relevance for Christians in 1805, but it does point to the inherently limited and provisional nature of any such attempt. Josef's apophatic speech destabilizes any final confidence the reader might have, especially in seeing the men's three speeches as the culmination and end point of the entire *Christmas Dialogue*, as though their speeches unify the whole and tie up loose ends. In fact, it is Josef who accomplishes that unity—not through dialectical, 'scientific' reflection, but through love and praise and communion with others. Josef echoes the speechless joy that is exhibited in all three of the women's stories, in Friederike's preference to play fantasias on the clavier rather than to relate a story, especially in Agnes's own apophatic words. It is not just that he *declares* that they have grasped the point better than the men; he also *shares* with them *how* they have grasped and experienced it. Similarly, he also identifies with Sofie, declaring himself to have become a child again.[107] The apophatic note at the end engenders a humility, which returns the *Christmas Dialogue* to the beginning, thereby uniting the various voices in a mystical "kiss" and in joyful song.

There are many reasons to read Schleiermacher's *Christmas Dialogue*. Simply as a literary and religious piece, it is accessible and charming. Its charm might in part be one of nostalgia for a by-gone era, but it also has to do with the simple joys to be found in a holiday feast, the possibilities of friendship, the heaviness of grief, the treasure of localized traditions, and the resistance to prescribed social norms. Its central question—namely, of how and why Christmas is celebrated, and of the relationship between the celebration and the historical event of the birth of Jesus of Nazareth—was new for 1805 but remains a question even

---

[106] *CD* 150; *WG* 97.23–24 (*verlangt oder erzeugt auch mir eine sprachlose Freude, die meinige kann wie ein Kind nur lächeln und jauchzen*).
[107] Sofie, in turn, is said to have a penchant for dogmatic theology (see *CD* 115; *WG* 58).

now. The *Christmas Dialogue* is also interesting for strictly historical and cultural reasons, insofar as it marks a shift in how Christmas was celebrated at the time (toward privatization) as well as a shift in how theologians reflected on Christmas (from dogmatic assertions to social and artistic expression). It also captures a parallel shift in ideas about gender roles, when older ideas were rejected and yet a new idealization of the feminine threatened to relegate women to the private sphere. Finally, of course, the *Christmas Dialogue* can be read as a theological work, in particular a Christological piece. On this point, however, understanding how Schleiermacher understood Plato has been instructive, in that it has exposed how most interpreters, in narrowly restricting their attention to the men's speeches, have violated Schleiermacher's own principles of interpretation and so have risked misunderstanding. The form (the formality of the men's speeches) cannot be separated from the content (the rest of the dialogue) if we are to try to understand Schleiermacher.

5.6 Concluding Remarks

The guiding question of this chapter has been whether Schleiermacher's *Christmas Dialogue* is a Platonic dialogue. I have argued that in order to answer that properly, we must attend to how Schleiermacher viewed the entire Platonic *corpus* as a single work of art, and then we can see that the more intriguing and illuminating comparison is between that *corpus* and the entire *Christmas Dialogue*, rather than between a particular dialogue and the men's speeches. This approach invites a reading of the *Christmas Dialogue* as an artistic whole wherein the integrity (literary, philosophical, theological, and religious) can be seen and the interrelated details better appreciated. Beyond offering new evidence for the importance of the 'Opening Scene' and the 'Stories,' this approach discloses something new that Schleiermacher did with the notion of Platonic dialogue. He reminded readers how the dialogue form is a matter not just of instruction but also of lively, mutual engagement. Whereas in his *Introductions* Schleiermacher insisted that the dialogue form could no longer be ignored (a point that was itself ground-breaking), in the *Christmas Dialogue* he went even further by expanding and modernizing the ideal of Platonic dialogue. It now includes women and children; and now, because of the intimacy and love of a Christian household, it also necessarily includes nonverbal communication.

The Platonic influences in the *Christmas Dialogue* were formal: they are found in the form of dialogue itself and the overall structure of the *Dialogue*, which, I have argued, mirrors Schleiermacher's interpretation of the overall structure of Plato's *corpus*. The content, however, was religious, specifically

Christian: the practices, rituals, the "object" of the occasion and the conversation, the specific affections aroused. This is not to draw a firm line between the religious and philosophical, or between what is Christian and what Platonic. Josef, the wise figure who appears at the end of the *Christmas Dialogue*, may be the avatar of a specific kind of pious Christian: a Moravian, perhaps; someone animated by love of his inner circle, humankind, and the world itself. He (like the female characters in the 'Stories') may just as well be considered a Socrates figure, as described by Schleiermacher in his "Introduction to the *Symposium*." Nevertheless, the Platonic influences in the revisions to the *Speeches*, in contrast to the *Christmas Dialogue*, operated on more than just a formal level. As we shall see in the next two chapters, they had to do with specific content, epistemology, and ontology.

6 The Presence of Plato in the *Speeches* (1806), Part 1: Revising, Reconceiving, and Recasting

> *You know this from my speeches, and if you have not yet figured it out for yourselves, then go and learn it from your Socrates.*[1]

6.1 Introduction

As we have seen in the previous chapter, Schleiermacher wrote his *Christmas Dialogue* in December 1805, his second Christmas in Halle. At that same time, he was also planning a new edition his *Speeches on Religion* (*Reden über die Religion*), which he had published anonymously in 1799 and which helped launch him onto the international stage.[2] Schleiermacher explained to his friend and publisher, Georg Reimer, that the revisions of his *Speeches* would need to be significant in order that "some confusion be made clear and excessive outgrowth be

---

[1] Schleiermacher, "On the Essence of Religion" (the second Speech on religion), OR^2 164–65; R^2 47 (... *das wisst Ihr aus meinen Reden, und wenn Ihr selbst es für Euch noch nicht einseht, so geht und lernt es von Eurem Sokrates*). See next note.

[2] Schleiermacher, *Über die Religion. Reden an die Gebildeten unter ihren Verächtern*, 1st ed. (1799), 2nd ed. (1806), 3rd ed. (1821). Text references become more difficult in this and the next chapter, where I compare the first two editions of the *Speeches*. That comparison is made possible by the relatively new study edition by Niklaus Peter: *Über die Religion. Reden an die Gebildeten unter ihren Verächtern 1799/1806/1821*, ed. Niklaus Peter, Frank Bestebreurtje, and Anna Büsching (Zürich: Theologischer Verlag, 2012); hereafter cited in text as "*R*" for *Reden*, with superscript number specifying first, second, or third edition. When citing the first edition, I also provide page and line numbers from the critical edition, in *KGA* 1/2: *Schriften aus der Berliner Zeit 1796–1799*, ed. Günter Meckenstock (Berlin and New York: Walter de Gruyter, 1984), 189–326. When citing the second edition, however, I refer exclusively to Peter ("R^{2n}"), since the *KGA* version of the later editions of the *Reden* prioritizes the fourth edition. See *KGA* 1/12: *Über die Religion (2. –)4. Auflage. Monologen (2. –)4. Auflage*, ed. Günter Meckenstock (Berlin: Walter de Gruyter, 1995).

English translation of first edition: *On Religion: Speeches to its Cultured Despisers*, trans. Richard Crouter (Cambridge: Cambridge University Press, 1988); hereafter cited in text as "OR^1." Second edition: "The Second Speech: "On the Essence of Religion'," in Lamm, *Schleiermacher*, 152–223; hereafter cited in text as "OR^2." Third edition: *On Religion: Speeches to its Cultured Despisers*, trans. John Oman (New York: Harper & Row, 1958; reprint, 1986); hereafter cited in text as "OR^3." Because my translation of the second edition is only of the second Speech, I cite Oman for passages from the second edition of the first Speech.

cut away."³ For this pruning, he would draw heavily from his interpretation of Plato for tools and materials alike. Schleiermacher worked on the second edition of the *Speeches* most intensely between March and August 1806. All the while, he was working on the fourth volume of *Platons Werke* (II,2), which included the *Cratylus, Sophist, Statesman,* and *Symposium*.⁴ During those years in Halle, when Schleiermacher was doing so much (lecturing, publishing, translating, preaching), Plato was his constant companion, so much so that he once complained that Plato "plagues"⁵ him (see table 1).

It is therefore stunning that, despite the considerable scholarly attention given to comparing the first two editions of the *Speeches* (and, in particular, changes made to the second Speech, "On the Essence of Religion"), virtually nothing has been written concerning any possible influence of Schleiermacher's Plato project on his revision of the *Speeches*. Increasingly, scholars have started noting the *fact* of Schleiermacher's simultaneous work on Plato and its possible relevance, without, however, investigating that in any sustained manner.⁶ This, despite the tantalizing fact that, in Rohls's words, "Schleiermacher not only initiated a new epoch in Protestant theology with his *Speeches on Religion*; with him also began a new epoch of the understanding of Plato."⁷ What is the significance of this intersection?

Due to the importance of Schleiermacher's *Speeches* for the philosophy of religion and for the study of religion more broadly, most of the secondary literature has been preoccupied with shifts between the two editions in Schleiermacher's employment of the terms *feeling* (*Gefühl*) and *intuition* (*Anschauung*) and their relation.⁸ Richard Crouter, who translated the first edition into English,

---

3 Schleiermacher to Reimer, 18 Mar. 1806 (#2167, lines 5 – 12), *Br.* 8:499. Most of those revisions were made to the second Speech. On his plans for the revisions, see Schleiermacher to Reimer, 9 Sept. 1805 (#2031, lines 89 – 90), *Br.* 8:314, where he also mentions plans for a new edition of his sermons.
4 The second volume of *Platons Werke* (I,2) appeared in November 1804, shortly after Schleiermacher had moved to Halle; the third volume (II,1) appeared at the end of 1805; the fourth volume (II,2) appeared in 1807, which means that Schleiermacher spent most of 1806 working on it.
5 Schleiermacher to Gaß, 5 Sept. 1805 (#2026, lines 4–5), *Br.* 8:303.
6 In a hefty volume of collected essays commemorating the two-hundreth anniversary of the publication of the *Speeches*, thirteen scholars mention Plato but none investigates the possible influence of the Plato project on the later editions of the *Reden*. See Ulrich Barth and Claus-Dieter Osthövener, eds., *200 Jahre "Reden über die Religion:" Akten des 1. Internationalen Kongresses der Schleiermacher-Gesellschaft, Halle 14. – 17. März 1999* (Berlin: De Gruyter, 2000).
7 Rohls, "Schleiermachers Platonismus," 467.
8 Two classic examples are Friedrich Wilhelm Graf, "Ursprüngliches Gefühl unmittelbarer Koinzidenz des Differenten: Zur Modifikation des Religionsbegriffs in den verschiedenen Auflagen

offers a consensus view of the significance of this change in terminology: Schleiermacher, in attempt to clarify "the problem of the cognitive status of religion," de-emphasized "the concept of intuition, which had been central to his original theory of religion," and for the most part replaced it with "feeling."[9] Crouter identifies two other notable shifts in the second edition: a mitigation of "the youthful author's theological radicality and his apparent indifference to the theistic view of God"; and the addition of an epilogue.[10] Günter Meckenstock, editor of all four editions of the *Reden* for the *KGA*, likewise identifies the matter of *Gefühl* and *Anschauung*, on the one hand, and the concept of God, on the other hand, as points of significant revision;[11] he recognizes, additionally, important structural changes to Schleiermacher's argument, a point to which we shall return.

As has so often been the case, it was Blackwell, who, almost forty years ago in his penetrating study of the early Schleiermacher, identified both the need for and the possibilities of examining the revisions of the *Speeches* in light of *Platons Werke*: "This immersion in Plato separates the first edition of the Speeches from the second edition of 1806, and because of this, alterations in the latter provide a particularly sensitive index of Plato's influence on Schleiermacher's thinking."[12] To my knowledge, no one to date has yet taken up this task. The task is made more possible than before by the recently published study-edition (*Studienausgabe*) of the *Reden* by Niklaus Peter, who lays out the first three editions on

---

von Schleiermachers 'Reden über die Religion'," *Zeitschrift für Theologie und Kirche* 75, no. 2 (1978): 147–86; and Van A. Harvey, "On the New Edition of Schleiermacher's: *Addresses on Religion*," *Journal of the American Academy of Religion* 39, no. 4 (1971): 488–512.
9 Crouter, "Introduction," OR^1 57–58. Given the influence and importance of Schleiermacher's *Speeches*, it can be overwhelming sometimes to know where to begin in learning about the context of the work or its legacy. I recommend three essays by Crouter, all conveniently included in a single volume: "Schleiermacher, Mendelssohn, and the Enlightenment: Comparing *On Religion* (1799) with *Jerusalem* (1783)"; "Schleiermacher's Theory of Language: The Ubiquity of a Romantic Text"; and "*On Religion* as a Religious Classic: Hermeneutical Musings after Two Hundred Years" (in *Friedrich Schleiermacher: Between Enlightenment and Romanticism* [Cambridge: Cambridge University Press, 2005], 39–69, 195–206, and 248–270, respectively).
10 Crouter, "Introduction," OR^1 58; see pp. 57–68 for his full treatment of what he says are the three main changes in the 1806 edition. In the past fifty years, scholars have underscored (and expressed their preference for) the "radical" nature of the first edition as opposed to the later editions. See, e.g., Harvey, "On the New Edition," 489; and Laurens ten Kate, "Intuitions of the Other: An Analysis of *Anschauung* on Schleiermacher's *On Religion*—With References To Kant," pt. 2 in Erik Borgman, Laurens ten Kate, and Bart Philipsen, "A Triptych on Schleiermacher's '*On Religion*'," *Literature & Theology* 21/4 (December 2007): 394.
11 See Meckenstock, "Historische Einführung," *KGA* 1/12:xix–xxiii.
12 Blackwell, *Schleiermacher's Early Philosophy of Life*, 128.

the same page so that readers may have a keener sense of what Schleiermacher changed, where he inserted major additions, and how he moved certain passages around.[13] Where the text remained relatively unchanged between editions, it fills the page from margin to margin, with small changes given in footnotes; where the text was significantly altered, the two versions are set side-by-side in columns, with later editions set in smaller font since, more frequently than not, they were expansions. Peter's synoptic edition marks a major contribution to Schleiermacher studies. Relying on it, I offer (in this chapter and the next) a close textual analysis of the first four major revisions to the famous second Speech. I refer to these major block revisions as the "revised blocks" (see table 8).

Table 8: Revised Blocks in the Second Speech, 2nd ed. (1806)

Revised Block N°	Location of revised blocks in 2nd & 3rd editions			Insertion points of revised blocks in 1st edition	
	R^2 (Peter), pp.	OR^2 (Lamm), pp.	OR^3 (Oman), pp.	KGA 1/2, begins on p./line	OR^1 (Crouter), begins on p.
1	35–42	153–59	26–32	207.39	197
2	43–46	160–64	33–37	211.7	101 (top)
3	47–49	164–167	38–40	212.22	102 (bottom)
4	49–56	167–75	41–49	213.34	104 (middle)

In my analysis, I compare the first two editions of the *Speeches* (1799, 1806) as I simultaneously examine parallels between the revised blocks and his *Introductions to the Dialogues of Plato*.[14]

---

13 See above, n. 2.

14 Because of the complicated nature of this investigation, an explanation of how texts are treated and cited is in order. Over the course of this chapter and the next, I have to juggle two (and sometimes more) editions of the *Speeches*, examining new additions and tracking the movement of other passages, as I also compare those revisions with passages from *Platons Werke*. Many of those passages are dense and multivalent, and we will sometimes need to revisit them from different angles. So as not to be repetitious in my quotations, I set the most significant and lengthy passages in indented block quotations and assign them a numerical designation to facilitate cross-reference. These passages will be designated by the chapter number in which they are first quoted, followed by a letter indicating their placement in that chapter. So, for instance, "Passage 6B" indicates that the passage is the second major indented block quotation in chapter 6.

My overall thesis in these two chapters is necessarily a complex one, given the almost impossibly complicated nature of Schleiermacher's intellectual cross-fertilization during this decade of Plato and given the challenges of teasing out the changes he made to the *Speeches* along with his motivations for them. At a more superficial level, the influence of Plato on the second edition of the *Speeches* seems straight-forward. Whereas in the first edition Plato could perhaps be recognized in the background in a general sense, in 1806 Schleiermacher's Plato is present in a specific and pervasive way in that the revised blocks contain numerous new and scattered allusions to Plato, Socrates, and recognizably Platonic themes. Yet the influence is more substantial than allusions alone might suggest. Schleiermacher's Plato informs his most significant revisions. I list here but three ways in which that is true, but the full list is even longer. First and foremost, Schleiermacher's reconceptualization of what I refer to as "The Three"—from *metaphysics* (*Metaphysik*), *morality* (*Moral*), and *religion* (*Religion*) in 1799 to *thinking* (*Denken*), *acting* (*Handeln*), and *religion* in 1806—reflects his theory of the role of *physics* and *ethics* in Plato's dialogues as well as his notion of the pedagogical progression of ideas; that reconceptualization, moreover, reshapes the dynamic flow of his argument of the second Speech. Second and relatedly, Schleiermacher's refinement in 1806 of the organic monism first articulated in 1799, which had invited accusations of pantheism, reflects his interpretation of Plato's ontology, especially as he found that in the *Sophist*. Third and finally, there were other natural alignments with Plato and with ancient philosophy more generally that Schleiermacher cultivated even more in the second edition than he had in the first. For instance, his appreciation of the contemplative aspect to Plato's thought—and of the ancients' holding together of theory and practice—confirmed his own prior commitments.

A fair question might be why, if these influences are so pervasive, no one has noticed them before, at least not enough to pursue them at length. The answer likely has to do with the fact that Schleiermacher's Plato is very particular, and too few Schleiermacher scholars have delved into his *Introductions*. Schleiermacher's Plato is defined by his view of Plato as artist and all which that entails; by his view of the two series (ethics and physics) and how they come together; by an emerging modern historical consciousness and his Romantic sensibilities, as he further shaped those in his inter-Berlin period; and by his modern, post-Kantian interpretation of the *Sophist*. Schleiermacher's Plato, in short, is not recognizable as a form of Plato*nism*. It only becomes recognizable through the lens of his *Introductions*. To return to Schleiermacher's own metaphor of gardening, it is fair to say that Schleiermacher's Plato provided him with new topsoil, clippers, and some stakes that helped him fertilize, prune, and straighten out his

Speeches, which in their first version could at times be as overgrown as they were brilliant.

I argue my thesis through a close, systematic analysis of the first four major revised blocks of the second Speech. That will bring us only to about a quarter of the way through that Speech but nonetheless to the culmination of what, I maintain, was Schleiermacher's revised argument regarding the relationship of The Three. Because the revised blocks are lengthy and the parallels numerous, the case about Plato's presence in the *Speeches* will take two chapters comprising five sequentially numbered sections. In this chapter, I focus on revised block n°s 1 and 2, showing how his revisions there, which fundamentally reshape his argument, reflect his view of the role *physics* and *ethics* in Plato's dialogues (sections 6.3 and 6.4). In the next chapter, I focus on revised block n°s 3 and 4, showing how they reflect ontological commitments influenced especially by his reading of the *Sophist* and how in his revisions there Schleiermacher worked out a new understanding of *intuition*, which addressed some of the inconsistencies from 1799 and, moreover, which also happened to be consistent with his use of that term in his *Introductions* (sections 7.2 and 7.3). I begin my analysis, however, with a discussion of another line of revision, starting in the first Speech and climaxing at the end of the second, which straightens out another inconsistency and, in so doing, resets the entire tone of the *Speeches* (section 6.2). This line of revision involves the holding together of philosophy and life, which was one of the things he admired about the ancients. Although not the result of his work on Plato in a narrow sense, this starting point will serve both to provide an overview of Schleiermacher's revisions and also to remind us of a unique feature of Schleiermacher's *Speeches*—namely, that it is at once a book about religion (theory) and a religious text (praxis).

6.2 Re-Writing as Spiritual Exercise: Holding together Theory and *Praxis* in the *Speeches*

When it comes to comparing the first and later editions of the *Speeches*, I suggest that the penchant among scholars for focusing on the question of whether Schleiermacher's theory of religion changed in any significant way has constricted our understanding of the different dimensions of that classic text. Such preoccupation has overshadowed two facts: first, that there were other changes, some of which, although neglected, were arguably momentous; and second, that his *Speeches* is itself a religious text. Indeed, part of the genius of the *Speeches* lies precisely in how, in writing it, Schleiermacher held together theory and practice, an especially difficult task since *theory about religion* continually threatens to undermine *religion*. The truth of the matter is that, at several points in the first edition, it did just that. Schleiermacher seemed to be aware of this, since in his revisions he corrected several contradictions as he also extended and tightened other threads of thought. He thereby heightened the creative tension between theory and practice in his *Speeches*. Telling is his new complaint to the cultured despisers: "you convert what I say into your concepts and seek precepts in them, and thus the misunderstanding has become ever more deeply rooted."[15] Schleiermacher's own formulation of theory in 1799 had done just that, but his revision of 1806 undid those contradictions.

In this section, influenced in part by Pierre Hadot's notion of *writing as a spiritual exercise* as applied to ancient philosophy,[16] I view Schleiermacher's re-writing of the *Speeches* as, in part, a spiritual exercise. I highlight three specific revisions in the first and second Speeches in order to demonstrate just how, in 1806, Schleiermacher was more successful at holding together *theory* and *practice* than he had been in 1799.[17]

6.2.1 The Two Impulses (*Triebe*)

In both editions, at the beginning of the first Speech, Schleiermacher identifies two "opposing"[18] or "primal forces" (*Urkräfte*);[19] he proceeds to describe every human soul both as a product of these two forces and also as engaging in

---

15 OR^2 173; R^2 54. Likely an allusion to the *Sophist* 239d: "he will easily take advantage of our poverty of terms to make a counter attack, twisting our words to the opposite meaning" (trans. Fowler, in *PDL*).
16 See Pierre Hadot, *Exercices spirituels et philosophie antique* (Paris: Études Augustiniennes, 1981). English translation: *Philosophy as a Way of Life: Spiritual Exercises from Socrates to Foucault*, ed. Arnold I. Davidson and trans. Michael Chase (Oxford and Cambridge, Mass.: Blackwell, 1995). I have pursued this at more length in Lamm, *Schleiermacher*, 36–44, and in "Schleiermacher's Re-Writing as Spiritual Exercise, 1799–1806," in *Der Mensch und seine Seele. Bildung—Frömmigkeit—Ästhetik. Akten des Schleiermacher-Kongresses 2015*, ed. Arnulf von Scheliha and Jörg Dierken (Berlin and Boston: Walter de Gruyter, 2017), 293–302.
17 Note: I here use "theory" and "practice" differently from how Schleiermacher uses these terms in the *Speeches*. I mean here Schleiermacher's *theory of religion* and his *practice of religion*.
18 R^1 10 ≈ R^2 10 (*Kräften* → *Tätigkeiten*); OR^1 79. Working with the various editions of the *Reden*, and citing them, is a notoriously difficult task. In this section my method of citation is slightly different from the remaining sections. Since I am tracking specific retentions and alterations, I cite the page numbers from the Peter edition for both versions. I use "=" to indicate a passage is the same in both editions and "≈" to indicate a passage was only slightly revised, with an → to note the change from one term to another.
19 R^1 10 ≈ R^2 10; OR^1 80.

these two "original functions of spiritual nature."[20] He notes the problem when these two impulses are not held together—when, therefore, life is lived at the extremes. Then he counterposes such extreme souls with the ideal soul, who by uniting the two forces attains a "perfect equilibrium."[21] If we map out the trajectory from this starting point through to the end of the second Speech, we might detect a continual process whereby those two forces are brought into harmonious relation,[22] a process culminating in a dizzying oscillation[23] that yields equilibrium.[24] In other words, Schleiermacher sets his own task as one of leading the cultured despisers from one state to the next—not just theoretically but also in practice. He explains, "Only the thoughtful expert penetrates into the secrets of such a combination brought to rest."[25] Importantly, he identifies himself as one such spiritual expert: "I wish to lead you to the innermost depths from which religion first addresses the heart [Gemüth]. I wish to show you from what capacity of humanity religion proceeds."[26] Throughout these first two Speeches, Schleiermacher reiterates, "let me lead you";[27] he "directs" their attention elsewhere;[28] he invites them to "follow" him.[29] And what they are to follow is not just an argument. He is asking his friends, the cultured despisers of religion, to do something—but that doing is a different kind of doing from that associated with *metaphysics* and *morality* because it is not an imposing. It is a doing that begins, so to speak, in undoing. It is, arguably, an ongoing act of contemplation (*Betrachtung*)—meditation, reflection, careful consideration—which involves the whole self and requires self-reflection.[30]

The contemplation to which he is calling the cultured despisers requires that they step back, free themselves of prejudices and preconceptions, consider

---

[20] R^1 11 ≈ R^2 11; OR^1 80. Whereas in the first edition he described these as "thirsty attraction and the expansion of the active and living self" (R^1 10; OR^1 80), in the second edition, as we shall soon see, he redefined them.

[21] R^1 12 ≈ R^2 12; OR^1 81.

[22] See R^1 98 = R^2 98; OR^1 132, OR^2 212.

[23] See R^1 91 ≈ R^2 91; OR^1 126, OR^2 206.

[24] See R^1 98 = R^2 98; OR^1 132, OR^2 212.

[25] R^1 12 (*In die Geheimnisse einer solchen zur Ruhe gebrachten Mischung dringt nur der gedankenvolle Kenner ein*); OR^1 81. Compare R^2 12: *Denn in die Geheimnisse einer so getrennten oder einer so zur Ruhe gebrachten Mischung dringt nur der tiefere Seher*.

[26] R^1 19 ≈ R^2 19; OR^1 87 (slightly altered).

[27] See, e.g., R^1 19, 68, 73, 83, 92.

[28] E.g., R^1 26.

[29] E.g., R^2 72; OR^2 189.

[30] As we shall see below in 6.4, 7.3.2, and 7.3.6, Schleiermacher's appeal to *Betrachtung* increases in the second edition and can be traced partly to his engagement with Plato.

things from a distance, and make distinctions. Schleiermacher demands of his addressees an "impartial sobriety of mind."[31] He re-presents and critiques their mistaken views, challenging them to see their inconsistencies. "You do not," he cautions, "want to have fought against a shadow."[32] All of this is an apophatic move, so to speak, to clear a space. Schleiermacher informs them that what he wants them to see cannot be completely conveyed by an argument; rather, something must take place within them. He explains, "in spiritual things" the aim is "to create the original in no other way than producing it by means of an original creation in you, even then only for the moment when you produce it."[33] Again, this activity, this producing, is different from other forms of activity: it comes through intuiting, feeling, longing, overhearing, and undergoing; it comes through falling in love with another person, with the world-spirit,[34] and with humanity;[35] it comes through entering "into that realm where you are also most properly and best at home, where your most inner life opens up to you."[36] The despisers must cultivate certain emotions and attitudes as they trim away others.[37] We must, he says, first master ourselves and our pious feelings.[38] The exercise of repeated movements from inner to outer and back to inner, the losing of oneself in order to discover oneself—it is all a spiritual practice that brings about transformation as it moves toward equilibrium.

There is, in other words, a pattern and a rhythm to the *Speeches* that is meditative as it builds to a point, pulls back, and repeats. Schleiermacher builds, bidding the cultured despisers to admit what they presently hold to be true, even though they may not be aware of it; he points to problems with that; he suggests a new movement of the mind or heart; he continues with this pattern by taking it further, extending and interweaving his points. Then he invites them, again and again, to turn to their own experience and consider what their experience really tells them; he offers them example after example to reflect on as an aid in opening that experience to contemplation. At the same time, as he addresses his friends, asking them to do this, he himself is in the process of doing the

---

[31] R^1 34 = R^2 34; OR^2 152–53; see OR^1 96.
[32] R^1 42 ≈ R^2 42; OR^2 159; see OR^1 100.
[33] R^1 42 ≈ R^2 42; OR^2 160; see OR^1 100.
[34] "For to love the world-spirit and joyfully to behold its works is the aim of our religion, and in love there is no fear" (R^1 74 = R^2 75; OR^2 191; see OR^1 115).
[35] "...a person must first have found humanity, and humanity is only found in love and by means of love" (R^1 82 = R^2 82; OR^2 198).
[36] R^1 83 = R^2 83; OR^2 198, see OR^1 120.
[37] See R^1 26 = R^2 26; OR^1 92.
[38] See R^1 66; OR^1 110.

same, and so he himself arrives at a deepened understanding of process. That deepened understanding is inscribed in his revisions of 1806.

The goal of this process is nothing less than human life: what it means to live a fully human life, which in turn is nothing less than a social life in relation to all the rest of life and to the infinite. It is a way of living that resists idolatry, the dead letter, and willful ignorance. It is a way of living that cultivates joy, humility, and openness. Yet, unlike the ancients, it turns out, this way of life is not only for the philosopher; it is for any open, pious heart. This is why it is a mistake to approach Schleiermacher's *Speeches* merely as a philosophical or theological *argument*, and why it may be instructive to read it rather (or also) as an exercise in philosophy as a way of life, reframed as *religion as a way of life*.

Let us look more closely at these two impulses (*Triebe*), as Schleiermacher presented them at the beginning of the first Speech, in order to see how both logical consistency and spiritual practice required that he re-work his description of them when he revised his *Speeches*.[39] In 1799, he described the second impulse as one that "longs to extend its own inner self ever further, thereby permeating and imparting to everything from within"; this impulse "goes on to ever-increasing and heightened activity; ... it wants to penetrate and to fill everything with reason and freedom, and thus it proceeds directly to the infinite and at all times seeks and produces freedom and coherence, power and law, right and suitability."[40] Notice the problem. This description of the second impulse came perilously close to what he had said about metaphysics and morals in the first edition: it wants to impose reason and freedom.

Now notice how differently he describes that second impulse in the second edition. He redefines it in 1806 as the "longing to surrender oneself to [the whole], and to feel oneself grasped and determined by it."[41] Surrender cannot be confused with either metaphysics or morals; it is distinctly religious. Schleiermacher has thereby set the second impulse in a more coherent relation to the first impulse (that of striving to be an individual) and has aligned both impulses together with what he says about piety. From the perspective of a spiritual exercise, this makes much more sense: what needs to be exercised is precisely the movement between the striving toward individuality and the willingness to sur-

---

[39] The importance of the notion of moral *impulses*, as opposed to *instincts*, figured also in Schleiermacher's earliest philosophical essays. See Lamm, "Early Philosophical Roots."

[40] R^1 10–11; OR^1 80. For discussion of these two impulses in first edition of the *Reden*, see Schmidt, *Konstrucktion der Endlichen*, 60.

[41] R^2 10 (... *die Sehnsucht hingebend sich selbst in ihm aufzulösen, und sich von ihm ergriffen und bestimmt zu fühlen*).

render. Each impulse in itself needs to be exercised, just as bringing them into relation requires practice.

6.2.2 Rhetorical Shifts

Arguably, the most significant shift in 1806 pertains to Schleiermacher's restructuring of The Three. In 1799, he designated them simply as *metaphysics, morals,* and *religion*.[42] In 1806, however, he presents the first two of The Three in terms of a much more complex typology in which metaphysics becomes *a way of thinking,* and morals *a way of acting*.[43] We shall examine this in detail in the next main section (6.3), where I argue that this shift closely mirrors his interpretation of Plato. For now, what is especially compelling about this substantial revision is not so much how he changes his *theory* as how those changes alter what he does in relation to the cultured despisers. It shifts the rhetorical force.

In 1799, Schleiermacher's categorization of The Three did little to challenge his friends, the despisers of religion. On the contrary, he *knew* that they shared his assessment of the "practical people" and of speculative philosophers. Although he wanted the cultured despisers to think differently about religion, he nonetheless confirmed their view of things. In 1806, however, he *does* challenge them. Not only does the more complex typology he introduces require more work on their part to understand it, but it also catches them in their own mistaken views and even chides them for not having rightly examined themselves. Moreover, rather than help orient the cultured despisers with the same sequence of (relatively) clear definitions of religion offered in 1799, he poses a series of questions in 1806, throwing his hearers back upon themselves, so to speak, and disorienting them, perhaps making them doubt themselves. The ground he thus lays is purposively destabilizing and disorienting. As a result, the dialogue between speaker and audience is actually more engaging, more intense. It would not be unreasonable to question whether his reflection on the importance of the dialogue form in Plato was a contributing factor to this revision.

---

42 See, e.g., R^1 36; OR^1 97.
43 *Denkungsart, Handlungweise, R^2* 36; OR^2 154.

6.2.3 Intuition as the 'Hinge' of the Argument

In 1799, Schleiermacher entreated the cultured despisers to "become familiar with this *concept:* intuition of the universe. It is the hinge of my whole speech; it is the highest and most universal formula of religion."[44] His deletion of that passage in 1806 suggests that he realized such an assertion had actually undermined his own theory, since it so explicitly tied religion to a particular *concept—* and thus made it into an argument and a theory—which would make it either an example of *metaphysics* (1799) or a *way of thinking* (1806). Schleiermacher's own theory of religion in the *Speeches*, however, cannot be like other theories; to work, it must be sustained in a tensive relationship to a religious way of being. If we compare the two editions, we see that in his revision Schleiermacher not only dropped his assertion about *intuition of the universe*, but he also added a substantial revision that includes a six-page addition.[45]

Notice the new entreaty he makes in 1806. Instead of asking them to understand a concept, he bids the cultured despisers towards self-reflection:

[Passage 6A: *Speeches*, 1806]

So that you understand, however, what I mean by this unity of science, religion, and art— and, at the same time, what I mean by their distinction—*try to descend with me into the innermost sanctuary of life*. Perhaps there we may find some common bearings. Only there will you *find the original relation* of feeling and intuition, and only out of this relation will their being-one and their distinction be understood. But *I must refer you to your own selves, to the apprehension of a living moment.* You must understand it by *eavesdropping on your own selves* before your consciousness, or at the very least by reconstituting this condition for yourselves out of that consciousness. What you should notice is the coming-to-be of your consciousness, but you shouldn't reflect on some already-having-become.[46]

Damit ihr aber versteht wie ich es meine mit dieser Einheit der Wissenschaft, der Religion und der Kunst und mit ihrer Verschiedenheit zugleich: so <u>versucht mit mir hinabzusteigen in das innerste Heiligtum des Lebens</u>, ob wir uns dort vielleicht gemeinschaftlich zurechtfinden können. Dort allein findet Ihr das ursprüngliche Verhältnis des Gefühls und der Anschauung, woraus allein ihr Einssein und ihre Trennung zu verstehen ist. Aber <u>an Euch selber muss ich Euch verweisen, an das Auffassen eines lebendigen Moments</u>. Ihr müsst es verstehen <u>Euch selbst gleichsam vor Eurem Bewusstsein zu belauschen</u>, oder wenigstens diesen Zustand für

---

44 *OR*¹ 104, emphasis added; *R*¹ 49–50 (KGA 1/2:213.34–36) (*Anschauen des Universums, ich bitte befreundet Euch mit diesem Begriff, er ist der Angel meiner ganzen Rede, er ist die allgemeinste und höchste Formel der Religion*).
45 See below, 7.3.
46 *OR*² 168, emphasis added.

> *Euch aus jenem wiederherzustellen. Es ist das Werden Eures Bewusstseins, was Ihr bemerken sollt, nicht etwa sollt Ihr über ein schon gewordenes reflektieren.*[47]

The despisers must examine themselves and train their attention in order to realize something, although what they are to realize is not a fixed concept. It is a living moment, and they must "capture [themselves] in the process."[48] It comes down to another line added in 1806: "Contemplation is essential to religion."[49]

Schleiermacher was a virtuoso of spirituality. His act of re-writing the *Speeches* was as much a spiritual exercise as an intellectual one. To neglect this, to try to understand his theory about religion apart from his practical advice about being religious, would be to fail to understand why his *Speeches* remains a masterpiece. It is impossible to assign a single cause to his revisions. In this case, the claim regarding *intuition* as the "hinge" of his argument was a logical contradiction that involved a practical inconsistency. His decision to rework it in so fundamental a manner can certainly not be directly attributed to his work on Plato. It just happens to align, however, with one of the insights of the ancients that he himself so valued: the holding together of "philosophy and life."[50]

6.3 Revised Block N° 1: A New Three of Thinking, Doing, and Feeling

The first main revised block begins early in the second Speech (on the second page of most editions) and extends for about seven (split-column) pages in the Peter edition.[51] As is true for most of the revised blocks, not everything in it is new, but much is, and what Schleiermacher retained from the first edition he reframed. The original text had set forth The Three: *metaphysics, morality, and religion*. The revised text also introduces The Three, although they are renamed and reconceptualized. This first major revision is a substantial one that is systemic in nature insofar as, with it, Schleiermacher recasts his entire argument and establishes a new dynamic and flow. It also just happens to closely reflect his interpretation of Plato in *Platons Werke*.

---

47 R^2 50, emphasis added.
48 OR^2 168; R^2 50 (*Ergreift Euch dabei*).
49 R^2 45; OR^2 162. See below, 6.4 and passage 6I.
50 Schleiermacher criticized the philosopher Johann Gottlieb Fichte (1762–1814) because "philosophy and life are for him ... entirely separate"/*Philosophie und Leben sind bei ihm ... ganz getrennt* (Schleiermacher to Brinckmann, 4 Jan. 1800 [#758, lines 26–27], *Br.* 3:313–14).
51 See R 35–42; OR^2 153–59. See table 8.

6.3.1 A More Complex Typology

In this revision, Schleiermacher fundamentally alters how he conceives of the three basic categories that shape so much of the second Speech: from the more static spheres of *metaphysics, morality, and religion* (1799) to the broader, gerundive categories of *thinking, acting, and religion/piety* (1806). He adds further complexity to his typology by subdividing *acting* into *life* and *art*, and *thinking* into theory about *physics/metaphysics*, on the one hand, and theory about *human behavior*, on the other hand. As Meckenstock puts it so well, Schleiermacher moves from a "duplicity of metaphysics and morals" (*Duplizität von Metaphysik und Moral*) to a "quadruplicity" (*Quadruplizität*):[52]

> [Passage 6B: *Speeches*, 1806]
>
> Religion is to you, in one moment, a kind of thinking, a faith, a distinct manner of observing the world and of connecting whatever we encounter in it; in another moment, it is a manner of action, a particular desire and love, a special kind of conducting and moving oneself inwardly. Without this separation of the theoretical and the practical, you can hardly think, and although religion belongs to both sides, you are nevertheless accustomed, every time, to looking at it selectively from one of the two sides.[53]
>
> *Die Religion ist Euch bald eine Denkungsart, ein Glaube, eine eigene Weise die Welt zu betrachten, und was uns in ihr begegnet in Verbindung zu bringen; bald eine Handlungsweise, eine eigene Lust und Liebe, eine besondere Art sich zu betragen und sich innerlich zu bewegen. Ohne diese Trennung eines Theoretischen und Praktischen könnt Ihr nun einmal schwerlich denken, und wiewohl die Religion beiden Seiten angehört, seid Ihr doch gewohnt jedesmal auf eine von beiden vorzüglich zu achten.*[54]

This is no mere substitution of terms but a reconceptualization with far-reaching consequences. This more complex typology requires considerably more elaboration on Schleiermacher's part. For the purposes of this book on his understanding of Plato and the degree to which it influenced his own thought, I focus here, first, on how, in broader terms, Schleiermacher's understanding of *thinking* and *acting*, including his positive casting of both, reflects his reading of Plato's dialogues; and second, on how, more specifically, his introduction of the terms *virtue* (*Tugend*) and *knowledge* (*Wissen*), and his treatment of both, make more sense when seen in the context of his deep engagement with Plato's philosophy (in both *Platons* Werke and *Grundlinien*) during the seven years between the pub-

---

52 Meckenstock, "Historische Einführung," *KGA* 1/12: xxi-xxii.
53 OR^2 154.
54 R^2 36.

lications of the first and second editions of the *Speeches*.⁵⁵ Whereas in 1799 Schleiermacher had cast *metaphysics* and *morals* in a largely negative light, in 1806 he presents the human activities of *thinking* and *acting* quite positively, as he also presents the normative goals of those activities—*knowledge* and *virtue*—as desirable. In doing so, moreover, he begins to argue for a dynamic interrelationship of The Three in a way that reflects his understanding of Plato's dialectical method.

In 1799, Schleiermacher presented both *metaphysics* and *morals* in dismissive, simplistic terms, using them as foils. He used them to set up his initial definitions of religion by way of strong opposition. At that time, he had identified metaphysics foremost with Fichte's transcendental philosophy, without expanding much on the point. He used that to delimit the sphere of religion: "religion must not venture too far. It must not have the tendency to posit essences and to determine natures, to lose itself in an infinity of reasons and deductions, to seek out final causes, and to proclaim eternal truths."⁵⁶ He then immediately transitioned to morality, which he also portrayed negatively insofar as it "develops a system of duties out of human nature and our relationship to the universe; it commands and forbids actions with unlimited authority."⁵⁷ As before, he followed this quick, mono-dimensional description with another apophatic definition of religion: "religion must not ... use the universe in order to derive duties and is not permitted to contain a code of laws."⁵⁸

In contrast, in his newly revised typology in 1806, Schleiermacher spends considerably more time explaining the dimensions of both *thinking* and of *acting*, thereby setting up a more complex relationship with *feeling*; he flips the order in which he treats them; and, crucially, he treats them in a more positive light than he had *metaphysics* and *morals* in the first edition. Most critically, his

---

55 Again, this is not to claim a unidirectional causal influence from *Platons Werke*. Schleiermacher had grappled with these issues since his university days. As Brent Sockness argues, his interest in virtue and his appeal to Plato as a "hero" goes back to his 1789 essay "On the Highest Good" ("Was Schleiermacher a Virtue Ethicist? *Tugend* and *Bildung* in the Early Ethical Writings," *Zeitschrift für Neuere Theologiegeschichte / Journal for the History of Modern Theology* 8, no. 1 [2001]: 17).
56 OR^1 98; R^1 38 (*KGA* 1/2:208.20–23) (... *die Religion nicht versteigen, sie darf nicht die Tendenz haben Wesen zu sezen und Naturen zu bestimmen, sich in ein Unendliches von Gründen und Deduktionen zu verlieren, lezte Ursachen aufzusuchen und ewige Wahrheiten auszusprechen*).
57 OR^1 98; R^1 38 (*KGA* 1/2:208.24–26) (*Sie entwikelt aus der Natur des Menschen und seines Verhältnißes gegen das Universum ein System von Pflichten, sie gebietet und untersagt Handlungen mit unumschränkter Gewalt*).
58 OR^1 98; R^1 38 (*KGA* 1/2:208.26–28) (*Auch das darf also die Religion nicht wagen, sie darf das Universum nicht brauchen um Pflichten abzuleiten, sie darf keinen Kodex von Gesezen enthalten*).

expansions reflect his work in *Platons Werke:* he speaks extensively of *virtue* (*Tugend*) and *knowledge* (*Wissen*). This expansion and added complexity require that *acting* and *thinking* each be addressed on its own.

6.3.2 Acting: Life and Art

Schleiermacher's discussion of *acting* extends to about two pages, which is much longer than the few lines devoted to *morality* in the first edition. In describing *acting* as it pertains to *life* (*Leben*), he introduces the term *virtue* and presents the virtuous life in a positive, or at least neutral, sense:[59]

> [Passage 6C: *Speeches*, 1806]
>
> ... when it comes to *life*, duty ought to be the motto, your moral law ought to regulate it, and virtue ought to demonstrate itself in life as *the ruling principle by means of which the individual harmonizes with the universal orderings of the world*, without ever acting in a disruptive or bewildering manner.[60]
>
> *Für das Leben soll die Pflicht die Losung sein, Euer Sittengesetz soll es anordnen, die Tugend soll sich darin als das Waltende beweisen, dass der Einzelne mit den allgemeinen Ordnungen der Welt harmoniere, und nirgends störend oder verwirrend eingreife.*[61]

Such language about virtue—as that by means of which we harmonize ourselves with universal laws and thus regulate our behavior—seems to echo Schleier-

---

[59] In his *Grundlinien* (1803), Schleiermacher developed the three "ideas" of ethics: duty, virtue, the artist. As Wallhausser explains, "The three 'ideas' of ethics refer to different aspects of the same moral process and correspond respectively to the formal, efficient and final causes of moral activity. All are equally necessary for ethics and there is no *logical* priority or subordination possible amog them" ("General Introduction," *Notes on Ethics*, 9). In his *Brouillon* (his lectures on ethics delivered at the University of Halle, 1805–1806), Schleiermacher distinguished between ancient and modern practices of virtue: "The ancients focus on the highest good and virtue, the moderns on virtue and duty. These two foci stand in a relation of contrast: if virtue is present, then duty ceases; and so long as one must inculcate duty, virtue is not yet present" (*Notes on Ethics*, 38); *Brouillon*, 8 (*Bei den Alten höchstes Gut und Tugend, bei den Neuen Tugend und Pflicht. Diese beiden stehn in einem Gegensaz: wenn die Tugend gegeben ist, hört die Pflicht auf; so lange man die Pflicht einschärfen muß, ist die Tugend noch nicht da*).
[60] OR^2 155, emphasis added.
[61] R^2 36, emphasis added.

6.3 Revised Block N° 1: A New Three of Thinking, Doing, and Feeling — 159

macher's account of the virtuous life as set forth in his *Introductions*. For instance, in his "Introduction to the *Laches*,"[62] Schleiermacher writes,

> For what Laches in his innocence says of the nature of moral wisdom, as being harmony of the mind, and coincidence of knowledge [*Wissens*] and of life, this is the right key to the Platonic Theory of Virtue, and to the meaning of his opinion that it is knowledge [*Erkenntniß*], or, a knowing [*Wissen*].[63]

> Denn was in seiner Unschuld Laches über das Wesen der sittlichen Weisheit sagt als Harmonie der Seele und Uebereinstimmung des Wissens und Lebens, dies ist der rechte Schlüssel zu der Platonischen Theorie der Tugend, und wie er es meinen könne, daß sie eine Erkenntniß sei oder ein Wissen.[64]

In the first edition of the *Speeches*, the word *virtue* and its cognates occurred only four times (and then only on two pages) and never in the second Speech; in the second edition, it occurs five times in the second Speech alone, four of them here in revised block n° 1. It would be difficult to understand this change as not having been influenced by *Platons Werke*.

Schleiermacher identifies *art* as the second aspect of *acting*. This provides another illustration of how, in his revisions, he paints the ethical category in a more positive light than he had *morality* in the first edition, where bourgeois moralists were contrasted with the Romantic ideal of the artist. Here in 1806, he is not merely appealing to the fact that art is highly prized by the cultured despisers; more, he is making a broader claim about human nature. In his lectures on ethics, delivered in the same year he revised his *Speeches*, Schleiermacher proclaimed that "all people are artists," by which he meant: "Making feeling ethical ... to the extent that it should become communal, consists in this: that every feeling carry over into presentation."[65] He is making a similar point here in revised block n° 1. Schleiermacher challenges his interlocutors more than he had before, asking them to reflect not just on the relation between *art* and *virtue* but also on the relation between *art* and *piety*. He chastises them for trying to separate *art* from virtue and from piety alike. Then, departing from

---

62 See also his "Introduction to the *Symposium*," where he refers to the "harmony of the [whole]" (*IDP* 280)/*die Harmonie des Ganzen* (*EÜP* 276) and the "harmony of the world"/*in der Harmonie der Welt* (*EÜP* 285, not in *IDP*).
63 *IDP* 101.
64 *PW* 1/1:879.21–26.
65 Schleiermacher, *Notes on Ethics*, 126; *Brouillon*, 108 (*Die Ethisirung des Gefühls aber, inwiefern es ein gemeinschaftliches werden soll, darin, daß jedes Gefühl in Darstellung übergehe: all Menschen sind Künstler*). Whence the title of Patsch's book: *Alle Menschen sind Künstler* (see above, chap. 1, 5n16).

his characteristic tact and simplistic definitions in the first edition, Schleiermacher poses a series of probing questions, issues his interlocutors a warning, and closes with a rather harsh conditional criticism: "be so kind also to communicate to me, if you find another way out, how your opinion about religion cannot appear as nothing. Until then, there is nothing left for me to do than accept that you have not yet rightly examined, nor have you yourselves understood, this side of religion."[66] This pattern repeats itself in Schleiermacher's treatment of a *manner of thinking* (*Denkungsart*).

6.3.3 Thinking About Nature—and About Human Nature

Although Schleiermacher rebukes the cultured despisers for assuming that there are "two antagonistic sciences" (*zwei gegenüberstehende Wissenschaften*),[67] he himself treated *metaphysics* and *morals* in a similar fashion in 1799. In this first revised block from 1806, while he distinguishes the sciences that seek to describe the "nature of things" (*die Natur der Dinge*) from those concerned with "human nature as determined through the relations of the universe, what this is for a person, and how we necessarily discover it,"[68] he categorizes *both* as kinds of thinking. The former he designates as "*physics* or *metaphysics*," the latter as "*ethics* or *deontology* or *practical philosophy*."[69] What is more, he affirms that both forms of thinking can lead to actual *knowledge* (*Wissen*). As with *virtue*, so too with *knowledge*: in 1799, Schleiermacher used *Wissen* only five times; in his revision of 1806, his use of it triples to fifteen, eleven of which appear here in the first revised block. In the next main section (6.4), I argue how this more optimistic treatment of *knowing* is best viewed in light of his embrace of Plato. For now, I want to comment on how, in revised block n° 1, this shift complexified his presentation of the relation among The Three.

---

66 OR^2 156, altered; R^2 38 (... *seid mir auch wieder gefällig, und teilt mir mit wenn Ihr wo einen anderen Ausweg findet, wie Eure Meinung über die Religion nicht als nichts erscheinen kann, bis dahin mir dann nichts übrig bleibt als anzunehmen, dass Ihr es noch nicht recht untersucht hattet, und Euch selbst nicht verstanden habt über diese Seite der Religion*).
67 OR^2 156–57; R^2 38.
68 OR^2 157; R^2 39 (... *die Natur des Menschen und seine dadurch bestimmten Verhältnisse zum Universum, was dieses für ihn sein, und wie er es finden muss*).
69 OR^2 157; R^2 39 (*Wir mögen nun die eine Physik nennen oder Metaphysik, mit Einem Namen, oder wiederum geteilt mit zweien, und die andere Ethik oder Pflichtenlehre oder praktische Philosophie*).

6.3 Revised Block N° 1: A New Three of Thinking, Doing, and Feeling — 161

Unlike in the first edition, Schleiermacher in his revision does not immediately set religion over and against the other two. He grants that religion, *to a certain extent*, might be taken as a manner of thinking, insofar as it shares the same basic objective: "What else does faith know but the relation of human beings to God and to the world, the purpose for which God has made them, and the harm the world can do, or not do, to them?"[70] He nevertheless denies that faith is some "mixture of opinions about God and the world, about commandments for one life or two."[71] Yet, meanwhile, Schleiermacher presses the cultured despisers to reflect on procedures for attaining knowledge—procedures which they themselves employ in trying to educate people about their "enlightenment" (*Aufklärung*).[72] He criticizes them for dismissing religious ideas that may really only be intended for beginners. After all, in teaching their philosophy, they too must develop "a method ... of teaching something to beginners about the results of knowledge and to make them desire the subject-matter itself."[73] Progress sometimes requires tossing aside "some other pre-existing thing" or preventing the entrance of something else.[74] Arguably, what is said here about pedagogy and the need for a method for constructing knowledge echoes what in his *Introductions* he calls Plato's pedagogical progression of ideas: the teacher must sometimes start with myth and work with *erōs* (the impulse of desire), and then by means of the dialectical method guide the student in moving toward knowledge, eventually leaving myth behind.[75]

To be sure, some patterns of thought that hint at Plato can be found in the first edition and are carried over to the second. In both editions, Schleiermacher challenged the cultured despisers to give an account of the grounding and unifying principles for their practical and theoretical sciences. In both editions, he pestered the cultured despisers "with all kinds of Socratic questions," although in 1806 he newly confronts them: "Could a person, by some means or another,

---

[70] OR^2 157; R^2 39 (*Was weiß der Glaube anderes als das Verhältnis des Menschen zu Gott und zur Welt, wozu jener ihn gemacht hat, was diese ihm anhaben kann oder nicht?*).
[71] OR^2 158; R^2 40 (*... als ein solches Gemisch von Meinungen über Gott und die Welt, und von Geboten für Ein Leben oder zwei*).
[72] OR^2 158; R^2 40.
[73] OR^2 158; R^2 40 (*... eine Methode etwa Anfängern von den Resultaten des Wissens etwas beizubringen um ihnen Lust zu machen zur Sache selbst*).
[74] OR^2 158; R^2 40 (*und dabei findet Ihr eben nötig erst ein anderes noch Vorhandenes auszutreiben, oder wo es nicht wäre ihm den Eingang zu verhindern*).
[75] See above, 40–41, 81–82, 137–38.

possibly be wise and pious at the same time?"⁷⁶ Finally, in both editions, he followed that pestering with a reference to the ancient principle that "like is compared to like, and the particular subordinated to the universal."⁷⁷ Plato, after all, had been in the deep background of the first edition of the *Speeches*, hence such general references to him should not surprise us. In the second edition, however, this particular passage—this appeal to Socratic questions and to the ancient principle—takes on a different resonance, coming as it does after his point about pedagogical method and leading to a more direct challenge at the end of this revised block:

[Passage 6D: *Speeches*, 1806]

It may be so—or it may be that both of those [the theoretical and the practical sciences], which you are accustomed to contrasting, are one, only in *a still higher original knowledge*. You cannot believe that religion is this highest restored unity of knowledge—religion, which you most dearly want to detect in and to deny to those who are far enough removed from science. I myself do not want to hold you to this, since I do not want to take a position I would not be able to argue. You will probably admit, however, that for the first time you have to deal with this part of religion in order to discover what religion really means.⁷⁸

Aber es mag nun so sein oder jenes beides welches Ihr entgegenzusetzen pflegt, mag nur in <u>*einem noch höheren ursprünglichen Wissen*</u> *eins sein, Ihr könnt doch nicht glauben dass die Religion diese höchste wiederhergestellte Einheit des Wissens sei, sie die Ihr bei denen am meisten findet und bestreiten wollt, die von der Wissenschaft weit genug entfernt sind. Hierzu will ich selbst Euch nicht anhalten; denn ich will keinen Platz besetzen, den ich nicht behaupten könn, aber das werdet Ihr wohl zugeben, denn ich will keinen Platz besetzen, den dass Ihr auch mit diesem Teil der Religion Euch erst Zeit nehmen müsst, um zu ich nicht behaupten könnte, aber zu dem untersuchen was er eigentlich bedeute.*⁷⁹

The notion here of a *higher original knowledge*⁸⁰ is without doubt indebted to Schleiermacher's immersion in Plato, as we shall explore more fully in the

---

76 *OR*² 158; *R*² 41 (*Ich hätte Lust, wenn Ihr es so meint, Euch durch allerlei sokratische Fragen zu ängstigen, manche endlich zu einer unverhohlenen Antwort zu nötigen auf die Frage, ob einer wohl auf irgendeine Art weise und fromm sein könnte zugleich*).
77 *OR*² 159, altered; *R*² 41 (*das Ähnliche zusammengestellt und das Besondere dem Allgemeinen untergeordnet wird*). See, e. g., *OR*¹ 99; *R*¹ 40 (*KGA* 1/2:209.15–18).
78 *OR*² 159, altered, emphasis added. In 1821, Schleiermacher would add an explanation to this passage denying that his opinion "really [had] been that religion is this restored unity of knowledge" (*OR*³ 102)/... *wenn auch meine Meinung wirklich gewesen wäre, die Religion sei selbst diese wiederhergestellte Einheit des Wissens* (R 115).
79 *R*² 41–42; emphasis added.
80 Schleiermacher's use of the modifier *original* (*ursprünglich*) doubles in the second edition of the second Speech.

next chapter, but for now I want to continue focusing on his re-conceptualization of The Three.

Were it only a matter of the introduction of the terms *Wissen* and *Tugend* here, that itself might suggest an influence of *Platons Werke* on his revisions to the *Speeches* but would not necessarily establish any profound depth of influence. The influence, however, was indeed profound insofar as it was pervasive and structural in nature. Schleiermacher begins a Platonic recasting of his argument right here in revised block n° 1, with his reconceptualization of The Three, and carries it forward. Since by "Platonic" I mean a distinctly Schleiermacherian interpretation of Plato, we need to attend to how, in *Platons Werke*, Schleiermacher treats the two principal activities, *thinking* and *acting*; their highest expression in *knowledge* and *virtue*; and the relation between their corresponding sciences, *physics* (*Physik*) and *ethics* (*Ethik*). Much as Schleiermacher's interpretation of Plato on these points determined his ordering of the dialogues, so it likewise contributed to his revised argument in the second Speech, particularly in how The Three function, each on its own and each in relation to one another. He continues that argument in the second revised block.

6.4 Revised Block N° 2: "Contemplation is Essential to Religion"

The second revised block begins just less than a page after the first ends and runs for about four (split-column) pages.[81] Its immediate context is a brief discussion of scripture and the cultured despisers' disdain for it. The original text from 1799 was significant in that, among other things, it included Schleiermacher's first use of the term *intuition*, which was also the first time he coupled *intuition* with *feeling*,[82] and it also contained the memorable phrase that "religion lives its whole life in nature, but in the infinite nature of [the whole], the one and all."[83] In the revised text, Schleiermacher tempers his earlier glib treatment of scripture; describes the educational process as a dialectical one; drops the reference to *intuition*, develops the notion of *Gefühl*, and introduces a new term, *contemplation*; elaborates on The Three and, in doing so, resituates the memorable phrase ("religion lives its whole life…"); introduces the two sciences, ethics and physics; and, finally, employs a new type of language, such as the *science of*

---

81 See *R* (Peter) 43–46; *OR²* 160–64. See table 8.
82 See *OR¹* 102; *R¹* 45 (*KGA* 1/2:211.33).
83 *OR¹* 102; *R¹* 46 (*KGA* 1/2:212.5–7) (*Die Religion lebt ihr ganzes Leben auch in der Natur, aber in der unendlichen Natur des Ganzen, des Einen und Allen*).

being. Each of these changes is significant, and each reflects Schleiermacher's work on Plato. Revised block n° 2 is a lengthy revision that must be carefully unpacked.

6.4.1 Appearances, Education, and the Higher Nature of Knowing

At this point in both editions, Schleiermacher addressed the problem of literalness in interpreting scripture and uttered in exacerbation, "If only you but knew to read between the lines!"[84] His revision commences with a seemingly minor switch in metaphor that nonetheless suggests the influence of Plato. In both editions, Schleiermacher made the point that "religion never appears pure" and that the despisers must therefore beget it "by means of an original creation" in themselves.[85] Yet, whereas in 1799 Schleiermacher (mixing metaphors somewhat) encouraged the despisers to "crack open this shell"[86] in order to get at the hidden diamond, in 1806 he addresses them as philosophers and educators rather than as miners: "You, however, are expected to penetrate through this appearance [*Schein*]."[87] Although he returns to a metaphor of finding riches in the earth, he alters the imagery from miner to the alchemist-artist who reconstitutes fine metals "in their glorious splendour."[88] In other words, in this struggle against appearances, Schleiermacher tries to enlist the despisers in the struggle against modern sophists.

In the first edition, speaking in the third person, Schleiermacher admitted that religious leaders, in trying to win over proselytes, rarely broke through that shell and consequently too often confused religion with metaphysics and morals. After briefly conceding this was perhaps due to the very nature of rhetoric, he hastened on to the next point.[89] In his revision of that passage in 1806, however, Schleiermacher presents a defense of scripture and religious education. Mid-stream, he shifts from third- to second-person plural, directly addressing his interlocutors and pointing to their own pedagogical practices. He de-

---

[84] *OR*² 160 (cf. *OR*¹ 101); *R* 43 (*KGA* 1/2:211.4) (*Wüßtet Ihr doch nur zwischen den Zeilen zu lesen!*).
[85] *OR*² 160 (cf. *OR*¹ 100); *R* 42 (*KGA* 1/2:210.30,36–38) (... *daß die Religion nie rein erscheint, ... in geistigen Dingen ist Euch das Ursprüngliche nicht anders zu schaffen, als wenn Ihr es durch eine ursprüngliche Schöpfung in Euch erzeugt*).
[86] *OR*¹ 101; *R*¹ 43 (*KGA* 1/2:211.9) (... *diese Schale zu spalten*).
[87] *OR*² 160; *R*² 43 (*aber Euch wird zugemutet durch diesen Schein hindurchzudringen*).
[88] *OR*² 160; *R*² 43 (*So bringt auch die Natur edle Metalle vererzt mit geringeren Substanzen hervor, und doch weiß unser Sinn sie zu entdecken, und in ihrem herrlichen Glanze wiederherzustellen*).
[89] See Crouter's salient discussion of this passage and debates concerning it (*OR*¹ 101n5).

scribes the educational process as a "dialectical" one. At the very least, this injection of the term *dialectical* could fairly be interpreted as an allusion to Plato, given how Schleiermacher focused on Platonic dialectics in his *Introductions*, but it is really much more than just an allusion. His description of the educational process in this revised passage of the *Speeches* maps neatly onto the pedagogical progression of ideas that served as an organizing principle in *Platons Werke:*

[Passage 6E: *Speeches*, 1806]

The sacred scriptures were not for perfected believers alone but principally for the children in the faith, for the newly dedicated, for those standing on the threshold and wanting to be invited in. How could they do it otherwise than exactly as I have just done it with you? They had to attach themselves to the given, seeking in it the means towards *a kind of spark by which, out of dark presentiments, the new sense could then be excited*. And do you not recognize the aspiration to break through from a lower sphere to a higher sphere in the way in which those concepts are treated in the *educational pursuit*—even if often in the sphere of a paltry and ingrate language? As you well see, this kind of communication could not be other than *poetic* or *oratorical* [*rednerisch*]. And what lies closer to the latter than the *dialectical?* What, since time immemorial, has been utilized more magnificently and successfully in revealing the *higher nature of knowing and of the inner feeling?* But, certainly, this objective will not be reached if you remain fixated on its *dressing* alone.[90]

Die heiligen Schriften waren nicht für die vollendeten Gläubigen allein, sondern vornehmlich für die Kinder im Glauben, für die Neugeweihten, für die welche an der Schwelle stehen und eingeladen sein wollen. Wie konnten sie es also anders machen, als jetzt eben auch ich es mache mit Euch? Sie mussten sich anschließen an das Gegebene, und in diesem die Mittel suchen zu <u>einer solche Spannung, bei welcher dann auch der neue Sinn aus dunklen Ahnungen konnte aufgeregt werden</u>. Und erkennt Ihr nicht an der Art wie jene Begriffe behandelt werden, an <u>dem bildenden Treiben</u>, wenngleich oft im Gebiet einer armseligen undankbaren Sprache, das Bestreben aus einem niederen Gebiet durchzubrechen in ein höheres? Eine solche Mitteilung, das seht Ihr wohl, konnte nicht anders sein als <u>dichterisch</u> oder <u>rednerisch</u>; und was liegt wohl dem letzteren näher als <u>das Dialektische</u>? was ist von jeher herrlicher und glücklicher gebraucht worden um <u>die höhere Natur des Erkennens und des inneren Gefühls</u> zu offenbaren? Aber freilich wird dieser Zweck nicht erreicht, wenn Ihr bei der Einkleidung allein stehen bleibt.[91]

This revision to the second Speech reflects Schleiermacher's Plato in at least five concrete ways, as I have indicated with italics (in the English version). I now take each point in turn.

First, Schleiermacher explains how beginners must start with *presentiments* (*Ahn[d]ungen*) and are propelled along by an energizing pressure or spark, so

---

90 OR^2 161, altered, emphasis added.
91 R^2 43–44, emphasis added.

that they move into *higher spheres*, and thus is their education deepened. Although the term *Ahnung* is not new to the second edition, Schleiermacher's use of it in this particular context reflects his theory of interpreting Plato in his *Introductions*,[92] and it also happens to be the same language he used to describe Plato in the *Grundlinien*.[93] Furthermore, it recalls his reason for placing the *Phaedrus* as the first dialogue: whereas the second part of the dialogue lays forth the method (*dialectics*) for proceeding towards knowledge, the first part identifies the impulse for proceeding—namely, *erōs*.[94] This is where learners begin their quest for knowledge. In Plato's dialogues, according to Schleiermacher, myth plays a key role in the earlier dialogues, before the student possesses real knowledge and virtue. In the second edition of the *Speeches* (and more so in later editions), Schleiermacher assigns a similar role to more naïve readings of scripture as he simultaneously points to other layers of meaning, hence to the need for sophisticated exegesis. Scripture thus seems here to take on a role analogous to that of myth in the earlier Platonic dialogues: it is that on to which the novice holds, that attractive force which draws the novice forward. The difference (and it is a significant one) is that, whereas in Plato's dialogues myth is eventually abandoned as vehicle (although it does return in Book I of the *Republic*), in religion the holy scriptures need not (indeed cannot) be. Piety requires that literalness, not scripture itself, be left behind. As Paul Nimmo argues in his careful study of Schleiermacher's treatment of scripture in various editions of the *Speeches*, the "potentially reductive comments on Scripture from the first edition," although sometimes retained verbatim in later editions, were also as frequently "amended to reflect a more expansive view of the significance of Scripture."[95]

Second, in this revised passage Schleiermacher frames the process of education much more positively than he had in 1799, when he seemed to grant that the making of proselytes in religion was a form of manipulation. In 1806 he points instead to a genuine progression whereby education is deepened; what is more, this *educational deepening* is aided by the poetic and by attraction to what is beautiful. This closely resembles his idea of the pedagogical progression of ideas in the Platonic dialogues and, once again, what he said about Plato in the *Grundlinien*. This revision might be deemed problematic in that it appears to reveal an inconsistency in his argument—namely, that religion can be taught,

---

[92] See, e.g., *IDP* 5, 42, 44, 67, 79; *PW* 1/1:20, 54, 56, 79, 427.
[93] See above, chap. 1, 15–17.
[94] See above, 3.3.
[95] Paul T. Nimmo, "Schleiermacher on Scripture and the Work of Jesus Christ," *Modern Theology* 31, no. 1 (January 2015): 25, 26.

that it is therefore a kind of knowing. As we shall see shortly, however, Schleiermacher goes on, almost in the next breath, to distinguish knowing from piety. Here the topic is not religion *per se* but the use of scripture. Although beginners might be more literal-minded and might attach themselves to simpler stories, that is often a phase. The cultured despisers, who have experience with the difficulty of educating people, should not mistake a *lower* form for a *higher*. If they do, Schleiermacher noted, then they themselves are being too literal.

Third, in this revised passage Schleiermacher explicitly ties the *oratorical* or *rhetorical* to the *dialectical*. Interestingly, he replaces "rhetorical" (*rhetorisch*) with "oratorical" (*rednerisch*).[96] Arguably, his earlier suspicion of rhetoric in 1799 is replaced by a more nuanced understanding of the communication of religion. In 1806, he embraces a *poetic and oratorical* practice, which is not manipulation but, employed rightly, aids in the movement towards something *higher*; it is rightly employed when it is connected to *dialectics*. This closely mirrors Schleiermacher's interpretation of Plato's critique of sophistical rhetoric. For instance, in his "Introduction to the *Phaedrus*," Schleiermacher explains:

[Passage 6F: "Intro. to *Phaedrus*"]

To blind the understanding of the hearers by sophistical means, and then, in particular passages, to excite their minds emotionally—this was their whole object; as likewise an extremely deficient and uniform method of instruction in composition, with uselessly accumulated subdivisions and technical terms, and some maxims upon the use of language, leading at most only to harmony and fulness of sound, or to the production of striking and brilliant effect, made up the whole secret. And thus the [art of speaking] was altogether devoid of internal substance. All this then, which up to this time had passed for the art itself, is degraded by Plato to the rank of technical knack, and while he exposes in its nakedness the principle of the sophistical rhetoricians, that he who would convince need not himself know the true and right, he shews, that in order really to produce conviction, that is, to compel as it were others to certain thoughts and judgments, if this is to be done at all, however without reference to the truth, yet with that degree of certainty which alone can lay claim to the name of art—he shews, I say, that an aptitude at deceiving and undeceiving is requisite, an art of logical semblance, which can itself rest on nothing but a scientific method of comprehending similar notions under higher; and a like knowledge of the difference of notions, *that dialectics, therefore, must be the true foundation of rhetoric, and that only what is connected with its principles, properly belongs to the art.*[97]

---

[96] Bart Philipsen lends further insight into this passage, arguing that Schleiermacher's view of rhetoric can be read as a retort to F. Schlegel's aesthetic account of religion. See "Inoculations of the Other: The Rhetorics and Politics of Religious Formation in Schleiermacher's *On Religion*," pt. 1 in Borgman, ten Kate, and Philipsen, "Triptych on Schleiermacher's *On Religion*," 381–93.
[97] *IDP* 51–52, emphasis added.

Den Verstand der Hörer durch sophistische Hülfsmittel zu blenden, und dann in einzelen Stellen auf leidenschaftliche Weise ihre Gemüther aufzuregen, dieses war die ganze Absicht, so wie eine sehr dürftige einförmige Anweisung zur Composition mit unnüz angehäuften Unterabtheilungen und Kunstworten, und einige fast nur auf den Wohllaut und die Wortfülle oder auf das Auffallende und Glänzende hinführende Vorschriften über die Behandlung der Sprache das ganze Geheimniß ausmachten; auf welche Art es freilich der Kunst an aller Haltung fehlte. Dieses alles nun, was bisher für die Kunst selbst gegolten, sezt Platon zurük auf den Rang technischer Handgriffe, und indem er den Grundsaz der sophistischen Redekünstler, daß derjenige, welcher überreden wolle, das Wahre und Richtige selbst nicht zu wissen brauche, in seiner Blöße darstellt: so zeigt er, daß um wirklich Ueberredung hervorzubringen, das heißt Andere zu gewissen Gedanken und Urtheilen gleichsam zu nöthigen, wenn dies anders wenn gleich ohne Hinsicht auf die Wahrheit doch mit derjenigen Sicherheit geschehen solle, die allein auf den Namen Kunst Anspruch machen kann, eine Fertigkeit der Täuschung und Enttäuschung erfordert werde, eine Kunst des logischen Scheines, welche selbst wiederum nur auf einer wissenschaftlichen Methode des Zusammenfassens gleicher Begriffe unter höhere, und auf einer eben solchen Kenntniß von der Verschiedenheit der Begriffe beruhen könne, <u>daß also die Dialektik das wahre Fundament der Rhetorik sei, und nur was mit ihren Principien zusammenhängt, eigentlich zur Kunst gehöre</u>.[98]

Fourth, Schleiermacher's appeal regarding the *higher nature of knowing and of the inner feeling* is clearly Platonic, as he understood that. For example, in his "Introduction to the *Parmenides*," he connects a *higher knowledge* with *intuition*: "The difficulties, which are here put forward in opposition to every theory of ideas, are not to be solved in the philosophy of Plato otherwise than by an exact comparison of the purer or higher knowledge with the empirical, and furthermore by the doctrine of original intuition and recollection."[99] We shall explore this connection further in the next chapter.

Fifth and finally, the reference to *dressing* or *outer garment* (*Einkleidung*) seems to echo a signature point he makes in *Platons Werke*. As we have seen, in his "General Introduction" Schleiermacher criticizes previous interpreters of Plato for dismissing the dialogic form as mere *dressing* (*Einkleidung*) that can be easily discarded, rather than as a necessary part of Plato's philosophy. They made the mistake, in other words, of separating form from content.[100]

---

[98] *PW* 1/1:66.7–30, emphasis added.
[99] *EÜP* 145 (*Die Schwierigkeiten nämlich, welche hier gegen jede Theorie von den Begriffen vorgebracht worden sind in der Philosophie des Platon nicht anders zu lösen als durch genaue Vergleichung der reineren oder höheren Erkenntnis und der empirischen, ferner durch die Lehre von der ursprünglichen Anschauung und der Rückerinnerung*); cf. *IDP* 132.
[100] See above, chap. 2, 42.

6.4.2 The Science of Being, the Infinite, and Contemplation

The two editions of the second Speech seem to come back together at this point, where Schleiermacher declares that religion "renounces all claims on whatever belongs to science and ethics," except that in 1799 it was "metaphysics" and "morals."[101] Yet that is not in fact the case, since the conceptual shift to *thinking* and *acting*, hence to *science* and *ethics*, reshapes the flow of the entire argument in the second Speech. We witness the extent to which this is true in the remainder of this revised block. A litmus test is found, I suggest, in tracing the fortunes of what Schleiermacher does differently with the following well-known line from the first edition, already cited: *Religion also lives its whole life in nature, but in the infinite nature of [the whole], the one and all.* In what follows, I refer to this as "our line."

In both editions, our line appears early in the Speech. In 1799, our line stood alone, tucked in amidst a quick cascade of strong contrasts between religion, on the one hand, and metaphysics and morals, on the other. That entire comparison occupied about a half of a page. The purpose of our line (underscored in 6G) in the first edition was to help distinguish religion from metaphysics in particular:

[Passage 6G: *Speeches*, 1799:]

Metaphysics proceeds from finite human nature and wants to define consciously, from its simplest concept, the extent of its powers, and its receptivity, what the universe can be for us and how we necessarily must view it. <u>Religion also lives its whole life in nature, but in the infinite nature of [the whole], the one and all</u>; what holds in nature for everything individual also holds for the human being; and wherever everything, including man, may press on or tarry within this eternal ferment of individual forms and beings, religion wishes to intuit [*anschauen*] and to divine [*ahnden*] this in detail in quiet submissiveness.[102]

Die Metaphysik geht aus von der endlichen Natur des Menschen, und will aus ihrem einfachsten Begriff, und aus dem Umfang ihrer Kräfte und ihrer Empfänglichkeit mit Bewusstsein bestimmen, was das Universum für ihn sein kann, und wie er es notwendig erblicken muss. <u>*Die Religion lebt ihr ganzes Leben auch in der Natur, aber in der unendlichen Natur des Ganzen, des Einen und Allen*</u>; *was in dieser alles Einzelne und so auch der Mensch gilt, und wo alles und auch er treiben und bleiben mag in dieser ewigen Gärung einzelner Formen und Wesen, das will sie in stiller Ergebenheit im Einzelnen anschauen und ahnden.*[103]

---

101 OR^2 161 (cf. OR^1 101); R^2 44 (... *entsagt die Religion vorläufig allen Ansprüchen auf irgendetwas das jenen angehörte*).
102 OR^1 102, emphasis added.
103 R^1 46 (*KGA* 1/2:212.2–10), emphasis added.

In the very next sentence, Schleiermacher moved on to draw the sharp contrast between religion and morality, which he also portrayed negatively.

By contrast, in 1806 the overall comparison of piety with what Schleiermacher now calls the *science of being* and the *science of ethics* is considerably longer (three to four split-column pages), in no small part because he is no longer so dismissive of the two *sciences*. (Because the revision is so lengthy, I break his account of the *science of being* down into two main parts, labeled as passages 6H and 6I.) Schleiermacher begins by offering a favorable view of knowing, hence a confidence in our ability to know, which reflects his engagement with Plato:

> [Passage 6H: *Speeches*, 1806]
>
> For what does your *science of being* strive after—your natural science, in which everything real must unite itself to your theoretical philosophy? To know things, I imagine, each in its distinctive essence; to identify the specific relations through which each one is what it is; to determine its place in the whole and to distinguish it from others; to situate every actual thing in its reciprocal, contingent necessity; and to state the unity between all appearances and their eternal laws. This is truly beautiful and divine, and I have no intention of disparaging it.[104]
>
> *Denn wonach strebt Eure* Wissenschaft des Seins, *Eure Naturwissenschaft, in welcher doch alles Reale Eurer theoretischen Philosophie sich vereinigen muss? Die Dinge, denke ich, in ihrem eigentümlichen Wesen zu erkennen; die besonderen Beziehungen aufzuzeigen, durch welche jedes ist, was es ist; jedem seine Stelle im Ganzen zu bestimmen und es von anderen zu unterscheiden; alles Wirkliche in seiner gegenseitigen bedingten Notwendigkeit hinzustellen und die Einerleiheit aller Erscheinungen mit ihren ewigen Gesetzen darzutun. Dies ist ja wahrlich schön und göttlich, und ich bin nicht gemeint es herabzusetzen.*[105]

In short, whereas in 1799 Schleiermacher criticized *metaphysics* for its speculative impulses along with its desire to impose order and to control, in 1806 he honors the *science of being* for being about discovery, for uniting the theoretical and the real, for understanding each thing on its own and in reciprocal relation—and, crucially, for examining fleeting *appearances* in terms of *eternal laws*. This, for Schleiermacher, was at the heart of Platonic epistemology.[106]

Having thus extolled the science of being, Schleiermacher pivots back to reaffirm the contrast between religion and knowledge: "religion has nothing to do with knowledge and ... its essence is perceived quite apart from any association

---

104 OR^2 161–62, emphasis added.
105 R^2 44, emphasis added.
106 See Schleiermacher, "Introduction to the *Gorgias*," *IDP* 171; *PW* 2/1:11.18–29. See below, passage 7L, 218–19.

6.4 Revised Block N° 2: "Contemplation is Essential to Religion" — 171

with knowledge."¹⁰⁷ He insists that the pious are humble and will concede their ignorance (a Socratic theme he repeats often in his revisions), and that they respect scientific knowledge. Then he proceeds, at considerable length, to delineate the differences between knowledge and piety, yet without the stark, antagonistic oppositions he employed in 1799. This part of revised block n° 2 is almost entirely new, except that it is here where he inserts our line about religion (underscored in 6I, whereas significant new additions are italicized). The new context and the redeployment of some wordings are significant not only for what they say about religion but also for how they reflect Schleiermacher's interpretation of Plato:

[Passage 6I: *Speeches*, 1806:]

What I actually want to do is to translate for you, with clear words, what most of them [the pious] only suspect but do not know themselves how to express. When you place God at the apex of your science as the ground of all knowing, they do honor and respect this, but this is not the same as their way of having and knowing about God—nay, neither science nor knowing arises out of their way. For, indeed, *contemplation [Betrachtung] is essential to religion.* You will never want to call anyone pious whose sense for the life of the world is not open, anyone who goes there in impenetrable obtuseness. This *contemplation*, however, does not attend to the essence of one finite thing in opposition to other finite things. It is, rather, simply the immediate perception [*Wahrnehmung*] of the *universal existence [Sein] of everything finite in the infinite and through the infinite, of everything temporal in the eternal and through the eternal*. This seeking and finding in all that *lives and moves*, in all *becoming and change*, in all *doing and suffering*, and just having and knowing life itself in immediate feeling as this existence [*Sein*]—this is religion. Religion is satisfied wherever it finds this; wherever this lies hidden, there is for religion inhibition and anxiety, necessity and death. <u>And so religion is certainly a life in the infinite nature of the whole, in the one and all, and it sees everything in God and God in everything</u>. It is not, however, knowledge [*Wissen*] or knowing [*Erkennen*], neither of the world nor of God—but it simply appreciates this without being it. To religion, knowledge is also *a stirring and revelation of the infinite in the finite*, which religion also sees in God and God in it.¹⁰⁸

... ich will Euch sogar mit klaren Worten dolmetschen, wie die meisten von ihnen nur ahnen aber nicht von sich zu geben wissen, dass wenn Ihr Gott an die Spitze Eurer Wissenschaft stellt als den Grund alles Erkennens, sie dieses zwar loben und ehren, dies aber nicht dasselbige ist wie ihre Art Gott zu haben und um ihn zu wissen, aus welcher ja das Erkennen und die Wissenschaft nicht hervorgeht. Denn freilich <u>ist der Religion die Betrachtung wesentlich</u>, und wer in zugeschlossener Stumpfsinnigkeit hingeht, wem nicht der Sinn offen ist für das Leben der Welt, den werdet Ihr nie fromm nennen wollen; aber diese <u>Betrachtung</u> geht nicht auf das Wesen eines Endlichen im Gegensatz gegen das andere Endliche; sondern sie ist nur die un-

---

107 *OR*² 162; *R*² 44 (... *aber doch behaupte ich, dass die Religion es mit dem Wissen gar nicht zu tun hat, und dass auch ohne Gemeinschaft mit demselben ihr Wesen wahrgenommen wird*).
108 *OR*² 162–63, emphasis added, trans. altered.

> mittelbare Wahrnehmung von <u>dem allgemeinen Sein alles Endlichen im Unendlichen und durch das Unendliche, alles Zeitlichen im Ewigen und durch das Ewige</u>. Dieses Suchen und Finden in allem was lebt und sich regt, in allem <u>Werden und Wechsel</u>, in allem <u>Tun und Leiden</u> und das Leben selbst nur haben und kennen im unmittelbaren Gefühl als dieses Sein, das ist Religion. Ihre Befriedigung ist wo sie dieses findet; wo sich dies verbirgt, da ist für sie Hemmung und Ängstigung, Not und Tod. <u>Und so ist sie freilich ein Leben in der unendlichen Natur des Ganzen, im Einen und Allen, in Gott, und sieht alles in Gott und Gott in allem</u>. Aber das Wissen und Erkennen ist sie nicht, weder der Welt noch Gottes, sondern dies erkennt sie nur an ohne es zu sein; es ist ihr auch <u>eine Regung und Offenbarung des Unendlichen im Endlichen</u>, die sie auch sieht in Gott und Gott in ihr.[109]

Blackwell similarly chooses to highlight (part of) this passage for its "Platonic aspects," which he identifies as being threefold: "Schleiermacher's sense for the infinite"; his "emphasis upon life and motion, becoming and change"; and the "sense for 'the organic whole'."[110] Let us take Blackwell's insight a step further by comparing Schleiermacher's revision here with its earlier version in order to track more specifically the reciprocating influences between the *Introductions* and the *Speeches*. Before we can identify any such influences, however, we need to be clear about what is new in this passage.

Contemplation (Betrachtung).[111] What should stand out immediately, yet what has gone largely unnoticed in commentaries, is Schleiermacher's introduction of the term *contemplation*. He uses it twice here (6I) in connection with the infinite and eternal, and once more in revised block n° 2; overall in the second Speech, his use of the term more than triples in the second edition (from five times in 1799 to eighteen times in 1806). That this has been overlooked is curious, given that, as we see here, he newly declares that *contemplation is essential to religion.*[112]

The infinite (das Unendliche). Another point that stands out is how Schleiermacher here changes how he speaks of the infinite. In the first edition, when he referred to the infinite at this early point in the Speech, it was in terms of what the moralists and metaphysicians had gotten wrong about the infinite, so that the reader had to infer what the correct stance towards the infinite might be. In the second edition, not only does he refer to the infinite more often (four times as opposed to once), but he does so more directly and positively, as he

---

109 R^2 45, emphasis added. See Harvey's criticism of Terrence Tice's decision to translate the end of that last line as "… and God sees it in religion" ("On the New Edition," 496).
110 Blackwell, *Schleiermacher's Early Philosophy of Life*, 134.
111 See *DWB* s.v. BETRACHTUNG: "*f. contemplatio, consideratio.*"
112 Patsch also notes increased use of *Betrachtung* in the second edition and attributes it to a more Christian readership (see "Schleiermachers theologische Schriften," 48–49).

6.4 Revised Block N° 2: "Contemplation is Essential to Religion" — 173

also connects it with the *eternal* (*das Ewig*) and with *God* (*Gott*). Furthermore, in this expanded revision Schleiermacher highlights the dynamic, immanental relation between the finite and the infinite by introducing language about the finite existing *in* the infinite, about the infinite revealing itself *in and through* the finite (twice here in revised block n° 2 and once again in revised block n° 3). It is not so much that this was a new idea in 1806 (indeed, it had been key to his organic monism in 1799) as it is that Schleiermacher lends it fuller expression in his revision.[113] In 1799, Schleiermacher referred frequently to "the infinite," but he never actually bound it so explicitly or closely to "the finite." In marked contrast, in 1806 he relates the infinite and finite more intimately together by speaking (as in this passage) of how the finite exists only *in* and *through* the infinite, the temporal *in* and *through* the eternal; moreover, he underscores the importance of this close relation through repetition; finally, he identifies the infinite as God.

Omissions: Intuition, the Universe. Not just additions but omissions, too, need to be counted as something new in any significant alteration, even as we need to remember that passages from the two editions do not always line up cleanly, so that what appears to be dropped in one place might reappear in another revised block. Nonetheless, there are two noteworthy omissions here. First, Schleiermacher no longer pairs *intuition* and *feeling*.[114] Instead, he drops *intuition* at this point but retains *feeling*, which is newly modified by *immediate* (*unmittelbaren*).[115] Second, whereas in the (roughly) corresponding text from 1799 Schleiermacher referred to *the universe* four times, he no longer does so at all in 1806. As we shall see, he does refer to both *intuition* and the *universe* several times in revised block n° 4, so that these two key terms are not altogether dropped, but their use is more restricted. For instance, *universe* is dropped here (6I), and his use of it throughout the first and second Speeches is reduced by two-thirds to three-quarters (from about seventy-five times in 1799 to twenty-one times in 1806). While these omissions could be related to his work on Plato, it is not immediately clear how that might be. Nonetheless, the first two changes (regarding *contemplation* and *the infinite*) do align in interesting ways with his discussions of the middle dialogues in *Platons Werke*, especially with his introductions to the *Symposium* and the *Phaedo*.

---

[113] For further elaboration on his organic monism of 1799, see Lamm, *Living God*, chap. 2: "Berlin and the *Speeches on Religion*," 57–94.
[114] See *R* 45: in the middle of left-hand column for 1799, in the middle of right-hand column for this new passage.
[115] He refers to *Gefühl* two more times in this revised block, once modified by "inner" (*inneren*) and the other time by "finest" (*feinste*).

Let us return to our line, using it as a guidepost. Schleiermacher's new elaboration of what it means to *live a life in the infinite nature of the whole, in the one and all* picks up at least two Platonic themes that preoccupied him in his interpretation of the dialogues he assigned to the middle trilogy: the holding together of the temporal and eternal, of change and changelessness, of becoming and being, and of the mortal and immortal; and the role of contemplation in that holding-together. In some ways, the terminology he adopts in the *Speeches* is different from that in his *Introductions*. Schleiermacher only refers to *the infinite* as a noun once in his *Introductions*, since it was not Plato's term, but when he does refer to it, he connects it to *eternity*. For example, in his "Introduction to the *Phaedrus*," referring to Socrates's second speech, he writes, "we have the inspired tone, the exaltation of beauty to an equal rank with the highest moral ideas, and its close connection with *the Eternal and Infinite*."[116] Note that in the revised passage from the *Speeches* under consideration (6I), he likewise associates the infinite with the eternal: *the universal existence [Sein] of everything finite in the infinite and through the infinite, of everything temporal in the eternal and through the eternal*. Even though Schleiermacher otherwise does not use the noun *the infinite* in his *Introductions*, there are illuminating parallels between his treatment of the dialogues and his revisions of the second Speech in 1806. Let us therefore direct our attention back to his *Introductions*.

6.4.3 Plato's Middle Dialogues on the Infinite and the Finite

As we have seen, Schleiermacher held that in the middle dialogues[117] Plato turned his attention from philosophical *method* to the *object* of philosophy, namely "the true and what-*is* [*Seienden*], ... the eternal and immutable."[118] We have furthermore seen how Schleiermacher reined in the more speculative moments in the *Sophist* and *Phaedo*, where Plato might seem to be separating absolute being from finite being, the immortal from the mortal. Schleiermacher resisted potentially more dualistic strains of Plato's metaphysics by means of his

---

116 *IDP* 54, emphasis added; *PW* 1/1:68.36–69.3 (... *das Begeisterte, die Erhebung der Schönheit zu gleichem Range mit den höchsten sittlichen Ideen und ihre genaue Verbindung mit dem Ewigen und Unendlichen*).
117 Schleiermacher identified the middle dialogues as the *Gorgias, Theaetetus, Meno, Euthydemus, Cratylus, Sophist, Statesman, Symposium, Phaedo*, and *Philebus*. See tables 2 & 3.
118 *PW* 1/1:11.12–14 (*Der Anschauung des Wahren und Seienden, welches eben deshalb das Ewige und Unveränderliche ist, mit der wie wir gesehen haben alle Darstellung der platonischen Philosophie anfing,...*); cf. *IDP* 171.

internal method—that is, by reading parts (individual passages or dialogues) in relation to larger wholes (a dialogue, a trilogy of dialogues, the entire *corpus*), and by seeking out what he called the natural and necessary connections.[119] A case in point is how he read the *Symposium* first in relation to the *Sophist* and then in relation to the *Phaedo*. Let us return to his treatment of those dialogues, this time reading them in light of his revisions of the *Speeches* and, simultaneously and correlatively, reading those revisions in light of his *Introductions*, all the while bearing in mind that Schleiermacher was actually revising his *Speeches* and preparing volume II,2 of *Platons Werke* at roughly the same time in 1806.

According to Schleiermacher, in contrast to the *Sophist*, which enunciates "the nature of all true philosophy" (*das Wesen aller wahren Philosophie*) and for the first time offers that "glance into that higher sphere of speculation" (*der Blick in jenes höhere Gebiet der Spekulation*),[120] the *Symposium* emphasizes the true philosopher as embodied in Socrates. The subject-matter of the *Symposium* is, he proposes,

[Passage 6J: "Intro. to *Symposium*"]

not the absolute being [*Sein*] and nature of wisdom, but its life and its appearance in the mortal life of the visible person, in whom wisdom itself—for this is clearly Plato's main point in all his explanations of philosophy—has put on mortality and shown itself as subject to time as a becoming and expanding, so that the life of the philosopher too is not some repose in wisdom, but is instead a striving to retain it and, taking up each excitable point throughout time and throughout space, to imagine that immortality becomes in the mortal.

... *also nicht etwa das absolute Sein und Wesen der Weisheit sollte dargestellt werden, sondern ihr Leben und ihre Erscheinung in dem sterblichen Leben des erscheinenden Menschen, in welchem sie selbst, denn dies ist offenbar die Hauptansicht des Platon in allen seinen Erklärungen über die Philosophie, das sterbliche angezogen hat und der Zeit unterworfen als ein werdendes und sich verbreitendes sich offenbart, so daß auch das Leben des Philosophen nicht etwa ein Ruhen in der Weisheit ist, sondern ein Streben sie festzuhalten und an jeden erregbaren Punkt anknüpfend der ganzen Zeit und dem ganzen Raume einzubilden, auf daß eine Unsterblichkeit werde in dem Sterblichen.*[121]

In other words, as a counterweight to any desire to be rid of the mortal body, Schleiermacher stresses Socrates's embodiment of wisdom along with his desire to be with friends and celebrate mortal life.

---

119 See above, 4.4.
120 *IDP* 253; *EÜP* 250.
121 *EÜP* 276; cf. *IDP* 279–80.

The *Phaedo*, with its focus on the immortality of the soul, presented a special problem for Schleiermacher because of the "passionate desire [expressed therein] to become pure spirit, that wish for death in the wise man"[122]—a desire that appears to devalue material, bodily, temporal existence. He resolves the problem by stressing the natural, necessary relation between the *Phaedo* and the *Symposium*. When these two dialogues are read together, as he insists they should be, the dualistic tendencies (immortal vs. mortal, soul vs. body) in Plato are mitigated to the point of disappearance:

[Passage 6K: "Intro. to *Phaedo*"]

Whoever then comprehends the connection of these two points in the sense in which Plato meant it, will certainly no longer hesitate to place the *Phaedon* and the *Symposium* together, and to recognise the reciprocal relation of the two. For, as the love there described [in the *Symposium*] exhibits the endeavour to connect the immortal with the mortal, that *pure contemplation* [*reine Betrachtung*] here [in the *Phaedo*] is the endeavour to withdraw the immortal, as such, away from the mortal; and the two are manifestly in necessary connection with one another.[123]

Wer nun so den Zusammenhang dieser beiden Punkte im Sinn des Platon aufgefaßt hat, der wird wohl nicht länger Bedenken tragen, den 'Phaidon' zum 'Gastmahle' zu stellen, und die Verwandtschaft beider anzuerkennen. Denn wie die dort beschriebene Liebe das Bestreben ist, das Unsterbliche mit dem Sterblichen zu verbinden: so ist die hier dargestellte reine Betrachtung das Bestreben das Unsterbliche als solches aus dem Sterblichen zurückzuziehn. Und beide sind offenbar notwendig mit einander verbunden.[124]

Notice here his reference to *pure contemplation* (*reine Betrachtung*) and his warning of the danger in separating immortality from mortality, soul from body.[125] Schleiermacher avoids this by connecting that pure contemplation to love, hence to sociability:

[Passage 6L: "Intro. to *Phaedo*"]

For, as the description of love in the speech of Diotima could not exist at all without reference made to pure contemplation [*reine Betrachtung*], so also in this dialogue [the *Phaedo*], where, properly speaking, that contemplation is represented, we find manifold allusions throughout to the passionate desire always to live with sympathetic minds, and to co-operate in creating truth within them, as a common task and profit; only, that as regards Soc-

---

122 *IDP* 292; *EÜP* 288 (... *das Verlangen reiner Geist zu werden, das Sterbenwollen des Weisen*).
123 *IDP* 294, emphasis added.
124 *EÜP* 289.
125 See also *IDP* 296, 299; *EÜP* 291, 294.

6.4 Revised Block N° 2: "Contemplation is Essential to Religion" —— 177

rates, in order as it were to secure him a tranquil departure, this is represented as already essentially completed in his own peculiar circle.[126]

Denn wie die Darstellung der Liebe in der Rede der Diotima gar nicht bestehen konnte ohne Rückweisung auf die reine Betrachtung: so blickt auch hier in der Darstellung der Betrachtung auf mannigfaltige Weise das Verlangen hindurch, immer mit Gleichgesinnten zusammen zu leben, und in ihnen das Wahre mit zu erzeugen als gemeinsames Werk und Gut, nur daß es für den Sokrates gleichsam um ein ruhiges Hinscheiden zu gewähren, als im wesentlichen vollendet dargestellt wird.[127]

For Schleiermacher, what is quintessentially Platonic is not the separation of body/spirit or mortal/immortal, but precisely their being held together and the contemplating of the one through the other.

If we can speak at all of Schleiermacher's Platonism, it can only be in these terms. Schleiermacher's would be a decidedly modern Platonism in that he explicitly rejected any dualism, any separation of body and spirit, including of the finite and the infinite.[128] He instead rotated the vertical plane, so to speak, so that transcendence is viewed neither dualistically nor hierarchically (i.e. as an escape from the body, from mortality, or from finitude) but rather in terms of a dynamic, living, immanental relationship.[129] Although Schleiermacher had begun to develop this immanentalism (a.k.a. organic monism) over a decade earlier (1793–94) with the help of Spinoza as filtered through Herder and neo-Spinozism, and although he developed it yet further in the first edition of the *Speeches* (1799) with additional energy from the early Romantic movement, in which of course he played a central role,[130] his decade of engagement with Plato prompted him to refine that ontology even further while addressing some of its earlier weaknesses in formulation.

Arguably, that is precisely what we see in the extended revised passage of the second Speech now under consideration (6I). It is religion that immediately

---

126 *IDP* 294–95.
127 *EÜP* 290.
128 As Rohls points out, Plato, according to Schleiermacher, struck a "middle way between Ionic dualism and Eleatic monism" ("Schleiermachers Platon," 717).
129 Scholtz demonstrates how, according to Schleiermacher, the Platonic ideas function as "the productive power of nature as such" ("Schleiermacher und die Platonische Ideenlehre," 861). He explains, "Schleiermacher has so interpreted the Platonic doctrine of ideas that the Aristotelian criticism hardly touches it... For the Platonic ideas form no second, separated and thus impotent world next to the given world of experience, rather they are its immanent, real powers; ... The dualism between the spiritual ideas and sensible things, which for Aristotle formed the fundamental structure of Platonism, resolves into a continuum in this Plato-interpretation" (867–68).
130 See Lamm, *Living God*, chapters 1–3.

grasps not the infinite as some absolute object but as *the universal existence [Sein] of everything finite in the infinite and through the infinite, of everything temporal in the eternal and through the eternal. This seeking and finding in all that lives and moves, in all becoming and change, in all doing and suffering, and just having and knowing life itself in immediate feeling as this existence [Sein]*.[131] The notion of a *coincidence of opposites* has historically been a feature of various forms of neo-Platonism. Even though Schleiermacher unequivocally broke from previous forms of Platonism metaphysically and methodologically speaking, he did construct a decidedly modern version of the notion of the *coincidence of opposites*, which arguably was deeply informed by Plato—that is, by his distinctive interpretation of Plato. Blackwell has already attuned us to the Platonic notes in the pairs of opposites implied this passage (6I) from the *Speeches* (movement and rest). Those Platonic notes are likewise to be found in his phrase *in all doing and suffering* (*in allem Tun und Leiden*), which mimics his translation of the *Phaedrus* 245c.[132]

6.4.4 Plato's Middle Dialogues on Contemplation

Yet further insight can be gained by reading this passage (6I) from the *Speeches*, where Schleiermacher declares *contemplation is essential to religion*, alongside his introductions to the *Symposium* and the *Phaedo*: it might help explain Schleiermacher's use of the term *contemplation* three times in this revised block alone, even though it did not occur in the comparable passage from the

---

131 Arndt finds the parallels between Schleiermacher's "Introduction to the *Symposium*" and his *Soliloquies* (*Monologen*) of 1800 to be stronger than any parallels with the *Speeches*, but he cites only the first edition. He therefore misses the many parallels in the second edition. See Arndt, "'Das Unsterbliche mit dem Sterblichen verbinden': Friedrich Schleiermacher und Platons *Symposion*," chap. 2 in *Schleiermacher als Philosoph*, 282.

132 *Phaedrus* 245c: "Zuerst nun muß über die göttliche sowohl als menschliche Natur der Seele durch *Betrachtung ihres Thuns und Leidens* richtige Einsicht vorangehn" (*PW* 1/1:195.1–197.1–3); "First, then, we must learn the truth about the soul divine and human by *observing how it acts and is acted upon*" [trans. Fowler, in *PDL*, emphasis added). Another example is his translation of *Sophist* 248c: "Wir setzen das als eine hinreichende Erklärung des Seienden, wenn einem auch nur im geringsten ein Vermögen bei wohnte *zu leiden oder zu tun*?" (*PW* [Eigler] 6:331); "We set up as a satisfactory sort of definition of being, the presence of the power *to act or be acted upon* in even the slightest degree" (trans. Fowler, in *PDL*, emphasis added). Compare *Sophist* 247d–e. Regarding the role that the pairing of *Handeln/Tun* with *Leiden* plays in Schleiermacher's thought, see Schmidt, *Konstruktion des Endlichen*, 24.

first edition.[133] Schleiermacher's appeal to *Betrachtung* has been neglected in the secondary literature, with the term being treated or translated more neutrally as *reflection, consideration,* or *observation*.[134] Such neglect is harder to carry off, however, once one sees that it is the same term Schleiermacher used in his translation and interpretation of *contemplation* in Plato's dialogues—for instance, in connection with Diotima's speech in the *Symposium*. In fact, his appeal to *contemplation* at this point in the second Speech seems to have created a problem for him, since in the third edition (1821) he would feel compelled not just to temper it ("the contemplation of the pious is only the immediate consciousness"[135]) but also to address the issue in one of his "Explanations" (*Erläuterungen*).[136] The worry cannot be dismissed as a modern one about a pre-critical speculative claims, since Schleiermacher himself railed against speculation; the worry, rather, might better be read in part as a distinctly Protestant one about (neo-)Platonic (and certain Catholic) practices of contemplation.[137] This warrants further investigation.

Betrachten is a fairly common verb when it comes to subject-matter requiring careful reflection. In his translations of Plato's dialogues, Schleiermacher used *betrachten* to render different ways of saying *to see, to behold, to consider, to look at closely, to examine,* etc.[138] In his *Introductions*, he employed it not only

---

[133] See the next sub-section (6.4.5) for discussion of his third use in this revised block. He also employs the term four times in revised block n° 4.

[134] For instance, even though Thomas Curran gives a nuanced discussion of *speculation* (*Spekulation*) in Schleiermacher, and thus would seem to be more open to the idea of *contemplation*, he decides to render *Betrachtung* as *reflection* (*Doctrine and Speculation in Schleiermacher's Glaubenslehre*, Theologische Bibliothek Töpelmann 61 [Berlin and New York: Walter de Gruyter, 1994], 150).

[135] ... *die Betrachtung des Frommen ist nur das unmittelbare Bewusstsein* (R 45n109; KGA 1/12:53.11–12).

[136] "The connection shows that the expression *contemplation* is to be taken in the widest sense, not as speculation proper, but as all movement of the spirit withdrawn from outward activity" (OR³ 103)/*Aehnliches dieser Stelle steht schon S. 42, wo nur dem Zusammenhange nach der Ausdruk Betrachtung in dem weitern Sinne genommen werden muß, wie nicht nur die eigentliche Speculation darunter zu begreifen ist, sondern alles von äußerer Wirksamkeit zurükgezogene Erregtsein des Geistes* (R 116 [KGA 1/12:131.3–7]).

[137] See Julia A. Lamm, "Schleiermacher on 'The Roman Church': Anti-Catholic Ideology and the Future of Historical-Empirical Dogmatics," in *Schleiermacher, the Study of Religion, and the Future of Theology*, ed. Brent Sockness and Wilhelm Gräb (Berlin and New York: Walter de Gruyter, 2010), 243–56.

[138] Take this innocuous example from his translation of the *Protagoras* 311b: "*Ich nun wollte gern des Hippokrates Stärke versuchen, betrachtete mir ihn daher recht, und fragte ihn: Sage mir, Hippokrates ...*" (PW 1/1:599.8–11); "... and I, to test Hippocrates' grit, began *examining*

to interpret Platonic texts but also to instruct readers how to read a text. For that reason, Dobson usually and not incorrectly translated it as *to consider*. In the first edition of the *Speeches*, Schleiermacher used the verb frequently, such that any uptick of occurrence in the second edition is not particularly noteworthy.

It is a different matter, however, with the noun *Betrachtung*. In *Platons Werke*, Schleiermacher did use that term to convey a careful *consideration* or *reflection*—sometimes as it pertains to reading a text closely but sometimes, too, in a more specific Platonic sense of a focused attention necessary for discerning the difference between appearances and reality in order thereby to behold the beautiful, the good, and true existence. Hence, the practitioner who strives for such a goal is "*der Betrachtende*."[139] *Consideration*, *reflection*, or *observation* do not always capture the sense as well as *contemplation* sometimes can. Let us ourselves consider some more examples from his *Introductions* in the middle trilogy, where Schleiermacher indicates that *contemplation* is a necessary tool in moving the novice from mere appearances to being. Unfortunately, Dobson's translation is unhelpful due to inconsistencies when it comes to this term (and others).

In his "Introduction to the *Gorgias*," Schleiermacher makes the case that the dialogue is a transitional one that serves as the gateway to the second main division (the second trilogy) more than as a conclusion to the first.[140] The *Gorgias*, he says, lays important groundwork for the all-important sub-trilogy *Sophist-Symposium-Statesman*, the center of the central trilogy. The dialogue is preparatory, first, because it "lays bare" the "worthlessness" of what had been mistaken as "science and art"[141] and, second, because it identifies the "innermost disposition" (*innerste Gesinnung*) as the "root" (*Wurzel*) of the problem of "arrogance" (*Anmaßung*).[142] Such "contemplation of the seemingly scientific" (*Betrachtung des scheinbar wissenschaftlichen*) sets the stage for the "idea of true science" (*Idee der wahren Wissenschaft*).[143] Here, *contemplation* is that close observation and attentiveness that results in recognition of what is false (in understanding as well as in disposition), which is a necessary step before forming a clear idea of a positive truth, as opposed to a negative truth (recognizing the untruth of something). Schleiermacher repeats this association of *preparation-disposition-con-*

---

him with a few questions. Tell me, Hippocrates,..." (trans. W. R. M. Lamb, in *PDL*, emphasis added).
139 See, e.g., *PW* 1/1:20.27, 667.35.
140 See table 2.
141 *IDP* 172; *PW* 2/1:12.14–16 (... *theils das bisher für Wissenschaft und Kunst gehaltene in seinem Unwerth aufgeldekkt wird*).
142 *PW* 2/1:12.21–22; cf. *IDP* 172. Dobson renders *Gesinnung* here as "spirit."
143 *PW* 2/1:12.24–26; cf. *IDP* 172. Dobson renders *Betrachtung* here as "observation."

templation a few pages later. He explains, "In this, then, Socrates, in accordance with the ethical and *preparatory* nature of the work, concludes with a development resting upon the *disposition of the mind*, and expressing it mythically"; after comparing the role of myth in the *Gorgias* with the earlier *Phaedrus*, he concludes, "time is only an image, but the essential thing is the [*contemplation*] of mind[,] divested of personality [*die Betrachtung des Geistes, entblößt von der Persönlichkeit*]."[144] The meaning of *contemplation* has moved further along the continuum as the mind, aided by a more proper disposition (*Gesinnung*), sheds its needs for images. Schleiermacher insists that there is a "necessary connection between method and [disposition]";[145] this connection, furthermore, is how the dialectical method carries the student forward, out of appearances to true existence. *Contemplation*, therefore, plays an important role in this connection between method and disposition insofar as Schleiermacher means it in a Socratic–Platonic sense: that quiet, disengaged attentiveness which fixes itself both outwardly (on the world of appearances) and inwardly (on one's own disposition). At the end of his "Introduction to the *Gorgias*," Schleiermacher makes one more stop on the continuum, this time at what he calls "sheer contemplation" (*bloßen Betrachtung*),[146] as he discusses the tension between Plato's philosophical life (withdrawal) and his public life (immersion). In short, in the *Gorgias* Schleiermacher identifies three iterations of *contemplation* as it operates along a continuum.

In his "Introduction to the *Symposium*," Schleiermacher rehearses the Platonic graduated progression from the beginner in the *Phaedrus* to one who be-

---

[144] *IDP* 177, emphasis added (Dobson renders *Betrachtung* here as "consideration"); *PW* 2/1:16.1–13 (*Auf diese Auseinandersezung folgt dann, sobald Kallikles einen Unterschied zwischen dem Angenehmen und Guten, wenn auch nur ganz im Allgemeinen eingeräumt hat, der dritte die beiden vorigen verbindende und zusammenfassende Abschnitt, in welchem Sokrates nun der ethischen und vorbereitenden Natur des Werkes gemäß mit einer auf die Gesinnung sich gründenden und sie mythisch aussprechenden Entwickelung endiget. Will man auch diesen Mythos, was theilweise sehr nahe liegt, mit dem im Phaidros, in wiefern ja dieser als Grundmythos ist angerührt worden, vergleichen: so ist zu bedenken, daß zum Willen und zur Kunst hier die Zukunft sich gerade so verhält, wie dort die Vergangenheit zur Wissenschaft und zur Erkenntniß, und daß in jenem wie in diesem die Zeit nur Bild ist, das Wesentliche aber die Betrachtung des Geistes, entblößt von der Persönlichkeit*).
[145] *IDP* 180 (Dobson renders *Gesinnung* here as "thought"); *PW* 2/1:18.7–8 (*… und des nothwendigen Zusammenhanges der Methode mit der Gesinnung*).
[146] *PW* 2/1:24.6; cf. *IDP* 186. Dobson renders it as "abstract thought."

holds the beautiful and then absolute beauty—or, "what Diotima says of the gradual advances in the mysteries of love":[147]

[Passage 6M: "Intro. to *Symposium*"]

For first of all, the Phaedrus with its enamoured preference for one object, is excused as a work of youth; then the beginner rises to the *contemplation [Betrachtung] of the beautiful*, in practical exertions and laws; consequently, to investigations into the political virtues, such as we find in the Protagoras, and the dialogues connected with it, and in the Gorgias. Then come the modifications of knowledge, in their plurality indeed, but still as modifications of knowledge, consequently, with the consciousness of the peculiar character of knowledge as exhibited from the Theaetetus onwards; and thus the mind rises at last to the *conscious [intuition] of the absolutely beautiful*, as it is beheld in disconnection with any individual beauty.[148]

Zuerst nämlich wird der Phaidros mit seiner Verliebtheit in Einen als ein Werk der Jugend entschuldiget, dann erhebt der Anfänger sich zu der <u>Betrachtung des Schönen</u> *in den Bestrebungen und Gesetzen, also zu Untersuchungen über die bürgerlichen Tugenden, wie wir sie im 'Protagoras' und den ihm anhängenden Gesprächen finden und im 'Gorgias'. Dann kommen die Erkenntnisse in ihrer Vielheit freilich, aber doch als Erkenntnisse, also mit dem Bewußtsein des eigentümlichen der Erkenntnis wie es vom 'Theaitetos' an aufgestellt wird; und so erhebt sich der Geist endlich zur* <u>bewußten Anschauung des absolut Schönen</u>*, wie es ohne an ein Einzelnes gebunden zu sein, sondern als jedes Einzelne hervorbringend in der Harmonie der Welt der sittlichen sowohl als der leiblichen angeschaut wird, und sich uns in dem letzten späteren Teile seiner Werke offenbaren wird.*[149]

Here, *contemplation* seems to be preparatory to *intuition*. Yet, in his "Introduction the *Phaedo*," Schleiermacher twice uses *contemplation* in a way that suggests that it is itself that absolute beholding which comes about through withdrawal:

[Passage 6N: "Intro. to *Phaedo*"]

For, in the Symposium, Socrates is eminently exhibited in the joyousness and pride of life, though it is not forgotten at the same time how he is plunged in *philosophical contemplation*, and can postpone all else to that; in the Phaedon, on the contrary, what appears most prominent is the tranquillity [sic] and cheerfulness with which he expects death, as the liberator from everything that interrupts *contemplation*; and on the other hand, he does not nevertheless interrupt his accustomed social practice, but even with the fatal goblet will observe the sacred ceremonies of the festive meal.[150]

---

147 *IDP* 289; *EÜP* 285 (... *was Diotima von den allmähligen Fortschritten in den Mysterien der Liebe sagt*).
148 *IDP* 289–90, emphasis added. Dobson renders both *Betrachtung* and *Anschauung* ("intuition") as "contemplation," thus conflating two important terms.
149 *EÜP* 285, emphasis added.
150 *IDP* 295, emphasis added.

> Im 'Gastmahl' nämlich ist Sokrates vorzüglich dargestellt in der Festlichkeit und dem Glanze des Lebens, aber doch auch nicht vergessen, wie er in <u>philosophische Betrachtung</u> versunken alles übrige hintansetzen konnte; im 'Phaidon' hingegen ist das am meisten hervorragende die Ruhe und Heiterkeit, mit welcher er den Tod erwartet, als den Befreier von allem was die <u>Betrachtung</u> stört, und wiederum unterbricht er auch so nicht das gewohnte Zusammenleben, sondern will noch mit dem tödlichen Becher die heiligen Gebräuche des festlichen Mahles begehen.[151]

Comparing how Schleiermacher employed the term which he used to speak about Platonic contemplation in these various passages from his *Introductions*, we may draw some preliminary conclusions at least. For Schleiermacher's Plato, *contemplation* is both a mode of reflection and a way of positioning oneself along a kind of continuum; it requires a degree of detachment in the sense of withdrawal from distractions; it involves an ability to perceive not just objects but relations, virtues, laws (patterns), and beauty; it is a prerequisite for seeing the good and the true, for being virtuous and gaining knowledge; it is associated with the imagery of rising to something "higher"; it is an attentiveness that requires and yields quietude, peace, and tranquillity; its aim is absolute beauty (and, as we shall see in the next section, true being); it is related to but is not the same as intuition; and, finally, there are degrees and kinds of contemplation (e. g., "pure," "philosophical").

6.4.5 Return to the Science of Being in Revised Block N° 2

Now let us return at long last to our revised passages (6H–I) from revised block n° 2 of the *Speeches* in order to see what more insight we might gain when it is set in relief against his *Introductions*. *Contemplation* in revised block n° 2 seems to occupy the middle position on the continuum indicated in *Platons Werke*. It is not associated with that kind of transition (accompanied by a transformation of disposition) to knowledge of finite things as distinct entities and in relation to other beings, a knowledge which requires making a distinction between appearances and eternal laws as it also recognizes their relation. That would be scientific knowledge, which is important and honorable, but it *is not the same as their* [*the pious people's*] *way of having and knowing about God* (6I). Nor is it itself *feeling*. What knowing and contemplation have in common, according to this passage (6I), is an openness to reality, a sense for the *life* of the world, and an acknowledgement of higher laws. Keep in mind that the opposition which

---

[151] *EÜP* 290, emphasis added.

Schleiermacher draws in 1806 between piety and knowing is not as stark as it was in 1799, although the differences remain crucial. One key difference is that *feeling* is receptive, whereas *thinking* is active, albeit in a different way from *acting*.[152] Another difference is attitudinal. A third difference is that, while *knowing* might entertain the idea of the infinite, piety is the *immediate perception of universal existence [Sein] of everything finite in the infinite and through the infinite* and, significantly, *a life in the infinite nature of the whole* (6I). Contemplation signals each of these differences: it is a concentrated activity that initiates a concentrated inactivity; it involves attunement and attitudinal adjustment; and it calls for a participatory way of *being*, of *living*. Again, it is related to, but is not itself, *feeling*. It involves that kind of quieting, hence a dispositional stance, which in suspending activity (as self-imposition) can aid in opening oneself up so as to make the *seeking and finding* possible (6I). It is a form of receptivity, hence *immediate perception*.

It is instructive to read Schleiermacher's new employment of *contemplation* in relation to his revisions about the need for the cultured despisers to examine themselves, their own experience, and the need to integrate life and theory: it is a *life*, not just an observation. Yet it is directed not to any finite thing or system of things, nor even to an infinite somehow outside the finite. What *contemplation* contributes, and what *immediate perception* alone would not convey, is the involvement of oneself, through an attitudinal posture, in the process.

6.4.6 The Science of Acting and Piety

Revised block n° 2 in the second Speech ends with Schleiermacher completing his expanded, revised introduction of The Three by training his attention on *acting*.[153] His revision of the comparison between religion and what in 1799 he called *morality* follows a similar pattern to that between religion and what he

---

152 For Schleiermacher, both *thinking* and *acting* are activities, but *thinking* has more to do with the impression the world makes on consciousness, whereas *acting* is the impression humans make on the world. In revised block n° 3, he writes, "For what is all science, other than the existence of things in you, in your reason? What is all art and culture, other than your existence in things, in its measure and its form?" (OR^2 166)/ *Denn was ist alle Wissenschaft als das Sein der Dinge in Euch, in Eurer Vernunft? was ist alle Kunst und Bildung, als Euer Sein in den Dingen, in ihrem Maße und ihrer Gestalt?* (R^2 48). Compare *Sophist* 248d–e for description of knowing (*Erkennen*) as an acting (*Tun*), and of being-known (*Erkannte*) as a suffering or being-acted-upon (*Leiden*); trans. Schleiermacher, *PW* (Eigler) 6:331
153 See OR^2 163–64 ; R^2 45–46.

had called *metaphysics:* he newly frames what he now calls *ethics* (*Sittenlehre*) or the *science of acting* (*Wissenschaft des Handelns*); he more positively portrays that *science* than he had *morality*; he expands on the *science of acting* in terms of his new complex typology; and he specifies that there is a form of pious *contemplation* that is distinct from any kind of contemplation in which *ethics* might engage. In the first edition, Schleiermacher devoted only one sentence to drawing the opposition between morality and religion. There he identified "the consciousness of freedom" as the point of contention:

[Passage 6P: *Speeches*, 1799]

Morality proceeds from the consciousness of freedom; it wishes to extend freedom's realm to infinity and to make everything subservient to it. Religion breathes there where freedom itself has once more become nature; it apprehends man beyond the play of his particular powers and his personality, and views him from the vantage point where he must be what he is, whether he likes it or not.[154]

Die Moral geht vom Bewußtsein der Freiheit aus, deren Reich will sie ins Unendliche erweitern, und ihr alles unterwürfig machen; die Religion athmet da, wo die Freiheit selbst schon wieder Natur geworden ist, jenseit des Spiels seiner besondern Kräfte und seiner Personalität faßt sie den Menschen, und sieht ihn aus dem Gesichtspunkte, wo er das sein muß was er ist, er wolle oder wolle nicht.[155]

In the second edition, Schleiermacher expands his discussion of the differences to include three key points, each of which involves an attitudinal posture and at least one of which shows influence from *Platons Werke*.

First, we find in this part of his discussion Schleiermacher's third use of *contemplation* in revised block n° 2. It mirrors what he has just said about *contemplation* in contrast to the science of being. The pious, Schleiermacher explains, "certainly contemplate human action, but their contemplation is simply not the kind that results in such a system";[156] rather, as before, it has to do with a seeking and a finding, this time of observing "acting from God, the efficaciousness of God in human beings."[157]

Second, Schleiermacher uses the term "surrender" in order to stress the importance of this kind of contemplation on the part of the pious and to describe the passive nature of *piety* itself:

---

154 OR^1 102. Crouter breaks the sentence down into two.
155 R^1 45–46 (*KGA* 1/2:212.10–15).
156 OR^2 163; R^2 46 (*Er betrachtet ja freilich das menschliche Handeln, aber seine Betrachtung ist gar nicht die aus welcher jenes System entsteht, ...*)
157 OR^2 163; R^2 46 (*... sondern er sucht und sieht nur in allem dasselbige, nämlich das Handeln aus Gott, die Wirksamkeit Gottes in den Menschen*).

[Passage 6Q: *Speeches*, 1806:]

For piety also has a passive side, it appears also as a *surrender*, a letting oneself be moved by the whole that the person faces, while ethics always and only shows itself as an intervention in the whole, as a self-moving. And that is why ethics depends on the consciousness of freedom ... Piety, in contrast, is not at all bound up with this side of life but stirs in the opposite sphere of necessity, where no particular acting of an individual appears. Hence the two are indeed different from each other. If, in fact, religion *lingers with pleasure* on every acting from God, on every activity through which the infinite reveals itself in the finite, then it is not itself this activity.[158]

... *denn [Frömmigkeit] hat auch eine leidende Seite, sie erscheint auch als ein <u>Hingeben</u>, ein Sichbewegenlassen von dem Ganzen, welchem der Mensch entgegensteht, wenn die erste sich immer nur zeigt als ein Eingreifen in dasselbe, als ein Selbstbewegen. Und die Sittlichkeit hängt daher ganz an dem Bewusstsein der Freiheit, ...; dem entgegengesetzten Gebiet der Notwendigkeit, wo kein eigenes Handeln eines Einzelnen erscheint. Also sind doch beide verschieden voneinander, und wenn freilich auf jedem Handeln aus Gott, auf jeder Tätigkeit durch welche sich das Unendliche im Endlichen offenbart, die Religion <u>mit Wohlgefallen verweilt</u>, so ist sie doch nicht diese Tätigkeit selbst.*[159]

Schleiermacher's connecting of pious contemplation here with surrender aligns his reconceptualizing of the distinction between *religion* and *acting* with his revising of the two impulses in the first Speech: on the one side, the striving to establish oneself as an individual, and on the other side, "the longing to surrender oneself and be absorbed into a great, to be taken hold of and determined."[160]

Third, the new language of *lingers with pleasure* from that last sentence of the passage (6Q), which is also the last line of revised block n° 2, is not unlike Schleiermacher's description of Socrates's attitude in the *Phaedo*. This is not to imply that it is directly the effect of his interpretation of Plato. These three points of revision (contemplation, surrender, lingering enjoyment) regarding *acting* and piety, however, do reflect certain patterns of thought Schleiermacher had settled on by 1806, in part through his engagement with Plato. At the heart of that was the integration of theory and practice, philosophy and life.

Discussion of the next two revised blocks in the second Speech continues in the next chapter.

---

158 OR^2 163–64, emphasis added.
159 R^2 46.
160 OR^3 4; R^2 10.

7 The Presence of Plato in the *Speeches* (1806), Part 2: Being, Non-Being, and Intuition

> ... what an ancient sage has taught you is also true in this sense: every knowing is a remembering of what is outside time and is thus justifiably placed at the apex of all that is temporal.[1]

7.1 Introduction

This chapter continues the argument begun in the previous one as I make the case that Schleiermacher's revision of his *On Religion: Speeches to Its Cultured Despisers* in 1806 bears the imprint of his scholarly immersion in Plato during the first decade of the nineteenth century, when he translated the Platonic dialogues, ordered them, and wrote introductions to each. In chapter six, I considered changes Schleiermacher made to the flow of his argument in the first two speeches, whereby he cleaned up certain inconsistencies in theory as well as in practice (section 6.2); I then examined revised blocks n[os] 1 and 2 in the second Speech and argued how Schleiermacher's reconceptualization of The Three reflected his interpretation of Plato's dialogues, especially when it came to *physics* and *ethics*, but also when it came to *contemplation* (sections 6.3 and 6.4). I now continue that close textual analysis, shifting attention to revised block n°s 3 and 4. Schleiermacher's revisions in these two revised blocks are arguably among the weightiest he made to his *Speeches* in that he was sorting through difficult epistemological and ontological issues. It is there, for instance, where he started revising his understanding of *feeling* (*Gefühl*) and *intuition* (*Anschauung*) and the relation between them. I proceed as I did before: moving systematically through each revised block, reading his revisions to the *Speeches* alongside his *Introductions to the Dialogues of Plato*, identifying crosscurrents and tracing possible influences. My thesis in this chapter is that revised blocks n[os] 3 and 4 bear significant imprints of Schleiermacher's "Introduction to the *Sophist*," especially in his new discussion of the nature of being and existence (section 7.2) and in his new, more restricted definition of *intuition* (section 7.3). More so even than before, the material treated here is incredibly dense due both to the subject-matter itself and

---

1 Schleiermacher, Second Speech on Religion, OR^2 170–71, altered; R^2 52 (... *was ein alter Weiser Euch gelehrt hat, dass jedes Wissen eine Erinnerung ist an das nämlich was außer der Zeit ist, ebendaher aber mit Recht an die Spitze jedes Zeitlichen gestellt wird*).

to the fact that reading two editions of the *Speeches* alongside his *Introductions* is an inherently complicated endeavor.

A note of terminology is in order, given the abstract nature of the philosophical discussion in the *Sophist* regarding being, beings, existence, and non-being—something made even more challenging here by the task of having to juggle three languages. It is not just a matter of translating Schleiermacher but of translating (1) his translation of Plato and (2) his particular take on notoriously difficult philosophical discussions in the Platonic *corpus*, all while (3) trying to make it readable in English. To complicate the matter further, as Peter Steiner points out, Schleiermacher not infrequently sought to improve Plato's texts.[2] For the most part, but not always, Schleiermacher translated Plato's *to on* as *das Seiende* (and *to mē on* as *das Nichtseiende*), thus retaining the participial form of the Greek, and he translated Plato's *ousia* and *to einai* as *das Sein*. The former term, *das Seiende* (*what-is, the existing, that-which-is, existent, being*), is a nominalized present participle and can refer to different modes of being, at various levels of abstraction: from concretely existing things (entities or beings) to *existing* more generally (existence); it can also refer to timeless things, and he sometimes modifies it with *eternal* and *immutable*. The latter term, *das Sein*, is a nominalized infinitive; Schleiermacher usually, but not always, reserves it for *being* in the sense of *the highest being*;[3] with the indefinite article it means *a being*. The dilemma for the English translator is that most Anglophone classicists and philosophers, in translating Plato or in writing about these same ideas, do not sustain, as Schleiermacher tried to, the distinction between the grammatical forms of *being/be-ing*; rather, most simply use *being* (or *non-being*), letting the context convey particular meaning. Therefore, trying to maintain Schleiermacher's distinction between *das Seiende* and *das Sein* can prove difficult and often awkward, making consistency nearly impossible and rendering discussion of certain passages from the *Sophist* confusing, even unrecognizable, for the Anglophone reader. Dobson clearly ran into this problem and opted sometimes to translate *das Seiende* as "existent" (a finite being) and *das Sein* as "existence,"[4] but he could not sustain that. However sympathetic one might be with Dobson's attempt, his translation does not always make philosophical sense, and more consistency than he was able to accomplish in his translation is both possible and necessary, although no perfect solution is available. Adding to the difficulty is the fact that Schleiermacher's terminology in the *Speeches* is somewhat different

---

[2] See Steiner, "Zur Kontroverse um Schleiermachers Platon," xxv.
[3] See below, 196–98, for his distinction between *being* and *the highest being*.
[4] See, e.g., *IDP* 252–53.

from that in *Platons Werke*, where he tried to adhere more closely to Plato's Greek. For example, in the *Speeches*, while he newly incorporated the language of *being* (*das Sein*) in 1806 in a way that, I maintain, reflected his engagement with Plato, he nevertheless used it in a broader sense than he did in his *Introductions*. He did not, for example, import the term *das Seiende* to his *Speeches*, with the sole exception that he used it once in a compound form, *das Nichtseiende* ("non-being").⁵ I try to navigate these treacherous waters by acknowledging the inherent difficulties and, in a departure from my usual practice of consistency in translating Schleiermacher's technical terms, will translate *das Seiende* usually as *what-is*, but also as I think the context warrants (sometimes in English *being* and *becoming* just go together); in contrast, *das Sein* is more straight-forward and will almost always be rendered as *being*, although occasionally as *existence*, again as meaning dictates. In every case, I provide the German so that readers may be reminded and remain informed, and so, too, that they may judge for themselves.

7.2 Revised Block N° 3: "... go and learn it from your Socrates"

The third revised block starts just a few lines after the end of the second revised block and runs for about two-and-a-half (split-column) pages.⁶ The two editions come back together in the famous passage where Schleiermacher praises Spinoza. The mere two sentences which separate revised blocks n°ˢ 2 and 3 are not unimportant in that Schleiermacher there describes religion as "the necessary and indispensable third,"⁷ although in 1806 he changes the derogatory term *speculation* (*Spekulation*) to the more laudable *science* (*Wissenschaft*), in keeping with his new typology. The original text from 1799 was significant in that it contained his pithy description of The Three, which includes what may be his most famous definition of *religion* as "the [sense] and taste for the infinite"⁸; his rebuke of (Fichte's) "completed rounded idealism" (*dem vollendeten und gerundeten Idealismus*) and his embrace of "a higher realism" (*einen höhern Realismus*);⁹ and a pair of references to the phrase "the feeling of the infinite" (*das Gefühl des Un-*

---

5 OR^2 164; R^2 47.
6 See R 47–49; OR^2 164–67. See table 8.
7 OR^2 164; R^2 47 (*das notwendige und unentbehrliche Dritte*).
8 See below, passage 7E.
9 OR^1 103; R^1 49 (*KGA* 1/2:213.20–22).

endlichen).¹⁰ These three ideas are mostly retained, with some adjustments, in 1806. Yet, once again, Schleiermacher reframes recognizable ideas within a new and expanded understanding that reflects insights he had forged and refined through, in part, his work on Plato. In this third revised block, Schleiermacher is keen on continuing (from the previous revised blocks) the emphasis on a positive relationship among The Three; on affirming the possibility and necessity of true knowing; on rejecting the perceived opposition between knowing (hence, science) and religion; and on carrying through the theme of surrender.

The influence of Plato can be seen in the obvious (e.g., a new, explicit reference to Socrates) but, more revealingly, can also be detected in Schleiermacher's new discussions of a virtuous form of ignorance, dialectics, being and non-being, appearance and truth, and the unity of nature and reason. In this one revised block, Schleiermacher refers to *being* (*das Sein*) or *non-being* (*das Nichtseiende*) eight times; in contrast, the corresponding text from 1799 included no mention of such weighted philosophical terms. Indeed, in the second edition of the *Speeches*, there is a sevenfold increase in the use of the noun *being* (*Sein*) and its cognates.¹¹ Schleiermacher's employment of the term simply cannot be properly understood apart from his intense engagement with Plato's dialogues—and with the *Sophist* in particular. In case the cultured despisers of religion would not recognize the obvious allusions to Plato in this revised block, Schleiermacher admonishes them: "You know this from my speeches, and if you have not yet figured it out for yourselves, then go and learn it from your Socrates."¹²

7.2.1 Socratic Ignorance, Being and Non-Being

At this point in both editions of the *Speeches*, Schleiermacher attempted to establish how, despite their differences, The Three cannot exist independently from one another. In 1799, a more positive relationship among them was difficult to tease out given the oppositions he had erected from the onset of the second Speech. Consequently, his claim regarding the interdependence of The Three

---

10 OR^1 103; R^1 49 (*KGA* 1/2:213.12, see also lines 3–4, 17).
11 In 1799, *being* (or a cognate or compound) is only used four times in the second Speech; in 1806, it (or a cognate or compound) is used twenty-seven times.
12 OR^2 164–65; $R.^2$ 47 (for German, see passage 7A just below).

came in the form of rhetorical questions.[13] In 1806, however, all he needs to do is simply continue (from revised blocks n[os] 1 and 2) his more nuanced discussion of the relationship among The Three by appealing to a Socratic distinction between ignorance understood as, on the one hand, a not-knowing and, on the other hand, a false-knowing (*falsch wissend*). Schleiermacher insists that it is impossible for someone to "be scientific without religion" and yet, just as strongly, he stipulates, "piety is not the measure of science."[14] He explains,

> **[Passage 7A: *Speeches*, 1806:]**
>
> Yet just as a person can hardly be truly scientific without being pious, so as certainly the pious person can be truly *ignorant* [*unwissend*], but never *false-knowing* [*falsch wissend*]. For the pious person's own being [*Sein*] is not of that subordinated kind, which (according to the ancient principle that like can only be known by like) would have nothing knowable except *what-is-not* [*das Nichtseiend*] under the deceptive appearance of being [*Schein des Seins*]. On the contrary, it is *a true being* [*ein wahres Sein*] that also recognizes true being [*wahres Sein*]. And where this is not encountered, the pious person also believes there is nothing to see. In my opinion, for someone still entangled by that *false appearance*, *ignorance* [*Unwissenheit*] is a priceless nugget of science. You know this from my speeches, and if you have not yet figured it out for yourselves, then go and learn it from your Socrates.[15]
>
> *Aber so wenig einer wahrhaft wissenschaftlich sein kann ohne fromm: so gewiss kann auch der Fromme zwar wohl unwissend sein, aber nie falsch wissend. Denn sein eigenes Sein ist nicht von jener untergeordneten Art, welche, nach dem alten Grundsatz, dass nur von Gleichem Gleiches kann erkannt werden, nichts Erkennbares hätte als das Nichtseiende unter dem trüglichen Schein des Seins. Sondern es ist ein wahres Sein, welches auch wahres Sein erkennt, und wo ihm dieses nicht begegnet, auch nichts zu sehen glaubt. Welch ein köstliches Kleinod aber nach meiner Meinung die Unwissenheit ist für den, der noch von jenem falschen Schein befangen ist, das wisst Ihr aus meinen Reden, und wenn Ihr selbst es für Euch noch nicht einseht, so geht und lernt es von Eurem Sokrates.*[16]

In these few lines alone, we can detect reverberating echoes of his interpretation of Plato (see italicized words in English). Let me highlight just a few of these, offering parallel evidence from his *Introductions*.

Ignorance. In his *Introductions*, Schleiermacher identifies Socratic ignorance as a marker of Platonic thought. In his "General Introduction," for example, he criticizes as "unplatonic" interpreters who presumed too much and who forgot

---

13 "Without religion, how can praxis rise above the common circle of adventurous and customary forms? How can speculation become anything better than a stiff and barren skeleton?" (*OR*^{1} 103; see R^1 47–48 [*KGA* 1/2:212.32–35]).
14 *OR*^{2} 164, altered; R^2 47 (*Aber ebenso unmöglich, bedenkt es wohl, ist ja nach meiner Meinung, dass einer sittlich sein kann ohne Religion, oder wissenschaftlich ohne sie*).
15 *OR*^{2} 164–65, altered and emphasis added.
16 R^2 47.

the value that Plato himself had placed on "the consciousness of ignorance."[17] As we have seen in chapter three, not-understanding and misunderstanding became for him a crucial step in the process of understanding, as he set forth in his *Hermeneutics*. Here in the second Speech, Schleiermacher holds up ignorance as a virtue of the pious. The pious will grant what they do not know and that there is much they do not know, but they do not cling to falsehoods. Not ignorance but the conceit of knowledge is the opposite of knowledge.[18]

The ancient principle. This is the second time in the second Speech that Schleiermacher appeals to the *ancient principle* that *like can only be known by like*.[19] Although the first instance is a carry-over from the first edition, this second instance is new in 1806 and is inserted nearby a new reference to Socrates. What is more, it is given almost verbatim in his "Introduction to the *Phaedo*";[20] it surfaces in his "Introduction to the *Lysis*," where he applies it to the moral life;[21] and it appears in his university lectures on ethics, delivered around this same time.[22]

Falsehood, non-being, and being. Most broadly speaking, the issues Schleiermacher touches on in this passage from revised block n° 3 reflect what he took to

---

[17] IDP 5; PW 1/1:19.30–20.3 (*So daß jene Zufriedenheit etwas unreif zu sein scheint, welche behauptet, wir könnten den Platon jezt schon besser verstehen, als er sich selbst verstanden habe, und daß man belächeln kann, wie sie den Platon, welcher auf das Bewußtsein des Nichtwissens einen solchen Werth legt, so unplatonisch suchen will*).

[18] Schleiermacher would clarify this point in the third edition. See OR^2 165n20; R 47n128.

[19] See OR^2 159; R^2 41; see above, 6.3.3.

[20] "And if the soul is to apprehend the essentially existent [*das Seiende*], which is not subjected to origination and destruction, and to all the conditions of imperfect existence, it can only do so, (according to the old principle, and one, which in this argument must be always born in mind, that like is only apprehended by like, [sic]) as existing similarly, and in the same manner with that essential existence" (*IDP* 293)/*Und wenn die Seele das Seiende, welches nicht dem Entstehen und Vergehen und der ganzen Form des Werdens unterworfen ist, erkennen soll: so kann sie es, nach dem alten immer mit zu verstehenden Grundsatz, daß Gleiches nur vom Gleichen erkannt wird, auch nur als eine eben so seiende und auf eben solche Weise* (*EÜP* 289).

[21] "Like is only then unprofitable to like when a man confines himself to his own external personality, and to an interest in his own sensuous being; not to him who, taking interest in the consciousness of [an ideal], possible at the same time among many and for the good of many, enlarges the sphere of his being beyond those limits; a process, in the course of which, first, every man universally meets with something like and related to himself, and not at war with his own endeavours" (*IDP* 77)/*Nemlich das Aehnliche ist nur dann dem Aehnlichen unnüz wenn Jeder sich auf seine äußere Persönlichkeit und auf das Interesse der Sinnlichkeit beschränkt, nicht aber wenn er sich durch Bewußtsein eines in mehreren möglichen Ideals, wodurch es erst für Jeden ein Verwandtes giebt das nicht entgegengesezt wäre, über jene Schranken hinaus erweitert* (*PW* 1/1:422.13–18).

[22] See Schleiermacher, *Notes on Ethics*, 105; *Brouillon*, 84.

be one of the main tasks of Plato's middle dialogues—namely, to distinguish being from appearance, truth from falsehood. This new addition in the *Speeches*, in its reference to non-being and falsehood, is at the very least an allusion to the *Sophist*. Let us first consider a passage from the *Sophist* which sets up the problem, and then look at Schleiermacher's assessment of that. In the *Sophist*, the Stranger signals a transition in the dialogue when he says,

> We are really, my dear friend, engaged in a very difficult investigation; for the matter of appearing and seeming, but not being, and of saying things, but not true ones—all this is now and always has been very perplexing. You see, Theaetetus, it is extremely difficult to understand how a man is to say or think that falsehood really exists and in saying this not be involved in contradiction.... This statement involves the bold assumption that not-being [*to mē on*] exists, for otherwise falsehood could not come into existence.[23]

Schleiermacher describes this transition to what he calls the "core" (*Kern*) of the dialogue as one that begins with a laden question. He comments in his "Introduction to the *Sophist*":

> For with the question 'whether there can be anything false in speech or representation' he raises the question whether what-*is-not* [*Nichtseiendes*] can somehow be, and along with that the question whether the non-being [*Nichtsein*] of something can be predicated.
>
> *Denn mit der Frage, ob es Falsches geben könne in Reden und Vorstellung, hebt er an, rein aufgelöset in die ob Nichtseiendes irgendwie sei, und ihm etwas beigelegt, oder das Nichtsein von etwas könne ausgesagt werden.*[24]

The resonances found among Schleiermacher's translation of the *Sophist*, his interpretation of it in his introduction to that dialogue, and his revised passage (7A) from the *Speeches* are undeniable. The question for us is whether this is just a passing allusion or whether there is something else going on here. I maintain that it is the latter, but to make that argument I need to direct our attention to Schleiermacher's larger discussion in his "Introduction to the *Sophist*." Krapf

---

23 Plato, *Sophist* 236d–237a, trans. Fowler, in *PDL*. Schleiermacher's translation from the Greek: *In Wahrheit, du Guter, wir befinden uns in einer höchst schwierigen Untersuchung. Denn dieses Erscheinen und Scheinen ohne zu sein und dies Sagen zwar aber nicht Wahres, alles dies ist immer voll Bedenklichkeiten gewesen schon ehedem und auch jetzt. Denn auf welche Weise man sagen soll, es gebe wirklich ein falsch Reden oder Meinen ohne doch schon, indem man es nur ausspricht, auf alle Weise in Widersprüchen befangen zu sein, dies, o Theaitetos, ist schwer zu begreifen.... Diese Rede untersteht sich ja vorauszusetzen, das Nichtseiende sei. Denn sonst gäbe es auf keine Weise Falsches wirklich* (*PW* [Eigler] 6:289).
24 *EÜP* 248; cf. *IDP* 250. Schleiermacher is paraphrasing *Sophist* 241a, which he translates as *wenn wir wagten zu sagen, Falsches sei in Vorstellungen und Reden?* (*PW* [Eigler] 6:305).

was on to something in claiming that, in what amounts to about three pages of that introduction, we can detect the "point at which Schleiermacher's relation to Plato comes to light most clearly."[25]

7.2.2 *Platons Werke*: The *Sophist* on Being and Non-Being

As we have seen, Schleiermacher considered the "inner" part of the *Sophist* (236d–263b) to be "the most valuable and precious core of the dialogue, ... as here for the first time almost in the writings of Plato, the innermost sanctuary of philosophy is opened in a purely philosophical manner, and as, generally, being [*das Sein*] is better and more noble than non-being [*das Nichtsein*]."[26] Schleiermacher's excitement here had as much to do with insights he gleaned from Plato as it did with his belief that he had grasped Plato. His exposition focuses on the basic principle that *being is better and more noble than non-being*. His is a dense treatment of a challenging philosophical text, which he was reading in a particular (post-Kantian) philosophical context. Scholtz and Rohls have both argued persuasively that Schleiermacher took up ideas from the *Sophist* (as he interpreted that in *Platons Werke* and later in his lectures on the history of philosophy, delivered between 1807 and 1823) and incorporated those into his *Dialectics*. Building on their research, I would add that Schleiermacher also incorporated them into his revisions of the second Speech in 1806. Let me first distill Schleiermacher's interpretation of the *innermost sanctuary* of Plato's philosophy into four main interrelated points, all of which, I suggest, have bearing on his revision of the *Speeches*. Then I will highlight three insights each from Scholtz's and Rohl's analyses in order to draw out further connections.

First, Schleiermacher notes that the entry point into the "core" of the *Sophist* is the investigation of the meaning of non-being and whether it can be predicated of anything. The analysis of non-being involves the further issue of the association of ideas. Plato's notion of the association (*Gemeinschaft*) of the greater "kinds" or "classes,"[27] Schleiermacher says, is that "upon which all real thinking

---

25 Krapf, "Platonic Dialectics," 92.
26 *IDP* 251, altered; *EÜP* 248 (... *gerade hierin den edelsten und köstlichsten Kern des Ganzen um so gewisser erkennen, als sich hier fast zuerst in den Schriften des Platon das innerste Heiligtum der Philosophie rein philosophisch aufschließt, und als überhaupt das Sein besser und herrlicher ist als das Nichtsein*). See above, chap. 4, 97–99.
27 In Greek the term is *genos*, which Schleiermacher usually translated as *Begriff* (see, e.g., *Sophist* 254b–258c; trans. Schleiermacher, *PW* [Eigler] 6:351–69); sometimes, though, he renders it *Gattung* (see *PW* [Eigler] 6:371).

7.2 Revised Block N° 3: "... go and learn it from your Socrates"   — 195

[*Denken*] and all scientific life depends."[28] In the *Sophist* 254b–e, Plato identifies those greater kinds as existence itself (*Seiende selbst*), movement (*Bewegung*) and rest (*Ruhe*), sameness (*Selbige, Einerleiheit*) and difference (*Verschiedene, Verschiedenheit*). Schleiermacher interprets Plato's association of kinds as dynamically reciprocal, mutually participatory relations.[29] Consequently, the analysis of non-being in the *Sophist* discloses, he maintains,

[Passage 7B: "Intro. to *Sophist*"]

the intuition [*Anschauung*] of the life of what-*is* [*Seienden*] and of the necessary being-one and being-in-one-another of being [*Sein*] and of knowing [*Erkennnes*].

... *die Anschauung von dem Leben des Seienden und von dem notwendigen Eins- und Ineinandersein des Seins und des Erkennens.*[30]

In other words, for Schleiermacher's Plato, the highest pair of "kinds" is *being* (*Sein*) and *knowing* (*Erkennens*), with the other paired kinds and sub-kinds falling under each of these.

Second, the break-through point for Schleiermacher is Plato's insight that non-being or what-*is-not* (*Nichtseiende*) is not the opposite of what-*is* (*Seiende*) in the sense of being incompatible or mutually exclusive but is better understood as *difference* within the sphere of oppositions. Schleiermacher explains, for instance, that movement and rest, as representing the sphere of oppositions, show

[Passage 7C: "Intro. to *Sophist*"]

how, first, association with opposites is grounded in the associated sameness and difference of what-*is* [*das Seiende*] and how in this sphere of difference what-*is* exhibits itself necessarily and in diversified manner also as what-*is-not* [*Nichtseiendes*], so that for the highest being itself [*das höchste Sein selbst*] there can be nothing opposed whatsoever; the person, however, who has not penetrated into the light of true being [*des wahren Seins*] is generally incapable of yielding further than to this non-being [*Nichtsein*] of true knowing and non-knowing of true being [*Sein*].

wie erst in der Einerleiheit und Verschiedenheit gemeinschaftlich des Seienden Gemeinschaft mit den Gegensätzen gegründet ist, und wie auf diesem Gebiete der Verschiedenheit das Sei-

---

28 *EÜP* 248–49 (*Denn in dem Lauf der Untersuchung über das Nichtseiende entsteht, gerade wie sie selbst als ein höheres in der über den Sophisten entstanden war, die Frage über die Gemeinschaft der Begriffe, von welcher alles wirkliche Denken und alles Leben der Wisenschaft abhängt, und es eröffnet sich auf das bestimmteste die Anschauung von dem Leben des Seienden und von dem notwendigen Eins- und Ineinandersein des Seins und des Erkennens*); cf. *IDP* 251.
29 Twentieth-century philosophers such as Martin Heidegger and Edith Stein would do something similar in their respective interpretations of Plato's *Sophist*.
30 *EÜP* 249; cf. *IDP* 251. See below, 202–204, 219.

> ende sich notwendig und auf mannigfaltige Weise auch als Nichtseiendes offenbart, so daß es
> für das höchste Sein selbst gar kein entgegengesetztes irgend geben kann; derjenige aber, der
> nicht zu dem Lichte des wahren Seins hindurchgedrungen ist, es überall nicht weiter zu bringen
> vermag als bis zu diesem Nichtsein des wahren Erkennens und Nichterkennen des wahren
> Seins.[31]

As this passage indicates, for Schleiermacher it follows that *true being*, a.k.a. the *highest being*, has no opposite because it does not belong to the sphere of oppositions; nor, however, is it some "empty unity."[32] The *highest being* is, rather, the ground of the unity of *being* (*Sein*) and *knowing* (*Erkennen*), the unity which makes any knowledge possible. This dictates the need to keep in mind Schleiermacher's distinction between *the highest being* (*das höchste Sein*) and *being* (*Sein*), on the one hand, and between *being* (*Sein*) and beings or what-is (*das Seiende*), on the other hand. According to Schleiermacher, (1) *das höchste Sein* is the ground of unity of all oppositions, which is active in and through all *Seiende*, *Sein* and *Erkennen*; (2) *das Sein* is the most general concept for being and existence, for the *real*, and stands in polar opposition to (albeit always in dynamic relation with) *Erkennen*, the most general concept for thought, for the *ideal*; and (3) *das Seiende* refers usually to what exists (not just material objects but also, for example, forces and laws of nature), all of which are interrelated and interpenetrate one other; in some instances, however, he modifies it to signal that he means eternal and unchanging *being*. Neither *being* nor *the highest being* can be represented in thought.

Third, Schleiermacher emphasizes that Plato thereby avoids the futility and skepticism of those philosophers who either "proceed from an empty unity" or "remain standing within the sphere of opposites."[33] Plato begins where we all do, in "the sphere of representation" (... *dem Gebiete der Vorstellung*), and proceeds by means of the "purest dialectics" (*reinsten Dialektik*),[34] which is the combinatory art of carefully and accurately examining how the kinds apply in any particular situation and which requires recognizing the interpenetration of all opposition within the life of the existing, of what-*is*.

Fourth, according to Schleiermacher, Plato's dialectical method presupposes the *highest being* and requires a breaking through *into the light of true being*

---

[31] *EÜP* 250; cf. *IDP* 252–53.
[32] *EÜP* 249; cf. *IDP* 252. For German, see next note.
[33] *EÜP* 249 (... *welche von einer leeren Einheit ausgehn, oder auch die, welche innerhalb des Gebietes der Gegensätze stehen bleiben*); cf. *IDP* 252. These are the same two tendencies that, by the way, he thought defined philosophy in the early nineteenth century.
[34] *EÜP* 250; cf. *IDP* 253.

(7C).³⁵ Schleiermacher explains that this "glance into that higher sphere of speculation" is "the only defence against the pretensions, not to be otherwise repulsed, of sophistical contentiousness."³⁶ Knowledge, it follows, is not subjective since it participates in the highest being, in the unity of being and knowing, of physics and ethics. For that reason there can be no knowledge of true being itself, since the highest being has no opposite, and knowledge by definition is acquired through the dialectical process within the realm of oppositions.

Scholtz's and Rohls's respective analyses of these dense few pages from Schleiermacher's "Introduction to the *Sophist*" are lengthy and detailed. I lift up three insights from each of them that are particularly helpful for our present discussion.

Scholtz contends that in the *Sophist* Schleiermacher encountered "a sort of speculative theology"³⁷ which served as a basis for his own philosophy in his *Dialectics*. Schloltz describes three influences of Plato's *Sophist* on Schleiermacher. First, the doctrine of being provided a "defined structure, namely the distinction between an absolute being [*eines absoluten Sein*] as *Coincidentia oppositorum* and existence [*Seiende*] as the realm of opposites. Plato has shown that all opposites interpenetrate each other in the 'highest being', while 'existence' [*das Seiende*] participates in these opposites and through them acquires determinateness. Therein the 'essence of all true philosophy' is uttered."³⁸ Second, "... for Schleiermacher being [*das Sein*] is not the most important *formal* category; rather, *substantial being* and plentitude-of-being is, as 'highest being.' He borrows Plato's arguments against those who know being [*das Sein*] only as empty unity or as sphere of opposing existents."³⁹ And third, "Accordingly,

---

35 He made the same point in the passage from the *Grundlinien* comparing Plato and Spinoza (see above, chap. 1, 15–16).
36 *IPD* 253; *EÜP* 250 (... *der Blick in jenes höhere Gebiet der Spekulation Allen die hineinzudringen vermögen als die einzige Hilfe eröffnet wird gegen die sonst nicht abzuweisenden Ansprüche der sophistischen Streitsucht*).
37 Scholtz, "Schleiermacher und die Platonische Ideenlehre," 852.
38 Scholtz, "Schleiermacher und die Platonische Ideenlehre," 850 (*Aber Schleiermacher erkennt in dieser Seinslehre sogleich eine bestimmte Struktur, nämlich die Unterscheidung eines absoluten Seins als Coincidentia oppositorum und dem Seienden als Reich der Gegensätze. Platon habe gezeigt, daß in dem 'höchsten Sein' sich alle Gegensätze durchdringen, während das 'Seiende' an diesen Gegensätzen teilhat und durch sie seine Bestimmtheit erfährt. Darin sei das 'Wesen aller wahren Philosophie' ausgesprochen*).
39 Scholtz, "Schleiermacher und die Platonische Ideenlehre," 851 (... *ist für Schleiermacher das Sein nicht die wichtigste formale Kategorie; sondern als 'höchstes Sein' ist es ihm substantielles Sein und Seinsfülle. Er entnimmt das Platons Argumenten gegen die, welche das Sein nur als leere Einheit oder als Gebiet von entgegengesetztem Seienden kennen*).

'being' [*Sein*] has for Plato two main meanings in the *Sophist*. It is absolute being [*das absolute Sein*], which has no opposite; and it is existence [*das Seiende*], which stands in opposition to non-existence [*das Nichtseiende*]. Schleiermacher adopted this distinction in his *Dialektik*.... That he sees an ontology carried out in the *Sophist* has great significance for his understanding of the ideas."[40]

In three essays on the topic, Rohls stands in basic agreement with Scholtz, arguing that Schleiermacher found in the *Sophist* a "philosophical theology"[41] that he appropriated for his own *Dialectics*. Rohls contributes three additional explicit points which, in elaborating upon the post-Kantian philosophical context, can further aid our present investigation. First, whereas "Plato characterizes the idea of the good as the highest being [*das höchste Sein*]," Schleiermacher "conceives of this highest being furthermore as the identity of being [*Sein*] and knowing [*Erkennen*] or consciousness [*Bewußtsein*]."[42] Second, in the post-Kantian context, the *highest being*, understood as the identity of being and knowing, is the presupposition of all knowledge.[43] The *highest being*, therefore, is not something "transcendent" so much as it is "a transcendental ground."[44] And third, that absolute unity of *being* and *knowing*, in Schleiermacher's view, indicates "the theistic character of the Platonic, indeed, of Greek philosophy after Socrates."[45] For Schleiermacher's Plato, we can know nothing real "without presupposing the idea of the good."[46] Nevertheless, the theological difference is crucial: for Plato, God and the world are correlates; for Schleiermacher, metaphysics (as presented in his *Dialectics*) "culminates in the idea of God as the oppositionless unity."[47]

---

40 Scholtz, "Schleiermacher und die Platonische Ideenlehre," 852 (*'Sein' hat demnach bei Platon im 'Sophistes' zwei Hauptbedeutungen: Es ist das absolute Sein, das keinen Gegensatz hat; und es ist das Seiende, dem das Nichtseiende als Verschiedenheit gegenübersteht.... Schleiermacher hat diese Unterscheidung ähnlich in seine Dialektik übernommen.... Daß er im 'Sophistes' eine Ontologie durchgeführt sieht, hat große Bedeutung für sein Verständnis der Ideen*).
41 Rohls, "Schleiermachers Platonismus," 483.
42 Rohls, "Schleiermachers Platonismus," 482 (*Die Idee des Guten wird von Platon ja als das höchste Sein charakterisiert. Schleiermacher faßt dieses höchste Sein zudem als Identität von Sein und Erkennen oder Bewußtsein*).
43 See Rohls, "Schleiermachers Platonismus," 482; and "Schleiermachers Platon," 729.
44 Rohls, "Schleiermachers Platonismus," 485.
45 Rohls, "Schleiermachers Platonismus," 484 (*Gerade dies macht in Schleiermachers Augen den theistischen Charakter der platonischen, ja, der griechischen Philosophie nach Sokrates überhaupt aus*).
46 Rohls, "Schleiermachers Platon," 731.
47 Rohls, "Schleiermachers Platonismus," 485.

Schleiermacher found in Plato's *Sophist* an ontology correlated to an epistemology. He took that up in his own way in his *Dialectics*—as Scholtz, Rohls, and others have established in some detail. What has not been recognized, however, is the degree to which that modified Platonic ontology also served to shape the second edition of the *Speeches*. Schleiermacher's Plato lent Schleiermacher a more supple and defined armature for the higher realism and organic monism he had begun to develop in the first edition of the *Speeches*.

7.2.3 The Second Speech and the *Sophist*: The Two Series, Physics and Ethics

If we hold together the four distilled points from Schleiermacher's "Introduction to the *Sophist*" together with the six summary points drawn from Scholtz and Rohls, and if we reflect those back on what we have already examined in revised blocks n°s 1 and 2 and thus far here in n° 3, then the presence of Plato in the second edition of the second Speech should emerge even more clearly. Schleiermacher's treatment of the Platonic association of kinds in his *Introductions* sheds new light on his reconceptualization of The Three—or, more precisely, of his reconceptualization of those two of The Three that are not *piety*. We have already looked closely at *thinking* and *acting* and their connection to *knowledge* and *virtue*—hence to *physics* and *ethics*, respectively.[48] We are now in a position to investigate the Platonic ontology behind that connection.

Here in revised block n° 3 of the *Speeches*, just beyond the passage we have been considering (7A), Schleiermacher speaks of "the eternal unity of reason and nature" (*die ewige Einheit der Vernunft und Natur*).[49] Similarly, in his "Introduction to the *Sophist*," he refers to the unity (and reciprocating relation) of *knowing* (*Erkennen*) and *being* (*Sein*).[50] In other words, *thinking* and *acting* function in the second edition of the *Speeches* as the highest (most universal and general) pair of opposing yet correlative human activities, and they function at various levels of associations (see table 9).

---

48 See above, 6.3.
49 OR^2 166; R^2 48. Schmidt explains that, for Schleiermacher in the *Brouillon*, "nature and reason are the boundary concepts of the absolute opposition, absolute unity and absolute diversity and express themselves as functions: endowing unity or structuring and granting material or matter" (*Konstruktion des Endlichen*, 336).
50 See *EÜP* 246, 249, 251; *IDP* 249, 251, 254.

Table 9: Reciprocal Relations of Opposites in the *Speeches: Thinking (Denken)* and *Acting (Handeln)*

basic human activity (neutral category):	thinking/*Denken*	doing, acting/*Tun, Handeln*
goal, or proper realization of basic activity (normative category):	knowledge/*Erkennen*, *Erkenntniß* (Schleiermacher's translation for *epistēmē*), *Wissen*	virtue/*Tugend*
ideal:	the true/*das Wahre*	the good/*das Gut*
form:	science/*Wissenschaft*	art/*Kunst*
discipline:	physics/*Physik*	ethics/*Ethik*
application of activity:	theoretical	practical

Beneath this highest pair (of what in *Platons Werke* are "kinds") fall other oppositions, the two poles of which are actually complements that mutually, reciprocally, dynamically relate in ways also reminiscent of Plato: through movement and rest, by acting upon (*tun*) and being acted upon (*leiden*), etc. We can recognize here a structure that has a definite *telos* and that includes within itself countless dynamic relations between opposites at various levels and in countless combinations. This structure, in turn, shapes Schleiermacher's more developed argument in the 1806 edition of the *Speeches*. Much as Schleiermacher saw a pedagogical progression of ideas throughout Plato's *corpus*, so he inscribed a prescribed progression of intellectual and moral attunement in the *Speeches*, a progression informed and propelled by the increasing harmonization of the two impulses introduced at the beginning of the first Speech and brought to that dizzying oscillation by the end of the second Speech.

Moreover, the ontological reflections we find in Schleiermacher's "Introduction to the *Sophist*" supply us with a clearer understanding of Schleiermacher's description of the relation between the infinite and finite existence in a passage from revised block n° 2, which we have already examined: *It is, rather, simply the immediate perception [Wahrnehmung] of the universal existence [Sein] of everything finite in the infinite and through the infinite, of everything temporal in the eternal and through the eternal. This seeking and finding in all that lives and moves, in all becoming and change, in all doing and suffering, and just having and knowing life itself in immediate feeling as this existence [Sein]—this is religion* (6I).[51] In the first sentence, the terminology differs from that in the *Introductions*.

---

[51] OR^2 162–63; R^2 45. For full text, see above, chap. 6, 171–72.

Schleiermacher retains his language of *the infinite* from the first edition of the *Speeches*, and *the infinite* is not the language of Plato or, therefore, the language found in *Platons Werke*. Nonetheless, the incorporation into the second Speech of the language of *being/existence* (*Sein*), and the manner in which he exercises that in order to expand upon the immanental relation between being and beings (between the infinite and the finite, between the eternal and temporal) is consistent with what he emphasizes in his "Introduction to the *Sophist*." Along those same lines, the second sentence reflects the dialectical movement between opposites which so captured Schleiermacher in his reading of the *Sophist*, although there is a more passive note in the activity described here in the *Speeches*. Since the seeking and finding is religious, it requires that kind of observation or contemplation which does not try to impose.

Up to this point in the second edition of the *Speeches*, in contrast to the first edition, Schleiermacher continues to hold back somewhat on definitions of *religion* or *piety*—the third term of The Three—because the logic of his argument requires that he first establish these other two. Still, here in revised block n° 3 we can detect hints about where he is heading.

7.2.4 Intuition and the Unity of Theory and *Praxis*, Reason and Nature

The revisions in the second half of revised block n° 3 are subtle and reflect developments in Schleiermacher's thinking that were in part developed and formed in his engagement with Plato—but not Plato alone. Schleiermacher clears away some of the logical and terminological problems relating to *intuition* as he prepares the ground for *feeling*. Sometimes the imprint of *Platons Werke* is clear, but even when it is not altogether clear the wider Platonic view, in a Schleiermacherian sense, is still discernible.

Tellingly, Schleiermacher chooses to delete a sentence from 1799 that identified *intuiting* (*Anschauen*) as the *touchstone* (*Prüfstein*) in relation to the infinite.[52] This change reflects similar omissions of *intuition* in revised blocks n°s 2 and 4. Schleiermacher, however, does not altogether eliminate the term *intuition* or its cognates (*Anschauen, anschauen*) in 1806. Even though he chooses to restrict its use, he also more pointedly defines it. Hence, while he omits this one reference, he does employ *intuition* three times elsewhere in revised block n° 3; at least two of those times, the meaning carries certain resonances with what he wrote in his *Introductions*.

---

[52] See OR^1 103; R^1 49 (*KGA* 1/2:213.16–19). See above, 6.2.3.

The first time Schleiermacher uses *intuition* in revised block n° 3 is shortly after his reference to Socrates:

[Passage 7D: *Speeches*, 1806]

Because you do not recognize religion as the third, the other two—knowledge [*das Wissen*] and action [*das Handeln*]—are so fractured from one another that you cannot catch sight of their unity, but you think instead that someone could have right knowledge without right action, and *vice versa*. I allow the separation only in contemplation [*Betrachtung*], where it is necessary. You disdain it there and, in contrast to me, transfer it to life, as though what we are speaking about could itself exist in life separated and independently, one from the other. That is why you do not have *a living intuition* of any of these activities; rather, to you, each is an abstraction, something torn away. Hence your conception is a meager one—the impression of nothingness bearing in on itself, because it does not engage with the living in a living way.[53]

... weil Ihr die Religion nicht anerkennt als das Dritte, treten die anderen beiden, das Wissen und das Handeln so auseinander, dass Ihr ihre Einheit nicht erblickt, und meint man könne das rechte Wissen haben ohne das rechte Handeln, und umgekehrt. Eben weil Ihr die Trennung, die ich nur für die Betrachtung gelten lasse wo sie notwendig ist, für diese verschmäht, dagegen aber auf das Leben übertragt, als ob das wovon wir reden im Leben selbst getrennt könnte vorhanden sein und unabhängig eines vom anderen; deshalb eben habt Ihr von keiner dieser Tätigkeiten <u>eine lebendige Anschauung</u>, sondern es wird Euch jede ein Abstraktes, ein Abgerissenes, und Eure Vorstellung ist überall dürftig, das Gepräge der Nichtigkeit an sich tragend, weil sie nicht lebendig in das Lebendige eingreift.[54]

This differs from his criticism of the cultured despisers at this point in the first edition, which began as one directed specifically at the despisers but then morphed into a more general criticism: he shifted from the second-person plural, addressing them directly, to the third-person singular, describing what happens to a person in general when "he" loses intuition as the touchstone. In his revision, Schleiermacher maintains his directed focus on the cultured despisers, criticizing them because *they* have separated theory from practice, *they* have given themselves to abstraction, and thus *they* have lost the living connection between life and philosophy, praxis and theory. A subtle point, admittedly, but one consonant with the ideals of ancient philosophy as, in Hadot's words, a way of life. Additionally, this particular use of *intuition* (7D), which emphasizes livingness, carries faint echoes of the passage from the "Introduction to the *Sophist*" already quoted (7B): *the intuition of the life of what-is [Seienden] and of the necessary being-one and being-in-one-another of being [Sein] and of knowing [Erkennnes]*. In both instances, *intuition* occurs in the arena of a dynamic interrelat-

---

[53] OR^2 165, emphasis added.
[54] R^2 48, emphasis added.

ing of opposites; both times, it pertains to an actual apprehension of some circumstance in life, as opposed to a mere abstraction; and, importantly, both times it is the criterion for distinguishing what is real from what is only a projection or construction.

The second time Schleiermacher introduces *intuition* anew here in revised block n° 3, it is part of his reformulation of his well-known, pithy line differentiating The Three, which includes his most famous definition of *religion*. In 1799, he pronounced:

[Passage 7E: *Speeches*, 1799]

Praxis is an art, *speculation* is a science, religion is the sensibility and taste for the infinite.[55]

Praxis ist Kunst, Spekulazion ist Wißenschaft, Religion ist Sinn und Geschmak fürs Unendliche.[56]

In 1806 he rewrites the passage:

[Passage 7F: *Speeches*, 1806]

True science is perfected *intuition*; true praxis is self-generated cultivation and art; true religion is sensation and taste for the infinite.[57]

Wahre Wissenschaft ist vollendete Anschauung; wahre Praxis ist selbsterzeugte Bildung und Kunst; wahre Religion ist Empfindung und Geschmack für das Unendliche.[58]

Schleiermacher's reformulation of what science is (*speculation* is dropped, and *intuition* added) is certainly part of his reconceptualization of *knowing* in more positive terms, as we have seen in chapter six. In this case, it also happens to be consonant with the role of *intuition* in gaining knowledge of what-*is* in the "Introduction to the *Sophist*," as passage 7B again suggests. Moreover, the new triple iteration in 1806 of the modifier *true* may well be a nod to Plato and the search for truth, as it also aligns with and carries forward Schleiermacher's treatment of the two series (*thinking* and *acting*, *physics* and *ethics*) in the *Speeches*.

As Schleiermacher expands upon this revised definition of The Three (7F) in the next several lines of revised block n° 3, we see him incorporating into the *Speeches* what, in his philosophical works during this decade of engagement with Plato, he came to formulate as the reciprocal, dialectical relation between

---

55 *OR*¹ 103, emphasis added.
56 *R*¹ 47 (*KGA* 1/2:212.31–32).
57 *OR*² 165, emphasis added.
58 *R*² 48.

the two sciences, ethics and physics, whose unity is grounded in the infinite. Schleiermacher poses a series of questions:

[Passage 7G: *Speeches*, 1806]

What can the human person possibly want to cultivate in life and in art that is worthy of speech other than what has come to be in the self through the excitations of that former sense [i.e. sense of the infinite]? Or how, without that sense, can a person wish to comprehend the world scientifically? Or yet how, without that sense, when the cognition presses itself upon that person in a definite talent, can this talent be exercised? For what is all science, other than the existence [*Sein*] of things in you, in your reason? What is all art and culture, other than your existence [*Sein*] in things, in its measure and its form? And how can both flourish and come to life in you, other than insofar *as the eternal unity of reason and nature*—and insofar as the universal existence [*Sein*] of everything finite in the infinite —lives immediately in you?[59]

Was kann wohl der Mensch bilden wollen der Rede Wertes im Leben und in der Kunst, als was durch die Aufregungen jenes Sinnes in ihm selbst geworden ist? oder wie kann einer die Welt wissenschaftlich umfassen wollen, und wenn sich auch die Erkenntnis ihm aufdrängte in einem bestimmten Talent, selbst dieses üben ohne jenen? Denn was ist alle Wissenschaft als das Sein der Dinge in Euch, in Eurer Vernunft? was ist alle Kunst und Bildung, als Euer Sein in den Dingen, in ihrem Maße und ihrer Gestalt? und wie kann beides in Euch zum Leben gedeihen als nur sofern <u>die ewige Einheit der Vernunft und Natur</u>, sofern das allgemeine Sein alles Endlichen im Unendlichen unmittelbar in Euch lebt?[60]

Here we find a fuller and more consistent articulation of his higher realism than Schleiermacher was able to give in 1799, possible in part because his reconceptualization of The Three in 1806 no longer employs negative oppositional language. That reconceptualization helps him reframe *thinking* and *acting*—now science and art—in a positive manner, and consequently aids him in presenting more clearly and coherently than he could before the role of religion in relation to the other two. In this passage, we see a quite particular point of influence by Schleiermacher's Plato: it is because of the *eternal unity of reason and nature* (7G), what in the "Introduction to the *Sophist*" he thrice refers to as the unity of *being* and *knowing* (7B).[61] This fundamentally (Schleiermacherian) Platonic insight and commitment serves to reinforce, inform, and refine his earlier post-Kantian realism. At the same time, interestingly, in the second edition of the *Speeches* Schleiermacher drops the modifier "higher" for his claim about realism at the end of this block. Finally, notice how in this passage (7G) we see another

---

59 *OR*² 165–66, emphasis added.
60 *R*² 48, emphasis added.
61 *EÜP* 246, 249, 251; *IDP* 249, 251, 254.

instance of the newer, more dynamic phrase regarding the relationship of the finite in the infinite, and the immediate and living quality of that.

The third time Schleiermacher employs *intuition* in revised block n° 3, it is bound with *feeling:*

> **[Passage 7H: *Speeches*, 1806]**
>
> The person who does not become one with the universe in the immediate unity of intuition and feeling remains eternally separated from it, in the derived unity of consciousness.[62]
>
> Wenn der Mensch nicht in der unmittelbaren Einheit der Anschauung und des Gefühls eins wird mit dem Universum bleibt er in der abgeleiteten des Bewusstseins ewig getrennt von ihm.[63]

He elaborates on this *unity of intuition and feeling* in the next revised block, as we shall soon see. For now, two points about its immediate context here should be of interest. The first point is that, in the few lines between this passage and the previous use of *intuition* (7F), Schleiermacher offers what sounds like a rebuke of his contemporary sophists. The sharp challenge to "speculation" and "rounded idealism" is retained, but it is also broadened somewhat beyond a particular philosophical school to include other deceptive habits: "Hence the sovereignty of the pure concept! Hence, instead of the organic structure, the mechanical stunts of your system! Hence the empty game with analytical formula, whether categorical or hypothetic, in whose fetters life refuses to rest comfortably!"[64] The second point is that this reference to the *unity of intuition and feeling* (7H) immediately follows a reference to the "yearning for the infinite" (*Sehnsucht nach dem Unendlichen*), a line which also appeared in the first edition, except that here in 1806 Schleiermacher casts it in relation to *surrendering* (*hinzugeben*), one of the two impulses he has revised and further developed in the second edition.[65]

The two editions of the *Speeches* come back together again in the ode to Spinoza:

> Respectfully offer up with me a lock from the mane of the holy, repudiated Spinoza! The high world spirit permeated him, the infinite was his beginning and end, the universe his sole and eternal love. In holy innocence and deep humility, he was mirrored in the eternal world, and he also beheld how he himself was a most genial mirror to it. He was filled

---

[62] OR^2 166–67.
[63] R^2 49.
[64] OR^2 166; R^2 49 (*Daher die Herrschaft des bloßen Begriffs! daher statt des organischen Baues die mechanischen Kunststücke Eurer Systeme! daher das leere Spiel mit analytischen Formeln, seien sie kategorisch oder hypothetisch, zu deren Fesseln sich das Leben nicht bequemen will*).
[65] OR^2 166; R^2 49.

with religion and full of holy spirit. And, for that reason, he also stands there alone and unsurpassed, master in his art, yet exalted beyond the profane guild, without apprentices and without citizenship.[66]

Keep in mind that, in both his *Grundlinien* and his lectures on the history of philosophy, Schleiermacher held up Spinoza and Plato together as the pinnacle of ethics and philosophy.

7.3 Revised Block N° 4: "the original relation of feeling and intuition"

The fourth revised block is especially substantive and lengthy, running over the course of seven pages, five of them full (not split-column) pages; in other words, this revision is extensive and most of it is entirely new, with some rearrangement of previous material.[67] The original text replaced by revised block n° 4 was only one-and-a-half, split-column pages. It was significant in that it opened with the declaration that the concept *intuition of the universe* is the "hinge" of his entire argument,[68] and in it Schleiermacher elaborated upon his "higher realism" by explaining *intuition* and how it "proceeds from an influence of the intuited on the one who intuits."[69] Revised block n° 4 begins with a significant omission—not just the omission of Schleiermacher's declaration about intuition being the hinge of argument, but also an omission of the ensuing discussion of *intuition*. It thus disrupts the 1799 comparison of *intuition* and *feeling*, replacing a discussion of the former and displacing a definition of the latter; instead, it picks up and develops at length the notion of *the immediate unity of feeling and intuition* (7H) introduced in revised block n° 3. It expands the ode to Spinoza, including now a tribute to the poet Novalis, who had died tragically young in 1801.[70] It in-

---

66 OR^2 167; R^2 49 (*Opfert mit mir ehrerbietig eine Locke den Manen des heiligen verstoßenen Spinoza! Ihn durchdrang der hohe Weltgeist, das Unendliche war sein Anfang und Ende, das Universum seine einzige und ewige Liebe, in heiliger Unschuld und tiefer Demut spiegelte er sich in der ewigen Welt, und sah zu wie auch Er ihr liebenswürdigster Spiegel war; voller Religion war Er und voll heiligen Geistes; und darum steht Er auch da, allein und unerreicht, Meister in seiner Kunst, aber erhaben über die profane Zunft, ohne Jünger und ohne Bürgerrecht*).
67 See R^2 49–56; OR^2 167–75. See table 8.
68 See above, 6.2.3 and 7.2.4.
69 OR^1 104; R^1 50. For fuller discussion of intuition and higher realism in the first edtion of the *Speeches*, see Lamm, *Living God*, 80–87; and Schmidt, *Konstruktion des Endlichen*, 59–71.
70 Georg Philipp Friedrich von Hardenberg (1772–1801). "... when the philosophers, like Spinoza, will be religious and seek God, and when the artists, like Novalis, will be pious and love

cludes his famous analogy of the marital embrace, which occurred at a much later point in the first edition. It offers, for the first time in the speech, a full-fledged account of the relation of *feeling* to both *acting* and *knowing*. And it also happens to include at least three allusions to Plato, which become all the more obvious once the Plato question is posed.

Revised block n° 4 is the culmination of Schleiermacher's argument concerning his new typology of The Three. Having just spent almost the first quarter of his revised second Speech developing the two of The Three that are not religion, he now circles back to *religion*. The influence of Plato can be glimpsed in the scattered allusions but, once again, is especially found in how he sets up the dynamic ontology grounding The Three. The presence of Plato is not found in his understanding of religion *per se*, but in how Schleiermacher describes The Three in terms of "series," no longer just as "spheres." The presence of Plato in the *Speeches*, it must be remembered, is very much Schleiermacher's Plato.

As before, I proceed through the revised block systematically, closely examining what Schleiermacher did in his revision of the *Speeches* and reading that in light of his *Introductions*, in order to see what further insight we might glean than were we to read it simply at face value. As much as possible, I try to focus on the matter of Plato's presence here and not try to solve every issue of *intuition* and *feeling*. As before, we find Schleiermacher articulating ideas and patterns of thought that he had developed since at least 1803 and was continuing to hone throughout 1806—ideas and patterns of thought which he formed, in part, through studying Plato's dialogues. Here, at the culmination of his new argument of The Three, we begin to recognize Schleiermacher's Plato most clearly. In order, however, to grasp the full significance of Schleiermacher's extensively re-worked argument in revised block n° 4, we need to start with that telling omission.

7.3.1 The Replaced 1799 Version: Intuition as the "Hinge" of the Second Speech

In 1799, Schleiermacher was neither consistent nor sufficiently clear about the relation between the key terms *feeling* and *intuition*. At times the two appeared as identical and thus interchangeable, at other times as distinct or even separate

---

Christ, then the great resurrection will be celebrated for both worlds" (OR^2 168)/... *wenn die Philosophen werden religiös sein und Gott suchen wie Spinoza, und die Künstler fromm sein und Christum lieben wie Novalis, dann wird die große Auferstehung gefeiert werden für beide Welten* (R^2 50).

functions.⁷¹ In 1806, Schleiermacher does not discard the term *intuition* as some have maintained,⁷² although he does significantly reduce his use of it and, when he does employ it, defines its relation to *feeling* more precisely than he had in the first edition. At the same time, he dramatically increases his use of the term *feeling*.⁷³ This more deliberate defining and drawing of the relation between *feeling* and *intuition* occurs at the very beginning of revised block n° 4. To appreciate the significance of his revision, we need to return to the first edition to gain a clear understanding of what he deemed problematic.

The 1799 passage which Schleiermacher deleted in 1806 at the insertion point of this fourth major revision began with the declarative statement: "I entreat you to become familiar with this concept: intuition of the universe. It is the hinge of my whole speech."⁷⁴ At the beginning of chapter six, I argued how, logically speaking, Schleiermacher *had* to drop that claim since it contradicted his basic point that religion is not a concept.⁷⁵ Now let us put that original claim in context in order to see what he was trying to accomplish with it and why, therefore, his removal of it in 1806 is so significant.

At this point in the first edition, Schleiermacher was drawing an analogy between *intuition* and *feeling*.⁷⁶ Following what amounted to a thesis statement, he

---

71 For example, in his first reference to the terms in the second Speech, Schleiermacher appeared to conflate them but then went on to describe the work of intuition, leaving the question of whether feeling operates in the same way or functions differently: "Religion's essence is neither thinking nor acting, but *intuition and feeling*. It wishes to *intuit* the universe, wishes devoutly to overhear the universe's own manifestations and actions, longs to be grasped and filled by the universe's immediate influences in childlike passivity" (*OR*¹ 102, emphasis added)/*Ihr Wesen ist weder Denken noch Handeln, sondern Anschauung und Gefühl. Anschauen will sie das Universum, in seinen eigenen Darstellungen und Handlungen will sie es andächtig belauschen, von seinen unmittelbaren Einflüßen will sie sich in kindlicher Paßivität ergreifen und erfüllen laßen* (*R*¹ 45 [*KGA* 1/2:211.32–36]).
72 For example, Harvey claimed a "virtual elimination as a technical term" ("On the New Edition," 499); and Emil Fuchs asserted that "this concept *Anschauung* disappears in the second edition" ("Wandlungen in Schleiermachers Denken zwischen der ersten und zweiten Ausgabe der Reden," *Theologische Studien und Kritiken* 76 [1903]: 74).
73 A comparative word search of *Anschauung* and *Gefühl* in the the second Speech reveals the following shifts, in approximate numbers: *Anschauung* is used (independently of *Gefühl*) 44 times in 1799 but only 22 times in 1806, for a fifty-percent reduction; *Gefühl* is used (independently of *Anschauung*) 35 times in 1799 but 134 times in 1806, for an almost four-fold increase; the two terms are bound tightly together 13 times in 1799 and 7 times in 1806, for an almost fifty-percent reduction, and four of those times occur in our revised block n° 4.
74 *OR*¹ 104. For German, see above, chap. 6, 154n44.
75 See above, 6.2.3.
76 See *R*¹ 49–51 (*KGA* 1/2:213.34–214.18); *OR*¹ 104–105 (from "I entreat you ..." to "empty mythology").

spent about fifteen lines on *intuition*, tying it closely to *perception*[77] and describing it as the receptive point of contact with the activity of the universe that then becomes spontaneous as the universe's activity is "grasped, apprehended, and conceived by the [individual] according to one's own nature."[78] This was the key to his *higher realism* in the post-Kantian context. He used that description of *intuition* as a parallel illustration of *religion*, similarly described as receptivity to the universe:

[Passage 7I: *Speeches*, 1799]

The same is true of religion. The universe exists in uninterrupted activity and reveals itself to us every moment. Every form that it brings forth, every being to which it gives a separate existence according to the fullness of life, every occurrence that spills forth from its rich, ever-fruitful womb, is an action of the same upon us. Thus to accept everything individual as a part of the whole and everything limited as a representation of the infinite is religion. But whatever would go beyond that and penetrate deeper into the nature and substance of the whole is no longer religion, and will, if it still wants to be regarded as such, inevitably sink back into empty mythology.[79]

So die Religion; das Universum ist in einer ununterbrochenen Thätigkeit und offenbart sich uns jeden Augenblik. Jede Form die es hervorbringt, jedes Wesen dem es nach der Fülle des Lebens ein abgesondertes Dasein giebt, jede Begebenheit die es aus seinem reichen immer fruchtbaren Schooße herausschüttet, ist ein Handeln deßelben auf Uns; und so alles Einzelne als einen Theil des Ganzen, alles Beschränkte als eine Darstellung des Unendlichen hinnehmen, das ist Religion; was aber darüber hinaus will, und tiefer hineindringen in die Natur und Substanz des Ganzen ist nicht mehr Religion, und wird, wenn es doch noch dafür angesehen sein will, unvermeidlich zurüksinken in leere Mythologie.[80]

The analogy he was trying to draw between *intuition* and *religion* was evidently twofold: a receptive mode in relation to reality (an active universe conceived as an organic system of forces) acting upon us; and a relationship to the universe as a whole rather than to particulars *qua* particulars. The distinction he appears to have intended was that, whereas *intuition* was caused by and responded to the

---

77 "If the emanations of light ... did not affect your sense [organ/*Organ*], ... you would *intuit nothing and perceive nothing*, and what you thus *intuit and perceive* is not the nature of things, but their action upon you" (*OR*¹ 104–105, emphasis added)/*Wenn die Ausflüße des Lichtes nicht ... Euer Organ berührten, ... so würdet Ihr nichts anschauen und nichts wahrnehmen, und was Ihr also anschaut und wahrnehmt, ist nicht die Natur der Dinge, sondern ihr Handeln auf Euch* (R¹ 50 [KGA 1/2:214.1–8]). See Schmidt, *Konstruktion des Endlichen*, 61–63, for discussion of *Anschauung* in the first edition of the *Reden*.
78 *OR*¹ 104; R¹ 50 (*KGA* 1/2:213.40–214.1) (... *welches dann von dem lezteren seiner Natur gemäß aufgenommen, zusammengefaßt und begriffen wird*).
79 *OR*¹ 105.
80 R¹ 50–51 (*KGA* 1/2:214.9–18).

impressions left on our senses, *religion* (in this passage he did not use *feeling*) was caused by and responded to the *infinite* as it reveals itself in and through the *universe*, or the *whole*. Religion sees everything finite as an action of the infinite, and it accepts every action affecting oneself as likewise an action of the infinite.

In 1806, Schleiermacher drops the separate discussion of *intuition* and displaces the religion as *ever-fruitful womb* line (7I) to the very end of revised block n° 4. In thus deciding to delete half of the original text, shift the other half, and add five pages of mostly new material, what did he place in its stead? Schleiermacher still seeks to explain the relation between *intuition* and *feeling*, and that relationship remains that upon which his larger argument turns, but he has fundamentally re-thought the matter. He begins with what he now calls with *the original relation of feeling and intuition* (6A), but to grasp what that means the cultured despisers must enter *the innermost sanctuary of life* (6A), which requires *contemplation* (6I). In chapter six, we considered all this from the vantage point of praxis; now let us return to it from the vantage point of theory.

7.3.2 Contemplation and the Innermost Sanctuary of Life, *Redux*

After opening revised block n° 4 with his expanded ode to Spinoza and Novalis, which rhetorically serves both to establish a common ground of shared admiration and to plant aspiration, Schleiermacher delivers the main point of his argument about The Three. Having spent a quarter of his revised second Speech carefully laying forth what he means by *thinking* and *acting*, he is now ready to explain *this unity of science, religion, and art—and, at the same time, what I mean by their distinction* (6A). The key has to do with *the original relation of feeling and intuition* (6A). We see immediately that this is a different kind of argument, different even from the dialectical challenges posed in his revised argument regarding *thinking* and *acting*. This is why Schleiermacher had to omit reference to *intuition* as the *concept* on which his entire argument turned in 1799. As we have seen, Schleiermacher's argument requires praxis as much as the exercise of reason; it requires *contemplation*, a term which we have already encountered in revised block n°s 2 and 3 and which he uses five times here in revised block n° 4. It is not the case, as his critics have maintained, that Schleiermacher therewith retreated into some privatized experience or, as Wayne Proudfoot put it, some "autonomous moment … invulnerable to rational and moral criticism."[81] It is simply the kind of argument that requires contemplation—pause, stepping back, careful consideration, self-examination—but it is not irrational. Schleiermacher offers several examples of common experiences of what he calls those "living moment[s]"[82] that have shaped the cultured despisers' lives: art, a clear idea, sex.[83] He advises them, *You must understand it by eavesdropping on your own selves before your consciousness, or at the very least by reconstituting this condition for yourselves out of that consciousness* (6A). Conceding the difficulty of his task, Schleiermacher nonetheless continues to insist on holding praxis together with theory. He tries to get them to see—as philosophers, artists, human beings—that "everything living in your life"[84] depends on some kind of union, an *original being-one:*

[Passage 7]: *Speeches,* **1806]**

As soon as you try to turn a given, definite activity of your soul into an object of communication or *contemplation,* you are already within the divorce, and your thought can only comprehend that which is disjoined. That is why my speech cannot lead you by any definite example. Precisely because what I want to point out in my speech is one, it is also already past. And here I could point out to you only a faint trace of *the original being-one* [*von dem ursprünglichen Einssein*] of that which is disjoined. Yet even this I do not wish to scorn prematurely.[85]

Sobald Ihr eine gegebene bestimmte Tätigkeit Eurer Seele zum Gegenstande der Mitteilung oder der Betrachtung machen wollt seid Ihr schon innerhalb der Scheidung, und nur das Getrennte kann Euer Gedanke umfassen. Darum kann Euch meine Rede auch an kein bestimmtes Beispiel führen; denn eben weil es eins ist, ist auch das schon vorüber was sie aufzeigen will, und hier könnte ich Euch von dem ursprünglichen Einssein des Getrennten nur eine leise Spur aufzeigen. Aber auch die will ich vorläufig nicht verschmähen.[86]

---

81 Wayne Proudfoot, *Religious Experience* (Berkeley: University of California Press, 1985), 2. Proudfoot has since reconsidered aspects of his argument from 1980s (see, e. g., "Intuition and Fantasy in *On Religion,*" in *Interpreting Religion: The Significance of Friedrich Schleiermacher's Reden über die Religion for Religious Studies and Theology,* ed. Dietrich Korsch and Amber L. Griffioen [Tübingen: Mohr Siebeck, 2011], 87–98; and "Immediacy and Intentionality in the Feeling of Absolute Dependence," in Sockness and Gräb, *Schleiermacher, the Study of Religion, and the Future of Theology,* 27–37), but *Religious Experience* continues to have an inordinate influence in shaping the assumptions of scholars of religion concerning Schleiermacher.
82 OR^2 168; R^2 50 (... *eines lebendigen Moments*).
83 The most extended example he offers is the analogy of sexual intercourse, which in 1806 he moves from its later position in the first edition up to this point. Compare OR^2 170 (R^2 52) with OR^1 112–13 (R^1 70–71 [*KGA* 1/2:221.72–222.7]).
84 OR^2 170; R^2 52 (*alles Lebendigen in Eurem Leben*)
85 OR^2 168, emphasis added. See passage 6A for lines immediately preceding these.
86 R^2 50.

212 — 7 The Presence of Plato in the *Speeches* (1806), Part 2

This is not a "protective strategy," as Proudfoot charges.[87] If the cultured despisers resist or still cannot grasp it, Schleiermacher does not seal himself off from them. On the contrary, we witness him continuing to engage his interlocutors: "Capture yourselves in the process. How do you sketch an image of any one object?"[88]

Such preparation is necessary because, at least at this point in his presentation, the "object" of the *feeling(-intuition)* is not a definite object but is instead object-less-ness, so to speak: some experience of a union of subject and object, of the interpenetration of opposites. The "object" of inquiry here is the *coming-to-be of [one's] consciousness* (6A), possible only through an awareness of oneself as existing (or, sharing "common being [*Sein*]"[89]) with other beings and the "whole" (*Ganze*), which because being is never static can be understood "only as act, as moment."[90] How did he get from *an image of any one object* to a *whole*?

7.3.3 The "Original Relation of Feeling and Intuition"

In a matter of three dense pages, Schleiermacher presents his basic (and newly honed) epistemology. Rather than unpack that entirely here, I set forth his basic pattern of thought with the aim of demonstrating the influence of Schleiermacher's Plato. One influence may seem minor, since it has to do with imagery, but it actually signals a shift in content, form, and flow: although he retains the 1799 imagery of three *spheres* (*Gebiete*) in describing The Three, he supplements that in 1806 with the imagery of three *series* (*Reihen*). *Series* serves his revised argument better than does *sphere* because it is less static and insular, allowing for movement and dynamic interrelationship among The Three.[91] It also happens to be the language Schleiermacher uses in his *Introductions* to describe *physics*

---

87 Proudfoot, *Religious Experience*, xv–xvi.
88 *OR*² 168, altered; *R*² 50 (*Ergreift Euch dabei, wie Ihr ein Bild von irgendeinem Gegenstand zeichnet ...*).
89 *OR*² 171, altered; *R*² 53 (*... gemeinschaftlichen Seins*).
90 *OR*² 169, altered; *R*² 51 (*nur als Akt, als Moment*).
91 Proudfoot focuses on what he calls an "autonomous moment in human experience" and "radical independence" of religious experience in Schleiermacher (*Religious Experience*, 2, 3; cf. 10–11). Although this criticism might apply to a certain extent to the 1799 edition, it does not apply to the 1806 edition, where Schleiermacher went out of his way to explain the reciprocal relations among The Three. Like other critics, Proudfoot mistakenly conflates Schleiermacher's views with those of Rudolph Otto (see *Religious Experience*, 8). On such a conflation in the history of Schleiermacher interpretation, see Andrew Dole, "Schleiermacher and Otto on Religion," *Religious Studies* 40, no. 4 (December 2004): 389–413.

7.3 Revised Block N° 4: "the original relation of feeling and intuition" — 213

and *ethics*. Recall how, in his *Introductions*, Schleiermacher describes the two "series" (knowing and acting, knowledge and virtue, the theoretical and practical), which, by means of the dialectical method, are brought together in the middle dialogues and, by means of ever more advanced dialectics, culminate in the two sciences of *physics* (in the *Timaeus*) and *ethics* (in the *Republic*). Recall, too, how he argues there that the two series can and ought to be brought together in the life of the individual since being and thought, truth and goodness are already united in the highest being. We find a strikingly similar template in the 1806 edition of the *Speeches*, except that in the *Speeches* Schleiermacher adds a third series—*feeling* (*Gefühl*), or *religion*—which does not merely run alongside the other two series but also enhances, connects, and corrects them as it roots the person in reality, which is the life of the finite in the infinite. In short, the presence of Schleiermacher's Plato in revised block n° 4 is detectable in how Schleiermacher describes the two series of *thinking* and *doing*, their reciprocal relation, and their relation to existence; in a similar fashion, it is detectable in how he applies that reciprocity to the relation between *intuition* and *feeling*, although only to a degree; and, finally, it is detectable in his treatment of *intuition*, specifically. That notwithstanding, what Schleiermacher does with the third series (*intuition* and *feeling*) is something different from what he does with the two series in *Platons Werke*, even if we can recognize certain common ontological commitments operative in the *Speeches* and the *Introductions*.

At the simplest level, Schleiermacher's post-Kantian epistemology (what he called his "higher realism" in 1799 and "an other realism" in 1806)[92] begins with a sense perception of external objects: "How do you sketch an image of any one object? Do you not still find bound up with it a being-stimulated and being-determined, as it were, of your very selves by the object?"[93] Any encounter stimulates a response—both a thinking and an acting. The two series, *thinking* and *acting*, thus begin in some encounter between object and subject (sense), but due to the "constant cessation and recurrence"[94] that reciprocal relation (along with awareness of that reciprocity) builds: "How is it you now exist in the whole? Through your senses, I hope, if indeed you must exist with the senses in order to exist in the whole. And how is it you exist for yourselves? Through the unity of your consciousness, which unity you initially have in sensation, in

---

92 See R^1 49 (*KGA* 1/2:213.22); R^2 49.
93 OR^2 168, altered; R^2 50–51 (*wie Ihr ein Bild von irgendeinem Gegenstand zeichnet ob Ihr nicht noch damit verbunden findet ein Erregt- und Bestimmtsein Eurer selbst gleichsam durch den Gegenstand*).
94 OR^2 169; R^2 51 (*das Resultat seines beständigen Aufhörens und Wiederkehrens*).

the contrast and change of its varying degrees."⁹⁵ Consciousness emerges out of the most basic experience of being in relation to the world, in being part of that world.

At this point in his revision, Schleiermacher invokes (not for the sole or last time) the two impulses, which he introduced at the beginning of the first Speech (and which, as we have seen, he had to revise in 1806) in order to capture the basic dynamics of each moment of life.⁹⁶ Notice the language of *being* and *becoming*:

> Therefore, to be sure, it is a becoming of a being [*Sein*] for itself and a becoming of a being [*Sein*] in the whole, both at the same time; it is a striving to return to the whole, and a striving to exist on its own, *both at the same time.*⁹⁷

> Also wohl ein Werden eines Seins für sich, und ein Werden eines Seins im Ganzen, beides zugleich; ein Streben in das Ganze zurückzugehen, und ein Streben für sich zu bestehen, beides zugleich.⁹⁸

Schleiermacher sees each moment of life as an act, a movement, a becoming: a movement of interactions between self and world, and simultaneously a movement within oneself involving two opposing-yet-reciprocal impulses. Notice how those two impulses, in their interrelation, are not unlike the pairs of Platonic "kinds" of *movement* and *rest*, *difference* and *identity:* one is an active creating, the other is more passive in the sense of being a surrender; one emphasizes distinct differentiation, the other a being-one-with. Again, Schleiermacher envisions this in terms of polar opposites (one impulse moving towards identification with the other or the whole, the other moving back from that towards individuation) which act reciprocally. In that reciprocity is found a kind of union: "this flowing-into-one-another and having-become-one of sense and object, before each returns to its place, this is what I mean: it is that moment that you always experience yet also do not experience."⁹⁹ In other words, the reciprocating influences and movements are experienced in that they are always there and always active,

---

95 OR^2 169; R^2 51 (*Wodurch nun seid Ihr im Ganzen? Durch Eure Sinne hoffe ich, wenn Ihr doch bei Sinnen sein müsst um im Ganzen zu sein. Und wodurch seid Ihr für Euch? Durch die Einheit Eures Bewusstseins, die Ihr zunächst in der Empfindung habt, in dem vergleichbaren Wechsel ihres Mehr und Weniger*).
96 See above, 6.2.1.
97 OR^2 169, emphasis added.
98 R^2 51.
99 OR^2 169, altered; R^2 51 (*dieses Ineinandergeflossen- und Einsgewordensein von Sinn und Gegenstand, ehe noch jedes an seinen Ort zurückkehrt, das ist es was ich meine, das ist jener Moment den Ihr jedesmal erlebt aber auch nicht erlebt*).

7.3 Revised Block N° 4: "the original relation of feeling and intuition" — 215

but they are not experienced in the sense of being objects of perception. In encouraging the cultured despisers to reflect on their experience, Schleiermacher asks them to isolate a particular living moment of their lives for examination and then to imagine their lives as a chain or necklace made up of such moments as links.[100] A human life, for Schleiermacher, is a continual process of creation by bringing the two series together through the dialectical interplay of the two impulses. Every act of consciousness presupposes a prior union of subject and object, also of individual and whole, but to try to represent that in thought means you are "already within the divorce."[101] If Schleiermacher has succeeded in getting his cultured despisers to recognize in their own lives some experience of being-one—whether in any simple moment or in the more exhilarating moments of experiencing beauty, knowledge, or love—he then bids them to reflect on how that "immediate union" (*unmittelbaren Vereine*)[102] arose, how it affected them, and how it contributed to their own coming-to-be.

Here is where *feeling* and *intuition*, and their newly specified relationship, enter into his argument. Schleiermacher devotes thirty-eight lines to delineating the relation between them.[103] In the second edition of the *Speeches*, the difference between *intuition* and *feeling* is not so much a difference in the cause (what is stimulating the intuition or feeling) or in the receptors (what is doing the perceiving, responding, or apprehending) as it is the *direction* which that being-stimulated predominantly takes within a given person at a given moment. The difference is as crucial as it is subtle since, with it, Schleiermacher tries to clear up problems with his 1799 account of how *feeling* is related to cognition. There is evidence here of how his engagement with Plato helped him clarify certain things and yet, at the same time, how his argument in the *Speeches* differed from other, philosophical arguments he was making around the same time.

In any experience of being-one, Schleiermacher explains, either "the *intuition* comes up before you, living and ever clearer" or "the consciousness issues forth the *feeling* out of your interior and, spreading, takes up your entire being [*Wesen*]."[104] The former, *intuition*, thus represents what might be called an outward-moving vector (my language, not his) in that it tends towards cognition and objectivation, and in that sense may be said to be more objective; it is the

---

100 See OR^2 169; R^2 51.
101 OR^2 168; R^2 50 (... *seid Ihr schon innerhalb der Scheidung*).
102 OR^2 170; R^2 52.
103 See OR^2 170–71; R^2 52–53.
104 OR^2 170, emphasis added; R^2 52 (... *und nun tritt entweder lebendig und immer heller die Anschauung vor Euch hin, ... oder es arbeitet sich das Gefühl aus Eurem Inneren hervor und nimmt verbreitend Euer ganzes Wesen ein*).

root of a knowing and of knowledge, where something begins to be conceived. The latter, *feeling*, would then represent an inward-moving vector in that it starts in one's interior and remains there, expanding, and in that sense may be said to be more subjective; it shapes who one is, not just cognitively but in terms of one's entire being and, therefore, one's way of being in the world. Depending on the person and the moment itself, one or the other vector will likely predominate, even though both will be in play. Schleiermacher continues,

> [Passage 7K: *Speeches*, 1806]
>
> And when your consciousness has first established itself as either one, as intuition or as feeling, then—if you are not wholly self-conscious in this separation, if you have not wholly lost the true intuition of your life in the particular—what remains to you is nothing other than *the knowledge [Wissen] of the original unity of both separated things*, about their identical emergence out of *the fundamental relationship of your existence*.[105]
>
> Und, wenn sich erst als eines von beiden, als Anschauung oder Gefühl Euer Bewusstsein festgestellt hat, dann bleibt Euch, falls Ihr nicht ganz in dieser Trennung befangen die wahre Anschauung Eures Lebens im Einzelnen verloren habt, nichts anderes übrig als das Wissen um die ursprüngliche Einheit beider Getrennten, um ihr gleiches Hervorgehen aus dem Grundverhältnis Eures Daseins.[106]

No longer parallel faculties and no longer conflated, in 1806 *feeling* and *intuition* might better described as two sides of the same coin: closely bound together yet distinct. They are bound even more closely than, but in a different fashion from, The Three are in relation to one another. Like *thinking* and *acting* (and like *being* and *thought* or the other Platonic "kinds" such as *movement* and *rest*, *difference* and *identity*), *feeling* and *intuition* are set closely together in tensive, active reciprocity—except that Schleiermacher presents them as even closer together than those other pairs.[107] Where the other pairs are separable, this pair appears to be inseparable. Unlike the pair *thinking* and *acting*, *feeling* and *intuition* do not constitute two different series or spheres but together constitute one series, called *feeling*, *religion*, or *piety*. Furthermore, unlike *thinking* and *acting*, *feeling(-intuition)* is receptive in nature. Finally, unlike *thinking* and *acting*, *feeling(-intuition)* apprehends the unity of subject and object (the shared

---

105 OR^2 170, emphasis added.
106 R^2 52.
107 In introducing a distinction between *intuition* and *feeling* in revised block n° 4, Schleiermacher complicates his terminology even as he tries to clear up a confusion. The term *feeling* takes on both a more comprehensive meaning (a genus) when it refers to his third "sphere" or "series," and a particular meaning (a species or kind) when it stands in contradistinction to *intuition*.

being) before the separation that occurs precisely by means of thinking and acting. That is what he calls *the fundamental relationship of your existence* (7K).[108] The thinking and the acting that become knowing and virtue arise out of that *fundamental relationship*.

With that, Schleiermacher inserts a reference to Plato. He reminds the cultured despisers about what that *ancient sage* has taught them—namely, that *every knowing is a memory of what is outside time and is thus justifiably placed at the apex of all that is temporal*.[109] This is characteristic of Schleiermacher's Plato: Schleiermacher points not to a pre-existing time, but to the moment *just before*, or the moment *now* just at the cusp of reflection; he underscores the simultaneity, the *coincidence*. This reference to Plato is neither accidental nor incidental, and in it we glimpse an epistemological convergence between the *Speeches* and the *Introductions*. For it is here that *thinking*, as a generalized activity, becomes a *knowing* (*Erkennen* or *Wissen*). Below, we will examine more closely how Schleiermacher explains the complex relationship between the series *feeling* with the other two series, *knowing* and *acting*.[110] Before that, however, let us see what we might learn by comparing what he says about *intuition* in his *Introductions* with what he says about it here in revised block n° 4 (in this condensed discussion of about one page) regarding this distinction between *intuition* and *feeling*. His revisions here regarding *intuition*, I maintain, reflect how he employs *intuition* in *Platons Werke*. The parallels between the *Speeches* and *Introductions*, however, exist in relation to *intuition* and *knowing*, not in relation to *feeling*.

7.3.4 Intuition in *Platons Werke* and the Second Speech

In his *Introductions*, Schleiermacher consistently uses *intuition* to convey two connected ideas: first, a "living" grasp or apprehension of something active and existing; and second, an apprehension of reality in terms of the unity of opposites, a unity which is possible because of their shared existence in the "high-

---

108 This reflects Schleiermacher's asymptotic approach in epistemology and in human life more generally: an identity between two "opposites" that is ever more closely approached yet never fully attained because we always already exist within the realm of opposition and diversity. The difference in this case seems to that that unity of *feeling* and *intuition* is not so much a goal to be realized as it is an originating point.
109 See epigraph to this chapter and note 1 above.
110 See below, 7.3.5.

est being." I offer three examples, listed according to Schleiermacher's ordering of the dialogues.

First, in his "Introduction to the *Gorgias*," Schleiermacher offers a summary of the importance of *intuition* for *knowing*, and indeed of the possibility of knowledge within the world of appearances and oppositions.[111] It is a long and difficult passage, which I quote at length:

[Passage 7L: "Intro. to *Gorgias*"]

As we have seen, every presentation of Platonic philosophy commences with the intuition of what is true and what-*is* [*Seienden*]—in other words, of the eternal and immutable. Standing opposed to this intuition is the just as universal (and, for common thinking and being [*Sein*], no less original) intuition of what is becoming, ever flowing and mutable, with which all doing and thinking, insofar as it can be grasped in reality, remains bound up. Therefore, the highest and universal task of science is none other than apprehending that *being* [*jenes Seiende*] in this *becoming*, and presenting it as the essential and good. Thus, the apparent opposition between those two intuitions, by being brought rightly to consciousness, is at the same time resolved. This coalescence, however, always dissolves into two moments; the difference of method is based on the different relation each moment has to the other. The immediate manner of proceeding, in relation to science, is to start from the intuition of what-*is* [*Anschauung des Seienden*] in the presentation and progress to demonstration of appearance, and thus only then to excite and to explain the solution of the opposition together with consciousness of that opposition. The other way is to start from consciousness of the opposition as a given and progress to that intuition as the means of resolving the opposition, and to lead towards that precisely through the necessity of such a means. This way, which we have called the mediate way and which for many reasons is especially befitting to someone who has taken up the ethical, was placed by Plato at the center, the true means of linking and forming the original intuition (with which he starts, preliminarily) to the constructive presentation (with which he concludes, systematically).

Der Anschauung des Wahren und Seienden, welches eben deshalb das Ewige und Unveränderliche ist, mit der wie wir gesehen haben alle Darstellung der platonischen Philosophie anfing, steht gegenüber die eben so allgemeine und für das gemeine Denken und Sein nicht minder ursprüngliche Anschauung des Werdenden, ewig Fließenden und Veränderlichen, unter welcher doch zugleich alles Thun und Denken, wie es in der Wirklichkeit kann ergriffen werden, mit befaßt bleibt. Daher denn die höchste und allgemeine Aufgabe der Wissenschaft keine andere ist, als daß jenes Seiende in diesem Werdenden ergriffen, als das Wesentliche und Gute dargestellt, und so der scheinbare Gegensaz zwischen jenen beiden Anschauungen, indem er recht zum Bewußtsein gebracht wird, zugleich aufgelöt werde. Diese Vereinigung aber zerfällt immer in zwei Momente, auf deren verschiedener Beziehung auf einander die Verschiedenheit der Methode beruht. Von der Anschauung des Seienden ausgehend in der Darstellung bis zum

---

111 Recall that he interpreted the *Gorgias* as the gateway to the middle trilogy of Plato's *corpus* but not as itself a first-ranked dialogue (see table 2). He used his introduction to it to provide an overview of what Plato accomplishes in that middle trilogy, which is to bring *physics* and *ethics* together, so that real knowledge and virtue become possible.

7.3 Revised Block N° 4: "the original relation of feeling and intuition" — 219

> *Aufzeigen des Scheins fortzuschreiten, und so erst mit der Lösung des Gegensazes zugleich dessen Bewußtsein aufzuregen und zu erklären, das ist die in Beziehung auf die Wissenschaft unmittelbare Verfahrungsart. Von dem Bewußtsein des Gegensazes aber als einem Gegebenen ausgehend zu jener Anschauung als dem Auflösungsmittel desselben fortzuschreiten, und eben durch die Nothwendigkeit eines solchen Mittels auf sie hinzuleiten, das ist die Weise, welche wir die mittelbare genannt haben, und welche aus vielerlei Ursachen dem der ethisch angefangen hat vornemlich geziemend, vom Platon in die Mitte ist gestellt worden, als das wahre Bindungs- und Bildungsmittel von der ursprünglichen Anschauung, mit welcher er elementarisch anhebt, zu der constructiven Darstellung, mit welcher er systematisch endiget.*[112]

Schleiermacher emphasizes that both kinds of intuition are of something real, whether it be existence or some existing thing; both are of some kind of unity and relatedness; and both serve as the basis for science and knowing.

Second, in his "Introduction to the *Sophist*," as we have seen, Schleiermacher writes more succinctly of *the intuition of the life of what-is [Seienden] and of the necessary being-one and being-in-another of being [Seins] and knowing [Erkennens]* (7B).

Third, in the "Introduction to the *Statesman*," he speaks of the "intuition of the life of the world as alternating in opposite movements, and reproducing itself."[113] In these cases and in others, the intuition occurs in the midst of and in response to the activity of existence; it apprehends as it participates in the uniting of opposites.

In his revision of the *Speeches*, Schleiermacher's redefines and repositions *intuition* in a way consistent with these (and other similar) passages from his *Introductions*. We have seen in general how Schleiermacher curtails his use of *intuition* in 1806 and how, in revised block n° 3, he begins to assign to it a specific role. Now we see how, in revised block n° 4, he even more specifically relates *intuition* to *feeling* (in both the wider and narrower senses of *feeling*) and how he positions *intuition* as a crucial epistemological link. *Intuition* turns *thinking* into *knowing*. *Intuition* provides a point of connection between *feeling* and *knowing* without turning *feeling* into a form of *knowing* or *knowing* into *feeling*. *Knowing* occurs when the living interconnection of existence, grounded in the higher unity of *being* and *knowing*, is immediately apprehended. Schleiermacher claims that *knowing* (*Wissen*) occurs "when it encompasses both intuition and feeling in itself."[114]

---

[112] *PW* 2/1:11.12–12.3; cf. *IDP* 171–72. See Rohls's discussion of Schleiermacher's comparison of ancient and medieval scholastic dialectics („Wahrheit, Dialog und Sprache," 184–85).
[113] *EÜP* 268 (… *Anschauung des Lebens der Welt als in entgegengesetzten Bewegungen wechselnd und sich wieder erzeugend*); cf. *IDP* 272.
[114] OR^2 171; R^2 52 (… *mit dem Wissen, als beides unter sich begreifend*).

7.3.5 The Three Series and Their Association

In the new paragraph immediately following his extolling of Plato, that *ancient sage*, Schleiermacher continues to exposit what he means by the *original relation of feeling and intuition* (6A), although now he does so in terms of how *feeling* and *intuition*, in their *unity* (7H), are related to the other two series, *knowing* and *acting*: "As it is on the one side with intuition and feeling, so it is too on the other side with knowing, when it encompasses both intuition and feeling in itself, and with acting."[115] He imports into the *Speeches* the very language and the conceptual schema he uses in his *Introductions*:

> **[Passage 7M: *Speeches*, 1806]**
>
> For these latter two, knowing and acting, are the opposites through whose continual play and reciprocal stimulation your life expands and attains composure over time... Therefore, you only give back, confirm, and relinquish in the world what has been formed and effected through that kind of *associative being* [Sein], and only in the very same way can what they imagine in you be such an existence. For that reason, each must excite the other *in a reciprocal way*, and only in *the exchange of knowing and acting* can your life persist.[116]
>
> *Denn dies sind die Gegensätze durch deren beständiges Spiel und wechselseitige Erregung Euer Leben sich in der Zeit ausdehnt und Haltung gewinnt.... [A]lso gebt Ihr nur zurück und befestigt, und legt nieder in die Welt, was in Euch ist gebildet und gewirkt worden durch jene Art des gemeinschaftlichen Seins, und ebenso kann auch was sie Euch einbilden nur ein solches sein. Daher muss wechselseitig eines das andere erregen, und nur im Wechsel von Wissen und Handeln kann Euer Leben bestehen.*[117]

The language and pattern of thought Schleiermacher employs here in revised block n° 4 reflect parallel patterns of thought in his *Introductions*. Look back to passage 7C: the reciprocal, continual play of opposites within associative or common being (*gemeinschaftliches Sein*); the association of opposite "kinds" and the expansion and progression of life precisely through the active exchange between the two series. Consider, similarly, this other passage from his "Introduction to the *Sophist*":

---

[115] OR^2 171; R^2 52 (*Wie es sich nun auf der einen Seite mit der Anschauung und dem Gefühl verhält, so auch auf der anderen mit dem Wissen, als beides unter sich begreifend, und dem Handeln*).

[116] OR^2 171, altered, emphasis added. Current English usage cannot well convey the close connection between *gemeinschaftliches Sein* and *Gemeinschaft*, which is the word Schleiermacher uses for the association of kinds in Plato.

[117] R^2 52–53.

7.3 Revised Block N° 4: "the original relation of feeling and intuition" — 221

[Passage 7N: "Intro. to *Sophist*"]

... the true life of what-*is* [*Seiende*], in which all opposites interpenetrate one another, is pointed out, and at the same time it is shown that knowledge can endure neither without rest nor without motion, neither without fixure nor without flux, neither without persistence nor without becoming; rather, it requires both combined.

... auf das wahre Leben des Seienden, in welchem sich alle Gegesätze durchdringen, hingewiesen, und zugleich daruf, daß Erkenntnis weder ohne Ruhe noch ohne Bewegung, weder ohne Stehendes noch ohne Fließendes, weder ohne Beharren noch ohne Werden bestehen könne, sondern beider in einander bedürfe; ...[118]

Much as, in *Platons Werke*, Schleiermacher tracks the correlated pairs (*knowing/ doing, being/knowledge, physics/ethics, knowing/willing, true/good, movement/ rest*)[119] throughout the Platonic dialogues, so too in his revision of the second Speech he describes *knowing* (*Wissen*) and *acting* (*Handeln*) as opposites existing in dynamic, reciprocal relation to each other due to their shared existence in something higher.

The difference is that in the *Speeches* Schleiermacher introduces the third series of *feeling* (and *intuition*). *Feeling* roots *acting* and *thinking* in being and allows for *thinking* to become a *knowing*; *feeling* integrates *acting* and *knowing*; *feeling* governs the expansiveness and composure of a human life. Schleiermacher explains the precise mechanism of how this occurs by again incorporating the two impulses into his discussion of The Three. In any given moment, "your wanting-to-become-one with the universe through an object"[120] will either take the form of a surrender (the object predominately acts on you), in which case it becomes a *knowing*, or manifest itself as self-assertion (you predominately act on the object), in which case it is an *acting*. The relationship he sketches among The Three in this paragraph is too complex to be diagrammed in any two-dimensional table. *Feeling* might better be imaged as a third dimension which both grounds and connects the other two series, but which does so *via* a fourth dimension of time-movement as it functions continually in and through the two impulses of human life.

In this same paragraph, Schleiermacher shifts the discussion from an epistemological one (*feeling* as it relates to *knowing*) to a moral one in the broadest sense: what it means to live a full human life (*feeling* as it relates to *acting* and as it connects *knowing* to *acting*). Recall that in his *Speeches* Schleiermacher is not

---

[118] *EÜP* 249; cf. *IDP* 252.
[119] *Wissen/Tun, Sein/Erkenntnis, Physik/Ethik, Wissen/Wollen, Wahre/Gut, Bewegung/Ruhe*. The exact pair depended on the subject matter and vocabulary of any particular dialogue.
[120] OR^2 171; R^2 52 (... *Euer Einswerdenwollen mit dem Universum durch einen Gegenstand*).

just making an argument about religion but is also offering spiritual guidance: he is explaining how life *expands* and ideally, through that exercise of bringing The Three in ever closer relation to each other, *attains composure* (7M). A similar pattern occurs in the *Introductions*, where Schleiermacher orders Plato's dialogues according to the pedagogical progression of ideas, which includes the increasing interconnecting of *knowledge* and *virtue*, of the *true* and the *good*.

Notice how, thus far in his new discussion of *feeling* and *intuition* in revised block n° 4, Schleiermacher has not yet referred to *religion*, to *the infinite*, or to *feeling* by itself. He has instead undertaken the necessary preparatory work: rhetorically and practically, of getting the cultured despisers to reflect on their own experience; theoretically, of specifying how *feeling* and *intuition* are not two separate functions. Yet that preparation has taken him a full quarter of his revised second Speech, and it has been accomplished to a significant degree with ideas consistent with those developed in *Platons Werke*. He concludes his argument thus far:

[Passage 7P: *Speeches*, 1806]

You have here before you, therefore, these three: knowing, feeling, and acting. Up to this point, my speech has revolved around them. And you can understand what I mean when I say that they are not all the same and yet they are inseparable.[121]

Hier also habt Ihr diese drei, um welche sich meine Rede bis jetzt gedreht hat: das Erkennen, das Gefühl und das Handeln, und könnt verstehen wie ich es meine, dass sie nicht einerlei sind und doch unzertrennlich.[122]

With that, Schleiermacher transitions, at last, to explaining the third "series": *religion* or *piety*.

7.3.6 Religion and Contemplation

Having preliminarily described *feeling* and its relation to *intuition*, Schleiermacher proceeds in the second half of revised block n° 4 to delineate the relation of *feeling* to the other two, *knowing*[123] and *acting*—in order, he says, to clear up the "confusion" (*Verwechslung*) which conflates *religion* with *concepts* and *precepts*.[124] In three full (not split-column) pages, mostly new in 1806, Schleier-

---

121 OR^2 171.
122 R^2 53.
123 Recall that *thinking* (*Denken*) has become *knowing* (*Erkennen*). See table 9.
124 OR^2 172–73; R^2 54. See above, chap. 6, 149.

macher brings his argument regarding The Three to a climax.[125] Finally, he believes, the proper distinctions have been established and he can now get at the crux of the matter. In these pages, we find a concentrated employment of four terms, all key to Schleiermacher's second Speech: *religion, feeling, piety*, and *contemplation*. And we can recognize therein the presence of Schleiermacher's Plato, even though it does not map exactly onto his definition of religion. Schleiermacher's Plato lends some ontological and epistemological supports, but the argument he is making belongs uniquely to the *Speeches*. Bearing in mind that the task here is a limited one—to trace the presence of Plato and not to expound all the revisions—I focus on those two places where characteristics of Schleiermacher's Plato manifest themselves: within a two-fold definition of *religion*, and within yet another discussion extolling the virtue of *contemplation*.

Religion. In this culmination of his argument regarding The Three, Schleiermacher uses the word *religion* seventeen times. He opens by distilling "the distinctive sphere that I want to assign to religion"[126] down to two elements (presented between the dashes here [7Q] in the English translation). In the first element, but not in the second, we can catch glimmers of Schleiermacher's Plato:

[Passage 7Q: *Speeches*, 1806]

> Your feeling—insofar as it expresses, in the way described, the being [*Sein*] and life common to you and to the universe, and insofar as you hold the individual moments of this being and life as an operating of God in you by means of the universe—this is your piety.[127]

> *Euer Gefühl insofern es Euer und des Universums gemeinschaftliches Sein und Leben auf die beschriebene Weise ausdrückt, insofern Ihr die einzelnen Momente desselben habt als ein Wirken Gottes in Euch durch das Universum, dies ist Eure Frömmigkeit.*[128]

The language of the *common* (or *shared, associative*) *being and life* of the individual and the universe is clearly reminiscent of the language Schleiermacher uses in his *Introductions*, including in those three passages quoted in the previous subsections regarding his use of *intuition* there (7C, 7L, 7N) but also in other passages where he addresses the Platonic association of kinds (*Gemeinschaft der Begriffe*). The language of the *universe*, however, is particular to the *Speeches*. In contrast, the language of holding the *individual moments of this being* [or, *exis-*

---

125 See R^2 53–56; OR^2 170–75.
126 OR^2 172; R^2 53 (*Dieses ist demnach das eigentümliche Gebiet, welches ich der Religion anweisen will*).
127 OR^2 172, altered.
128 R^2 53.

tence] *and life as an operating of God in you by means of the universe* distinguishes the *Speeches* from the *Introductions* (see 6I). The difference is a theological one having to do with the nature and activity of the highest being, the infinite, or God. We have seen Rohls differentiate the theology of Plato in the *Sophist* from that of Schleiermacher in his *Dialectics*.[129] The religious and theological claim made here in the *Speeches* is different further still: the infinite, here called *God*, actively operates on the individual, and the *feeling* of that, including how one takes that up and holds that in one's being, is *piety*. Both elements described in this passage together define *religion*, but only one of those elements is coextensive with Schleiermacher's Plato.

Contemplation. In the space of a few lines in the same culminating argument, Schleiermacher uses the noun *contemplation* four times and the verb *to contemplate* twice. At several points along the way in these two chapters on the *Speeches*, I have emphasized the significance of *contemplation* in the revisions of 1806 and pointed out certain parallels with his *Introductions*. That significance is captured in his line *contemplation is essential to religion* (6I).[130] It is no accident, therefore, that Schleiermacher would return to the matter at this point in his argument. *Contemplation* is not *feeling*, nor is *feeling* a kind of *contemplation*. If we recall how in his *Introductions* Schleiermacher depicted contemplation as a continuum, we might recognize here the early stage (as a stepping back, pausing, and close observation) or middle stage (as exercising a stance and interior sensibility), but not the final stage (as a glance into that higher sphere). The object of contemplation in the second Speech is not the highest being or the infinite, but is instead oneself:

[Passage 7R: *Speeches*, 1806]

In this way, therefore, as feeling persons, you can become objects to yourselves and can contemplate your feeling. Yes, you could so become an object to yourself as a "feeling you" that you have a formative effect on that "object" and impress your inner existence [*Dasein*] on it more and more.[131]

Auf diese Art also könnt Ihr als Fühlende Euch selbst Gegenstand werden, und Euer Gefühl betrachten. Ja auch so könnt Ihr als Fühlende Euch Gegenstand werden, dass Ihr auf ihn bildend wirkt, und ihm mehr und mehr Euer inneres Dasein eindrückt.[132]

---

129 Rohls comments on the different theologies of the *Sophist* and Schleiermacher *Dialectics* (see "Schleiermachers Platonismus," 484–85); see above, chap. 7, 198.
130 R^2 45; OR^2 162.
131 OR^2 173.
132 R^2 54.

7.3 Revised Block N° 4: "the original relation of feeling and intuition" — 225

Contemplation is directed attention at one's own *feeling* as that produces either *principle/precept* ("the general description of your feeling according to its essence") or *concept* ("the description of each individual feeling emerging in it"); those, however, are "really the scientific treatment of religion—it is knowledge about religion, not religion itself."[133] Disease enters when those are conflated and confused, and contemplation is the antidote. Schleiermacher reminds the cultured despisers:

[Passage 7S: *Speeches*, 1806]

Do not forget that contemplation already presupposes the original activity and rests entirely on it, and that those concepts and principles, if they are not the reflection of your own feeling, are nothing other than an empty essence, superficially taught from the outside.[134]

Vergesst nicht dass die Betrachtung schon die ursprüngliche Tätigkeit voraussetzt und ganz auf ihr beruht, und dass jene Begriffe und Grundsätze gar nichts sind als ein von außen angelerntes leeres Wesen, wenn sie nicht eben die Reflexion sind über Euer eigenes Gefühl.[135]

Contemplation is that quiet kind of attunement that recognizes *feeling* within oneself and realizes how *feeling* relates to and informs (or fails to relate and inform) *acting* and *thinking*; it thus aids in clearing away unhealthy connections, as it also aids in fostering healthy connections.

Interestingly, Schleiermacher at this points makes two allusions to Plato in order to describe the unhealthy results when *feeling* becomes disconnected from the other two series. Without *feeling*, he says, you have only "decompositions of the religious sense."[136] This seems to hearken back to Socrates's somatic imagery regarding the composition of a living body and the problem of dissection. Consequently, he goes on to say, "You have only memory, and you have imitation—but not religion."[137] The *imitation* here might well be read as a criticism of the sophists.

---

133 OR^2 173; R^2 54 (*Wollt Ihr nun das Erzeugnis jener Betrachtung, die allgemeine Beschreibung Eures Gefühls nach seinem Wesen Grundsatz nennen, und die Beschreibung jedes einzelnen darin Hervortretenden Begriff, und zwar religiösen Grundsatz und religiösen Begriff: so steht Euch das allerdings frei, und Ihr habt recht daran. Aber vergesst nur nicht, dass dies eigentlich die wissenschaftliche Behandlung der Religion ist, das Wissen um sie, nicht sie selbst*).
134 OR^2 173.
135 R^2 54.
136 OR^2 174; R^2 55 (*Zersetzungen des religiösen Sinnes*).
137 OR^2 174; R^2 55 (*Gedächtnis habt Ihr und Nachahmung, aber keine Religion*).

7.4 Concluding Remarks on the *Speeches* (1806) and the *Introductions*

Evidence of cross-fertilization between Schleiermacher's revisions of the second Speech and his *Introductions* by no means ends with revised block n° 4. Both references to and extended discussions of such topics as *being* and *existence*, *opinion* versus *knowledge*, the association of *knowing* and *acting*, etc., fill subsequent revised blocks as well. Throughout the second Speech, where he made most of his revisions in the second edition, Schleiermacher continued to develop the lines of argument he introduced earlier in the Speech. Nonetheless, the basic points of connection between *Platons Werke* and the *Speeches* of 1806 are set forth in revised block n°s 1–4. I trust that the close textual analysis and comparison undertaken in this and in the previous chapter, as detailed and dense as that has been, has established that Schleiermacher's continued engagement with Plato between the publication of the first and second editions of the *Speeches* did indeed impact his revisions of 1806. The impact was profound in that his quite particular interpretation of Plato informed fundamental changes he made to his main argument about "the essence of religion." We find the presence of Schleiermacher's Plato in his reconceptualization of The Three; in his discussions of being, existence, and non-being; in his notion of the dynamic "association" of opposites; in his refinement of *intuition*; and in his appeal to contemplation. At the same time, it must be kept in mind that the influence was never unidirectional. Schleiermacher's interpretation of Plato, as presented in *Platons Werke*, was itself shaped by ideas he held prior to 1800, certainly, but also by the complex of ideas developed during that formative decade from 1800–1810.

8 Conclusion: Schleiermacher's Plato

> *No one should be discouraged, Theaetetus, who can make constant progress, even though it be slow. For if a man is discouraged under these conditions, what would he do under others—if he did not get ahead at all or were even pressed back?*[1]

I began this book with two questions, both of which have been addressed from the perspective of Schleiermacher studies: *How did Schleiermacher understand Plato?*, and *In what ways might Schleiermacher's religious thought have been influenced by Plato?* In my Introduction above, I tendered some provisional answers. Now, having argued my thesis and sub-theses in detail, it is time to step back and offer some reflections. At this point, those two questions can be broken down further, into four.

Who is Schleiermacher's Plato? Schleiermacher's Plato is the *perfect artist* whose form is the dialogue form and whose medium is the written dialogue. It follows from this that Plato's dialogues constitute a single work of art, wherein everything has a purpose and all parts together form an organic, beautiful whole. This also means that Plato did not change his mind in any fundamental way, which means we cannot neglect some dialogues for being immature. Schleiermacher's Plato, rather, is the *consummate pedagogue* who has in mind the full body of material to be taught as well as a textured understanding of the learning process and stages of intellectual and moral development. It follows from this that the ordering of the dialogues is at least as student-centered as it is author-centered: it is determined through the pedagogical progression of ideas. Together, these two characteristics (Plato as artist and as pedagogue) paint the portrait of a Plato who is accessible, whose philosophy is not reserved for a private elite. In the history of modern Plato interpretation, Schleiermacher stands firmly on the end of the spectrum maintaining the unity and continuity of Plato's thought and works. Schleiermacher's Plato is primarily the Plato of the *Phaedrus*, *Sophist*, *Theaetetus*, and *Symposium*—and that leads us to the next question.

What is Schleiermacher's Plato's philosophy? The answer must begin by underscoring that Schleiermacher's Plato is distinctly modern, but that itself is not sufficient since there are many modern and postmodern Platos.[2] On this point it may be helpful to recall (albeit with a twist) Beiser's distinction between the Ger-

---

[1] Plato, The *Sophist* 261b, trans. Fowler, in *PDL*.
[2] See, e.g., Kim, *Brill's Companion to German Platonism*, and Catherine H. Zuckert, *Postmodern Platos* (Chicago: University of Chicago Press, 1996).

man Romantics' "hyperrational" Platonic mystical stance and a Kantian "suprarationalism."[3] Some modern Platonisms tend toward immanental or monistic models, while others affirm newer dualistic models of the relation between the sensible world and the forms. Certainly, consistent with his earlier appropriation of Spinoza to counter Kantian dualisms (between noumenona and phenomena, freedom and determinism), Schleiermacher rejected any dichotomous interpretation of the Platonic forms. That is not to say, however, that he offered a strictly monistic alternative. He walked a middle course between the ancient alternatives of dualism and monism. Here we see his slight preference for Plato over Spinoza come into relief. Plato's philosophy, as Schleiermacher presented it, is perhaps best described as one that sustains a modern *coincidence of opposites* at every level. Based on the investigations laid forth in the preceding chapters, but now in reverse order, I offer the following six summary features of the content of Plato's philosophy as Schleiermacher understood it.

1. According to Schleiermacher, the *Sophist* is the heart, the core, of Plato's philosophy. We detected his excitement at discovering Plato's ontology in that dialogue. "The highest being" (*das höchste Sein*) has no opposite but is, rather, the absolute unity of being and knowing; it is not, however, what Schleiermacher called some "empty" unity or purely formal category. This is where he thought Plato was better than Spinoza, even though he set the two of them at the pinnacle of the history of philosophy. Schleiermacher's Plato's highest being is "generative" and "poeticizing,"[4] the ground of knowing and of the good, and active in and through all becoming. Relatedly, the Platonic ideas are best understood, in Scholtz's words, as "the productive power of nature as such."[5] In Schleiermacher's Plato-interpretation, attention shifts from the forms to method and process; it would be a mistake, however, to reduce this to interpretation. Schleiermacher never lost sight of the ontological, nor therefore of the highest being. He maintained the distinction between the opposition-less "highest being" and *das Sein* (as the opposite of *Erkennen*) or *das Seiende* (as the realm of oppositions).

2. According to Schleiermacher, the *Sophist* establishes that opposition is not cancelation but is really difference. The world of becoming, of what-*is* (*das Seiende*), is thus best understood in terms of the continual, dynamic associating of opposites. There are countless such oppositions, but the greater "kinds" are the Platonic ones (*movement* and *rest*, *difference* and *identity*),

---

[3] Beiser, *Romantic Imperative*, 64; see above, chap. 1, 11–12.
[4] Schleiermacher, *Grundlinien*, in *KGA* 1/4: 65.8–66.13; quoted above, chap. 1, 15–16.
[5] Scholtz, "Schleiermacher und die Platonische Ideenlehre," 861; see above, chap. 6, 177n129.

which for Schleiermacher's Plato fall under the highest two, *being* (*Sein*) and *knowing* (*Erkennen*). This world of becoming is neither devalued nor, therefore, meant to be escaped. Part of Schleiermacher's excitement on this point is that, while consistent with his earlier view of the universe as an organic system of dynamic forces, it also lent that a more definite form.
3. For Schleiermacher's Plato, *ethics* and *physics* are the two sciences corresponding to *being* and *knowing*, respectively; each relates to a basic human activity (*doing* and *thinking*) and is oriented toward a certain end (*virtue* and *knowledge*). This view of *ethics* and *physics* is so fundamental to Plato's thought, Schleiermacher maintained, that the entire Platonic *corpus* is ordered according to it: *ethics* and *physics* are treated separately in the early dialogues; they are brought together in the middle dialogues; and, finally, they are brought even closer together in the later dialogues. This, of courses, advances his view of the unity of Plato's thought.
4. For Schleiermacher, Plato's holding together of *being* and *knowing*, of the *good* and the *true*, and *ethics* and *physics* was simply part and parcel of the ancients' holding together of *praxis* and *theory*—or, as Schleiermacher put it, "philosophy and life."[6] In Schleiermacher's Plato's philosophy, this is reflected in the understanding of dialectics and contemplation in non-speculative terms. *Dialectics* remains dialogical—communicative, social, relational. *Contemplation* is not a speculative act but a way of being—consideration, composure, and (only then) a glance into the higher sphere.
5. For Schleiermacher's Plato, *erōs* is the philosophical impulse with which novice students begin the movement towards virtue and knowledge in the *Phaedrus*, and in which they mature as they consider the philosopher in the person of Socrates in the *Symposium* and *Phaedo*. *Erōs* helps to keep the philosophical endeavor communicative and social as it works ever more in concert with dialectics; it propels as it acts as attractive force.
6. Schleiermacher's recognition of the significance of the dialogue form, hence of the literary quality of Plato's philosophy, is arguably his most lasting contribution to Plato studies. It is important that we grasp how far-reaching this was for Schleiermacher's Plato. It is not just that form and content cannot be separated in treating the dialogues as objects of study; it has much broader epistemological, ontological, and anthropological implications. As Käppel says, the Platonic dialectical method is the "intersubjective communication about the ontologically given order of the world through idea-led assembly

---

6 See above, chap. 6, 155n50.

up to utter ideational abstraction, to the idea of the good."[7] The dialogue form permeates every aspect of Schleiermacher's Plato's philosophy and shapes it as social, intersubjective, interrelational, dynamic, and transformational.[8]

How did Schleiermacher's Plato influence Schleiermacher's own thought, especially his religious thought? As we have seen (chapters 3–4), both Schleiermacher's *Hermeneutics* and his *Dialectics* were directly rooted in his *Platons Werke*. I have argued (chapters 5–7) that his two major publications in religion and theology from his time in Halle, written while still working on the Plato project (1806), also bear the imprint of *Platons Werke*. Indeed, the influence of Schleiermacher's Plato on his *Christmas Dialogue* and on his second edition of the *Speeches* was both profound and pervasive in ways that have not heretofore been recognized. In my examination of the *Christmas Dialogue* in chapter 5, I focus mainly on form and structure and a little bit on content (e. g., *erōs* and *Mutterlieb*). I anticipate that further investigation might well reveal the cross-fertilization of much more specific content, especially when we consider that Schleiermacher wrote his introductions to the *Sophist*, *Symposium*, and *Phaedo* after he published his *Christmas Dialogue*, although he had sketched their general contours beforehand in his "General Introduction." This stands as a reminder that any influence cannot be assumed to have been unidirectional. In contrast to the *Christmas Dialogue*, the presence of Plato in Schleiermacher's revisions of his *Speeches* is stronger in content than in form. We catch glimpses of the effects of the dialogue form and Socratic questioning in the new ways in which Schleiermacher addresses the cultured despisers, but the parallels between the *Introductions* and his recasting of his main argument regarding The Three in the second Speech are definite and undeniable. What is more, all six of the features of Schleiermacher's Plato's philosophy just outlined are present in one way or another in the revised blocks of the *Speeches*—and, importantly, in ways that were not true of the first edition. That notwithstanding, we cannot assume that his revisions were due entirely to Plato. As I argue in 6.2 above, there were logical as well as spiritual inconsistencies in the first edition of the *Speeches*, and Schleiermacher's correction of those, while consistent with his thinking that had taken form during that decade of Plato, was particular to his argument and approach in *On Religion*. Moreover, it could well be that Schleiermacher's own gifts when it

---

[7] Käppel, "Schleiermachers Hermeneutik," 238.
[8] On moral transformation in Schleiermacher, see Jacqueline Mariña, *Transformation of the Self in the Thought of Friedrich Schleiermacher* (Oxford: Oxford University Press, 2008).

came to religion led him to appreciate and reclaim the ancients' view of philosophy as a way of life (to borrow from Hadot). Finally, however profound and pervasive the presence of Plato in the second edition is, Schleiermacher's understanding of religion cannot be reduced to that. Schleiermacher's Plato maps well onto his rethinking of *acting* and *thinking* but not so much onto *feeling* or *piety*. The significance of those influences for his theory of religion must be reserved for future investigations. My hope is that I have convincingly established here that Platonic influences on his 1806 *Speeches* go well beyond mere allusions; in fact, Schleiermacher's Plato was a shaping force in how he recast his argument.

Was Schleiermacher's Plato a form of Platonism? I have been reticent to refer to Schleiermacher's Plato and the ways in which he carried that over into his own thought as a form of Platonism for several reasons, chief among them: like any "*—ism*," the term is as loaded as it is indefinite; many of the features of his Plato-interpretation are not easily recognizable as Platonic; and, the influence of Plato on Schleiermacher has barely been recognized. Hence, it hardly makes sense to label it as a *Platonism*. Nevertheless, the fact that there was a definiteness and stability to his Plato-interpretation and to what he repeatedly did with that, at least during his decade of Plato, suggests that maybe the designation might do some work in helping us to understand Schleiermacher better. Schleiermacher's *Platonism*, if that be allowed, was distinctly modern in a Schleiermacherian way: it was non-dualistic and non-hierarchical; it was democratic in spirit (in that he thought Plato and Plato's thought was and should be accessible to all, and in that he included women and children as dialogue partners); it allowed for the new historical consciousness as it was itself subject to the new historical-critical method; it embraced new discoveries in the natural sciences; it was social and communicative; it affirmed the ordinary and the concrete; and it grounded, as it reflected, confidence about the unity and continuity of knowing. It was early-nineteenth-century modern in its assumption of progress and unity. At the same time, it did have certain affinities with some forms of neo-Platonism even as it jettisoned those: it never lost sight of the "highest being," which was understood not as distant, empty unity but as generative and redemptive; its universe was a harmonious whole teeming with activity, dynamic interrelating, and the association of kinds; it held together knowing and being, truth and goodness; it offered a formative path for moving toward knowledge and virtue; it connected knowledge to love; and its organizing force was a *coincidence of opposites*.

Even as we continue to sort out the significance of Schleiermacher's Plato for his thinking, especially for the development of his theory of religion and his theology, during that decade of Plato, other questions loom: What happened to

Schleiermacher's Plato during the next quarter-century of his career, when he moved to Berlin and became a founding faculty member at the University of Berlin? Is Schleiermacher's Plato at all present in his mature theological system, *The Christian Faith*? If so, how might that affect our understanding of his Christian theology? If not, why not? Hopefully, those important questions might be more clearly posed and answered now that we have met Schleiermacher's Plato.

Bibliography

1 Primary Sources

German Editions of Schleiermacher's Texts Cited

Briefwechsel. In *KGA* 5/1–12. Edited by Andreas Arndt, Wolfgang Virmond, Simon Gerber, and Sarah Schmidt. Berlin and New York: De Gruyter, 1985–2020.
Brouillon zur Ethik (1805/06). Philosophische Bibliothek 334. Edited by Hans-Joachim Birkner. Hamburg: Meiner, 1981.
Der christliche Glaube nach den Grundsätzen der evangelischen Kirche in Zusammenhange dargestellt, 2nd ed. Berlin: Reimer, 1830–31. In *KGA* 1/13, 2 vols.: *Der christliche Glaube 2. Auflage*. Edited by Rolf Schäfer. Berlin and New York: Walter de Gruyter, 2003.
Dialektik (1811–1831). In *KGA* 2/10, 2 vols.: *Vorlesungen über die Dialektik*. Edited by Andreas Arndt. Berlin and New York: Walter de Gruyter, 2002.
Die Einleitungen zur Übersetzung des Platon (1804–1828). In *Friedrich Daniel Ernst Schleiermacher: Über die Philosophie Platons*. Philosophische Bibliothek 486. Edited by Peter M. Steiner, 21–387. Hamburg: Felix Meiner, 1996.
Friedrich D. E. Schleiermacher Kritische Gesamtausgabe (KGA). Edited by Hans-Joachim Birkner, Gerhard Ebeling, Hermann Fischer, Heinz Kimmerle, Günter Meckenstock, Ulrich Barth, Konrad Cramer, Kurt Victor Selge, Lutz Käppel, Hermann Patsch, Wolfgang Virmond, Andreas Arndt, Jörg Dierken, André Munzinger, and Notger Slenczka. 58 volumes (out of 67 volumes projected). Berlin, New York, and Boston: Walter de Gruyter, 1980–.
Gelegentliche Gedanken über Universitäten in deutschem Sinn. Nebst einem Anhang über eine neu zu errichtende (1808). In *KGA* 1/6: *Universitätsschriften—Herakleitos—Kurze Darstellung des theologischen Studiums*. Edited by Dirk Schmid, 19–100. Berlin and New York: Walter de Gruyter, 1998.
Grundlinien einer Kritik der bisherigen Sittenlehre (1803). In *KGA* 1/4: *Schriften aus der Stolper Zeit 1802–1804*. Edited by Eilert Herms, Günter Meckenstock, und Michael Pietsch, 27–350. Berlin and New York: Walter de Gruyter, 2002.
Hermeneutik und Kritik. In *KGA* 2/4: *Vorlesungen zur Hermeneutik und Kritik*. Edited by Wolfgang Virmond, with Hermann Patsch. Berlin and Boston: De Gruyter, 2013.
Schleiermacher: Hermeneutik und Kritik. Edited by Manfred Frank. Frankfurt am Main: Suhrkamp, 1977.
Platons Werke von F. Schleiermacher. 6 vols. Berlin: Reimer, 1804–1828.
Platons Werke I,1: Einleitung · Phaidros · Lysis · Protagoras · Laches (Berlin 1804. 1817). In *KGA* 4/3. Edited by Lutz Käppel and Johanna Loehr. Berlin and Boston: Walter de Gruyter, 2016.
Platons Werke II,1: Gorgias · Theaitetos · Menon · Euthydemos (Berlin 1805. 1818). In *KGA* 4/5. Edited by Lutz Käppel and Johanna Loehr. Berlin and Boston: De Gruyter, 2020.
Platon. Die großen Dialoge. Translated by Friedrich Schleiermacher. Köln: Anaconda Verlag, 2016.

Platon. Werke in acht Bänden, Griechisch und Deutsch, 8 vols. Translated by Friedrich Schleiermacher. Edited by Gunther Eigler. Darmstadt: Wissenschaftliche Buchgesellschaft, 1970; 2nd ed., 1990.

"Rezension Von Friedrich Ast: *De Platonis Phaedro*," (1802). In *KGA* 1/3: *Schriften aus der Berliner Zeit 1800–1802*. Edited by Günter Meckenstock, 469–81. Berlin and New York: Walter de Gruyter, 1988.

Über die Religion: Reden an die Gebildeten unter ihren Verächtern (1799), 1st ed. Berlin: Johann Friedrich Unger, 1799. In *KGA* 1/2: *Schriften aus der Berliner Zeit 1796–1799*. Edited by Günter Meckenstock, 189–326. Berlin and New York: Walter de Gruyter, 1984.

Über die Religion. Reden an die Gebildeten unter ihren Verächtern 1799/1806/1821. Edited by Niklaus Peter, Frank Bestebreurtje, und Anna Büsching. Zürich: Theologischer Verlag, 2012.

Über die Religion (2.-)4. Auflage. Monologen (2.-)4. Auflage. In *KGA* 1/12. Edited by Günter Meckenstock. Berlin: Walter de Gruyter, 1995.

Die Weihnachtsfeier: Ein Gespräch (1806). In *KGA* 1/5: *Schriften aus der Hallenser Zeit 1804–1807*. Edited by Hermann Patsch, 43–98. Berlin and Boston: De Gruyter, 2011.

"Zum Platon" (1801–1803). In *KGA* 1/3: *Schriften aus der Berliner Zeit 1800–1802*. Edited by Günter Meckenstock, 341–75. Berlin and New York: Walter de Gruyter, 1988.

English Translations of Schleiermacher's Texts Cited

Lamm, Julia A., ed. and trans. *Schleiermacher: Christmas Dialogue, the Second Speech, and Other Selections*. Classics of Western Spirituality Series. New York: Paulist Press, 2014.

Schleiermacher, Friedrich. *Brouillon zur Ethik/Notes on Ethics (1805/1806)*. Translated by John Wallhausser. In *Brouillon zur Ethik/Notes on Ethics (1805/1806) and Notes on the Theory of Virtue (1804/1805)*, edited by John Wallhausser and Terrence N. Tice, Schleiermacher Studies and Translations 22, 33–172. Lewiston, Queenston, Lampeter: Edwin Mellen Press, 2003.

Schleiermacher, Friedrich. *The Christian Faith*. Translated by H. R. Mackintosh, J. S. Stewart, A. B. Macaulay, D. M. Baillie, W. R. Matthews, and E. Sandbach-Marshall. 2nd ed. Edinburgh: Clark, 1928.

Schleiermacher, Friedrich. *Christmas Eve: Dialogue on the Incarnation*. Translated by Terrence N. Tice. Richmond: John Knox Press, 1967.

Schleiermacher, Friedrich. *Dialectic, or the Art of Doing Philosophy, A Study Edition of the 1811 Notes*. Translated by Terrence N. Tice. Atlanta: Scholars Press, 1996.

Schleiermacher, Friedrich. *Hermeneutics and Criticism and Other Writings*. Translated by Andrew Bowie. Cambridge Texts in the History of Philosophy. Cambridge: Cambridge University Press, 1998.

Schleiermacher, Friedrich. *Introductions to the Dialogues of Plato*. Translated by William Dobson. Cambridge & London, 1836; reprint, New York: Arno Press, 1973.

Schleiermacher, Friedrich. *Occasional Thoughts on Universities in the German Sense: with an Appendix Regarding a University Soon to Be Established* (1808). Translated by Edwina Lawler and Terrence Tice. San Francisco: Edwin Mellen Press, 1991.

Schleiermacher, Friedrich. *On Religion: Speeches to Its Cultured Despisers*, 1st ed. (1799). Translated by Richard Crouter. Cambridge: Cambridge University Press, 1988. Page references are to the 1988 edition.

Schleiermacher, Friedrich, *On Religion: Speeches to its Cultured Despisers*, 3rd ed. (1821). Translated by John Oman. New York: Harper & Row, 1958; reprint, 1986.

Schleiermacher, Friedrich. *On the Different Methods of Translation*. Translated by André Lefevere. In *German Romantic Criticism*, edited by A. Leslie Willson, 1–30. New York: Continuum, 1982.

English Translations of Plato's Dialogues

Sophist. In *Plato in Twelve Volumes*, vol. 12. Translated by Harold N. Fowler. Cambridge, Mass.: Harvard University Press; London: William Heinemann Ltd. 1921. In *Perseus Digital Library*. Edited by Gregory R. Crane. Tufts University. http://www.perseus.tufts.edu.

Phaedo. In *Plato in Twelve Volumes*, vol. 1. Translated by Harold N. Fowler. Cambridge, MA, Harvard University Press; London, William Heinemann Ltd. 1966. In In *Perseus Digital Library*. Edited by Gregory R. Crane. Tufts University. http://www.perseus.tufts.edu.

Phaedrus. In *Plato in Twelve Volumes*, vol. 9. Translated by Harold N. Fowler. Cambridge: Harvard University Press, 1925. In *Perseus Digital Library*. Edited by Gregory R. Crane. Tufts University. http://www.perseus.tufts.edu.

Phaedrus. Translated by Alexander Nehamas and Paul Woodruff. Indianapolis & Cambridge: Hacket Publishing Co., 1995.

2 Secondary Sources

Albrecht, Christian. *Schleiermachers Theorie der Frömmigkeit. Ihr wissenschaftlicher Ort und ihr systematischer Gehalt in den Reden, in der Glaubenslehre und in der Dialektik*. Berlin: Walter de Gruyter, 1994.

Altman, William H. F. *Ascent to the Beautiful: Plato the Teacher and the Pre-Republic Dialogues from Protagoras to Symposium*. Lanham, Boulder, New York, and London: Lexington Books, 2020.

Annas, Julia. *An Introduction to Plato's Republic*. Oxford: Oxford University Press, 1981.

Arndt, Andreas. "La Dialectique de Friedrich Schleiermacher: Un projet de la philosophie classique allemande." *Archives de Philosophie* 77, no. 2, *Schleiermacher philosophe* (April–June 2014): 217–235.

Arndt, Andreas. *Friedrich Schleiermacher als Philosoph*. Berlin: De Gruyter, 2013.

Arndt, Andreas, ed. *Friedrich Schleiermacher in Halle 1804–1807*. Berlin: Walter de Gruyter, 2013.

Arndt, Andreas. "Geselligkeit und Gesellschaft. Die Geburt der Dialektik aus dem Geist der Konversation in Schleiermachers *Versuch einer Theorie des geselligen Betragens*." In *Salons der Romantik: Beiträge eines Wiepersdorfer Kolloquiums zu Theorie und Geschichte des Salons*, edited by Hartwig Schultz, 45–62. Berlin and New York: Walter de Gruyter 1997.

Arndt, Andreas, ed. *Wissenschaft und Geselligkeit: Friedrich Schleiermacher in Berlin 1796– 1802*. Berlin and New York: Walter de Gruyter, 2009.
Arndt, Andreas, and Jörg Dierken, eds. *Friedrich Schleiermachers Hermeneutik: Interpretationen und Perspektiven*. Berlin and Boston: De Gruyter, 2016.
Arndt, Andreas, Simon Gerber, and Sarah Schmidt, eds. *Wissenschaft, Kirche, Staat und Politik: Schleiermacher im Preußischen Reformprozess*. Berlin: De Gruyter, 2019.
Asmuth, Christoph. *Interpretation–Transformation: Das Platonbild bei Fichte, Schelling, Hegel, Schleiermacher und Schopenhauer und das Legitimationsproblem der Philosophiegeschichte*. Göttingen: Vandenhoeck & Ruprecht, 2006.
Baird, William. *History of New Testament Research*. Vol. 1: *From Deism to Tübingen*. Minneapolis: Fortress Press, 1992.
Balansard, Anne and Isabelle Koch, eds. *Lire les Dialogues, mais lesquels et dans quel ordre? Définitions du corpus et interprétations de Platon*. Sankt Augustin: Academia Verlag, 2013.
Barth, Karl. "Schleiermacher's 'Celebration of Christmas'." In *Theology and Church: Shorter Writings 1920–1928*, translated by Louise Pettibone Smith, 136–58. New York: Harper & Row, 1962.
Barth, Ulrich, and Claus-Dieter Osthövener, eds. *200 Jahre "Reden über die Religion." Akten des 1. Internationalen Kongresses der Schleiermacher-Gesellschaft, Halle 14.–17. März 1999*. Berlin: De Gruyter, 2000.
Behler, Ernst, ed. *Kritische Friedrich-Schlegel-Ausgabe*. Vol. 19. München, Paderborn, Wien, 1958.
Beiser, Frederick C. *The Romantic Imperative: The Concept of Early German Romanticism*. Cambridge, Mass. and London: Harvard University Press, 2003.
Beiser, Frederick C. "Romanticism and Idealism." In *The Relevance of Romanticism: Essays on German Romantic Philosophy*, edited by Dalia Nassar, 30–43. Oxford and New York: Oxford University Press, 2014.
Beiser, Frederick C. "Schleiermacher's Ethics." In *The Cambridge Companion to Friedrich Schleiermacher*, edited by Jacqueline Mariña, 53–71. Cambridge: Cambridge University Press, 2006.
Bekker, Immanuel, ed. *Platonis Dialogi graece et latine, ex recensione Immanuelis Bekkeri*. 3 Vols. Berlin: Reimer, 1816–18.
Birus, Hendrik. "Hermeneutische Wende? Anmerkungen zur Schleiermacher-Interpretation." *Euphorion* 74, no. 2 (Spring 1980): 213–22.
Birus, Hendrik. "Zwischen den Zeiten. Friedrich Schleiermacher als Klassiker der neuzeitlichen Hermeneutik." In *Hermeneutische Positionen: Schleiermacher-Dilthey-Heidegger-Gadamer*, edited by Hendrik Birus, 5–58. Göttingen: Vandenhoeck & Ruprecht, 1982.
Blackwell, Albert L. *The Sacred in Music*. Louisville, Ky: Westminster John Knox Press, 1999.
Blackwell, Albert L. *Schleiermacher's Early Philosophy of Life: Determinism, Freedom, and Phantasy*. Greenville: Scholars Press, 1982.
Blackwell, Albert L. "Schleiermacher's Sermon at Nathanael's Grave." *The Journal of Religion* 57, no. 1 (January 1977): 64–75.
Blackwell, Albert L. "Three New Schleiermacher Letters Relating to His Würzburg Appointment of 1804." *The Harvard Theological Review* 68, no. 3/4 (July–October 1975): 333–56.

Boeckh, August. Review of *Platons Werke von F. Schleiermacher*, I,1 (1804), I,2 (1805), Berlin. *Heidelbergische Jahrbücher der Literatur für Philologie, Historie, Literatur und Kunst* 1, no. 1 (1808): 81–121.

Boeckh, August. Review of P.G. van Heusde, *Specimen criticum in Platonem. Jenaische Allgemeine Literatur-Zeitung* 6, no. 1 (January 1809): 161–68.

Borgman, Erik, Laurens ten Kate, and Bart Philipsen. "A Triptych on Schleiermacher's '*On Religion*'." *Literature & Theology* 21, no. 4 (December 2007): 381–416.

Bowie, Andrew. *From Romanticism to Critical Theory: The Philosophy of German Literary Theory*. London and New York: Routledge, 1997.

Brandt, Richard B. *The Philosophy of Schleiermacher: The Development of His Theory of Scientific and Religious Knowledge*. New York: Greenwood Press, 1968.

Brandwood, Leonard. *The Chronology of Plato's Dialogues*. Cambridge: Cambridge University Press, 1990.

Brisson, Luc. "Présupposés et conséquences d'une interprétation ésotériste de Platon." *Les Études Philosophiques*, no. 4 (1993): 475–95.

Bukowski, Piotr de Bończa. "Zur Übersetzungstheorie bei Friedrich Daniel Ernst Schleiermacher und Friedrich Schlegel in der Zeit ihrer Zusammenarbeit." In *Wissenschaft, Kirche, Staat und Politik: Schleiermacher im Preußischen Reformprozess*, edited by Andreas Arndt, Simon Gerber, and Sarah Schmidt, 119–144. Berlin: Walter de Gruyter, 2019.

Cantana, Leo. *Late Ancient Platonism in Eighteenth-Century German Thought*. Archives internationales d'histoire des idées/International Archives of the History of Ideas Archives 227. Cham, Switzerland: Springer, 2019.

Cercel, Larisa, and Adriana Serban, eds. *Friedrich Schleiermacher and the Question of Translation*. Berlin and Boston: De Gruyter, 2015.

Christ, Franz. "Schleiermacher zum Verhältnis von Mythos und Logos bei Platon." In *Internationaler Schleiermacher-Kongress 1984*, edited by Hermann Fischer and Kurt-Victor Selge, 837–48. Berlin: Walter de Gruyter, 1985.

Cramer, Konrad. "'Anschauung des Universums.' Schleiermacher und Spinoza." In *200 Jahre "Reden über die Religion." Akten des 1. Internationalen Kongresses der Schleiermacher-Gesellschaft, Halle 14.–17. März 1999*, edited by Ulrich Barth and Claus-Dieter Osthövener, 118–41. Berlin: Walter de Gruyter, 2000.

Crouter, Richard. *Friedrich Schleiermacher: Between Enlightenment and Romanticism*. Cambridge, U.K.: Cambridge University Press, 2005.

Curran, Thomas H. *Doctrine and Speculation in Schleiermacher's* Glaubenslehre. Theologische Bibliothek Töpelmann 61. Berlin and New York: Walter de Gruyter, 1994.

De Vogel, Cornelia J. "On the Neoplatonic Character of Platonism and the Platonic Character of Neoplatonism." *Mind* 62, no. 245 (January 1953): 43–64.

De Vogel, Cornelia J. *Rethinking Plato and Platonism*. Leiden: Brill, 1986.

DeVries, Dawn. *Jesus Christ in the Preaching of Calvin and Schleiermacher*. Louisville: Westminster John Knox Press, 1996.

DeVries, Dawn. "Schleiermacher's 'Christmas Eve Dialogue': Bourgeois Ideology or Feminist Theology?" *The Journal of Religion* 69, no. 2 (April 1989): 169–83.

Dierken, Jörg, Arnulf von Scheliha, and Sarah Schmidt, eds. *Reformation und Moderne. Pluralität—Subjektivität—Kritik. Akten des Internationalen Kongresses der*

Schleiermacher-Gesellschaft in Halle (Saale), März 2017. Schleiermacher-Archiv 27. Berlin: Walter de Gruyter, 2018.

Dilthey, Wilhelm. *Leben Schleiermachers* [vol. 1, in 2 parts]. Berlin: Reimer, 1870. 3rd edition, edited by Martin Redeker, 1970; reprint, De Gruyter, 2019.

Dilthey, Wilhelm. *Leben Schleiermachers*, vol. 2 [in 3 parts]: *Schleiermachers System als Philosophie und Theologie*. Edited by Martin Redeker. Berlin: Walter de Gruyter, 1966; reprint, De Gruyter, 2011.

Dole, Andrew. "Schleiermacher and Otto on Religion." *Religious Studies* 40, no. 4 (December 2004): 389–413.

Ellison, Julie. *Delicate Subjects: Romanticism, Gender, and the Ethics of Understanding*. Ithaca: Cornell University Press, 1990.

Findlay, J. N. *Plato: The Written and Unwritten Doctrines*. London: Routledge, 1974.

Fischer, Hermann, and Kurt-Victor Selge, eds. *Internationaler Schleiermacher-Kongreß Berlin 1984*. Berlin: Walter de Gruyter, 1985.

Flashar, Hellmut, Gründer Karlfried, and Axel Horstmann. *Philologie und Hermeneutik im 19. Jahrhundert*. Göttingen: Vandenhoeck & Ruprecht, 1979.

Follak, Andrea. *Der 'Aufblick zur Idee': Eine vergleichende Studie zur Platonischen Pädgogik bei Friedrich Schleiermacher, Paul Natorp und Werner Jaeger*. Göttingen: Vandenhoeck & Ruprecht, 2005.

Forstman, H. Jackson. "The Understanding of Language by Friedrich Schlegel and Schleiermacher." *Soundings* 51, no. 2 (1968): 146–65.

Frank, Manfred. "Metaphysical Foundations: A Look at Schleiermacher's Dialectic." In *The Cambridge Companion to Friedrich Schleiermacher*, edited by Jacqueline Mariña, 15–34. Cambridge Companions to Religion. Cambridge: Cambridge University Press, 2005.

Fuchs, Emil. *Schleiermachers Religionsbegriff und religiöse Stellung zur Zeit der ersten Ausgabe der Reden (1799–1806)*. Giessen: J. Ricker'sche Verlags-Buchhandlung/Alfred Töpelmann, 1901.

Fuchs, Emil. "Wandlungen in Schleiermachers Denken zwischen der ersten und zweiten Ausgabe der Reden." *Theologische Studien und Kritiken* 76, no. 1 (1903): 71–99.

Gadamer, H. G. "Schleiermacher Platonicien." *Archives de Philosophe* 32, no. 1 (April–June 1969): 28–39.

Gaiser, Konrad, ed. *Das Platonbild. Zehn Beiträge zum Platonverständnis*. Hildesheim: Georg Olms Verlagsbuchhandlung, 1969.

Gaiser, Konrad. *Platons ungeschriebene Lehre. Studien zur systematischen und geschichtlichen Begründung der Wissenschaften in der Platonischen Schule*. Stuttgart: Ernst Klett Verlag, 1963.

Gauss, Hermann. *Philosophischer Handkommentar zu den Dialogen Platos*. 7 vols. Bern: Herbert Lang, 1952–61.

Geddes, James. *An Essay on the Composition and Manner of Writing of the Antients, Particularly Plato*. Glasgow: R. Goulis, 1748.

Gerson, Lloyd P. *From Plato to Platonism*. Ithaca: Cornell University Press, 2013.

Gleason, Patricia Guenther. *On Schleiermacher and Gender Politics*. Harrisburg: Trinity Press International, 1997.

Gómez-Lobo, Alfonso, "Plato's Description of Dialectic in the Sophist 253," *Phronesis* 22 (1977): 29–47.

Graf, Friedrich Wilhelm. "Ursprüngliches Gefühl unmittelbarer Koinzidenz des Differenten: Zur Modifikation des Religionsbegriffs in den verschiedenen Auflagen von Schleiermachers 'Reden über die Religion'." *Zeitschrift für Theologie und Kirche* 75, no. 2 (1978): 147–86.

Güthenke, Constanze. *Feeling and Classical Philology: Knowing Antiquity in German Scholarship, 1770–1920*. Cambridge: Cambridge University Press, 2020.

Hadot, Pierre. *Exercices spirituels et philosophie antique*. Paris: Études Augustiniennes, 1981. English translation: *Philosophy as a Way of Life: Spiritual Exercises from Socrates to Foucault*, edited by Arnold I. Davidson and translated by Michael Chase. Oxford and Cambridge, Mass.: Blackwell, 1995.

Hartlieb, Elisabeth. *Geschlechterdifferenz im Denken Friederich Schleiermachers*. Berlin: de Gruyter, 2006.

Harvey, Van A. "On the New Edition of Schleiermacher's: *Addresses on Religion*." *Journal of the American Academy of Religion* 39, no. 4 (December 1971): 488–512.

Hedley, Douglas. *Coleridge, Philosophy and Religion: Aids to Reflection and the Mirror of the Spirit*. Cambridge: Cambridge University Press, 2000.

Hegel, G.W. F. *Vorlesungen über die Geschichte der Philosophie*. Vol. 18. Edited by H. Glockner. 3rd ed. Stuttgart, 1959.

Heindorf, Ludwig. *Platonis Dialogi Quattuor: Lysis—Charmides—Hippias Maior—Phaedrus*. Berlin: E Libraria Nauckiana, 1802.

Helmer, Christine, Christiane Kranich, and Birgit Rehme-Iffert, eds. *Schleiermachers Dialektik: Die Liebe zum Wissen in Philosophie und Theologie*. Religion in Philosophy and Theology 6. Tübingen: Mohr Siebeck, 2003.

Hermann, Karl Friedrich. *Geschichte und System der Platonischen Philosophie*. Heidelberg: Akademische Verlagshandlung von C.F. Winter, 1839.

Hermans, Theo. "Schleiermacher and Plato, Hermeneutics and Translation." In *Friedrich Schleiermacher and the Question of Translation*, edited by Larisa Cercel and Adriana Serban, 77–106. Berlin and Boston: De Gruyter, 2015.

Herms, Eilert. *Menschsein im Werden: Studien zu Schleiermacher*. Tübingen: Mohr Siebeck, 2003.

Herms, Eilert. "Platonismus und Aristotelismus in Schleiermachers Ethik." In *Schleiermacher's Philosophy and the Philosophical Tradition*, edited by Sergio Sorrentino, 3–26. Lewiston: Edwin Mellen Press, 1992.

Herms, Eilert. "Religion, Wissen und Handeln bei Schleiermacher und in der Schleiermacher-Rezeption." In *200 Jahre "Reden über die Religion." Akten des 1. Internationalen Kongresses der Schleiermacher-Gesellschaft, Halle 14.–17. März 1999*, edited by Ulrich Barth and Claus-Dieter Osthövener, 142–166. Berlin: Walter de Gruyter, 2000.

Hösle, Vittorio. "Platonism and its Interpretations: The Three Paradigms and their Place in History of Hermeneutics." In *Eriugena, Berkeley, and the Idealist Tradition*, edited by Stephen Gersh and Dermot Moran, 54–80. Notre Dame, IN: University of Notre Dame Press, 2006.

Hösle, Vittorio. "The Tübingen School." In *Brill's Companion to German Platonism*, edited by Alan Kim, 328–348. Leiden: Brill, 2019.

Jaeger, Werner. "Der Wandel des Platobildes im neunzehnten Jahrhundert." In *Humanistische Reden und Vorträge*, 129–42. Berlin: Walter de Gruyter, 1936; reprint, 1960.

Jantzen, Jörg. "Schleiermachers Platon-Übersetzung und seine Anmerkungen dazu." In *Über die Philosophie Platons*, edited by Peter M. Steiner, xlv-lviii. Hamburg: Felix Meiner Verlag, 1996.

Jeanrond, Werner. "The Impact of Schleiermacher's Hermeneutics on Contemporary Interpretation Theory." In *The Interpretation of Belief Coleridge, Schleiermacher and Romanticism*, 81–96. New York: Palgrave Macmillan, 1986.

Käppel, Lutz. "Die frühe Rezeption der Platon-Übersetzung Friedrich Schleiermachers am Beispiel der Arbeiten Friedrich Asts." In *Geist und Buchstabe: Interpretations- und Transformationsprozesse innerhalb des Christentums. Festschrift für Günter Meckenstock zum 65. Geburtstag*, edited by Michael Pietsch und Dirk Schmid, 45–62. Berlin and Boston: De Gruyter, 2013.

Käppel, Lutz. "(Re-)Konstruktion von Antike als (Neu-)Konstruktion von Moderne. Schleiermachers Auseinandersetzung mit Platon und Heraklit." In *Reformation und Moderne. Pluralität—Subjektivität—Kritik*, edited by Jörg Dierken, Arnulf von Scheliha, and Sarah Schmidt, 699–717. Berlin and Boston: Walter de Gruyter, 2018.

Käppel, Lutz. "Schleiermachers Hermeneutik zwischen zeitgenössischer Philologie und 'Phaidros'-Lektüre." In *Schleiermacher-Tag 2005. Eine Vortragsreihe*, edited by Günter Meckenstock, 65–74. Göttingen: Vandenhoeck & Ruprecht, 2006.

Kerber, Hannes. "Strauss and Schleiermacher on How to Read Plato: An Introduction to 'Exoteric Teaching.'" In *Reorientation: Leo Strauss in the 1930s*, edited by Martin D. Yaffe and Richard S. Ruderman, 203–14. New York: Palgrave Macmillan, 2014.

Kim, Alan, ed. *Brill's Companion to German Platonism*. Leiden, The Netherlands: Brill, 2019.

Krämer, Hans Joachim. *Arete bei Platon und Aristoteles: Zum Wesen und zur Geschichte der platonischen Ontologie*. Heidelberg: Carl Winter Universitätsverlag, 1959.

Krämer, Hans Joachim. *Gesammelte Aufsätze zu Platon*. Beiträge zur Altertumskunde 321. Edited by Dagmar Mirbach. Boston and Berlin: De Gruyter, 2014.

Krämer, Hans Joachim. *Plato and the Foundations of Metaphysics: A Work on the Theory of the Principles and Unwritten Doctrines of Plato with a Collection of the Fundamental Documents*. Translated and edited by John R. Catan. Albany: State University of New York Press, 1990.

Korsch, Dietrich. "'Höherer Realismus': Schleiermachers Erkenntnistheorie der Religion in der zweiten Rede." In *200 Jahre "Reden über die Religion." Akten des 1. Internationalen Kongresses der Schleiermacher-Gesellschaft Halle, 14.–17. März 1999*, edited by Ulrich Barth and Claus-Dieter Osthövener, 610–628. Berlin: De Gruyter, 2000.

Krapf, Gustav-Adolf. "Platonic Dialectics and Schleiermacher's Thought: An Essay towards the Reinterpretation of Schleiermacher." Ph.D. diss., Yale University, 1953.

Kroker, Paul. *Die Tugendlehre Schleiermachers, mit spezieller Berücksichtigung der Tugendlehre Platos*. Erlangen: Junge & Sohn, 1889.

Körner, Josef. "Friedrich Schlegels 'Philosophie der Philologie'." *Logos* 17 (1928): 1–72.

Laks, André. "Plato Between Cohen and Natorp: Aspects of the neo-Kantian Interpretation of the Platonic Ideas." In *P. Natorp, Plato's Theory of Ideas: An Introduction to Idealism*, edited by Vasilis Politis, translated by Vasilis Politis and John Connolly. *International Plato Studies* 16 (2004): 453–83. Sankt Augustin: Academia, 2004.

Laks, André. "Platonicien malgré lui? Le statut de l'éthique platonicienne dans les Grundlinien." *Archives De Philosophie* 77, no. 2 (April–June 2014): 259–79.

Laks, André. "Schleiermacher on Plato: From Form (*Introduction to Plato's Works*) to Content (*Outlines of a Critique of Previous Ethical Theory*)." In *Brill's Companion to German Platonism*, edited by Alan Kim, 146–64. Leiden: Brill, 2019.

Lamm, Julia A. "The Art of Interpreting Plato." In *Cambridge Companion to Schleiermacher*, edited by Jacqueline Mariña, 91–108. Cambridge: Cambridge University Press, 2005.

Lamm, Julia A. "The Early Philosophical Roots of Schleiermacher's Notion of *Gefühl*, 1788–1794," *Harvard Theological Review* 87, no. 1 (1994): 67–105.

Lamm, Julia A. *The Living God: Schleiermacher's Theological Appropriation of Spinoza.* University Park: Pennsylvania State Univ. Press, 1996.

Lamm, Julia A. "Plato's Dialogues as a Single Work of Art: Friedrich Schleiermacher's *Platons Werke.*" In *Lire les Dialogues, mais lesquels et dans quel ordre? Définitions du corpus et interprétations de Platon*, edited by Anne Balansard and Isabelle Koch, 173–88. Sankt Augustin: Academia Verlag, 2013.

Lamm, Julia A. "Reading Plato's Dialectics: Schleiermacher's Insistence on Dialectics as Dialogical." *Zeitschrift für Neuere Theologiegeschichte / Journal for the History of Modern Theology* 10, no. 1 (April 2003): 1–25.

Lamm, Julia A. "Romanticism and Pantheism." In *The Blackwell Companion to Nineteenth-Century Theology*, edited by David Ferguson, 165–186. Oxford: Blackwell Publisher, 2010.

Lamm, Julia A. "Schleiermacher as Plato Scholar." *The Journal of Religion* 80, no. 2 (April 2000): 206–39.

Lamm, Julia A, ed. *Schleiermacher: Christmas Dialogue, The Second Speech and Other Selections.* Classics of Western Spirituality. Mahwah, NJ: Paulist Press, 2014.

Lamm, Julia A. "Schleiermacher on 'The Roman Church': Anti-Catholic Ideology and the Future of Historical-Empirical Dogmatics." In *Schleiermacher, the Study of Religion, and the Future of Theology*, edited by Brent Sockness and Wilhelm Gräb, 243–56. Berlin and New York: Walter de Gruyter, 2010.

Lamm, Julia A. "Schleiermacher's *Christmas Dialogue* as Platonic Dialogue." *The Journal of Religion* 92, no. 3 (July 2012): 392–420.

Lamm, Julia A. "Schleiermacher's Modern Platonism." In *Reformation und Moderne. Pluralität—Subjektivität—Kritik*, edited by Jörg Dierken, Arnulf von Scheliha, and Sarah Schmidt, 675–697. Berlin: Walter de Gruyter, 2018.

Lamm, Julia A. "Schleiermacher's Post-Kantian Spinozism: The Essays on Spinoza, 1793–94," *The Journal of Religion* 74, no. 3 (July 1994): 476–505.

Lamm, Julia A. "Schleiermacher's Re-Writing as Spiritual Exercise, 1799–1806." In *Der Mensch und seine Seele. Bildung—Frömmigkeit—Ästhetik. Akten des Schleiermacher-Kongresses 2015*, edited by Arnulf von Scheliha and Jörg Dierken, 293–302. Berlin, Boston: Walter de Gruyter, 2017.

Lesky, Albin. *A History of Greek Literature.* Translated by James Willis and Cornelis de Heer. London: Methuen, 1966.

Lincoln, Bruce. *Theorizing Myth: Narrative, Ideology, and Scholarship.* Chicago: University of Chicago Press, 1999.

Margolis, Joseph. "Schleiermacher among the Theorists of Language and Interpretation." *The Journal of Aesthetics and Art Criticism* 45, no. 4 (June 1987): 361–68.

Mariña, Jacqueline, ed. *The Cambridge Companion to Friedrich Schleiermacher.* Cambridge: Cambridge University Press, 2006.

Mariña, Jacqueline. *Transformation of the Self in the Thought of Friedrich Schleiermacher.* Oxford: Oxford University Press, 2008.

Massey, Marilyn Chapin. *Feminine Soul: The Fate of an Ideal.* Boston: Beacon Press, 1985.

Migliori, Maurizio, Alonso Tordesillas, and Luc Brisson. "De la Critique de Schleiermacher aux Commentaires Récents. Évolution et Articulation du Nouveau Paradigme de Tübingen-Milan." *Les Études Philosophiques*, 96, no. 1 (January–March 1998): 91–114.

Morgenroth, Matthias. *Weihnachts-Christentum: Moderner Religiosität auf der Spur.* Gütersloh: Kaiser, Gütersloher Verlag, 2002.

Mróz, Tomasz. "The Reception of Schleiermacher's View on Plato in 19th Century Poland." In *Literary, Philosophical, and Religious Studies in the Platonic Tradition: Papers from 7th annual conference of the International Society for Neoplatonic Studies*, edited by John F. Finamore and John Phillips, 179–89. Academia Philosophical Studies 45. Baden-Baden: Academia, 2013.

Natorp, Paul. *Platos Ideenlehre: Eine Einführung in den Idealismus.* Leipzig: Felix Meiner, 1921.

Nicol, Iain G., ed. *Schleiermacher and Feminism: Sources, Evaluations and Responses.* Lewiston: Edwin Mellen Press, 1992.

Niebuhr, Richard R. *Schleiermacher on Christ and Religion: A New Introduction.* New York: Charles Scribner's Sons, 1964. Reprint, Eugene: Wipf & Stock, 2009.

Nimmo, Paul T. "Schleiermacher on Scripture and the Work of Jesus Christ." *Modern Theology* 31, vol. 1 (January 2015): 60–90.

Nowak, Kurt. *Schleiermacher: Leben, Werk, und Wirkung.* Göttingen: Vandenhoeck & Ruprecht, 2001.

Nowak, Kurt. *Schleiermacher und die Frühromantik: Eine literaturgeschichtliche Studie zum romantischen Religionsverständnis und Menschenbild am Ende des 18. Jahrhunderts in Deutschland.* Göttingen: Vandenhoeck & Ruprecht, 1986.

Odebrecht, Rudolf. "Der Geist der Sokratik im Werke Schleiermachers." In *Geistige Gestalten und Probleme: Eduard Spranger zum 60. Geburtstag*, edited by Hans Wenke, 103–118. Leipzig: Quelle & Meyer, 1942.

Oehler, Klaus. "Der entmythologisierte Platon: Zur Lage der Platonforschung," *Zeitschrift für philosophische Forschung* 19, no. 3 (1965): 393–420.

Olesko, Kathryn M. "Germany." In *The Cambridge History of Science.* Vol. 8: *Modern Science in National, Transnational, and Global Context*, edited by H. R. Slotten, R. L. Numbers, and D. N. Livingstone, 233–277. Cambridge: Cambridge University Press, 2020.

Patsch, Hermann. *Alle Menschen sind Künstler: Friedrich Schleiermachers poetische Versuche.* Berlin: Walter de Gruyter, 1986.

Patsch, Hermann. "Friedrich Schlegels 'Philosophie der Philologie' und Schleiermachers frühe Entwürfe zur Hermeneutik." *Zeitschrift für Theologie und Kirche* 63 no. 4 (1966): 434–72.

Patsch, Hermann. " '... mit Interesse die eigentliche Theologie wieder hervorsuchen': Schleiermachers theologische Schriften der Hallenser Zeit." In *Friedrich Schleiermacher in Halle 1804–1807*, edited by Andreas Arndt, 31–54. Berlin: Walter de Gruyter, 2013.

Pohl, Karl. "Die Bedeutung der Sprache für den Erkenntnisakt in der 'Dialektik' Friedrich Schleiermachers." *Kant-Studien* 46, no. 1–4 (January 1955): 302–32.

Proudfoot, Wayne. "Immediacy and Intentionality in the Feeling of Absolute Dependence." In *Schleiermacher, the Study of Religion, and the Future of Theology: A Transatlantic Dialogue*, edited by Brent Sockness and Wilhelm Gräb, 27–37. Berlin: De Gruyter, 2010.

Proudfoot, Wayne. "Intuition and Fantasy in *On Religion*." In *Interpreting Religion: The Significance of Friedrich Schleiermacher's* Reden über die Religion *for Religious Studies and Theology*, edited by Dietrich Korsch and Amber L. Griffioen, 87–98. Tübingen: Mohr Siebeck, 2011.

Proudfoot, Wayne. *Religious Experience*. Berkeley: University of California Press, 1985.

Rade, Martin, ed. *Schleiermacher: Monologen, Die Weihnachtsfeier*. Berlin: Deutsche Bibliothek, 1914; Leipzig: Spamer, 1954.

Ravenscroft, Ruth Jackson. *The Veiled God: Friedrich Schleiermacher's Theology of Finitude*. Leiden: Brill, 2019.

Redeker, Martin. *Friedrich Schleiermacher. Leben und Werk*. Berlin: Walter de Gruyter, 1968. English version: *Schleiermacher: Life and Thought*. Translated by John Wallhausser. Philadelphia: Fortress Press, 1973.

Richard, Marie-Dominique. "La Critique d'A. Boeckh de l'Introduction Générale de F. Schleiermacher aux Dialogues de Platon." *Les Études Philosophiques*, no. 1 (January–March 1998): 11–30.

Richard, Marie-Dominique, ed. *Friedrich Daniel Ernst Schleiermacher. Introductions aux dialogues de Platon (1804–1828). Leçons d'histoire de la philosophie (1819–1823). Suivies des textes de Friedrich Schlegel, relatifs à Platon*. Paris: Éditions du Cerf, 2004.

Richard, Marie-Dominique. "Plato and the German Romantic Thinkers: Friedrich Schlegel and Friedrich Daniel Ernst Schleiermacher." *Faculty Philosophy Journal* 36, no. 1 (2015): 91–124.

Richardson, Ruth Drucilla. "Friedrich Schleiermacher's *Weihnachtsfeier* as 'Universal Poetry': The Impact of Friedrich Schlegel on the Intellectual Development of the Young Schleiermacher." Ph.D. diss., Drew University, 1985.

Richardson, Ruth Drucilla. *The Role of Women in the Life and Thought of the Early Schleiermacher (1768–1806): An Historical Overview*. Schleiermacher Studies-and-Translations 7. Lewiston, NY: Edwin Mellen Press, 1991.

Rieger, Reinhold. *Interpretation und Wissen: Zur philosophischen Begründung der Hermeneutik bei Friedrich Schleiermacher und ihrem geschichtlichen Hintergrund*. Berlin: De Gruyter, 1988.

Ringleben, Joachim. "Die Sprache bei Schleiermacher und Humboldt. Ein Versuch Zum Verhältnis von Sprachdenken und Hermeneutik." In *Schleiermacher und die wissenschaftliche Kultur der Christentums*, edited by Günter Meckenstock, 473–92. Berlin: de Gruyter, 1991.

Rohls, Jan. "Schleiermachers Platon." In *Schleiermacher und Kierkegaard*, edited by Niels Jørgen Cappelørn, Richard E. Crouter, Theodor Jørgensen and Claus-Dieter Osthövener, 709–731. Berlin and New York: De Gruyter, 2006.

Rohls, Jan. "Wahrheit, Dialog und Sprache in Schleiermachers *Dialektik*." In *Schleiermachers Dialektik: Die Liebe zum Wissen in Philosophie und Theologie*, edited by Christine Helmer, Christiane Kranich, and Birgit Rehme-Iffert, 181–206. Tübingen: Mohr Siebeck, 2003.

Rohls, Jan. "'Der Winckelmann der griechischen Philosophie': Schleiermachers Platonismus im Kontext." In *200 Jahre "Reden über die Religion." Akten des 1. Internationalen*

Kongresses der Schleiermacher-Gesellschaft, Halle 14.–17. März 1999, edited by Ulrich Barth and Claus-Dieter Osthövener, 467–496. Berlin: Walter de Gruyter, 2000.

Rowe, Christopher. "One Dialogue or Two? Reading Plato's *Republic*." In *Lire les Dialogues, mais lesquels et dans quel ordre? Définitions du corpus et interprétations de Platon*, edited by Anne Balansard and Isabelle Koch, 245–52. Sankt Augustin: Academia Verlag, 2013.

Schaerer, René. *La question platonicienne: Étude sur les rapports de la pensee et de l'expression dans les Dialogues*. 2nd ed. Neuchatel: Secretariat de l'Universite, 1969.

Scheliha, Arnulf und Jörg Dierken, eds. *Der Mensch und seine Seele: Bildung—Frömmigkeit—Ästhetik. Akten des Internationalen Kongresses der Schleiermacher-Gesellschaft in Münster, September 2015*. Schleiermacher-Archiv 26. Berlin and Boston: De Gruyter, 2017.

Schenkel, Daniel. *Friedrich Schleiermacher: Ein Lebens- und Charakterbild: Zur Erinnerung an den 21. November 1768*. Elberfeld, 1868.

Schlegel, Friedrich von. *Dialogue on Poetry and Literary Aphorisms*. Translated and edited by Ernst Behler. University Park: Pennsylvania State University Press, 1968.

Schmidt, Sarah. "Analogie versus Wechselwirkung: Zur 'Symphilosophie' zwischen Schleiermacher und Steffens." In *Schleiermacher in Halle 1804–1807*, edited by Andreas Arndt, 91–114. Berlin: Walter de Gruyter, 2013.

Schmidt, Sarah. "Éthique et physique chez Schleiermacher." *Archives de Philosophie* 77, no. 2, Schleiermacher philosophe (April–June 2014): 301–320.

Schmidt, Sarah. *Die Konstruktion des Endlichen: Schleiermachers Philosophie der Wechselwirkung*. Berlin and New York: Walter de Gruyter, 2012.

Schmidt, Sarah. "Wahrnehmung und Schema: Zur zentralen Bedeutung des bildlichen Denkens in Schleiermachers *Dialektik*." In *Schleiermacher und Kierkegaard*, edited by Niels Jørgen Cappelørn, Richard E. Crouter, Theodor Jørgensen and Claus-Dieter Osthövener, 73–92. Berlin and Boston: De Gruyter, 2006.

Schmidt, Sarah, ed. *System und Subversion: Friedrich Schleiermacher und Henrik Steffens*. Berlin and Boston: De Gruyter, 2018.

Schnitzer, Adam. "A History in Translation: Schleiermacher, Plato, and the University of Berlin." *The Germanic Review* 75, no. 1 (Winter, 2000): 53–71.

Schnur, Harald. *Schleiermachers Hermeneutik und ihre Vorgeschichte im 18. Jahrhundert: Studien zur Bibelauslegung, zu Hamann, Herder und F. Schlegel*. Stuttgart: J.B. Metzler, 1994.

Scholtz, Gunter. "Ast and Schleiermacher: Hermeneutics and Critical Philosophy." In *The Routledge Companion to Hermeneutics*, edited by Jeff Malpas and Hans-Helmuth Gander, 62–73. Oxfordshire, England: Routledge, 2016.

Scholtz, Gunter. *Die Philosophie Schleiermachers*. Darmstadt: Wissenschaftliche Buchgesellschaft, 1984.

Scholtz, Gunter. "Schleiermacher und die Platonische Ideenlehre." In *Internationaler Schleiermacher-Kongreß 1984*, edited by Hermann Fischer and Kurt-Victor Selge, 849–74. Berlin: Walter de Gruyter, 1985.

Schultz, Werner. "Das griechische Ethos in Schleiermachers Reden und Monologen." *Neue Zeitschrift für systematische Theologie und Religionsphilosophie* 10, no. 3 (January 1968): 261–288.

Schur, David. *Plato's Wayward Path: Literary Form and the Republic.* Hellenic Studies Series 66. Washington, DC: Center for Hellenic Studies, 2015. http://nrs.harvard.edu/urn-3:hul.ebook:CHS_SchurD.Platos_Wayward_Path.2015. Accessed 19 June 2020.
Shorey, Paul. *Platonism: Ancient and Modern.* Berkeley: University of California Press, 1938.
Shorey, Paul. *The Unity of Plato's Thought.* The Decennial Publications of the University of Chicago 6. Chicago: Chicago University Press, 1904.
Socher, Joseph. *Ueber Platons Schriften.* München: Ignas Joseph Lentner, 1820.
Sockness, Brent W. "The Forgotten Moralist: Friedrich Schleiermacher and the Science of Spirit." *Harvard Theological Review* 96, no. 3 (July 2003): 317–348.
Sockness, Brent W. "Schleiermacher and the Ethics of Authenticity." *Journal of Religious Ethics* 32, no. 3 (Fall 2004): 477–517.
Sockness, Brent W. 'Was Schleiermacher a Virtue Ethicist? *Tugend* and *Bildung* in the Early Ethical Writings." *Zeitschrift für Neuere Theologiegeschichte / Journal for the History of Modern Theology* 8, no. 1 (January 2001): 1–33.
Sockness, Brent W., and Wilhelm Gräb, eds. *Schleiermacher, the Study of Religion, and the Future of Theology: A Transatlantic Dialogue.* Berlin: Walter de Gruyter, 2010.
Spiegler, Gerhard E. *The Eternal Covenant: Schleiermacher's Experiment in Cultural Theology.* New York: Harper & Row, 1967.
Stallbaum, Gottfried. *Platonis Dialogos Selectos recensuit et commentariis in usum scholarum instruxit Godofredus Stallbaum.* Gotha and Erfurt: Hennings, 1827– . Reprinted as: *Platonis Opera omnia.* New York & London: Garland, 1980.
Stein, Heinrich von. *Sieben Bücher zur Geschichte des Platonismus: Untersuchungen über das System des Plato und sein Verhältniss zur späteren Theologie und Philosophie.* 3 vols. Frankfurt am Main: Minerva, 1965.
Steiner, Peter M. "Zur Kontroverse um Schleiermachers Platon." In *F. D. E. Schleiermacher: Über die Philosophie Platons,* ed. by Peter M. Steiner, xxiii–xliv. Hamburg: Felix Meiner, 1996.
Stock, Hans. *Friedrich Schlegel und Schleiermacher.* Ph.D. diss., Philipps-Universität zu Marburg, 1930. Marburg: Joh. Hamel, 1930.
Straus, David Friedrich. *Charakteristiken und Kritiken. Eine Sammlung zerstreuter Aufsätze aus den Gebieten der Theologie, Anthropologie und Aesthetik.* Leipzig: Wigan, 1839.
Szlezák, Thomas A. *Aufsätze zur griechischen Literatur und Philosophie.* International Plato Studies 139. Baden-Baden: Academia, 2019.
Szlezák, Thomas A. "Friedrich Schleiermacher's Theory of the Platonic Dialogue and Its Legacy." In *Brill's Companion to German Platonism,* edited by Alan Kim, 165–191. Leiden: Brill, 2019.
Szlezák, Thomas A. *Platon und die Schriftlichkeit der Philosophie.* Berlin: de Gruyter, 1985.
Szlezák, Thomas A. *Reading Plato.* New York: Routledge, 1999. Florence: Taylor & Francis Group, 1999.
Szlezák, Thomas A. "Schleiermachers 'Einleitung' zur Platon-Übersetzung von 1804: Ein Vergleich mit Tiedemann und Tennemann." *Antike und Abendland* 43, no. 1 (December 1997): 46–62.
Tennemann, Wilhelm Gottlieb. *System der platonischen Philosophie.* 2 vols. Leipzig, 1792.
Thesleff, Holger. *Studies in Platonic Chronology.* Commentationes Humanarum Litterarum 70. Helsinki: Societas Scientiarum Fennica, 1982.

Thandeka. "Schleiermacher, Feminism, and Liberation." In *The Cambridge Companion to Friedrich Schleiermacher*, edited by Jacqueline Mariña, 287–306. Cambridge: Cambridge University Press, 2006.

Thouard, Denis. "Tradition directe et tradition indirecte remarque sur l'interprétation de Platon par Schleiermacher et ses utilisations." *Les Études Philosophiques* 53, no. 4 (October–December 1998): 543–56.

Tice, Terrence N. "Schleiermacher's Interpretation of Christmas: 'Christmas Eve,' 'The Christian Faith,' and the Christmas Sermons." *The Journal of Religion* 47, no. 2 (April 1967): 100–126.

Tigerstedt, E. N. *The Decline and Fall of the Neoplatonic Interpretation of Plato: An Outline and Some Observations*. Commentationes Humanarum Litterarum 52. Helsinki: Societas Scientiarum Fennica, 1974.

Tigerstedt, E. N. *Interpreting Plato*. Uppsala: Almquist & Wiksell, 1977.

Turner, R. Steven. "Historicism, *Kritik*, and the Prussian Professoriate, 1790–1840." In *Philologie und Hermeneutik im 19. Jahrhundert II*, edited by Mayotte Bollack and Heinz Wismann, 450–77. Göttingen: Vandenhoeck & Ruprecht, 1983.

Virmond, Wolfgang. "Der fiktive Autor: Schleiermachers technische Interpretation der platonischen Dialoge (1804) als Vorstufe seiner Hallenser Hermeneutik (1805)." *Archivo di Filosofia* 52, no. 1–3 (1984): 225–32.

Virmond, Wolfgang. "*interpretari necesse est:* Über die Wurzeln von Schleiermachers Hermeneutik und Kritik." In *Friedrich Schleiermacher in Halle 1804–1807)*, edited by Andreas Arndt, 67–76. Berlin: Walter de Gruyter, 2013.

Virmond, Wolfgang. "Neue Textgrundlagen zu Schleiermachers früher Hermeneutik: Prolegomena zur Kritischen Edition." In *Internationaler Schleiermacher-Kongress, Berlin 1984*, edited by Hermann Fischer and Kurt-Victor Selge, 575–90. Berlin: Walter de Gruyter, 1985.

Vorsmann, Norbert. *Die Bedeutung des Platonismus für den Aufbau der Erziehungstheorie bei Schleiermacher und Herbart*. Düsseldorf: A. Henn, 1968.

Wallhausser, John. "Schleiermacher's Critique of Ethical Reason: Toward a Systematic Ethics." *The Journal of Religious Ethics* 17, no. 2 (fall 1989): 25–39.

Wehrung, Georg. "Einführung." In *Die Weihnachtsfeier: Ein Gespräch*. Darmstadt: Wissenschaftliche Buchgemeinschaft, 1953.

Wilamowitz-Moellendorff, Ulrich von. *Geschichte der Philologie*. Leipzig: Teubner, 1921.

Wilamowitz-Moellendorff, Ulrich von. *Platon: Sein Leben und seine Werke*. Berlin: Weidmannsche, 1948.

Williams, Robert R. *Schleiermacher the Theologian: The Construction of the Doctrine of God*. Philadelphia: Fortress Press, 1978.

Willson, A. Leslie, ed. *German Romantic Criticism*. New York: Continuum, 1982.

Wippern, Jürgen, ed. *Das Problem der ungeschriebenen Lehre Platons: Beiträge zum Verständnis der Platonischen Prinzipienphilosophie*. Darmstadt: Wissenschaftliche Buchgesellschaft, 1972.

Wolfsdorf, David. "Aporia in Plato's Charmides, Laches, and Lysis." Ph.D. diss., University of Chicago, 1997.

Zeller, Eduard. *Die Philosophie der Griechen in ihrer geschichtlichen Entwicklung*. Tübingen, 1856.

Zuckert, Catherine H. *Plato's Philosophers: The Coherence of the Dialogues.* Chicago: University of Chicago Press, 2009.
Zuckert, Catherine H. *Postmodern Platos.* Chicago: University of Chicago Press, 1996.

Index

aesthetics, 10, 11–12n29, 22n6, 38, 41, 67, 75, 114, 167n96
Altman, William H. F., 31n53, 45n124
Ameriks, Karl, 62n12
Annas, Julia, 87–89, 102
apophasis, 10, 115, 140, 151, 157
Aristotle, 11, 36, 41, 55, 177n129
Arndt, Andreas, viii, 1n1, 2n9, 5nn17–18, 12n32, 18n45, 56–57, 85n117, 87n6, 106n93, 178n131
art, 16, 211. *See also* Plato-as-artist
– art of understanding, 58, 62–64, 70, 84
– art of doing philosophy 106
– art and religion, 120, 125, 154, 210
– art and science 154, 180, 200, 210
– dialectics as art, 66–67, 69, 87, 91–92, 123, 167–68, 196
– "life and art" in the *Speeches*, 156, 158–60, 203–204, 206
– Schleiermacher's theory of the artistic whole, 38, 71–72, 118
– Schleiermacher's translation of Plato as work of, 22, 26
– Schleiermacher's translation of *technē* as, 92
Asmuth, Christoph, 5n18
association of kinds, 121n57, 194–96, 199–200, 214, 216, 220–21, 223, 228–29, 231
Ast, Friedrich, 14, 28–30, 48–49
authenticity. *See under* Platonic dialogues

Baird, William, 33n58
Barth, Karl, 109n10, 114n27
Barth, Ulrich, 6n19, 144n6
beauty, 68, 93, 115, 116, 123–25, 127, 129–31, 174, 182–83, 215
– the beautiful, vii, 119, 166, 170, 182, 227
becoming/*Werden*, 171–72, 174–75, 178, 189, 200, 214, 218, 221, 228–29
Behler, Ernst, 23n10, 81n103

being
– being, existence/*Sein*, 83, 84, 98, 164, 169, 171–72, 174, 178n132, 180, 183, 185, 187–96, 201, 202, 212, 219, 226
– being, existence, what-*is*/*Seiende*, 98, 100, 174, 178, 188–89, 192, 195–98, 202, 218, 219, 221, 228
– the highest being/*das höchste Sein*, 16, 188, 195–98, 213, 224, 228, 231
– being and knowing (unity or identity of), 10, 82–83, 88, 98, 195, 199, 202–203, 213, 216, 219, 221, 229, 231
– non-being/*Nichtseiende, Nichtsein*, 98, 188–93, 190–96, 226
Beiser, Frederick, 11–12, 15, 227, 228n3
Bekker, Immanuel, 1
Berlin, 8, 11, 13, 14–15, 18, 22, 27, 58n2, 106, 147, 232
– University of, 19, 232
Bestebreurtje, Frank, 143n2
Birkner, Hans-Joachim, 17n42
Blackwell, Albert L., ix, 2n9, 7, 17n41, 121n52, 135n96, 145, 172, 178
Bloom, Allan, 2n9
Boeckh, August, 28n35, 30–31, 49, 52n155
Bollack, Mayotte, 30n48
Borgman, Erik, 145n10, 167n96
Bowie, Andrew, 62n12
Brandt, Richard B., 7n23
Brandwood, Leonard, 50n145
Brinckmann, Carl Gustav von, 1n1, 24, 25n16, 155n50
Brucker, Jacob, 33–34
Bukowski, Piotr de Bończa, 2n9, 25n17, 28n35
Burnet, John, 53n162
Büsching, Anna, 143n2

Cantana, Leo, 33n60
Cappelørn, Niels Jørgen, 6n19
Cercel, Larisa, 2n9
Charité Hospital, 11, 22
Chase, Michael, 149n16

Christ, Franz, 5n16
Christ. *See* Jesus Christ
Clarke, Desmond M., 62n12
coincidence of opposites, 138–39, 178, 197, 217, 228, 231
consciousness / *Bewußtsein*, 82, 93–94, 122, 124, 154, 182, 184n152, 185–86, 192, 198, 205, 211–18
– modern historical or scientific, 31, 138, 147, 231
contemplation / *Betrachtung*, 99n71, 102, 129, 147, 150–51, 155, 163, 169, 171–86, 187, 201, 202, 210–11, 222–25, 229
– essential to religion, 155, 163–69, 171–86
Crane, Gregory R., 20, 39n89
criticism, 22, 33–34, 58–62, 65, 71, 85. *See also under* method, historical-critical
– the new criticism, 33, 59–64, 65, 71
– "conjectural criticism," 30, 30
Crouter, Richard E., ix, 6n19, 143n2, 144–45, 146, 164n89, 185n154
Curran, Thomas, 179n134

Davidson, Arnold I., 149n16
De Vogel, Cornelia J., 53n162, 53–54n163
DeVries, Dawn, ix, 111n20, 120n49, 137n101
dialectics, 7n25, 9, 12, 40, 41, 43, 50, 57, 66–69, 81, 85, 86–106, 107, 113, 115, 123, 126, 137, 167–68, 190, 196, 203, 213, 215, 229
– dialectical process, 163, 165, 197, 201
– dialectical method. *See under* method
– *See also Dialectics / Dialektik* (under Schleiermacher's works)
dialogue form, 9–10, 15, 41–44, 46, 55, 59, 69, 71–74, 80–81, 85, 87, 90–91, 94–95, 105, 110, 113, 126–27, 136–37, 141, 153, 168, 227, 229–30
– form and content, 32, 42, 71–73, 90, 101, 104, 113, 128, 168, 212
Dierken, Jörg, x, 6n21, 7n25, 18n45, 149n16
Dilthey, Wilhelm, 4, 21, 24n15, 28nn35–36, 31, 58, 84, 108n7, 114n27, 123n61
Diotima, 129, 176–77, 179, 182

Dobson, William, 3n10, 20, 68n40, 77n85, 101n79, 180, 181nn144–46, 182n148, 188–89
dogmatics, 8, 14, 18, 179n137
Dole, Andrew, 212n91
dualism, 9, 56–57, 102, 174, 176–77, 228, 231
Duke, James, 29n36
Dülon, Friedrich, 108, 135

Eberhard, Johann August, 38n85
Eigler, Gunther, 2n9, 178n132, 184n152, 193n23, 194n27
Ellison, Julie, 111n20
Enlightenment, the, 11, 36, 145n9, 161
epistemology, 8, 83, 85, 142, 170, 187, 212, 213, 217, 219, 223, 251
eros. *See under* impulse
esoteric (unwritten) tradition, 4, 37, 38, 43–44, 46–47, 53–56, 59, 64, 68–69, 71, 80–81, 90
eternal, the, 93, 101, 122, 129, 130, 132–33, 134, 157, 171–74, 178, 188, 196, 200–201, 205, 218
– eternal laws, 170, 183
ethics. *See also* "ethics and physics," *Brouillon* (under Schleiermacher's works), and *Grundlinien* (under Schleiermacher's works)
– Schleiermacher's, 4, 8, 13, 15nn36–37, 103, 158n59. *See also under* Schleiermacher
– Schleiermacher's Halle lectures on, 14, 17–18, 106, 108, 138, 159, 192, 200, 206
– as "science of acting" in 2nd edition of *Speeches*, 160, 170, 184–86, 229
– Aristotle's, 11
– Christian, 14, 17–18
– Plato's, 16, 81, 82–84, 104, 213, 221, 229
– *See also* "ethics and physics" (the two series)
"ethics and physics" (the two series), 10, 16–18, 82–84, 91, 99, 104, 137, 147–48, 163, 187, 197, 199–201, 203–204, 212–13, 218n111, 221, 229
exegesis, 8, 14, 18, 166

exoteric (written) tradition, 9, 37–38, 53, 55n175, 59, 80, 43–44, 46, 53–56, 61–62, 68–69, 71, 72, 75, 90, 227

faith, 8, 9, 133, 138
feeling / *Gefühl*
– in *Speeches / Reden*, 144–45, 151, 154, 157, 159, 163, 165, 168, 171–72, 173, 178, 184, 187, 189–90, 200, 201, 205, 206–207, 208–10, 212–13, 215–17, 219–25, 231
– "philological feeling," 42–43
– general uses of, 76n74, 106n92, 107, 117, 119, 124n63, 125, 127, 132
Fichte, Johann Gottlieb, 5n18, 15, 155n50, 157, 189
Ficino, Marsilio, 2
Finamore, John F., 21n5
Findlay, J. N., 54n167, 54n170, 55n172
Fischer, Hermann, 5n16, 59n5
Follak, Andrea, 5n18
Forstman, Jack, 29n36
Fowler, Howard N., 38–39n89, 66n28, 67n34, 68n41, 88n14, 92n25, 101n80, 149n15, 178n132, 193n23, 227n1
Frank, Manfred, 11n29, 29n36, 58n3, 86
freedom, 126, 152, 185, 208, 228
Friedrich Wilhelm III (king of Prussia), 17
Frommann, Karl, 24, 27
Fuchs, Emil, 208n72

Gaiser, Konrad, 54nn167–68
Gander, Hans-Helmuth, 29n36
Gaß, J. C., 58n1, 144n5
Gauss, Hermann, 2n9
Geddes, James, 36
Gerber, Simon, 1n1, 2n9
Gerson, Lloyd, 44, 56
Gleason, Patricia Guenter, 111n20
God, 16, 120n47, 134, 145, 161, 171–72, 173, 183, 185–86, 198, 206n70, 223–24
good, the, 16, 78, 83–84, 118, 122, 129, 180, 183, 198, 206, 218, 221–22, 228–30
– goodness, 125–26, 213, 231
– the highest good, 157n55, 158n59
Graf, Friedrich Wilhelm, 145–46n8

Grunow, Eleanor, vii, 1n3, 107
Güthenke, Constanze, 31n53, 43n110, 79n90

Hadot, Pierre, 149, 202, 231
Halle, 8, 11, 12–19, 108, 131n81, 143–44, 230
– University of, 8, 11, 14–19, 38n85, 58, 106, 158n59, 192
Hamann, J. G., 22
Hartlieb, Elisabeth, 111, 114, 120n51
Harvey, Van A., 144–45n8, 145n10, 172n109, 208n72
Hedley, Douglas, 88–89n17
Hegel, G. W. F., 5n18, 53, 55, 86, 89n17
Heidegger, Martin, 195n29
Heindorf, Ludwig Friedrich, 25, 28, 58
Helmer, Christine, ix, 6n19
Heraclitus, 11n28, 15, 108n6
Herder, J. G. 22, 177
Hermann, Karl Friedrich, 40, 42n108, 50, 52
Hermans, Theo, 2n9
hermeneutics, 2n9, 8, 9, 18, 30n48, 36, 45, 47, 58–85 *passim*, 90, 91n20, 101, 103, 104, 138n102
– grammatical explication, 26, 29, 32, 61, 63, 64, 72
– technical explication, 63
– *See also* Hermeneutics / *Hermeneutik* (under Schleiermacher's works)
Herms, Eilert, 5n16, 12n32
Herz, Henriette, 23, 25n18, 107n1
Heusde, P. G. van, 31n50
Hösle, Vittorio, 2n6, 4n12, 54n164, 71n54
humanism, 21, 56

idealism, 29, 61, 106, 189, 205
ideas, the, 11n29, 16–17, 78, 82, 92, 128–29, 177n129, 194, 198, 228, 230
ignorance, 83, 152, 171, 190–92
immortality, 100, 102, 175–76
impulse / *Trieb*
– *erōs* as philosophical impulse in Plato, 67–69, 92–95, 100, 105, 115, 118, 122–23, 124, 137, 161, 166, 229
– joy as impulse in *Christmas Dialogue*, 112, 115, 123–25

– two impulses in the *Speeches*, 149–53, 186, 200, 205, 214–15, 221
infinite, the, 16, 93, 111, 138, 152, 169–74, 177–78, 184, 186, 189, 200–201, 203–205, 209–10, 213, 222, 224
intuition/*Anschauung*, 11n29, 84, 98, 144–45, 148, 154–55, 163, 168, 173, 182–83, 187, 195, 201–226

Jaeger, Werner, 5n18, 50n143, 53n162
Jantzen, Jörg, 2n9, 5n17
Jesus Christ
– historical Jesus, 52, 140
– Christ, 109, 110n14, 120, 123n62, 124, 138, 140, 166n95, 206–207n70
– as Redeemer, 126n68, 129
– the Christ-child, 128, 129, 130, 134, 135
Jørgensen, Theodor, 6n19
joy
– Christian, 10, 108, 110, 112, 115, 117, 118–20, 121, 123–35, 136n97, 140, 151, 152
– in Socrates, 99, 129, 182–83

Kant, Immanuel, 11, 34, 47, 60–61, 86, 145n10, 147, 194, 198, 204, 209, 213, 228
– post-Kantian context, 147, 194, 198, 204, 209, 213
Käppel, Lutz, ix, 1n2, 6, 11n28, 25n19, 28n35, 29n36, 59, 108n6, 229–30
Kerber, Hannes, 55n175
Kim, Alan, 2nn6–7, 15n38, 31n53, 227n2
Kimmerle, Heinz, 29n36
knowing, 10, 17, 77, 82, 88, 98, 105, 138, 159, 160, 164–68, 170–71, 183–84, 187, 190, 191, 195–98, 199, 202–204, 207, 213, 216–22, 226, 228–29, 231
– not-yet-knowing, 43, 79
knowledge, 38, 43, 63, 67n34, 68, 77–78, 81–84, 85, 90, 99, 100–101, 129, 137, 156–58, 159, 160–63, 166, 168, 170–72, 182, 183, 196–97, 198, 199, 200, 202–203, 213, 215–16, 218n111, 221–22, 226, 229, 231
Krämer, Hans Joachim, 54–55
Kranich, Christiane, 6n19

Krapf, Gustav-Adolf, 6, 50, 86, 88–89n17, 114n27, 193–94
Kroker, Paul, 4n15

Laks, André, 15, 28n35, 40n98
Lamb, W. R. M., 180n138
Lamm, Julia A., 7n25, 15n39, 106n92, 107nn2–3, 13n2, 146, 149n16, 152n39, 173n113, 177n130, 179n137, 206n69
Leibniz, G. W. von, 33
Lesky, Albin, 51
Lincoln, Bruce, 81n103
Livingstone, D. N., 62n11
Loehr, Johanna, 1n2, 28n35, 108n6
love, 88, 101, 117, 120, 123, 125, 126, 127, 128, 13032, 133–35, 140, 141, 142, 151, 156, 176, 182, 205–206, 215, 231
– in the *Phaedrus*, 68, 93, 100, 118, 122
– mother-love/*Mutterlieb*, 128, 130, 132–33, 135
Luther, Martin, 38n84

Malpas, Jeff, 29n36
Mariña, Jacqueline, 7n25, 15n37, 86n2, 111n20, 230n8
Mary (mother of Jesus), 120, 130–31, 133, 134
Massey, Marilyn Chapin, 111
Meckenstock, Günter, x, 6n21, 12n32, 143n1, 145, 156
metaphysics, 9, 86, 174, 198
– "metaphysics"/*Metaphysik* (in the first edition of the *Speeches*), 147, 150, 152, 153, 154, 155, 156–57, 160, 164, 169, 170, 185
method, 14, 16, 30, 37–38, 69, 80, 91–97
– dialectical, 67–68, 77, 126, 140, 161, 166, 181, 196, 213
– historical-critical 2, 18, 28, 36, 38, 40n96, 41, 59, 138, 231
– Schleiermacher's internal, 32–36, 44, 46, 51, 59, 61–62, 67, 75, 174–75
– Schleiermacher's translation of *technē* as *Kunst*, 66–67
mimetic character of dialogue form, 73, 84, 101
monism, 147, 173, 199, 228

"morals," "morality"/ *Moral* (in the first edition of the *Speeches*), 147, 150, 152, 153, 155, 156–57, 158–59, 160, 164, 169–70, 172, 184, 185
Morgenroth, Matthias, 108–109n7, 114n27, 123n62
Mróz, Tomasz, 21n5
music, 115, 116, 118, 120–21, 127, 131
mysticism, 11, 114, 140, 228
myth, 5n16, 40–41, 52n156, 81–82, 90–91, 93, 98, 105, 136, 137–38, 161, 166, 181, 209

Napoleon, 14, 18, 131n81
Nehamas, Alexander, 51n148, 67n34
neo-Platonism. *See under* Platonism
Nicol, Iain G., 111n20
Niebuhr, Richard R., 7n23, 109–111, 123n61, 138
Nimmo, Paul, 166
non-being. *See under* being
Novalis (Georg Philipp Friedrich von Hardenberg), 131, 206–207, 210
Nowak, Kurt, 25n15, 108n7, 109n8, 133n88
Numbers, R. L., 62n11

Odebrecht, Rudolf, 5n16
Oehler, Klaus, 52, 54n167
Olesko, Kathryn, M., 62n11
Oman, John, 143–44n2, 146
ontology, 85, 98, 142, 147–48, 177, 187, 198–200, 207, 213, 223, 228, 229
opposition, realm of, 88, 98, 121, 130, 195–98, 199n49, 217–18, 228
– as difference, 195–96
– "highest being" as without opposition, 198, 228
Osthövener, Claus-Dieter, 6n19, 144n6
Otto, Rudolph, 212n91

Parmenides, 95–96
Patsch, Hermann, 5n16, 12n32, 18n45, 28n35, 58n2, 60n7, 108n5, 108–109n7, 159n65, 172n112
pedagogical progression of ideas, 39–41, 77, 78–82, 90–91, 94, 123, 137, 147, 161, 165, 166, 181–82, 200, 222, 227

perception/ *Wahrnehmung*, 76n74, 171–72, 184, 200, 209, 213, 215
Peter, Niklaus, 143n2, 145–46, 149n18, 155
Philipsen, Bart, 145n10, 167n96
Phillips, John, 21n5
philology, 3, 28–29, 30, 31n53, 32–33, 42–43, 54n164, 56, 64, 71–72
philosophy, 12, 26, 28, 29, 30, 34, 79, 122, 124, 170, 196n33
– Schleiermacher's, 6, 11, 12, 15, 17, 53, 83n113, 86, 106, 194–99, 206, 209
– Plato's, 21, 32, 34, 35, 37n83, 38, 40, 42, 44, 46, 49n137, 52, 53, 54, 55, 56, 57, 59, 60–61, 65, 68, 69, 74, 77–78, 82, 84, 90, 91–97, 97–102, 104, 113, 115, 118, 128–29, 156, 168, 174, 175, 194, 218, 227–30
– ancient, 147–49, 152, 198, 202
– and life, 148, 152, 155, 186, 202
– cultured despisers', 161
– critical (Kant's), 11, 34, 60–61, 138, 147, 179, 194, 198
– transcendental (Fichte's), 157
– of religion, 144
– practical, 160
physics. *See* "ethics and physics"
Pietsch, Michael, 6n21, 12n32
piety, 117, 120, 121–22, 123n62, 125, 131, 134, 135, 152, 156, 159, 166, 167, 170–71, 184–86, 191, 199, 201, 216, 222–24, 231
Plato. *See also under* ethics, impulse/ *Trieb*, philosophy, Platonic dialogues, Platonism
– as-artist, 9, 22, 30, 32, 36, 37–41, 42, 43, 44, 46, 51–52, 53, 56, 59, 65, 66, 67, 69–73, 78, 79, 84–85, 90, 93, 94, 95, 104, 113, 118, 147, 227
– Schleiermacher's Plato (summary points), 8–10, 227–32
– modern interpretations of, 32–57, 59–64, 227–28, 231
Plato, works
– *Alcibiades I*, 46, 74
– *Alcibiades II*, 45, 74
– *Apology*, 26, 45, 62, 74
– *Clitophon*, 46, 74

– *Craylus*, 46, 108n6, 144, 174n117
– *Critias*, 2n8, 44, 46, 75–78, 112, 136
– *Crito*, 45, 74
– *Erastae*, 46, 74
– *Gorgias*, 1n2, 41n100, 45, 49n137, 77n84, 82n104, 83, 128n72, 170n106, 174n117, 180–82, 218–19
– *Hipparchus*, 45, 74
– *Hippias Major*, 25n19, 46, 74
– *Hippias Minor*, 45, 74
– *Ion*, 45, 74
– *Laches*, 1n2, 30, 45, 83, 91, 159
– *Laws*, 2n8, 76n73
– *Letters*, 2n8, 76n73
– *Seventh Letter*, 55, 56n176
– *Lysis*, 1n2, 25n19, 30, 45, 83, 91, 192
– *Menexenus*, 46, 74
– *Minos*, 45, 74
– *Parmenides*, 7n23, 30, 44–45, 68, 76, 78, 88–89, 91, 95–97, 98, 112, 168
– *Phaedo*, 9, 46, 77–78, 88, 89, 97, 100–102, 105, 108, 112, 127, 129, 134, 173–78, 182, 186, 192, 229, 230
– *Phaedrus*, 9, 25, 26, 29, 36, 41n100, 59, 64–71, 79, 89, 91–95, 108, 112, 115–17, 118, 122–25, 137, 167–68, 174, 178, 181, 182, 227, 229
  – as first of the dialogues, 40, 44, 45, 47, 48–51, 53, 65, 76, 77–78, 166
  – contains the 'seeds' / *Keime* of philosophy, 40, 49n137, 50, 65, 77, 94, 115–16, 118–22, 139
  – on writing, 43, 55, 68–69
  – relation of two parts of, 39, 51, 65–68, 104
– *Philebus*, 46, 77–78, 112, 174n117
– *Protagoras*, 1n2, 30, 31n53, 36n76, 44, 45, 49, 68, 76, 78, 79, 83, 91, 94–95, 112, 179n138, 182
– *Republic*, 2nn8–9, 31n53, 44, 46, 57, 75–76, 78, 79, 81, 83, 85n115, 89, 91, 99, 102–104, 105, 112, 115, 136–39, 166, 213
– *Sophist*, 5–6, 9, 44, 46, 57, 77–78, 79, 83, 88n15, 89, 94, 96, 97–100, 105, 108n6, 112, 121nn56–57, 128–30, 144, 147–48, 149n15, 174–75, 178n132, 180, 184n152, 187–88, 190–201, 202, 203, 204, 219, 220–21, 224, 227, 228, 230
  – as center of center, 97–99
– *Statesman*, 46, 77–79, 83, 99, 108n6, 112, 128–29, 144, 174n117, 180, 219
– *Symposium*, 9, 46, 78, 89, 97, 99–101, 108, 112, 115, 118, 128–35, 137, 139n104, 142, 144, 159n62, 174n117, 175, 176, 178–82, 227, 229, 230
– *Theaetetus*, 16, 44–45, 77–78, 83, 98–99, 108n6, 112, 174, 182, 193, 227
– *Theages*, 26, 44, 74
– *Timaeus*, 2n8, 44, 46, 75–76, 78, 79, 83, 91, 99, 103, 104, 112, 136–38, 213
Platonic dialogues
– determining authenticity of, 2, 3n11, 9, 17, 26, 28, 30, 32, 33–34, 36, 42, 44–48, 55, 56n175, 59, 61–63, 70, 71–74, 75, 113, 136
– ordering of, 2, 23, 26, 27, 28, 31, 32, 35–36, 40, 44–48, 49, 50n143, 51–53, 59, 65, 71, 74, 75–84, 90, 113, 118, 136, 137, 158, 163, 218, 227
– developmental theory, 40, 42n108, 52, 96
– stylometric theory, 50, 52–53
– trilogies of (Schleiermacher's theory of), 44–46, 68, 75–78, 79, 82–83, 89, 91–106 *passim*, 113, 115, 128–29, 136–37, 174–75, 180, 218n111
– "natural sequence and necessary relation of," 32, 34, 38, 40, 41, 44, 51–52, 80
– unity of, 37–38, 53, 55n175, 64–65, 67–68, 73, 75, 85, 113, 123, 227, 229
Platonism, 1, 2–3, 7n23, 9, 11, 13, 44, 53–54n163, 56, 57, 80, 126n68, 147, 177–78, 228, 231–32
– neo-Platonism, 33, 34, 37–38, 53, 53–54n163, 57, 178, 231
Pohl, Karl, 50
presentiment / *Ahn[d]ung*, 16, 68, 119, 165
Proudfoot, Wayne, 210–12

Rade, Martin, 108–109n7
Ravenscroft, Ruth Jackson, 7n26, 113n26
realism, 106n92, 189, 199, 204, 206, 209, 213

reason / *Vernunft*, 12n29, 138, 152, 184n152, 190, 199
– unity of reason and nature, 190, 199, 201–206
Redeker, Martin, 4n14, 5n16
Rehme-Iffert, Birgit, 6n19
Reimer, Georg A., x, 21n1, 27, 49, 143–44
rhetoric, 66–68, 92, 137n101, 167–68
Richard, Marie-Dominique, 28n35, 29n38, 30n48, 38n84
Richardson, Ruth Drucilla, 108n5, 110–11, 114n27, 138
Rohls, Jan, 5–6, 21n5, 83n113, 86, 144, 177n128, 194, 197–99, 219n112, 224
Romanticism, 11–12, 21–22, 25n15, 55, 67, 75, 81n103, 145n9, 227–28
– Schleiermacher as Romantic, 8, 11–12, 55, 69–70, 81n103, 88n17, 106, 118, 147, 159, 177
Rowe, Christopher, 85
Ruderman, Richard S., 55n175

Scheliha, Arnulf von, x, 6n21, 7n25, 18n45, 149n16
Schelling, F. W. J., 28n36, 53
Schenkel, David, 109
Schlegel, A. W., 56
Schlegel, Friedrich, 9, 13, 22, 23–31 *passim*, 40n98, 47–49, 51, 56, 60–62, 75, 81n103, 108n5, 110, 167n96
– Schlegel's "Hypotheses," 26, 48
Schleiermacher, Friedrich. *See under* art, ethics, method, philosophy, Plato, Platonic dialogues, Romanticism
Schleiermacher, works
– *Brouillon / Notes on Ethics*, 12n31, 14, 17–18, 19, 158n59, 159n65, 192n22, 199n49. *See also under* ethics
– *The Christian Faith / Glaubenslehre*, 103n84, 137n101, 138n102, 232
– *Christmas Dialogue / Die Weihnachtsfeier*, ix, 7n23, 8, 9–10, 14, 18, 107–142 *passim*, 143, 230
– *Dialectics / Dialektik*, 6, 50n146, 87n6, 138n102, 198–99, 224, 230
– *Grundlinien einer Kritik der bisherigen Sittenlehre / Baselines of a Critique of Previous Ethics*, 8, 13, 14, 15–17, 19, 106, 156, 158n59, 166, 197n35, 206, 228n4
– *Hermeneutics / Hermeneutik*, 6, 9, 28–29n36, 138n102, 192, 230
– *Occasional Thoughts on Universities in the German Sense / Gelegentliche Gedanken über Universitäten in deutschem Sinn*, 19n48, 80n97
– *Platons Werke*, *passim*
– *Speeches on Religion / Reden*, ix, 8, 10, 12, 14, 19, 23, 84, 106n92, 107, 143–226 *passim*, 230–31
Schmid, Dirk, 6n21
Schmidt, Sarah, 1n1, 2n9, 6n20, 7n25, 18nn45–46, 152n40, 178n132, 199n49, 206n69, 209n77
Schnitzer, Adam, 2n9
Schnur, Harald, 33n58, 48n131
Scholtz, Gunter, 5n16, 29n36, 17n129, 194, 197–99, 228
Schultz, Hartwig, 106n93
Schultz, Werner, 5n16
science / *Wissenschaft*, 16–17, 39, 62, 64, 66, 81, 82, 84, 90, 92, 99, 105, 137, 154, 160–63, 169, 180, 189–90, 200, 203, 204, 210, 213, 218–19, 229
– natural science(s), 17–18, 170, 231
– "science of being," 169–72, 183–84
– "science of acting," 184–85
– and piety, 91
– the two sciences. *See under* "ethics and physcis"
scripture, 163–67. *See also* exegesis
Selge, Kurt-Victor, vii, 5n16, 59n5
Serban, Adriana, 2n9
Shaftesbury, Anthony Ashley Cooper (3rd Earl of Shaftesbury), 4
Shakespeare, William, 22
Shorey, Paul, 52–53, 57
Slotten, H. R., 62n11
Smith, Louise Pettibone, 109n10
Socher, Joseph, 49–50
Sockness, Brent, ix, 157n55, 179n137, 211n81
Socrates, 5, 9, 35, 38n89, 43, 55, 65–70, 75, 79, 88n14, 92–96, 97, 99–102, 105, 127, 129–30, 134–35, 142, 143,

147, 174–75, 181–82, 186, 189–206, 225, 229
sophists, 105n91, 164, 205, 225
– sophistical attitudes, 90, 95, 100, 130, 167, 197
Sorrentino, Sergio, 5n16
soul, 67, 81n103, 88n14, 94, 101n80, 102, 122, 149–50, 176, 178n132, 192n20, 211
– body and soul, 57, 100, 102, 176
Spalding, G. L., 28
speculation,73, 81, 87–89, 90, 95, 96–98, 100–101, 102, 104, 105, 106, 122, 126, 128, 129, 138–39, 153, 170, 174–75, 179, 189, 191n13, 197, 203, 205, 229
Spiegler, Gerhard, 86n5
Spinoza, Benedict de (Baruch), vii, 4, 7, 15–16, 22, 86, 177, 189, 197n35, 205–207, 210, 228
Stallbaum, Gottfried, 49–50
Steffens, Henrik, 18
Stein, Edith, 196n29
Stein, Heinrich von, 1, 1n5, 3, 3n11, 31, 31n52, 51n147
Steiner, Peter M., 2n9, 3n10, 5n17, 188
Stock, Hans, 24n15
Stolp, 8, 11, 12, 13–17, 27
Strauss, David Friedrich, 108n7
Strauss, Leo, 55n175
Sturm und Drang (literary movement), 22, 81n103
surrender, 152, 185–86, 190, 205, 214, 221
Szlezák, Thomas A., 2n7, 32n56, 34n62, 54n164, 55–56, 57n183, 58n3, 69n43

Taylor, A. E., 53n162
Ten Kate, Laurens, 145n10, 167n96
Tennemann, Wilhelm Gottlieb, 32–35, 37, 40, 41–42, 46–47, 48, 55, 60–62
Thandeka, 111n20
The Three in the second Speech, 148, 153, 155–63, 184–85, 187, 189–91, 199, 201, 203–204, 207, 210, 212, 216, 221–23, 226, 230
theology, ix, 7, 8, 9, 12, 14, 17, 57, 103n84, 140n107, 144, 197, 198, 224, 230, 232

Thesleff, Holger, 3n11, 50n143
Tice, Terrence N., 19n48, 87n6, 109–110, 123n61, 172n109
Tieck, L., 56
Tiedemann, Dietrich, 32n56, 33–34
Tigerstedt, E. N., 33, 37n83, 46n125, 50n145, 54, 60n8
I Timothy, 15, 18

true, the, 16, 84, 167, 174, 183, 200, 218, 222, 229
– truth, 41, 71, 80, 88, 89, 95, 101, 157, 167, 176, 180, 190, 193, 203, 213, 231
Tübingen School, 2n6, 4, 54–56, 69n43
Turner, R. Steven, 30n48, 56

universe, 154, 157, 160, 169, 173, 205, 206, 208–209, 210, 221, 223–24, 229, 231

Virmond, Wolfgang, vii, 1n1, 5n16, 5n18, 25n19, 50n143, 58, 59n5
virtue, 4, 79, 84, 156–160, 163, 166, 182–83, 192, 200, 213, 217, 218n111, 222, 229, 231
Vorsmann, Norbert, 5n16

Wallhausser, John, 5n16, 12, 15n36, 158n59
Wehrung, Georg, 126n68
Wilamowitz-Moellendorff, Ulrich von, 2n9, 22
Williams, Robert R., 7n23
Willich, Heinrich von, 107nn3–4
Willson, A. Leslie, 22n6
Wippern, Jürgen, 54n167
Wismann, Heinz, 30n48
Wolf, F. A., 28–29n3656
Woodruff, Paul, 51n148, 67n34
Würzburg, University of, 17

Yaffe, Martin D., 55n175

Zeller, Eduard, 52
Zeno, 96
Zuckert, Catherine, 31n53, 40n95, 45n124, 85, 96n52, 227n2

www.ingramcontent.com/pod-product-compliance
Lightning Source LLC
Chambersburg PA
CBHW020225170426
43201CB00007B/318